JACQUES TATI

HIS LIFE AND ART

Also by David Bellos

GEORGES PEREC: A LIFE IN WORDS

BALZAC CRITICISM IN FRANCE, 1850–1900.
THE MAKING OF A REPUTATION

David Bellos

JACQUES TATI
HIS LIFE AND ART

THE HARVILL PRESS
LONDON

First published in Great Britain in 1999 by
The Harvill Press
2 Aztec Row
Berners Road
London N1 0PW

3 5 7 9 8 6 4 2

www.harvill.com

Copyright © David Bellos, 1999

David Bellos asserts the moral right to be
identified as the author of this work

A CIP catalogue record for this book
is available from the British Library

ISBN 1 86046 651 6

Designed and typeset in Bembo at
Libanus Press, Marlborough, Wiltshire

Printed and bound in Great Britain by Butler & Tanner Ltd
at Selwood Printing, Burgess Hill

Why do you look like a sad dog? a rather sharp young lady asked Jacques Tati in front of the cameras of Swedish TV, some time in the 1970s. *How lonely are you?*

The creator of Monsieur Hulot, that innocent intruder into the modern world, looked wearily at his acid interlocutor, and then straight at the lens, articulating very slowly in his accented but effective international English:

I am difficult to make me laugh

CONTENTS

ACKNOWLEDGMENTS

This book could not have been written without the permission and co-operation of Sophie Tatischeff, who allowed me access to her father's press books, photograph albums, and business correspondence, and also to her own precious collection of videotapes. I hope that this book – for which I alone take responsibility – will in some measure repay her uncommon kindness.

I owe thanks to many people in Paris, Stockholm and elsewhere who took the time to tell me of their memories of Jacques Tati, and also, in some cases, to lend me precious documents. Amongst them: Sylvette Baudrot, Michèle Brabo, Barbara Denneke-Ramponi, Gustaf Douglas, François Ede, Pierre Etaix, Karl Haskel, Maurice Laumain, Gilles L'Hôte, Germaine Meunier, Hyacinthe Moreau-Lalande, Fred Orain, Nicolas Ribowski, Anne Sauvy-Wilkinson, Marie-France Siegler, Lucile Terouanne, Norbert Terry, and Elisabeth Wennberg.

The illustrations in this book owe much to the technical skills of Jérôme Javelle. Patrizia Molteni – an unfailingly meticulous assistant – helped with library work and fact checking in Paris.

Steve Parker, Andrew Hussey, P. Adams Sitney, Gaetana Marrone-Puglia and many other colleagues answered queries, made suggestions, and helped me to avoid mistakes. Pascale Voilley put into this book (and its author) more than I can say.

Abbreviations

AJT	Archives Jacques Tati. Private Collection, Paris
AN	Archives nationales, Paris
BFI	British Film Institute, London
BiFi	Bibliothèque du Film, Paris
BN	Bibliothèque nationale
CC	*Cahiers du cinéma*
CNC	Centre national de la cinématographie
COIC	Comité d'organisation de l'industrie cinématographique (1940–1944)
MoMa	Museum of Modern Art (New York), Film Stills Archive
NYPL	New York Public Library, Performing Arts Collection
STO	Service du travail obligatoire
VdP	Vidéothèque de Paris

LIST OF ILLUSTRATIONS

PHOTOCREDITS

Canal+ : 84, 85, 86, 87
Dino, André: 13, 14, 64, 67
Fischer, Gunnar: 90
Gaumont: 20, 21
Lagrange, Estate of Jacques: 49, 51, 55, 59, 61, 62, 63, 65, 79, 93
Le Corbusier, Fondation: 60, 75
    ©FLC/ADAGP, Paris and DACS, London, 1999
MoMa, courtesy of: 34, 69
NYPL Performing Arts Collection: 50
Orain, Fred: 36, 37, 40, 41, 44
Panoramic/Specta-CEPEC: 8, 13, 14, 22, 26, 27, 28, 29, 36, 38, 39, 42, 43, 45,
    46, 47, 48, 52, 53, 54, 56, 57, 58, 71, 72, 73, 74, 76, 77, 78, 80, 81, 82, 88, 92
Saad, Georges: 23
Svensk Filmindustri, Ab: 91
Sveriges Radio: 94
Swedish Television, courtesy of: 11
Tatischeff, Sophie: 1, 2, 3, 4, 5, 6, 7, 9, 10, 12, 17, 18, 30, 32, 33, 35
All rights reserved: 11, 15, 16, 19, 24, 25, 31, 48, 50, 66, 68, 69, 70, 89

Film posters on verso of part titles

Part One	*Mon Oncle*	Panoramic/Specta-CEPEC © Pierre Etaix
Part Two	*Jour de fête*	Panoramic/Specta-CEPEC
Part Three	*Playtime*	Estate of Jacques Lagrange. Panoramic/Specta-CEPEC
Part Four	*Parade*	Estate of Jacques Lagrange

Preface

Jacques Tati – best known as his film persona, M. Hulot – was a mime of great genius, and the creator of four or five of the most entertaining yet mysterious films ever made: *Jour de fête*, *Les Vacances de M. Hulot*, *Mon Oncle*, *Playtime*, and, for some people, *Trafic* and *Parade*. All these films are commercially available on videotapes in France, Britain, the USA and many other countries; celluloid versions continue to be screened from time to time in commercial cinemas, and frequently in cinema clubs the world over. Jacques Tati's work is widely known. This book aims to show how it arose, and to make it a little better understood.

I am not a film critic, nor a film buff, and certainly not a fantasy film-maker (as I suspect many film critics are). What's more, at least a dozen books about Tati have been written over the past forty years. They range from a beautiful photo-album put together by Marc Dondey to a very personal essay by the distinguished music critic Michel Chion. They include a straightforward if imperfect biography in English by James Harding, and well-organised theses by Brent Maddock, Lucy Fischer and other American film-studies scholars. (Details of these and other works will be found on pp. 367 ff. below.) All are worth reading – I have drawn on many of them in the following pages – but they do not tell me all that I wanted to know.

"The unravelling of a riddle is the purest and most basic act of the human mind," wrote Vladimir Nabokov in a spoof review of his own autobiography. The life and work of Jacques Tati – and beyond that, the relationship between the two – constitute something of a brain-teaser: How did *that* man come to make *those* films? How and why do those films make a difference to the way we see cinema, and the world around us? What exactly does M. Hulot mean? These are puzzles that all art sets us. I cannot claim to have solved the Tati riddle once and for all; but this book sets out in a single work rather more of the clues than have been available before.

My decision to write this book was made on the intuition, now a conviction, that Tati did not simply make a sequence of movies, like many another respectable, professional film director. He made a *set* of films which, taken together, is much more than the sum of its parts. He is the author of an oeuvre which deserves to be known and to be studied with the same respect, and to be understood through many of the same methods, that we bring to the work of any artist, working in oils, in words, or in film.

Tati's films offer us a complex picture of a self-enclosed, imaginary, and gently poetic world, and also a rich commentary on the real, historical one. Made over a period corresponding almost precisely to the *trente glorieuses* – the thirty "glorious" years of rising prosperity in France from 1945 to 1975 – Tati's oeuvre is both an intensely objective history of France, and the expression of a highly individual sensibility. What I have tried to do in this book, as in my previous study of Georges Perec, is to show how the combination of craftsmanship, observation, sensibility and intelligence (though in Tati's case, of a rather special kind) lies at the source of meaningful art.

Jacques Tati was a man and an artist about as different from Georges Perec as can be imagined. Though I might perhaps have enjoyed a conversation with Perec, I doubt I would have lasted five minutes in the company of Tati. But I see no contradiction in seeking once again to present the man and the work as part of the same overall story, even if the relationship between the two – and the biographer's relationship to each – is not a close or even necessary one.

A life is longer and fuller than any biography can be. I have tried to include all I know about the man and his work, but I am aware of many gaps that remain. There must be a thousand missing anecdotes and hundreds of absent facts about Tati. Could he cook? What did he like to eat? I haven't been able to find out, in large measure because nearly all of Tati's contemporaries reached the ends of their lives some time ago. But some missing chapters of this book may some day be written – for instance, the full business history of Cady-Films, Specta-Films and CEPEC, and a less speculative account of how Tati got through the years 1939–44 – if and when the relevant documents, which must have once existed, come to light. Others, too, may be able to write a fuller account of Tati's relations with the artists, painters, musicians, and entertainers of his day. So this biography of Tati can hardly be considered the last word. I would rather see it as a part of a continuing, world-wide conversation about one of the outstanding creators of the twentieth century – surely the last of his kind.

D.B.
Princeton, N.J.
24 April 1999

Writing on Walls

As even occasional visitors grasp, the street-names of Paris embroider the urban fabric with a rich pattern of national history and culture. From Rue Clovis to Rue Charlemagne, from Quai Henri-IV to Pont Louis-Philippe, all the French kings have their places, as do scores of ministers, field marshals, physicists, biologists, war heroes and philosophers. Artists and creators are also commemorated in every *quartier*; in recent years, cultural heritage has spawned far more new place-names than military or political history. Pablo Picasso, Raymond Queneau and Louis Aragon now have their own metro stations, and streets have been named (or renamed) after Marcel Proust, Georges Perec and François Truffaut. But there has been another change in naming practice. As the old plates of blue-grey Volvic slate have been replaced with metal and now synthetic materials, the answers to the inevitable questions – "Papa, but who *was* Pierre Brossolette?" – have been supplied in small letters beneath the name: "French journalist and hero of the Resistance, 1903–1944". These legends are but tiny ramparts against the tide of time and oblivion. Tolbiac, Arago, Trousseau, Isabey – men of achievement and distinction in their different fields – have all merged in most people's minds into the streets and squares that bear their names.

Rue André Gide ("French writer, 1869–1951") forms the edge of a model housing estate in central Paris, up against the tracks leading into Gare Montparnasse. A slab wall – painted beige and ochre – shuts it off from the messy sheds at the back end of the station. On three of the slabs are life-size plaster bas-reliefs of a tall and angular, pipe-smoking gentleman in a soft hat, bearing alternately a butterfly-net, a tennis racquet and an umbrella. Here there is no plaque, no name, and no legend. You are expected to understand that the High-Speed Train gliding along behind the wall will whisk you westwards to Nantes and Saint-Nazaire, whence a rickety bus, a bicycle, or even an old Amilcar will soon get you to the Hôtel de la Plage at Saint-Marc-sur-mer, the actual and largely unchanged location of M. Hulot's unforgettable holiday.

Nearly fifty years after his creation, Jacques Tati's M. Hulot remains an instantly recognisable figure in France, and in many other parts of the world. No street is named after Hulot or his creator in Paris, yet few other film icons have kept their place in people's memory and imagination for so long. The obvious comparison is with the smaller but equally life-size image of a bowler-hatted tramp standing in the south-west corner of Leicester Square in London. The parallel with the "clever wee fellow" is inevitable, for American burlesque provides the essential context for Jacques Tati's work as a maker of comedy films. But even though "Hulot" rhymes with Chaplin's French nickname, "Charlot", what Tati's slow and dreamy films have to say lies in a quite different realm.

Tati's six feature films deal explicitly with many of the more striking changes that took place between 1945 and 1975: urban renewal, the growth of a leisure society, and the rise of the motor car, for example. They offer us a history of modern France – a material history, couched in benign and comic terms, lacking entirely the intellectual pretension of the "New Wave" cinema which belongs to the same period, and thus one which, in retrospect, seems all the more acute.

Those six films were made very slowly, by methods that were in some ways meticulous, not to say pernickety in the extreme, and yet in other ways amateur and dilatory. Tati sought and kept almost complete control over all aspects of his work, so his films were less directly constrained by commercial considerations than most film art. It is therefore quite proper to view them not just as charming comedies with a strong historical interest, but also as the crafted expression of a single creative personality. There is no reason not to approach them with the seriousness and respect we accord – for example – to the comedies of Molière.

The sources of Tati's vision of the world go back much further than 1945, obviously enough. Our starting point, which is also the earliest part of the stories that Tati allowed to be told about his background, and probably the earliest that he knew of in any case, goes back to a time when Louis and Auguste Lumière had not yet invented the *cinématographe*.

Part One

Years of Practice

1907–1946

SPECTA_GRAY_ALTER FILMS
Mon Oncle
UN FILM DE
JACQUES TATI
EN COULEURS

ONE

French Family Tatischeff

Il n'est tresor que de vivre a son aise
FRANÇOIS VILLON

Jacques Tati was born in 1907[1] – nine years after the making of the world's first comedy short (*L'Arroseur arrosé*, 1898), four years after the birth of Raymond Queneau, two years after Sartre. He thus belonged to a generation for whom the Great War of 1914–18 was not a personal experience, only the subject of adult conversations overheard. But the lives of all French men and women of Tati's age were broken in two by the Second World War and the German Occupation of France (1940–44).

The family name was (and remains) Tatischeff, which is to say, an aristocratic Russian name of great antiquity. Tati's paternal grandfather, a hereditary count and nominally commander-in-chief of the Alexandrisky Hussars, found himself posted to Paris as military attaché in the Imperial Russian Embassy in the 1870s. There, he fell in love with a French girl, Rose-Anathalie Alinquant, by whom he had a son in 1875, whom he named Georges-Emmanuel. Not long after, Count Dmitri's horse returned from the Bois de Boulogne without its rider: the count's body was later found by the wayside. Officially, the death of the military attaché was counted as a regrettable riding accident. But according to papers now lost, someone had tampered with the horse's stirrup straps.[2] Family legend has it that Dmitri's death was not an accident, but a murder, and that the commissioner if not the perpetrators of the crime were to be found in Moscow.

The supposition of a plot is made more plausible by what happened next. The following day, Dmitri's infant son was kidnapped, and it soon transpired that he had been whisked off to Moscow, to be brought up as the sole male issue of the great house of Tatischeff. The boy's mother – Jacques Tati's grandmother – had thus lost both her lover and her child. She reacted with remarkable fortitude. She taught herself Russian, then got a job as a nanny in Moscow, and found out where Georges-Emmanuel was being kept. After years of waiting and planning, she organised an abduction of her own and brought the eight-year-old boy back to France. As she lived in fear of reprisals from a powerful Russian family (Russia and France were close

Fig. 1: *Count
Dmitri Tatischeff in
the uniform of the
Alexandrisky
Hussars*

allies in the 1880s), she settled well outside Paris, in the village of Le Pecq,
nestling in one of the great loops of the Seine.

True or false, this myth of origins has a mad and violent energy in utter
contrast to the world of Jacques Tati's films. Even if the supposed plot
makes some kind of sense in terms of Russian rules about the transmission
of aristocratic titles and fortunes (as Balzac had discovered to his chagrin
thirty years before, Tsarist laws did not allow foreigners to come into titles
or money through marriage or inheritance), it seems quite self-defeating all
the same, since it involved disposing of the next-in-line with no assurance
that the illegitimate child would survive. But the death of Count Dmitri
and Georges-Emmanuel's early years in Moscow – stories manifestly retold
many times to Jacques Tati, and by him to his own children – left deep scars.

According to his granddaughter, Georges-Emmanuel never really came to terms with the brutal disruptions of his childhood. He started out in life an orphan, became the object of a confusing international tug-of-love, and from the age of eight was his mother's sole treasure. Was he Russian? Was he French? He resolved early on to owe nothing to Moscow. His illegitimacy was a stigma, to be hidden, or to be overridden, and he did so not by adopting another, or his mother's, name, but by defining himself very firmly as a respectable citizen of the French Third Republic. Assimilation was in any case expected in that optimistic and self-confident society; nationality was a much looser concept then than it is now, and social class a much more important reality.

Georges-Emmanuel grew up in Le Pecq and went into business locally. He set up or perhaps took over a coal-supply business at Port-Marly in the later 1890s, but he was happy to abandon it in 1903 when he married the daughter of a more prosperous local artisan-trader.[3] Claire Van Hoof was herself of mixed descent, Dutch on her father's side and Italian on her mother's. From her, Jacques acquired at least a smattering of Dutch, which would be re-awakened when he shot his last major fiction film, *Trafic*, with a largely Dutch crew on location in the Netherlands. So it is hardly correct to think of Tati as a French film-maker "of Russian descent", as many reference sources state: by descent, if that means anything very much nowadays, he was a European cocktail, part Italian, part Dutch, part Russian and part French, and in that sense not untypical of the twentieth-century population of France. Apart from the name of Tatischeff and a lumbering dreaminess that people describe as "typically Slav" – the man himself set his bouts of gloom and depression against his "Russian side" – Tati inherited nothing from his paternal grandfather.[4] Neither Jacques nor his elder sister Odette (born 1905, and later called by her middle name, Nathalie) ever spoke a word of Russian, nor did they have any contact with the country, save for Jacques's attendance at two film festivals when he was already a world-famous film director. Throughout his life, Tati seemed to others and to himself as French as garlic sausage; when asked, as he often was, what difference his Russian ancestry made, he would usually just shrug his shoulders, and pass on to the next question.[5]

Georges-Emmanuel, brought up an only child by a single parent in the village of Le Pecq, never moved away from his French roots, and it was there that Jacques Tati was brought up too. Le Pecq is really the lower part of the ancient and noble town of Saint-Germain-en-Laye. With its vast chateau (which now houses the National Museum of Antiquities), its cavalry garrison, and its extensive forest, Saint-Germain is more than a mere suburb of Paris. Even if it is now the terminus of the express metro line, it remains a

Fig. 2 (*left*): *Georges-Emmanuel Tatischeff in French military uniform, circa 1915*

Fig. 3 (*above*): *Jacques Tatischeff at his First Communion*

town with a distinctive, upper middle-class, not to say aristocratic identity. It was and remains a well-heeled, prestigious, and smart place to live.

Tati's mother was the daughter of a high-class picture-framer, whose business, Cadres Van Hoof, had premises in the very centre of Paris, near Place Vendôme. Georges-Emmanuel seems to have acquired rapidly both the technical and the managerial skills that made him his father-in-law's natural successor. Cadres Van Hoof was a flourishing firm from around the turn of the century, and supplied antique and modern frames to museums and collectors, and also to artists who did not always find it easy to pay in cash. But old man Van Hoof would not accept payment in kind; family legend had it that he had turned down three Van Goghs that would have made them all millionaires in due course.[6]

On their marriage, Tati's parents moved into a grand, brand-new house in Rue de L'Ermitage at Le Pecq. There was staff to keep the large garden in order, to run the stables and to drive the automobile that the Tatischeffs acquired in 1903; and at its peak the framing business employed as many as twenty-five workers.[7] Georges-Emmanuel was already a man of substance; he grew richer by clever operations on the Bourse. Later on, after the Russian Revolution, Georges-Emmanuel must have thanked his lucky stars for having turned out to be a French citizen instead of ending up like so many other Russian aristocrats as a cab-driver in Paris, Berlin or New York, with nothing more than a useless Nansen passport to their names.

As a prosperous middle-class family, the Tatischeffs brought up their children in a firm, conventional, one could say Edwardian manner. Mme

Fig. 4: *The family business, Rue de Caumartin, 1929*

Van Hoof, née Teresa-Maria Rizzi, Tati's Italian maternal grandmother, lived with the family, and insisted on the observance of religious as well as social proprieties. (All links with Russia having been abandoned, Catholicism was accepted as the family faith.) Fish on Fridays, without exception; attendance at church on Sundays was obligatory; and Jacques did service as a choirboy. The children did not dine with their parents until they were well into their teens.[8]

Both of Jacques's parents being only children, the boy had no first cousins, no aunts, and no uncle: *Mon Oncle*, Tati's Oscar-winning film of 1958, can thus only be about an uncle Tati never had. As for more distant family, no links were maintained on his father's Russian side; most of his mother's cousins were in Holland, Italy, and elsewhere. Jacques grew up as the only male of his generation, amongst his two grandmothers, his bewhiskered grandpa Van Hoof, his mother, and his elder sister. He was looked after by an English nanny, Miss Brammeld; he was tutored at the piano by a Mlle Saulx.[9] And what about the only adult male in his environment, Georges-Emmanuel? "My father was a man of strong character," Tati said to Penelope Gilliatt in the 1970s. "I wish he could have been a bit more like the Uncle in *Mon Oncle* . . ."[10] To a Swedish interviewer, he expressed his retrospective disappointment, and his childhood frustration, a little more firmly: "[My father] was the owner of the family. I think that was a little bit wrong."[11]

Fig. 5: *Georges-Emmanuel Tatischeff on horseback, circa 1925*

War broke out when Jacques was not quite seven years old. French cinema, which then dominated the world through the twin empires of Pathé Frères and Gaumont, went into sharp decline. If Jacques and Nathalie were taken to the movies in their childhood years, they would most likely have seen more American than French-made comedy films from 1915 on. All that is known about Jacques's early exposure to the popular arts, however, is that around the time that the war broke out, he was taken to see the strange exuberant dwarf entertainer known as Little Tich. This English music-hall performer wore shoes nearly as long as his little legs, and delighted audiences in Paris and London with acrobatic tomfoolery of a quite unique kind. Tati never forgot that experience, and in later life he often came back to his memory of Little Tich, who, he said, had invented the entire art of cinema burlesque. When he came to London in 1969 to give a lecture at the National Film Theatre, he insisted on running the one surviving clip of Little Tich doing his act.[12]

In 1914, Georges-Emmanuel joined the forces, as did all men of military age, and left for the duration. Unlike a very large number of his contemporaries, he survived that great butchery in the trenches. But during those four years of war, the children's environment became even more exclusively female. Young Jacques saw only women around him, except at school, and on those rare and unpredictable occasions when his father returned home on leave. One such occurred in the summer of 1916, when the women and children were on holiday at Mers-les-bains, on the Channel coast. The occasion stuck in Tati's mind.

> My father had some leave. He came to see us dressed in full uniform.
> He didn't have the right to take it off, except for a swim. There he
> stood, on the beach, in military blue. Like a gamekeeper keeping an
> eye on us. I often think of that scene.[13]

Thirty-five years later, with his painter-friend Jacques Lagrange, Tati searched far and wide for seaside locations in which to shoot *Les Vacances de M. Hulot*. Saint-Marc-sur-mer, near Saint-Nazaire, the location finally chosen, resembles Mers-les-bains only in the sense that it is a small seaside resort, with a hotel actually on the beach. All the same, the whole idea of the film was to recapture and to fix the essence of a "holiday-by-the-sea", an essence that is inextricably bound up with the memory of childhood, for Tati if not for most of us. For in all of Tati's many reminiscences, in scores of interviews published all over the world[14] as well as in memoirs dictated into a tape recorder, the earliest memory mentioned, and repeated many times, is of that holiday when the Father appeared as a stranger to the child.

Jacques was a placid boy, a natural idler – in contrast to his sister, forever in

Fig. 6: *Jacques and Nathalie Tatischeff, Mers-les-bains, circa 1916*

a rush. He could spend hours in his room doing nothing very much. On occasions, his sister surprised him at solitary games of make-believe in front of the mirror, putting on different hats; for a time, he spent much of his pocket money on fanciful headgear.[15] It was a form of fun and mime that he would take up again decades later, with his friends the Bergerons, who kept a supply of real and party hats in the cupboard in the hall of their flat in the sixteenth arrondissement. However late the hour, Tati would never leave one of the Bergerons' soirées without first trying on a hat or two, and miming a character to go with it. It became his regular way of saying farewell.[16]

Young Tatischeff grew quickly and seemed disinclined to stop. By the age of sixteen he was more a lamp-post than a lad, measuring 1m92.[17] Average heights were lower then than now, so we must imagine young Tatischeff not just as a tall adolescent, but as a beanstalk, an embarrassment to himself if not to others. Because of his precocious height, whenever there was a funeral, he was regularly chosen to carry the cross at the head of the procession of choirboys from the church to the graveside. As a consequence, he regularly stood by the freshly-dug grave, and close to the weeping mourners. Watching the coffin slowly descend into the earth, hearing the wails and sniffles of those around him, young Jacques wanted to cry too. But he couldn't. He had to behave like the big boy that he was.[10]

These two memories – of the Father by the sea, of stifled tears at the graveside – are of course not real memories of Jacques's childhood, but the traces that the celebrity Tati chose to leave, or to place, in interviews he gave to the press and in anecdotes recounted over canteen meals with his younger staff. Both of them suggest an awkwardness about emotion: they are not memories of a happy childhood, or of childhood happiness; they are perhaps best seen as signals of the adult Tati's awareness of some kind of emotional disarray in his early years.

Tati never rebelled directly against the values and the style of his stiff, respectable and perhaps rather cold home background. M. Hulot's manners, be they ever so ineptly implemented, are precisely those that Tati must have learned in the nursery and at table at Le Pecq. More striking is the almost complete absence of expressions of strong emotion from Tati's films, which is similarly identical to the *art de vivre* of the strictest bourgeoisie. Superficially, at least, Tati the film-maker remained faithful to the principles and style of his childhood home; the comedy of manners that he invented stops short of being satirical, and is in no sense a tool of revenge.

Tati in his teens was literally head and shoulders above his classmates, but academically he fell short of the mark. He went to a good school, and had all the home support that modest wealth could provide, including extra coaching at home; but little that he was taught stayed very long in his head. His father would have liked him to have a profession – say, to be an engineer – but there was never the slightest prospect of that. "Modern life is designed for the top boys in the class," Tati would repeat when asked to justify the superficial anti-modernism of some of his later work, "and I would like to defend all the others." Indeed, Tatischeff was so far from top at the lycée that he never even sat the baccalaureate examination. He dropped out of school around the age of sixteen, and went to work for his father.

Tati is only one of many clever and creative people to have appeared dull and dreamy at school – Einstein and Georges Perec are two other examples. Tati, though, is different: for he remained rather obtuse in the eyes of most others even when at the height of his powers. He was rarely at ease explaining himself in words; and at least one of Tati's close associates suspected that he never really got the hang of basic arithmetic.[19] An American journalist once asserted that Tati had "a much better mind than Steven's [Spielberg]",[20] but most people who actually crossed Tati's path could see that he was not, in any conventional or ordinary sense of the word, a clever man.[21] "Tati was not at all an intellectual," wrote Jean-Claude Carrière, who had been taken into an editing studio for the first time by Tati in 1957. "Anything but."[22]

Tati never sought to hide his dull start in life, and was only too ready to admit that he had no real education at all. "My academic credentials could be written out in full on the back of a postage stamp!" he declared to Jean L'Hôte; and to his old schoolmistress, who wrote to congratulate him once he had become famous, he replied without false modesty:

> I well remember the trouble you took to try to teach me something.
> I've forgotten everything you ever tried so patiently to get into my
> head, but I do remember you as a kind and gentle teacher.[23]

In his earlier films, Tati plays characters defined by stupidity: the make-believe boxer of *Soigne ton gauche*, the cycling postman of *L'Ecole des facteurs* and (even more markedly) the remodelled François of *Jour de fête* are variants on a single comic theme, that of the dimwit. M. Hulot is a more complex creation, but he too does not quite understand how things actually work (especially when confronted with gadgets and machines, as in *Mon Oncle*). Tati's retrospective descriptions of himself as an unintelligent child may be part of the creation of his public persona as a dimwit-clown, but that is not a reason to doubt the truth of it. Tati had no education to speak of, not for lack of opportunity, but for lack of ability and will. He was just a very dull boy.

Only one anecdote of Jacques's school years remains. The English teacher used an early form of "direct method", and got the boys to act out the sentences that they were learning by repetition and rote. Tati's turn came, and his sentences were: "I open the door" and "I close the door". He made his way to the door, held the handle, and mimed the role whilst the teacher said, "I open the door", "I close the door". Now Tati had to repeat: "I open the door," as he opened the door. Then an idea came to him. "I close the door," he said, as he closed it, from outside, having left the classroom, not in protest, but as a kind of experimental gag.

The stunt does not seem to have been motivated by hostility, or by the desire to make a point about language pedagogy. However, in his reminiscences, Tati claims to have learned a lot about comedy from the position he had put himself in, outside the classroom. The whole class was holding its breath waiting to see what would happen next. Should he go back in, with a big grin on his face? Should he go and hide in the lavatories until the next lesson? Which would be funnier – the suspense in the classroom as his absence grew longer, or his triumphant return? In the end Tati slipped out of school and went home, and only heard the next day what a furore his inconclusive stunt had caused.

Marc Dondey begins his excellent study of Jacques Tati with this anecdote, just as Tati began his own tape-recorded memoirs with it, as if to say: that was the birth of the comedian in me. It is a gag without a punch-line or a comic reversal, indeed without a conclusion at all; and like some of M. Hulot's strange antics, it seems motivated more by shyness than by malice.

The Tatischeff family continued to take summer holidays by the sea, in resorts that were at the height of fashion; and there are more recorded memories of Jacques's holiday escapades than there are of his times at school or at work. On one holiday, which must have been in the years immediately after the end of the First World War, he teamed up in Deauville with a school chum to enter a Charleston competition, which, to their delight, they won. The friend was called Bruno Coquatrix: he would become one of France's leading popular song-writers, and above all a musical impresario and the owner of the vast Olympia variety theatre. (Neither of them made it to the World Championships, held at the Albert Hall in London. It was won in 1926 by a Russian immigrant who later, under the name of Lew Grade, became Britain's biggest light entertainment impresario, and a member of the House of Lords.) Tati's dancing talent can be seen in several of his films (notably, in *L'Ecole des facteurs* and *Jour de fête*); but there is unfortunately no visual record of an evening at the Deauville film festival, one year in the 1970s, when he took the floor with . . . Marguerite Duras.

The Tatischeffs spent the summer of 1924 at Saint-Tropez, and it was there that seventeen-year-old Jacques first invented a mime sketch, which amused beach-goers no end. He acted out the movements and gestures of a football goalkeeper, and entitled his little act *Football vu par un gardien de but* ("Football from a goalkeeper's view"). Later on, for reasons of professional rivalry, Tati had the date and nature of this first performance certified by the general secretary of the *Fédération Française de Football Association*.[24] There is no reason to think that Tati had an inkling at the age of seventeen that his summer amusement bore the seed of a whole career; and Georges-Emmanuel Tatischeff could not have imagined that his only son might really be a clown. But the FFFA confirmed fifteen years later that the act as performed on the beach in Saint-Tropez was, "without the slightest alteration", identical to the one that Tati had gone on to perform, to vast acclaim, on the music-hall stage.

Apart from dancing and clowning, Jacques had no noticeable gifts. He wasn't much good at drawing, showed little musical talent (though he could hum in tune), and never really managed to bang out Beethoven's *Turkish March* on the keys, despite his mother's insistence on piano practice. Being very large, he could often win at tennis, which his father also played. But his favourite pastime, and the one activity at which he did acquire a high level of

Fig. 7: *Jacques Tatischeff in his teens*

skill, was horse-riding. Saint-Germain was a splendid place for riding practice; and in the bridleways and tracks of the forest he would often come across cavalry officers from the local garrison, who took some interest in the tall local lad so obviously at ease in the saddle. The happy result of these chance encounters turned out to be the most enjoyable year of Tati's youth, and his first real experience of comedy – in the French cavalry.

Fig. 8: *M. Hulot defeated by a white horse, 1953*

TWO

The Framing Business

When he left school, Tatischeff junior was taken on as an apprentice in a business managed by his father but still the property of his grandfather Van Hoof. The hierarchy was as simple as it was strict. Father and son would walk down to the suburban railway station every morning, where Georges-Emmanuel would board the first-class carriage, and young Jacques would get into a third-class compartment for the short journey to Gare Saint-Lazare, and thence on foot to the workshop, in Rue de Caumartin up to 1929, and in Rue de Castellane thereafter.

High-class picture framing is a skill, a business, and also a minor art in the service of a greater one. Its aim, in the account that Tati gave his assistants and hangers-on in a hundred if not a thousand working lunches later on, was to attract attention not to the frame but to the picture inside it: the perfect frame was supposed to be one you could hardly see.[25] A self-denying, not a self-designating work of art, a picture-frame is the embodiment of twin concepts of modesty and perfection. When holding court, Tati often irritated his younger listeners by asserting the transferability of those simple ideas to the cinema. For a film-frame (that is to say, the tableau to be seen on screen) is set in a picture-frame that is simply the absence of light, the blacked-out surround of the cinema screen. It might have been less confusing if in the cinema a frame were called a *tableau*; but there is no doubt that Tati's idea of what was worthy of being in a film frame was derived from his years of boredom and practice in the picture-framing trade.

Tati was supposed to be preparing himself for the competitive entrance examination to the Ecole Nationale des Arts et Métiers, which would in principle have given him a proper training and a recognised qualification. He attended classes at the Ecole professionnelle Hanley, at Choisy-le-Roi; but he failed the examination, because his maths papers were too weak. So he remained just an apprentice; there was no automatic staircase for him just because he was the next in line.[26]

It was his grandfather Van Hoof who taught him how to gild: by very slow, patient application of minuscule layers of gold paint into each little fold, each curl, each tiny scroll of the ornate classical frames that Cadres Van Hoof dealt with. Tati would certainly try his listeners' patience in later years with the slow, mimed repetition of how he had learned his first *métier*, making them feel the unending burden of the search for the perfect finish. Once, when Tati was particularly proud of a frame he had done, his grandfather made him take it all to pieces again – because it was allegedly too good for the picture, and thus too *visible*.[27] The anecdote is probably just an example of outdated ideas about how to train youngsters (by making them know their place – at the bottom), but it is one that also served to justify Tati's often erratic behaviour with respect to the work of his assistants, and to his own. Like his grandfather, he was perfectly capable of saying: No, that's not *quite* right. You'll have to do it all over again.

Fig. 9: *The workshop at Rue de Caumartin, 1929*

The painter Claude Schurr, whom Tati roped in for the dance-floor sequences of *Playtime*, recalls a quite maddening example of Tati's perfectionism. On the huge set of the "Royal Garden" restaurant, a very large cast had spent all day rehearsing and shooting a tiny three-second shot of the wildly dancing crowd. It seemed to have gone pretty well when it was time to break set and go home. But no. A waiter who crosses one part of the frame and who has had his trouser-seat torn on the knobs of the Royal Garden insignia that decorate all the dining chairs, was wearing plain white underpants that day. The continuity required striped underpants. In the multiple action seen in the shot, and in a shot so brief, no spectator could possibly notice the blemish. But that was not good enough. It would all have to be done again.[28]

In his youth and ever after, Tati never read anything very much nor did he like writing things down: "I hardly read anything and I don't watch many films. I am not a cultivated person."[29] Tati's cultural life in his formative years can thus only be guessed at. He must have gone to bars and cabarets, he must have listened to popular songs, and he presumably went to the cinema, like everyone in the 1920s. We can only assume that Tati saw the comic shorts made (mostly in America) by the French music-hall artist Max Linder, who took his own life in 1925; he could hardly have escaped Chaplin; and he must have acquired his fondness for Buster Keaton in the years of the silent screen. Over thirty years later Tati, in association with Raymond Rohauer, bought no less than 160 kilometres of early silent comic shorts (the whole stock of Educational Pictures, Inc.),[30] with a view to adding sound tracks to some and then re-releasing them throughout Europe, or at least in the single cinema he then leased in Rue de Rennes. He never quite got round to carrying out his plan, but it is hard to imagine that this act of fidelity to the classic comedies of the 1920s was not based on warm memories of seeing them when the films were still fresh and new.

If only by osmosis, he must also have acquired familiarity with the wide range of classical and contemporary European art that passed through the framing shop. This background explains why he felt at ease in later life with painters like Lagrange and Schurr, as well as with art dealers and art historians, such as René Huyghe, who became a family friend; but Tati himself never claimed to be a connoisseur, and he collected puppets and models of clowns much more than old masters, when he had the means to do so. Nonetheless, the "painterly eye" remained an important concept for him in his adult career. First in the scenario of Les Vacances de M. Hulot, and then in the remake of Jour de fête, he wanted a designated painter on screen to look in a particular way at the visible world of the film, so as to guide the spectator towards an appropriate way of viewing it. And if in his films there are quite a few frames that recall canvases by Dufy, Toulouse-Lautrec, and Cézanne, it is almost certainly due not to reading art history or to visiting museums, but to memories of actual pictures he had spent long hours trying to frame in the family atelier. But in his youth, Tati did not enjoy the learning experience; he did not enjoy working for his father, and, most obviously of all, he did not enjoy the experience of work as such. The subjects and titles of his films say it very simply: from a day off (*Jour de fête*) to a holiday by the sea (*Les Vacances de M. Hulot*), and to *Playtime*, Tati sought to celebrate leisure, not work, "time out" and not his time "in". It must have been a huge relief to the young man when he reached the age of twenty, and was called up. The dismal grind of the daily commute for eight hours' labour in the framing business came at last to a halt.

THREE

The Cavalier

France was at peace, and the army in clover. The survivors of the slaughter of 1914–18 were national heroes, and wore their decorations with pride. Thanks to the terms of the Treaties of Versailles, France was once again a wealthy nation: by 1929, there were but a thousand men unemployed in the entire country, and even as late as 1931, gold reserves stood at the mountainous total of fifty-five billion francs. France's military budget was consequently huge; army life was not especially unpleasant. Conscription was universal, but as France was not at war, it was not physically dangerous, nor was it unpopular. For many young men, Tatischeff amongst them, national service offered release from the home environment, and a memorable year of laddish fun.

The French, like the British, could not conceive that the millions who had died in the trenches had given their lives in vain: in 1928, few believed and even fewer dared suggest that the "war to end all wars" would ever have to be fought again. So the French army, and most especially its splendidly archaic cavalry regiments, organised themselves to make the most of everlasting calm.

Tati was very lucky. A cavalry regiment was stationed in the barracks in the centre of Saint-Germain-en-Laye, just over a mile from the family home, and the colonel had had plenty of occasion to notice a tall and competent young horseman showing off his skills in the local bridleways. Such a man could help solve one of the colonel's abiding problems. Although he had officers aplenty who rode well, he could hardly use them to groom, exercise and service the very large stable of racing and show horses that he had under his command; but in usual military fashion the recruitment bureau sent him conscripts most of whom hardly knew which end of a horse to tie a nosebag to. Experienced horsemen in "other ranks" were hard to find and keep. So strings were pulled, and Tati was allocated to the regiment that wanted him, the *XVIe Dragons* (Sixteenth Dragoons), just up the hill from home.

The regiment was at that time less a fighting force than a social institution. Many of its career officers were the dimmer sons of impoverished nobility, with little chance of restoring their fortunes in business or government service. For them, a cavalry regiment was both a refuge from the harsher environment outside, and a social launching ramp. It provided them with splendid uniforms and handsome mounts on which to display themselves to advantage in the unending round of gymkhanas and military parades. They got their keep and their pay for doing nothing much else, whilst waiting to be introduced to an acceptable heiress at one or another of the functions which the army put on for the local civilians.[31]

At the other end of the social scale, the regiment served also to give a common French identity to conscripts from widely different backgrounds and from many different regions of France: peasants, factory workers, carpenters, hairdressers, office clerks, and students, speakers of Gascon patois, Parisian slang, and Alsatian dialects – all had to learn to live together and to acquire at regulation speed the same military routines of mounting a horse, walking it, then trotting, learning to gallop, to jump, and finally to charge, drawn sabre in hand, screaming abuse at imaginary Boches in the bushes of the forest of Saint-Germain. It was the very model of a bonding experience.

Fig. 10: *Tati (far right) and comrades, Saint-Germain-en-Laye, 1928*

Tati had a whale of a time as a trooper. It is no coincidence that the only social background that is given to the M. Hulot of *Playtime* is his army service. In one key sequence, Hulot is hailed by the restaurant doorman (played by Tony Andall) driving the "Royal Garden" delivery van, in an episode designed to connect the hotel and exhibition "chapters" to the evening at the restaurant; and then by Schneider, the portly parvenu who lives in one of the "fishbowl" flats. Both these characters greet Hulot as a long-lost army friend: "*Alors, Hulot, l'Armée!*" is what we hear (just about) from Tony Andall; "*Hulot! Hulot! L'Armée!*" is Schneider's greeting. Despite all that happened to the French Army between 1928 and 1967, the military reference remains a notation of conviviality in the steel-and-glass newtown of *Playtime*.

Tati shared the life of the other conscripts, but was exempt from much of the suffering they endured during training, since he was a skilled rider already. "In retrospect," he recalled in his conversations with Jean L'Hôte in 1980, "I realise that, for sheer comic effect, no clown, no supposedly amusing film, can match the first riding lesson of a squad of raw recruits." The officer first gives a demonstration, repeating it several times over to underscore his control over the animal and over the troops. Then the recruits stand by their mounts, and, at the officer's bawled sequence of commands, try to jump on to their horses. "The show that is then put on really deserves an audience," Tati said.

> Faced with a task of such difficulty, the young soldiers' first reflex is to imagine that if they disregard the official method and invent one that they think will suit them better, they will manage to mount their horses more easily. So they look as though they are trying to jump a wall, and the result of such attempts obviously leaves a lot to be desired. The horses understand straight away that they can do what they like ... So they stroll around the ring, nodding to each other as they pass, or sniffing each other if they're interested ... No longer man's finest conquest, the horses behave like guests at a high-class equestrian garden-party ...

Of course it is mildly amusing to watch people doing something innocuous with incompetence; but the comedy Tati watched more closely was a comedy of manners, or more precisely, a comedy of social class. The working-class lad would hold on to the horse's neck or mane as if it was a handlebar (for cycling was then very much a working-class sport); the peasant lad would sit astride the stallion as if he was on a thickset shire horse; the office worker would sit up straight and pull the reins back tight as if he was sitting at a typing desk; and so on. There is one short film, *Cours du soir*, shot by Nicolas Ribowski on the set of *Playtime* in 1966, where Tati can be seen demonstrating his social theory of horseback-posture; the sequence is the only known movie record of Tati's equestrian skills, but it hardly seems very funny any more. Many of the social types satirised no longer exist; indeed, the whole concept of "social types" seems outmoded, if not downright reactionary. It is actually quite uncharacteristic of Tati's miming in general, which nearly always reproduces activities, not "types".

In the army, Tati's superior skills as a rider did not exempt him from the humbler tasks of an unpromoted cavalryman:

> I had done a lot of riding, but I had never been a stable boy. The job involves sacrificing a night's sleep to ensure that the thirty horses in your charge have an excellent rest. The problem is that you have to leave the stables in the morning in the same state of absolute cleanliness as you found them at the start of the watch. That means leaving not the slightest trace of dung on the floor.
>
> An old hand who had done plenty of nights before gave me some precious advice: "Tatischeff! If you wait until the morning to clean up, you'll never manage!"
>
> So there I sat on a stool at the end of the stable, with thirty equine haunches in my line of sight. I didn't have to wait long. Within minutes, the regular alignment of thirty tails was broken by one that rose up and thus provided necessary warning. I rushed to it with a bucket which I got into place just in time. My first victory. A good part of the night was spent in just such to-ing-and-fro-ing with a bucket. And sitting on my little stool, I began to smile. I had just thought of how proud my parents were when they told people that their "big boy was in the cavalry". – Yes indeed, I was in the cavalry! Up to my neck in it! [32]

With his skills and his local base, Tati seems to have been a ringleader when it came to larks and japes. The most curious of these was an elaborate plan, successfully executed, intended to scare the wits out of a junior officer who came back to his quarters every Sunday night with a skinful of drink. Although his room was on the first floor, above the stables, he stumbled back one night, fumbled with the latch, opened the door – and found a white horse standing over his bed. Tatischeff had organised a whole squad to get the horse up the stairs. But once the joke had been shared – the whole regiment apparently found it quite hilarious – it was up to Tatischeff to get the horse down again. And that was no simple task.

Nearly fifty years later, Elisabeth Wennberg, who knew Tati well from having worked for him on *Parade*, rang the maestro in Paris. She had heard he was coming to Stockholm for the re-release of *Trafic*; would he like to appear on the television talk-show she was then running? Sure, said Tati, in his approximate English. "All I need for my act is a white horse – in a cupboard." The request was bizarre, but Tati was firm: he would appear on the show only if there was a white horse in a cupboard. Swedish TV did the necessary. Tati's "act" on the show was to open the cupboard and to lead the horse round the studio, whilst the rock band "Kiss" played on. Nobody, bar an implausible French spectator of Swedish TV who had done his military service in the Sixteenth Dragoons in 1928, could possibly have got the joke. Indeed, nobody had much idea what Tati was up to, and put it all down to the whim of an ageing star for whom the Swedes had a particular affection.

Fig. 11: *Tati and a white horse, Stockholm, 1975*

Tati saw his army service as the time when he woke up to the comedy of life. Many scenes of military nonsense remained sharply etched in his memory, or at any rate came back to him with great vividness in his old age: more than half of the memoirs he spoke into Jean L'Hôte's tape recorder in 1980 consist of anecdotes from the mere twelve months that he spent in the Sixteenth Dragoons. The scenes that he then recalled have a family resemblance, naturally enough, and are also presented, perhaps too explicitly, as lessons about the construction of comic gags. But that is no reason to think of the anecdotes as anything but authentic.

Tatischeff, promoted to the rank of sergeant (*maréchal des logis*), had to do sentry duty. That was less easy than it sounds, because the barracks were right in the middle of town with the sentry post on the main street. On one such occasion, Tati's grandmother approached, bearing a neatly-tied paper package held by a fancy ribbon. The soldier standing at his post carried on looking straight ahead. Grandma came right up to him, smiling. "Look what I've brought you!" Tati tried not to bat an eyelid. "Jacques, say something to your grandma! I've brought you a cake!" Looking straight ahead, speaking in a whisper from the corner of his mouth, Tati tried to explain to his grandmother that she just couldn't approach a soldier on sentry duty like that. He failed, and ended up standing for the rest of his duty with a dainty cake-box hanging from his little finger, by a ribbon.

It was in the army too that Tati met men who were a lot dimmer than he was. One such simply could not memorise the names and insignia of military ranks, and Tati was detailed to tutor him. He found that he could indeed get the man to repeat the sequence by rote, but that when he asked him a question out of order, he got almost random replies. For fun, he taught him a ridiculous parallel sequence involving the height of the hats of the different echelons of the political ladder, from mayor to member of parliament to minister and president. So when his pupil underwent his formal interrogation by the captain, he reeled off in sequence not only the ladder of military ranks and their corresponding stripes and pips, but also the joke-hierarchy of politicians and their hats. "So who taught him this nonsense!!?" Tatischeff was the obvious and only possible culprit; but he seems to have got off scot-free, for all the laughter that his jape provoked.

Towards the end of his service, the regiment was modernised, at least to the extent of adding motorised half-tracks to the cavalry's traditional means of locomotion. Tati drove one of these vehicles a few times, and on one occasion felt the front tyre blow out. One of the troopers went to inspect the damage and came back quite relieved: "Don't worry, sarge, it's only the bottom bit that's burst."

However, the character that, according to Tati, had the greatest impact on his sense of comedy and of life was a hairdresser named Lalouette. Lalouette was a happy, inoffensive fellow who seemed simply not to notice that the army was different. He said "sir" to the officers, instead of *mon capitaine, mon colonel* and so forth as required, and, when rebuked, offered sincere apologies, saying once again, "I'm so sorry, sir." He was quite hopeless as a horseman, and was also forever losing things. But, undaunted and as it were blind to the reality of his situation, he would blithely walk up to senior officers and ask, with normal civilian deference, if they hadn't perhaps seen his grooming brush lying around somewhere . . . Lalouette wandered through his military service like the "Ivan Durak" of Russian folklore – stupid and innocent to a degree that made him untouchable, almost a holy fool. Even the rattiest of NCOs gave up trying to teach him a lesson, as it was obvious that Lalouette would take everything in the same impenetrably unruffled manner. On several occasions Tati explicitly attributed the original inspiration of Hulot to this irrecuperable conscript[33]; he also used the name in a comedy sketch on "Le Rugby militaire" that he put on with his rugby-club chums in the 1930s.[34] In Tati's description, Lalouette was never able to see or share the joke that he constituted; the humour of the situation lay in the exasperated reactions of the officers, rather than in the inappropriate, but unremarkable and never malicious behaviour of Lalouette. From this, Tati extracted the first principle of his own kind of comedy, which he was forever at pains to distinguish from Chaplin's: *Comedy lies not in the actions of the comedian, but in the comedian's ability to reveal the comic dimension of others.*

The few surviving anecdotes of Tati's school years, early training and military service hardly add up to the education of a comedy star, let alone of a creator. Yet the foundations of his later work must lie here, in these years of idling, in the proprieties of middle-class life that Tati never claimed to find stifling, in the horse-riding, and in the human comedy that opened up for him in the Sixteenth Dragoons. They must lie here, in holiday memories, in church parades, in classroom humiliations, not because all works of art are necessarily autobiographical, but because Tati was the very opposite of an inventor. He liked to say he was an observer and a realist. And nothing is so well observed, nothing is so real, as what we see for the first time, in childhood, adolescence and youth.

Fig, 12: *Military pageant, 10 June 1928. Tati in the uniform of a* carabinier *of 1809*

FOUR

Tati's University

When his twelve months of service were over, Tati left the Dragoons and went back to live at Le Pecq. The army had given him a good time, but as it had not given him another career, there was no alternative to taking up once again that dawdling apprenticeship at Cadres Van Hoof.

In the course of his long-drawn-out training in the picture-framing trade, Jacques was sent to London to see how other firms worked, to improve his English, and no doubt also to get him out of the family home for a while. He was placed with Spillers, in the centre of town, but he lodged with a family in Lewisham, a suburb as leafy as Saint-Germain. It was there that someone took the tall French youth to the nearby pitch at Westcombe Park, a branch of the famous Blackheath Rugby Club.

Tati took to rugby like a duck to water. He was large, fit and fast, and quickly turned into a good team player. On his return to Paris, he found a way of joining the Racing-Club de France, and was soon wearing the famous blue-and-white stripe as wing three-quarter in the third team, known, after the name of its unusual captain, as the "Equipe Sauvy" .

The youthful encounter of Alfred Sauvy and Jacques Tati on the turf of the Racing-Club's pitch at Colombes makes one of the oddest connections in French cultural history. Sauvy was ten years older than Tati, and a born leader of men. But he was also of an entirely different cast: a graduate of the elite engineering school, Polytechnique, he was a brilliant statistician, and an innovator of economic forecasting techniques. He applied himself in particular to population statistics (a matter of great concern in France, which has long had a lower birth-rate than England and Germany) and became an international authority in the emerging discipline of demography. But Sauvy was a man of many other parts, and at the time when he recruited the long-limbed Tatischeff for his team, he was also the part-time assistant to the immensely successful novelist, playwright, and sports-fancier Tristan Bernard. Rich both by inheritance and from his huge popularity, Bernard had been dashing off lightweight farces, one-acters, interludes and dialogue pieces for over thirty years; in the years before the Great War and again in the 1920s, Tristan Bernard had often had several works playing simultaneously on the Paris stage. Bernard's often acerbic verbal wit was the quintessence of French culture of *la belle époque*; and his varied extra-curricular activities – as the owner of a velodrome, a backer of football teams, an investor in early films (his son Raymond was already a well-established film director) and as an elegant man-about-town – make him seem like a one-man résumé of popular culture in the inter-war years.[35]

Tati obviously did not learn any statistics from his rugby captain, nor did he start reading Tristan Bernard just because the playwright sometimes came into the changing rooms after matches to chat with his secretary and encourage his team's sporting exploits. But the Racing-Club's rugby crowd must nonetheless have been Jacques Tati's real university, the milieu in which he first rubbed shoulders with clever people active in the sciences, the arts, and the wider world. They all also seem to have known how to have a good time. In their convivial company, Tati was first able to overcome the shyness that had made him such a dull and underperforming child; and it was there that he gained the conviction – no doubt very slowly – that he too might have something to give to the world.

Tati took rugby quite seriously, certainly rather more than picture-framing. He got into a routine of training after work on Thursdays and Fridays, playing practice matches on Saturdays and the real matches on Sundays, followed by late-night team binges which left him hung-over and half-asleep well into the following week. He began to adjust to a personal rhythm that made late nights easy and early mornings very hard. This did not go down well at the Cadres Van Hoof in Rue de Castellane, nor at home in Rue de L'Ermitage at Le Pecq. There must have been quite serious tensions between the feckless youth with no apparent talents for anything but sport and leisure, and the stiff-collared businessman with a serious trade to maintain.

Like the army, the amateur sporting scene was relatively free of the class rigidities of French society at large, and Tati felt at ease with his socially varied team-mates. The Sauvy Squad fielded, amongst others, a travelling salesman for a Swiss watch manufacturer (Broïdo), a worker at the Renault automobile factory at Boulogne-Billancourt (Lagrelat), and a medical student who would soon be a senior consultant (Gorodiche); Moutet was the son of a member of parliament, whereas Dupont lived in a gypsy caravan parked on waste land at Colombes[36]; and then there was Doug Schneider, an American diplomat, born in England but who had spent most of his life in France. These substantial differences of class, occupation, and circumstance could be seen when the team jogged on to the pitch at the start of the match.

Some (those who lived at home and had their washing done for them) had spotless shorts and shirts; some (those who lived alone, and most especially the students) still had the stains of the previous match; and some kept their shorts up with safety pins and bits of string. The differences were less visible by half-time; and by the end of the match, the generous mud of the pitch had obliterated all visible distinctions of background and wealth.[37]

The team's secret weapon was Colombel, a sturdy bull of a youth who was the son of the chief attorney to the Paris police. Colombel had a bad squint, which made him a terrible driver of his Citroën B14: for when he looked straight ahead, he saw to the side, and to see straight in front, he was obliged to turn his head to the side. On the rugby pitch, whenever he got the ball, the opposing team would mark the man to the side that Colombel appeared to be looking – except that he wasn't, and often had a clear run to the line all to himself.

When Tati's first feature film, *Jour de fête*, was finally released in 1949, critics were far from unanimous in their praise, despite the enormous public success of the film. One critic singled out the scene in which a cross-eyed peasant repeatedly fails to hit the maypole peg with his mallet. Postman François, played by Jacques Tati, invents a gag to solve the problem: he places a decoy peg a few inches to the side of the real one, and by inviting the squinting peasant to hit the wrong peg, succeeds in getting him to drive the right one into the ground. It is apparently a gag that figures in a Mack Sennett & Ben Turpin movie, and Tati was accused of copying it;[38] but if Tati found Sennett worth copying in this respect, it may have been because the situation depicted keyed in with his memory of the reality of the Racing-Club's third fifteen.

Tati was a good rugby player, but not an exceptional one. There was never any question of going professional: indeed, there was no professional rugby in France in those day. The sports that had acquired entertainment status and thus a commercial dimension were cycling (most of all), tennis, football, boxing and wrestling; but the 1930s were also the years of mass crazes for what now seem quite implausible and cruel events, such as six-day roller-skating contests, track-cycling behind wind-breaking motorcycles, and twenty-four-hour Charleston marathons. Rugby was then, as now, a popular sport in quite specific regions of France (in the Catalan and Basque areas of the south-west, most of all – Sauvy was from Perpignan – but also in Brittany and parts of the Massif Central), but elsewhere retained the cachet of an English gentleman's game, which was no doubt why it had its place in the otherwise rather exclusive Racing-Club de France.

As in the Army, so in the Racing-Club, Tati found a convivial, all-male environment that provided him with constant examples of natural comedy.

"Laughing together is easier than laughing alone," Tati explained in his dictated memoirs. "The oldest spring of comedy is simply the pleasure that a group of people feel on being together."[39] But the ribald and rumbustious fun that might be expected of fifteen large young males seems far removed from the gracious and subtle comedy of Tati's films; the connection that he makes in his memoirs between rugby-club junkets and the development of comic art depends absolutely on the very special nature of the entertainment that Tati invented spontaneously to celebrate each match that had been played. And it seems to have begun with his very first game for the Sauvy Fifteen:

> It was a rugby Sunday. There were only fourteen of us in the changing rooms. A young, shy, hulk of a chap came up to me. Jacques Tatischeff.
>
> We shook hands, I looked him up and down, and said: half-back.
>
> That evening the team, which was not yet a troupe, gathered at Barbe Jean, a restaurant in Montmartre which has kept its name but not its now historical telephone booth . . .
>
> In the middle of the dinner, all the lights went out in the room, save those in the little booth . . . and we all became the audience of the most hilarious shadow-mime you can imagine. A star was born: Jacques Tati.[40]

Tati's fourteen team-mates now expected a show after each match, and at the appropriate moment after dinner they would fall silent, as if the curtain was about to rise. Tati needed this audience to be able to perform; and the team had come to need his act, as an integral and crowning glory of the match. Sauvy's Fifteen, though it must have resembled in some respects any other group of healthy twenty-five-year-olds, was a good deal more sophisticated than most.

Tati found that he could amuse his team-mates most at dinner by play-acting the main events of the match that they had just played. He would mimic the moves and dodges of this player or that, just by altering the angle of his head or making a bend in his arm; and he soon came to realise that he was kept on in the team not so much for what he could do on the field, but for the instant replays he could provide in those fabulous "third halves".

The environment of the games and junkets was not quite exclusively male, as Tati's and Sauvy's published reminiscences always state or imply: la belle Catherine [41] may not have been a flapper, or a groupie, or just a hanger-on, but she came to all the matches, including away fixtures in far-flung corners of France, and naturally captured the hearts of all the players one by one, before she settled down as Mrs Douglas Schneider. By 1934, Sauvy and

Broïdo were also married; but Tatischeff carried on as a now slightly ageing *garçon* for many more years. No anecdotes – and certainly no facts – have survived about relationships he might have had with women in these foot-loose years: his own reminiscences and those of his team-mates focus exclusively on the all-male bunch of mates – *les copains*.

In the changing rooms after one successful match or another, Tristan Bernard noticed Sauvy's hefty half-back whirling around the lockers in a kind of trance, silently acting out the whole match over again, all for himself. (We see Tati doing something like that in *Jour de fête*, when, after saving the village maypole from collapse, he demonstrates his exploit in mime three times over, to villagers who cross his subsequent path.) He mimed the referee, the team, the opposition, even himself, apparently oblivious of the hoots of laughter of the entire team that had gathered to watch the performance.

> "You know", Tristan Bernard muttered, " I really don't see why you
> should carry on framing still-lifes."[42]

Tati had begun to find a skill, if not yet a *métier*, and one that is no doubt as old as human history itself. The art of *reprise* – the re-enactment, in comic or tragic mode, of acts of skill, daring, or import, on whatever scale or stage – is the common source of circus clowning and serious acting, and perhaps of all the arts of imitation. A gift for mimicry is shared by many, and there were plenty of lovable buffoons on stage and screen in 1930s France (Fernandel, for example, or the wonderful Raimu); but miming of genius is rare. Jean-Louis Barrault was as yet an unknown trainee at the Ecole du Vieux-Colombier, and Marcel Marceau (born 1923) still a schoolboy. Without any career models to look up to, Tati seems to have been happy enough just to fool around after his matches, entertaining his team-mates, and keeping his place as the master of post-match festivities. A word of encouragement from a famous playwright must have helped Tati to imagine how he might find a way out of Rue de Castellane. But off the rugby pitch, Tatischeff did not move fast.

FIVE

Les Copains

Tati's talent for instant improvisation in mime found free rein not only in after-match dinners, but more generally whenever he was in the company of members of the team. His later evocations of the collective jollity of his social life in the 1930s is uncannily reminiscent of Jules Romains's stylishly comic novel of male bonding, *Les Copains* (1922), which provides a model, if not for the actual behaviour of the rugby-club crowd, then certainly for ways of talking about it. Sauvy recalled Tati doing a stunning "impression" of a radio broadcast on the open rear platform of a Paris omnibus, which had passengers so rapt in attention that they missed their stops . . .

> Once we had got off the bus, I said, "Quick, Tati, you must write down that little masterpiece, it's a a real gem . . ." Only you had forgotten it all already and had your mind on some other expression of life. [43]

A significant turn came when Tati found himself selected for a higher-ranking team, far above his actual form, for an away match at Bordeaux – not because he was the best player in the Sauvy squad, but simply so as to perform in the "third half-time". It turned out to be a memorable occasion.

The team won, which put everyone in a suitably good mood, and, in addition, in the restaurant booked for the evening, Tati came across a stack of party hats and disguises, left over from some previous junket. He did a particularly high-spirited show that evening, acting out not just the after-noon's match, but other traditional mime numbers, such as the drunk trying to get back through his front door.

> I then realised that I had two audiences, one of whom was wildly supportive (my team-mates) and the other plainly hostile (the *patron* and the restaurant staff). I'll never forget the icy stare of the latter. Afterwards, when I thought back on the scene and put myself in their place, I discovered what real comedy would be for me. [44]

Tati's "discovery" is exemplified in his memory by what happened later that night. The team was moving on to Toulouse for another match, but he had to return to Paris on the night train to be at Rue de Castellane in the morning. The whole noisy bunch accompanied him to Gare Saint-Jean, and he carried on larking and japing even as he got on the train. He came to the window of his compartment, and with a circus nose on his face and a silly hat on his head, mimed an eccentric train driver, and then did his drunken act again. As the train finally got under steam, he closed the window, turned round and found himself facing five pairs of very dour eyes. With his red nose, his jacket on backwards, and a pink paper hat, he felt like a second-rate clown answering charges in some circus tribunal.

Tati adjusted his dress, stuffed his paper hat slowly into his pocket, and sat down in the last remaining seat. Then he began to watch his fellow-travellers. One by one, they settled down for the night. One undid his shoe-laces, another loosened his belt; one made a blanket out of an overcoat, another rolled up a scarf to make a pillow ... It was as if they were all pantomime artists themselves, *imitating* passengers on a night train, in Tati's much later interpretation of the scene. And it is in such scenes that are both entirely natural and completely hilarious when observed in a certain way that Tati claims to have found the real sources of his kind of comedy.

Tati's interpretation of the scene (in an interview done in 1980) is necessarily coloured by the views he formed later on about the difference between professional actors and what he thought of as real performers, that is to say, ordinary people doing ordinary things. In this view, trained actors simply could not achieve the "truth-effect" that he sought; Tati thus came to use mostly non-professionals to represent themselves on screen. For example, the concierge in the electronic lodge of the Strand Building in *Playtime* really was a retired concierge (he was brought by taxi every morning from the old people's home, where Tati had finally tracked him down); just as the businessman forever called to the telephone in *Les Vacances de M. Hulot* is not an actor playing a businessman, but an actual businessman (the leading lady's husband, in fact), playing himself.

Only in some specific instances does Tati's use of non-professionals seem close to naturalistic, documentary, or candid-camera styles – in the shots of drivers picking their noses at traffic lights in *Trafic*, most obviously (a sequence that was actually made by Bert Haanstra, in fact, not by Tati), and in the episodes of the cart-driver and the clean blouse in *Jour de fête* (see below, p. 129) and the infant ice-cream-cornet-carrier in *Les Vacances de M. Hulot*. Most often, however, Tati made his amateur cast members *learn how* to represent themselves. At rehearsals, which he enjoyed most enormously, he would mime his cast's particular ways of walking and standing – and then make them imitate his imitation of themselves . . .

This approach to the business of acting goes back to the observation that Tati made in his youth on the Bordeaux-Paris express. What he saw on the train was not just that ordinary actions can be comic. The insight that he had – even if it was never quite expressed in these terms – was into the nature of the real, and the ways in which it can be represented. Those real travellers – if observed with attention of a quite particular kind – performed gestures which, when repeated both with accuracy and with exaggeration, could become signs capable of representing precisely that reality and no other. The only school of acting required, the only "alphabet of mime" that was needed, was to observe quite precisely what it was that real people did.

The idea is reminiscent of Diderot's famous paradox about the emotional effects that actors create: an effect which the philosopher insisted was not the fruit of authentic feeling, but, on the contrary, the product of the intellectual observation and careful recomposition of the gestures of others. Diderot maintained that accurately simulated emotion is more communicative and in effect more "true" than the real thing. In her dithyrambic early work on the art of Tati, Geneviève Agel develops the same point with respect to the mime, who is, she declares, "such a sharp, precise and attentive observer that he can incorporate the beings and things he observes and render them to us more truthfully than when we see them ourselves."[45]

Such a concept of mime is at the antipodes of naturalistic art, with its various kinds of stress on the authentic, the sincere, or the unmediated representation of the world. If there is a unity to Tati's two careers as mime and film-maker, then it is based in these twin convictions – that art does represent the real, and that the real can only be represented by studied recomposition. This approach puts Tati much closer to the formalised acting styles of Brechtian theatre, and to fashions of experimental painting and writing in the post-war period than he himself probably imagined. However, there can be few scenes on film that are as formal, non-naturalistic and nonetheless "real" as the garden-party scene in *Mon Oncle*. When the guests gather on the "modern-style" front lawn of the Arpel residence, every movement of their legs, hands, and bodies contributes to the meaning of the overall scene. Every posture adopted, every tiny shift of neck or shoulder, had been designed and rehearsed as signifying elements in a complex tableau of (petit-bourgeois) stiltedness. All the movements come from a single school, a single teacher, and a single vision – that of Jacques Tati, who first mimed the parts before allowing his "amateurs" to copy him. The garden-party is thus rather like a piece of comic grand opera: a world intensified by exaggeration, but serving to express an overriding theme. It is not exactly caricature, for the exaggerations remain within the bounds of plausibility,

Fig. 13: *Tati giving a mime lesson on the set of* Mon Oncle

and are subtly composed; but it is also the very opposite of a documentary film-record of a petty-bourgeois party scene.

Around 1930-31, when the seeds of these ideas were sown, Tati's emerging comic talent was greatly encouraged and enhanced by other members of the Sauvy team. Jacques Broïdo, in particular, seems to have become for a while Tati's almost inseparable performing partner. He had already had an extraordinary life: born in Moscow in 1908, Broïdo had escaped the Revolution by making a long trek overland with his mother to Basle, and had then been brought up in Geneva, where he acquired Swiss nationality and a training in the watch-making trade. Though he had never been to university, and though he earned his living as a commercial traveller, Broïdo was a natural engineer, and was fascinated by the technology of photographic equipment, most particularly of movie cameras (at his death

Fig. 14: *The "garden-party" in* Mon Oncle *(1958)*

in 1987, Broïdo left no fewer than 750 industrial patents, many of which are still in use). In name the son of a celebrated Russian-Jewish architect, Hermann Broïdo, and thus the brother of the moderately successful French film and stage actress Colette Broïdo, with whom he had little contact, Jacques was thought to be the illegitimate son of Prince Dolgorukin, the former Russian Ambassador to Paris . . . and thus a descendant of that great Russian family that built St Petersburg, against the wishes of the local barons called . . . Tatischeff.

The two "Russian Jacques", Tati and Broïdo, worked up sketches and skits as a performing duo, involving the kind of verbal wit and repartee that would never be seen in Tatischeff's later stage and film work; according to Sauvy, they could keep up an improvised exchange of puns and quips for a whole evening, indeed for a whole night.[46] On one occasion, they were lunching with Sauvy at a restaurant opposite Gare Saint-Lazare when news of the first non-stop aeroplane crossing of the Atlantic by the Frenchmen Costes and Bellonte was the big story of the day.

> And thereupon . . . Jacques Tati and his friend and alter ego Jacques Broïdo stood up and declared without bombast that they were going to perform Costes and Bellonte crossing the Atlantic. They put out two chairs, one in front of the other: on the first, there was Tati-Costes, and behind him, Bellonte-Broïdo. And what we saw was an amazing dramatic representation, hard to imagine and even harder to reconstruct. The performance went from the gag-laden crossing itself, to the arrival in New York, the official reception, and so forth . . . [47]

This seems to have been a special moment in Tati's blossoming comic career, for at other times, and in most other circumstances, he does not seem to have had much of a talent for verbal improvisation, even if he did have a stock of jokes and sketches that he would perform, at his own slow pace, with ponderous panache. Far more typical, and far more promising for his future career, were improvised dumb-shows:

> One evening, in which not much had happened so far, at the *Trapèze volant*, which does indeed have a trapeze hanging from the ceiling, Tati and his disciple, J. Vigouroux, stepped up on to the little foothold as if they were acrobats about to do a turn, though without the faintest idea of what they were going to do. They managed to keep up an act for forty minutes, miming acrobats getting ready to do their turn. Now and again, one of them would launch the trapeze over the audience and grasp it firmly on its return, whilst the other limbered up or rubbed rosin into his hands. Then one or the other would silently mime the announcement of the somersault to come, but each time the trapeze would return empty because of some mimed obstacle or other . . . [48]

These post-match performances almost displaced the game as the team's centre of gravity: the rugby men were slowly turning into a theatrical troupe. One night they disported themselves with particular brio at the *Bon Bock*, a restaurant in Rue Dancourt, and left in a state of great gaiety, saying to all and sundry, "See you next Friday!" Lo and behold, when they arrived after the following week's match, there was a long line at the door. "Get in line!" the queuers said, "We're all waiting to see the jesters!" [49]

This kind of unsought-after celebrity inspired the team to make a speciality of comic acting, and to put on its own show at the end of the season. The

PROGRAMME

—

R.C.F. 31

Revue sportive de A. Sauvy et H. Janicot
Musique adaptée par M. Gaston Saux

PREMIÈRE PARTIE

1. Musique de disques.
2. LA RESQUILLE
   Le spectateur .. ..   MM. Jacques Keyser.
3. A LA MANIÈRE DE, par .. .. ..   Gabriel Lavoégie.
4. JARDINAGE ET CONSTRUCTION, par   Douglas Schneider.
5. LE COUP DU SAC, par   .. .. ..   Henri Colombel.
6. CEUX D'AUTREFOIS, sketch de G. Lavoégie et A. Sauvy.
   Le dirigeant .. ..   MM. P. Taffet.
   Le joueur. .. ..   A. Sauvy.
   L'ancêtre.. .. ..   G. Lavoégie.
7. DITES-MOI ROUSSEL, par .. .. ..   Goullet.
8. SPORT MUET, par .. ..   Jacques Tattischoff.
9. LA NUIT ARGENTINE, Parodie sonore de H. Janicot
   (D'après C. A. GONNET)
   Le bandit. .. ..   M. Douglas Schneider.
   Dolorès .. ..   Mlle Simone Millet.
   Manola .. ..   Mlle Denise Balensi.
10. DANSES DE STYLE par les JACK TWINS
    J. Tattischeff, J.-J. Cattier et J. Broïdo.

———

ENTR'ACTE
MUSIQUE DE DISQUES

Fig. 15: *"R.C.F. 31" : Gala Programme*

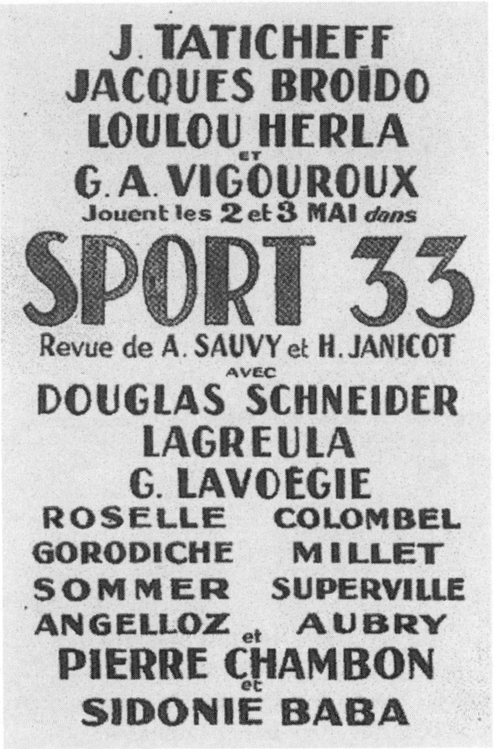

Fig. 16: *"Sport 33"*: *Gala Programme*

J. TATICHEFF
JACQUES BROÏDO
LOULOU HERLA
ET
G. A. VIGOUROUX
Jouent les 2 et 3 MAI dans

SPORT 33

Revue de A. SAUVY et H. JANICOT
AVEC
DOUGLAS SCHNEIDER
LAGREULA
G. LAVOÈGIE
ROSELLE   COLOMBEL
GORODICHE   MILLET
SOMMER   SUPERVILLE
ANGELLOZ et AUBRY
PIERRE CHAMBON
et
SIDONIE BABA

theme would be sport; and the occasion would be the Racing-Club's own annual "gala". So for four seasons, from 1931 to 1934, Sauvy scripted, in collaboration with all the team members, a collective entertainment first entitled *Ballon d'essai*.

In front of an audience that included wives, girlfriends, families, and old members, the rugby men sang songs, did dance routines and recitals; but most of all the gala consisted of comic sketches, and Alfred Sauvy, like his boss Tristan Bernard, was a dab hand at stringing a few jokes on a thin scenario to keep an audience in stitches for thirty minutes or more. It was for these galas that Tati worked up his one and only real music-hall act, which went by the title of *Sport muet* ("Silent Sport") before acquiring its definitive name of *Impressions sportives* ("Sporting Impressions"). The first attested performance was in the gala held in April 1931:[50] but at least one of the elements – the miming of a football goalkeeper – went back, as we have seen, to 1924.

Tati actually did at least two "acts" in the rugby-club revue: the first, never repeated elsewhere, was a standard male adolescent lark – dancing the *pas-de-deux* from *Coppelia* with Jacques Broïdo, both dressed in pink tights and tutu. *Impressions sportives*, on the other hand, even if it was not entirely unprecedented, seemed to all who saw it to be utterly original. The mime act tackled five different sports activities: the football goalkeeper; the boxer's first fight; the angler; the cyclist; and the show-horse and rider in one. Oddly enough, rugby, which had had so much to do with the emergence of Tati's skills as a mime, did not figure in the act; and the sports portrayed were not ones in which Tati indulged very much (or at all), even if he was a decent horse-rider and endowed with good enough legs to propel a bicycle at a fair pace.

Tati can be seen doing exactly the same routines more than forty years later, in the last film that he actually directed, *Parade* (1974). By then he had also added impressions of "Tennis at the Turn of the Century" and a set of innocuously racist mimes on traffic policemen in Paris, London, Mexico, Rome, and New York: but even those two additions went back to the early 1950s at least. [51]

The stability of Tati's act is characteristic of circus and music-hall turns. An acrobat has just one "number", a routine that is part imitation of models and masters, and – necessarily – in part entirely unique. The point of the act is not to be always different, but to be always exactly the same (it is for the act that the *artiste* is hired in the first place), and to be ever nearer perfection. Each performance is a rehearsal for the next time.

The gala performances went down really well, just as Tati's apprenticeship as a framer seemed to be turning into a life sentence. One day he panicked at the prospect of his whole life laid out before him, in an unending rut. Standing on the front step of the family business, he asked himself: "Do I have to look out on the shop on the other side of the street for the rest of my days?"[52] He had to get out. He went home and told his father that he was chucking it in.

> "To do what?"
> "To go on stage."
> "To do what? To go on stage! To be a clown?"

When Georges-Emmanuel calmed down, he told Jacques he could do as he pleased, but he wouldn't get a penny in support. So Tati threw in not only his job, but his home base too, and the pittance that Cadres Van Hoof paid him as an apprentice. It must have been in 1931 or perhaps 1932. Several years of poverty followed, for Tati left home at just the wrong moment. The Great Depression set off by the Wall Street Crash of October 1929 had just begun to make itself felt in France.

Fig. 17: *Father and Son, July 1931*

SIX

Down and Out

Tati left home with nothing. He lived in cheap hotels, or by cadging a bed off one friend or another, or even, when truly desperate, by getting his rugby-mate Gorodiche (now a qualified doctor) to sign a medical certificate entitling him to a free night in a hostel for the needy. Tati was not the only pauper in Paris. Though France still thought of itself as a rich country – had it not won the war barely more than a decade before? – its industrial base had begun to shrink as the effects of the American depression worked their way through the economy. Tati was no longer a middle-class lad with a boring job and a mad ambition; he was one of the rapidly growing number of unemployed and destitute on the streets.

All he had was a mime act that had delighted the audiences of the Racing-Club's annual galas, an act that could plausibly be performed on the music-hall stage, or even, at a pinch, in a circus ring; but the live music-hall was hardly in a position to take on much new talent in the early 1930s, as its audience had suddenly shrunk like a shrivelled balloon.[53]

In the 1920s, to be sure, music-hall and cabaret were to be found all over Paris – not just in the expensive entertainment district of the Champs-Elysées, but in every arrondissement and almost every *quartier*. Many ordinary restaurants and numerous bars that served mainly local clienteles had back rooms where variety entertainment was provided: not just the singers of the traditional and essentially working-class *caf'conc'*, but jugglers, accordionists, singers of ballads and popular songs, and, in larger establishments, more complicated acts such as acrobats and trick-cyclists were regularly put on for popular and not at all wealthy clienteles. But the *années folles* had pretty much come to an end when Tati first tried to get a toe-hold in the entertainment world.

The stock-market crash had already turned the flood of high-rolling American visitors into a mere trickle, and the more expensive cabarets and music-halls that relied on tourist custom had gone into a sharp decline. Between 1929 and 1931, all but two of the larger establishments closed down:

the Alhambra was destroyed by fire and not rebuilt; the Olympia closed down and remained empty for years; the Cirque de Paris went dark, Le Palace gave up variety for light opera, and – perhaps most symbolic of all – the Moulin-Rouge was converted into a cinema. All that remained of the major variety venues of the 1920s were the Empire and the Bobino. The smaller music-halls that survived could not accommodate all the displaced performers, and Tati found himself just one among many hundreds of unemployed entertainers. Some took to busking on the streets. Others looked elsewhere for ways of earning a living, and the cinema beckoned as the obvious alternative outlet for the talents that had previously filled the variety stage.

The start of the economic downturn that soon came to afflict the whole of Europe coincided almost exactly with the launch of the talking film, which created its own powerful wave of change in the entertainment world. The idea of joining sound and image was as old as the moving picture itself, and methods of recording voice and music – on waxed cylinders, to begin with, then on metallic and eventually bakelite disks – were developed in exactly the same time-frame as the cinema. However, despite strong industrial links between sound and screen (Charles Pathé made a fortune from copies of Edison's phonograph as well as from marketing his own film cameras, and Léon Gaumont patented a "talking picture" procedure which he failed to develop or exploit), cinema grew up in America and Europe as an art of silent drama, or, in Chaplin's words, as a reinvention of the pantomime. By the late 1920s, there were thus well-established cultural and intellectual barriers to the introduction of cinema sound. When Warner Brothers launched the first supposedly "one hundred per cent talking film" in 1927 – The Jazz Singer, with Al Jolson – not everyone in the industry, and certainly very few in France, thought it a serious threat. The system used (Vitaphone) was a cumbersome one, involving separate equipment for sound and vision; but very quickly, Fox and RKO acquired the patents of two rival versions of optical sound (Movietone and Photophone, respectively). In both systems, a thin strip on the side of the image-bearing film is used to record a sound track in analogue form, providing perfect synchronisation with the image. Optical sound was a runaway success with the public, and changed the nature of the industry – and of the art – of the cinema almost overnight. The first real sound films arrived in Europe in 1929, and, after a very short battle for technical and commercial supremacy, the market was divided straightforwardly between the American devices and the only slightly different Tobis-Klangfilm system created by a powerful German-Swiss industrial concern. It was a great blow to French pride: sound arrived as a foreign, not a home-grown invention, despite the historical priority of the French cinema industry. But even if the patents had been French, the talkies would have created serious – and also very interesting – problems for the home of the *cinématographe*.

The very first French talkies were made, or rather, commissioned in 1929. At one end of the social and cultural scale, Charles and Marie-Laure de Noailles gave 700,000 francs each to Luis Buñuel and Jean Cocteau to experiment with the new medium: from this aristocratic patronage came *L'Age d'Or*, which was eventually finished in 1930 and promptly banned for immorality; and *Le Sang d'un poète*, which was not released until 1932.[54] This could be taken to mark the end of cinema as a toy for wealthy aesthetes in Europe (and also, in another sense, as the last adventure of Surrealism), because by the time Cocteau's "first" sound movie appeared, the popular end of the film industry had already abandoned the silent screen entirely and had produced hundreds of more or less forgettable talkies. The first to appear on French screens seems to have been a 600-metre reel directed by Georges Lacombe. Entitled *Bluff*, this pioneering short was a compendium of music-hall celebrities: Yvette Guilbert, Georges Tschernogarow and his balalaika, Frédo Gardoni on the accordion, the Boyer Sisters, and someone called Jack Forrester performed their acts just as on the music-hall stage.[55] Sound cinema provided a potentially far more lucrative medium for music-hall artistes than the music-hall itself; and the decline of live variety shows proceeded in tandem with the rise of the talking, singing, moving picture. Like the Moulin-Rouge, many "*music-halls de quartier*", such as the Folies-Belleville, converted themselves into cinemas within a year or two.[56]

The silent cinema, unaffected by linguistic boundaries, could be seen as an intrinsically international art form. The potential audience for any silent movie, wherever it is made, is the whole world, and its potential profits correspondingly huge. Though that was not always the reality, the arrival of the talkies changed the fundamental equations, and also the whole idea of what a local – that is to say, a national – cinema industry was for. The Americans had the patents on the technology; they also had the largest linguistic community (there were approximately three times as many speakers of English as of French in the world at that time) and thus the greatest economies of scale. The risk – which has obsessed French governments, politicians, trade unions and film-makers ever since – was that French-language films would simply be squeezed out of existence. And, as at many other times in its history, the French film industry – financially fragmented, under-capitalised, and under-equipped – was not in a good position to resist.[57]

Tati left home to go into live performance as a mime just at a time when the music-hall was in crisis and decline. If he also wanted to become a movie star (and it would seem that he did), then his timing was just as bad – for *silent* acts were just what the industry could now do without. And it must have looked to many as if the world could probably do without a French cinema industry as well. Many talented French film technicians and creators left for Hollywood, to supervise French-language versions of American sound movies there: for prior to the development of dubbing techniques, the cheapest way to make a film in French was to reshoot a movie being made in English, on the same sets, with exactly the same shots, extras, stunts, and so forth, but with French actors standing in for the stars. Indeed, that was how Claude Autant-Lara learned his directorial skills – shooting French remakes of Buster Keaton shorts, on "location" in the sound-studios of Hollywood.[58]

SEVEN

Oscar, Roger and Rhum

We do not know exactly when Tati left home to go on stage, but it certainly happened while he was still a very active member of the Sauvy Fifteen, master of its after-match entertainments, and one of a jolly band of bachelor chums. It also happened at a time when French cinema was trying to develop its own brand of burlesque short films, to serve as "fillers" to precede the main feature, since audiences expected a full evening's entertainment at the talkies. That was how Robert Bresson began his career: his first film, *Les Affaires publiques* (Arc-Films, 1934) has a cast including the "girls" of the Folies Bergères, circus clowns, and comedians such as Marcel Dalio and Gilles Margaritis.[59] And that was also how Tati tried to start: not on stage, in fact, but on film.

That first film, which has been lost, despite Tati's later efforts to recover it ("I never found a single metre of it," he said in a radio interview in 1977)[60], was directed by the same Jack Forrester who performed in *Bluff*: in other words, by a music-hall artiste looking for a new career. Forrester certainly found one: he went on to direct numerous French versions of American "talkies" and home-grown thrillers throughout the 1930s, all produced by Forrester-Parant Productions. But all we know officially about his first short film, *Oscar champion de tennis* ("Oscar the Tennis Champ"), which received its *visa de production* in 1932, is that it was, or was to be, written and acted by Jacques Tati.[61]

Tati's first clearly documented professional engagement in the live music-hall did not come until 1935, at a half-private, half-public celebration of the winning of the Blue Riband (the fastest Atlantic crossing) by the French liner *Le Normandie*. Of course, he may have had less prestigious engagements in smaller places before then; he may of course have been performing "Oscar champion de tennis" as a live professional act simultaneously with his amateur shows for the rugby club; and the mimed sketch of "Tennis in 1900" which can be seen both in Tati's last film, *Parade*, and in the short film made by Nicolas Ribowski in 1966 (*Cours du soir*) may be nothing other than the core of that first, lost, and perhaps never really finished "Oscar".[62] There is a striking continuity between the image of Georges-Emmanuel in one of the few photographs of him that his son kept, the title of Tati's first projected film, and the contents of his very last – made all the more significant and repetitive by the unforgettable "tennis act" in Tati's most perfect film, *Les Vacances de M. Hulot*.

Fig. 18: *Georges-Emmanuel Tatischeff playing tennis*

The first of the shorts of which copies have survived was apparently made in 1934 (though the dating of these early works is at best hypothetical). According to Alfred Sauvy, *On demande une brute* was the title of a comic sketch he had written about rugby. Tati asked him if he could use it as the basis of a short film, which they planned together and began shooting in a still almost mediaeval village called Sournia.[63] Sauvy withdrew from the project and lost touch with it when he became head of the *Institut de Conjoncture* (Economic Forecasting Institute) in 1934 – just as he withdrew from amateur dramatics, from the rugby club, and from his job with Tristan Bernard. The original scenario got changed beyond easy recognition, and ended up as a film about boxing, under the title *Soigne ton gauche*.

> I developed the script of Tati's first film from a sketch that I wrote
> on the world of rugby. We worked for ages on the subject, cutting
> it up, debating the points, sometimes taking two hours over a tiny
> sequence which we then cut out altogether. Once the script was
> more or less done, Tati launched into making it. But he fell into the
> hands of illiterate producers . . . and the script became quite unrecog-
> nisable, losing everything it had, including its title. *Soigne ton gauche*
> doesn't even deal with rugby, but with boxing. I've never seen it,
> nor have I tried to.[64]

Sauvy's account seems very odd, because a film called *On demande une brute*
most certainly exists, and it is no more about rugby than is *Soigne ton gauche*,
which also exists. And although it is not very good, it was made not by
amateurs, but by a perfectly professional team. Sauvy's memory may have
been playing him tricks; titles and sketch material no doubt also migrated
from one more or less evanescent film project to another. Sauvy did write
a prophetic sketch entitled "Le Rugby en 1940", of which Tati kept a copy
in his files, but that also has nothing to do with any of the films Tati
actually made.

The director of *On demande une brute* was certainly not illiterate in filmic
terms: Charles Barrois had worked for the great silent director Jacques
Feyder and went on to make many a feature film of his own. *On demande
une brute*, which marks his transition from assistant and occasional actor to
director in his own right, is the story of Roger, a gormless out-of-work
actor in dire financial straits, played with wide-eyed passivity by the
incongruously tall and lanky Jacques Tati. His ambitious wife (played by
Hélène Pépée) responds to a classified advertisement for a well-paid part
on her husband's behalf; Roger does not realise until it is too late that the
"role" he has signed on for is to confront the reigning champion in the
wrestling ring. And it is a real wrestling champion, Kwariany, whom he has
to beat.

Tati plays opposite Enrico Sprocani, in a kind of Laurel and Hardy double
act: a willowy dimwit and a short, stocky wise-guy, always able to "fix
things" for his hapless chum. In fact, Tati and Sprocani were chums in real
life too, and together they eventually found a solution to their constant
lodging problems: a sort of glorified garden shed in the courtyard of number
30, Rue de Penthièvre, not far from Rue du Faubourg Saint-Honoré.
The courtyard also housed a dilapidated public bath, and a collection of
quaint and more or less down-at-heel Bohemian inhabitants. It was to be
Tati's base for nearly twenty years.

The first time I went into that courtyard, the house I had my eye on was utterly dilapidated. I told the manager that I planned to take up residence in it. He looked at me with wide-eyed astonishment, and shouted: "You are mad! I've got a madman on my hands!" But I insisted, and, finally, nodding his head in commiseration, he agreed to rent the shack to me for three thousand francs per year. [65]

Sprocani's real profession was that of circus clown, and he was already well-known as "Rhum" at the Cirque Medrano. Appearing in film was a natural sideline for him as for other variety artistes in those years: he appears, either as an actor or as himself, "le clown Rhum", in several dozen pre-war shorts.

In later reminiscences of his early adventures as a down-and-out entertainer, Tati spoke warmly of his long friendship with Rhum and of their joint efforts to break into commercial comedy film. "We had a lot of trouble trying to get producers interested in our proposals," he told his interviewer, making it also seem as if the pair had failed entirely to do so. "I must admit that we wasted our best years in such efforts,"[66] But if the poor quality of Tati's first film made the effort seem in retrospect like a waste of time, the circus and music-hall duo did not fail entirely to raise backing for their films.

Tati claimed that he saved up his music-hall earnings to buy blank film stock, reel by reel, and that he shot his first films piece by piece, as finances permitted: "In 1934 I began to shoot my first film with the income I got from my music-hall act; I used to buy ten metres of stock here, and ten metres there . . ." [67] That is hard to square with the fragments of evidence that exist. It may be how *Oscar champion de tennis* was envisaged, though if its recorded date of 1932 is correct, Tati did not at that point have any music-hall income to fund his purchases of reels. If the reminiscence concerns *On demande une brute*, then the cost of film stock could hardly have been a significant part of the budget : Barrois, the director, and the actors Rhum and Pépée (real name: Hélène Pierre) were not amateurs and are unlikely to have given their services free;[68] moreover, Tati could not have hired a professional wrestler, a full-size ring and a hundred or more real extras out of savings from a career that had barely begun. In fact, the credit sequence on the currently available copies of *On demande une brute* announces it as a film produced and distributed by "Les Films Fernand-Rivers", the production company founded and owned by the actor and music-hall artiste of the same name, who had once been almost a rival to Max Linder. However, more than twenty years later, when a negative of the lost film finally turned up at the Cinémathèque, Tati himself (through his administrative assistant, Bernard Maurice) described it as having been produced by MM. Rigault and Dolbert.[69] It thus seems very likely that *On demande une brute* was bought at some later stage – possibly even in the post-war period – by Les Films Fernand-Rivers, who added their own title sequence.

On demande une brute, like the later *Soigne ton gauche*, bears a general resemblance to many other French films of the period: for if there is one common thread to the 1,305 feature films produced in France in the 1930s, as Ginette Vincendeau says, it is the depiction of leisure[70] – in which sports played an inescapable, central role. A whole minor genre of French-made talkies presented sporting activities from points of view ranging from the heroic to the satirical: perhaps the classic example of the latter is *Les Rois du sport* (1937), starring the comic actors Raimu and Fernandel, who, like Tati, moved naturally between music-hall and cinema. According to contemporary résumés, this film tells the tale of two Marseillais bar-tenders who, through a crazy plot of which they are more victims than perpetrators, become respectively a boxing manager and a boxing champion.[71]

On demande une brute has a fairly clumsy two-act structure – a dramatic set-up, followed by the match itself. The set-up scenes, which switch between the Tati-Rhum duo rehearsing some drab theatrical role, then hearing that Roger has lost his job, with scenes at the impresario's office where the wrestling fixture is accepted, are, however, not exclusively functional narrative sequences. There is a kind of interlude where Roger and his pert and sharp-voiced wife eat a miserable dinner of soup and sardines in total silence. Entirely absorbed by the newspaper she is reading at table, the wife ladles not soup, but water from the goldfish bowl – and a live goldfish – into her plate. Tati silently switches plates, then tries to extract the goldfish, which plops into the open tin of sardines ... More plate-switching ensues in a kind of agonising embarrassment, as if Roger were incapable of saying anything at all to his wife, as if (in a vague intimation of the Hulot character Tati would later create) he were already guilty for the confusions of daily life ... and in a comic but also infinitely sad conclusion to the scene, he ends up swallowing the goldfish whole himself.

The wrestling-ring sequence, filmed in front of a live audience in an arena that looks rather like the Salle Wagram, provides Tati with a narrative frame for his "sports-miming" talents. He is twice the height and one-quarter the width of "Grossof le Tartare", his entirely bald and hugely muscular opponent, and has not got a clue how to cope. He is tripped, gripped, held to the floor, has his head thumped on the canvas and his limbs twisted into positions that look horribly painful. The only moment of graciousness is when he races away from the champion and runs around the ring, his knees riding up high like a show-jumping horse. The gong marks the end of round one. Enrico the artful dodger turns up and surveys the sorry scene. He plays the wise guy, the optimistic fixer and adjutant: and in round two, he helps his mate by two perfectly criminal devices. First, he drives a nail up through the floor of the ring and into the champion's buttock; and next, when Kwariany comes close to the ropes, Rhum hits his great shaven pate with a piece of lead piping concealed in a ladies' umbrella. As a result, young Roger wins the bout, and a fortune with it; and the last scene of the film shows the two chums departing in a taxi, leaving the martinet of a wife standing on the kerb.

Fig. 19: On demande une brute: *after the match*

On demande une brute thus has a generic resemblance to a thousand shorts of the silent era, pitting a loveable clown (or pair of clowns) against impossible odds, setting a representative of the poor against the rich (the impresario) and powerful (Kwariany), and setting the bonds of boyish friendship above those of family (the "wife" saved from a live sardine seems much more like a bossy mother, in fact, and Tati acts the "husband" as if he were a scolded child). There is little to distinguish this clumsily-made and indifferently-acted short from any number of similarly forgotten reels made in Hollywood, save for Tati's antics in the wrestling ring. They are not exactly acrobatic, nor are they entirely stylised: but at their best moments they fall half-way between ballet and mime.

Tati's entry into the film world, though it was barely a distinguished one, was thus probably a lot less amateur than he liked to make it seem in his post-war reminiscences and interviews.[12] It was certainly associated with the friends and contacts that Tati was making in the world of variety, circus and music-hall; but that was in no way exceptional at a time when the talkies had suddenly made it both possible and very necessary for variety artistes to find their audiences through film.

EIGHT

Sporting Impressions

Silence and mime sometimes achieve depths of feeling
that all the resources of oratory cannot reach
DENIS DIDEROT

Alongside his early ventures in film, Tati did his best to get engagements as
a mime in live variety theatre. But the years from 1929 to 1933 were a low
point in the fortunes of French music-hall, and there weren't many lucrative
opportunities. A new wave of investment in live entertainment began
around 1932: the first venue to reopen was the Lido, a luxurious restaurant
with a floor-show twice a night, built in what had once been a swimming
pool and Turkish bath. In 1934, the old Plaza on Boulevard Poissonnière
that had been dark for several years was bought by a consortium headed
by Mitty Goldin, who refurbished and reopened it as the A.B.C. (allegedly,
he chose the new name so it would always appear first on alphabetical listings
of theatres and cabarets). It put on top-level variety which soon made it
one of the main Paris "attractions", and it was there that stand-up comics,
wits and *raconteurs* like Pierre Dac, Fernandel and Raimu first appeared,
alongside cinema figures of great celebrity (Arletty, Noël-Noël), singers such
as Tino Rossi,[73] and at least one manifestation of the unbelievable Borrah
Minevich, the Russian-American inventor of the chromatic harmonica.[74]
And in the following year, the reconstructed Alhambra resumed its role as
"le music-hall de Paris", giving Borrah Minevich another stage, on which he
was quickly succeeded by the young Larry Adler, and also, in 1936, by a new
singer that the impresario, Louis Leplée, had heard busking on the streets,
and whom he dubbed (in honour of the song he had first heard her singing,
Les Moineaux de Paris ("The Sparrows of Paris")), *la môme Piaf* – "the bird
girl" in Parisian slang.[75]

Tati – whose stage-name was occasionally spelled Tatti or Taty – did the
rounds of auditions at these and no doubt many other less celebrated houses,
and for many a long month he got nothing but the conventional "Don't
call us, we'll call you." All sorts of anecdotes exist about how Tati got his
"first break": unsurprisingly, few of them are reliably dated. One account
(reproduced by Dondey, p.23) places the breakthrough at an after-match
dinner at *Le Gerny*'s, a restaurant run by Louis Leplée. At the end of the

meal, Tati borrowed a white jacket and a napkin, and invented (or repeated) his imitation-pantomime of the clumsy waiter. Leplée was delighted, and asked the rugby man to come back and do it again, and effectively hired him as an unavowed floor-show. Tati's act at Le Gerny's involved being rude to customers, getting their orders mixed up, dropping the odd plate, spilling soup on to the tablecloth, and, before the end of the evening, getting upbraided and sacked on the spot by the boss, Louis Leplée. Which is why Tati said, in other contexts, that his first real job was to be sacked . . .

According to Tati's sister, Nathalie, who now ran her own lingerie store on Rue Saint-Honoré, the true link between Tati's first performances in the sports galas at the Racing-Club de France and the professional entertainment scene was Léon Bailby, another impresario and man-about-town.[76] It might have been Bailby who introduced Tati to the producers of a sports documentary (Football quand tu nous tiens) who hired him to do his "silent sport" act before the curtain rose at a special presentation of the film for the French Football Association (FFFA) in 1934.[77] Or again, it might have been through this or a similar contact that Tati was hired to perform at the gala put on by Le Journal to celebrate the recent French victory in the competition for the fastest transatlantic crossing. Amongst the numerous celebrities watching Tati do his "Sporting Impressions" at this dinner was the writer Colette, who was also an influential commentator on the Paris arts and entertainment scene.[78]

But in Tati's own and almost contemporary account, his great chance came as the result of a charity function, the "Dîner des Trois-Cents", at which he performed his usual routine. His miming caught the attention of an impresario and theatre director, Max (Robert) Tréflin, who promptly offered him a "spot" in the interval of a comedy review due to go on at the Théâtre-Michel. But even before the show opened Tati's act was moved from the interval to the main show, and quickly became the star attraction.[79] At all events, the first pieces that Tati pasted into his cuttings book are reviews of that show, Lavalisons!, by Dorin and Saint-Granier, which opened in late September, 1935.

Dorin and Saint-Granier were actor-impersonators, who played their own material. In one sketch, for example, Dorin impersonated the socialist leader Léon Blum in the guise of Mephistopheles, whispering terrible thoughts into the ear of Prime Minister Pierre Laval, portrayed as Goethe's Gretchen; other numbers involved a satire of the National Lottery and a topical sketch about the demilitarisation of "Monte Carlo", strung along by interludes of song, trick-cycling, and acrobatic ballet. In those days of acute political strife – between the riots of February 1934, when Communists fought it out with the extreme right-wing Croix de feu on the streets of Paris, and the election of the Popular Front in 1936 – the political tone of a popular, but middle-class entertainment was obliged to remain pretty anodyne:

> Political satire is obviously suited to Dorin's biting wit, but Saint-Granier's good humour takes the cruel edges off it.[80]

Many of the cuttings that Tati kept and pasted into his press-book make it seem as if he stole the show:

> The theatre commissioned two wits, Dorin and Saint-Granier to write its revue, and that was a good idea. But the outstanding performance of the evening came from a wordless beginner, Jacques Tati. What a lesson! (Lucien Descaves, in *L'Intransigeant,* 22 September 1935)

> In Dorin and Saint-Granier's show, one of the acts that got the best reception was entirely silent, but no less funny for that. It was Jacques Tati's "Sporting Impressions" (*Juvénal,* 28 September 1935)

> "Sporting Impressions" is a novelty. Jacques Tati offers a very personal and perfectly rehearsed act. It's an attraction that is going to be famous in music-hall (J.D., in *L'Avant-Scène de Paris,* no. 297, 21 September 1935)

These and many other references in the press make it clear that Tati's success was made by the audiences at the Théâtre-Michel. It was the first time that Tati had appeared outside the private world of club reviews, galas, dinners, and charity functions, the first time he had met a real, entirely anonymous public that had no reason to pay for the evening other than for being entertained. Despite all this, Tati still expected to go back to work for his father in the picture-framing business fairly soon, even if what he really wanted was to appear on the London stage and meet the challenge of an English audience, "who are connoisseurs when it comes to music-hall". [81] But as far as can be told from the (not very reliably dated) materials that remain, the first thing he did after *Lavalisons!* closed ... was to make another film.

NINE

A Day in the Country

Though their first film together was at best a flop and may not even have been released, Tati and his friend Rhum managed to find another producer to finance their second venture, based on a story they wrote themselves. The title credits of *Gai dimanche* ascribe it to a now-forgotten production company called Atlantic-Film, whose backers were Micheline and Claude Fusée. It was probably made in 1935 or early 1936. Like *On demande une brute*, it is not a very polished object; but it is a much more interesting and elaborated piece.

The film opens with two tramps being thrown out of a metro station at dawn, for they have spent the night on the platform. Tati and Rhum adjust their dress, yawn, stretch and declare that they would like to spend a day in the country. But how? I can fix that, says the wise guy.

Cut to a second-hand car lot full of antiquated automobile junk. The sauntering pair peek into this jalopy and that, and are surprised to hear "brrrrr ... brrrrr ..." coming from one tall, square saloon. Rhum opens the bonnet to reveal a grimy urchin squatting where the engine should have been, playing at being a car. The gag is not developed; it is just a hint of the world of childhood and of make-believe that runs through all of Tati's later work like a nostalgic thread.

The destitute pair hire a dilapidated open-top twenty-seater charabanc from the motor-man: Tati pays with banknotes filched by Rhum from the man's own trouser-pocket. They then seek to attract tourists for a day in the country. See the chateaux, see the sights, lunch included, only thirty-five francs! they shout; but only a single punter shows up. Other tourist buses are filling up nonetheless, and Rhum understands why: their customers have pre-booked tickets. So he goes over the road, espies plausible excursionists making their way towards the far more modern buses parked in front of the hotel, and calls out: blue tickets this way! And so like sheep a whole group make their way to the fraudulent charabanc, and climb on.

The set-up of *Gai dimanche* is thus much less laborious than that of *On*

Fig. 20: Gai dimanche: *under the bonnet*

Fig. 21: Gai dimanche: *Tati and Rhum touting for customers*

demande une brute, and already contains at least three properly Tatiesque themes: that of leisure (though here in the context of the overweening ambition of two down-and-outs to have a "day off"), that of make-believe (the child in the engine compartment), and that of mechanical locomotion. The charabanc is in effect the precursor of an amazing variety of vehicles, all treated in humorous and passably satirical vein, in every one of Tati's subsequent films: bicycles in *Soigne ton gauche*, *L'Ecole des facteurs*, *Jour de fête*; M. Hulot's antiquated Amilcar in *Les Vacances*, his velosolex in *Mon Oncle*, and his camping-car in *Trafic*; as if from this point on Tati would never escape the contradictory passions attached throughout the twentieth century to the privileges and servitudes of individual mobility.

The main part of *Gai dimanche* is the story of a truly disastrous excursion. To begin with, the passengers, having already paid for their tickets, refuse to

Fig. 22: Les Vacances de M. Hulot: *the Amilcar*

cough up any more cash. Secondly, the charabanc is subject to all the mechanical peculiarities that the only moderately inventive minds of Tati and Rhum could think up (doors that won't close, a steering wheel that comes off). Then the vehicle arrives at a fork in the road. The spectators can see that behind the roadside bushes a workman is planting a post which carries a directional arrow at its top, and to get the thing into the ground, moves it around from side to side. What the charabanc duo see is just the arrow, pointing first this way, then that, and of course they take the wrong fork into a bosky lane, whose overhanging foliage decorates the bus and its passengers in quasi-military camouflage. The same gag was used no less than three more times by Tati in his post-war films: in *L'Ecole des facteurs* and *Jour de fête*, where the trailing members of a cycle-racing squad are misdirected by a road sign waggling in the same way, and in *Les Vacances de M. Hulot*, in the course of the picnic outing episode, which is in effect a vastly improved version of the main topic of *Gai dimanche*. Finally the party arrives at a country restaurant that advertises a full lunch for a modest price. The peasant restaurateur can offer them chicken and rice for even less if Tati and Rhum will act as waiters. This could have provided Tati with an opportunity for doing his clumsy waiter routine, but a different direction is taken in the film. Tati serves a minute portion of salami to one half of the party, and then, to distract their attention, Rhum does a conjuring act, whilst Tati quietly shifts the sad little slices of salami to the plates on the other side of the table.

These standard and painfully slow gags are the weakest part of the film, and are thankfully interrupted by an equally classic, but far better handled comedy routine: the cook-restaurateur announces a disaster – the chicken intended for lunch has escaped. A comic chase sequence ensues – poorly filmed, but full of Tati's elegant acrobatics, as the chicken forever scuttles just a little further off. The passengers join in the chase, and for a brilliant moment, turn into a pack of horses galloping across fields and hedges.

The last sequences show the still-hungry party touring the countryside and then getting stuck on a level-crossing. A stock shot of an approaching locomotive prepares the denouement: the party, still in charabanc formation, but with no vehicle to ride in, march back towards town, with the driver and his mate striding out at the front, still giving an incomprehensible commentary on the sights as they pass by.

Gai dimanche thus seems to have less to do with Tati's *métier* as a mime, and more to do with the early development of the themes that he would later elaborate into films of real imaginative quality. Unlike his later work, however, *Gai dimanche* sets leisure, locomotion and make-believe in a "miserabilist" context typical of the comedy of Chaplin and more generally of Hollywood burlesque; and, like *On demande une brute*, it tries to exploit the contrast between the tall guy and the short one, the dim and the bright. However, apart from a rather vulgar "fat lady" gag and the use of an observant and malicious child to undo the conjuring act, the film pays almost no attention to the comic potential of the group, only to the comedy created by the leading duo and by the machinery they use.

Gai dimanche also marks the end of Tati's collaboration with Rhum, but not the end of a friendship, to which Tati remained ever faithful. Through Rhum, Tati had also come to meet many of the leading personalities of the circus, and he enjoyed the company of clowns, trapezists, stunt riders and acrobats. It may be a cliché to say that there is nothing sadder than an ageing acrobat or a retired circus clown, but it was a sadness that Tati was to come to know, and to respect. When he was rich and famous, he continued to keep in touch with chums such as Edmond and Renée Naudy, circus acrobats "resting" in a caravan in the Dordogne;[82] in 1959, he committed himself for ten years to paying the nursing-home costs of André Bégaud, a famous circus clown of the 1930s under his stage-name of Drena.[83] But perhaps Tati's most touching and secret homage to the circus people who were his friends in those difficult years before the war is the comic car-parking sequence in *Mon Oncle*. Though there is no reason for the spectator to know this, the very aged, shuffling volunteer who tries to guide M. Arpel towards the kerb in his overlarge two-tone limousine is Georges Bazot, who had first appeared as a circus clown before Tati had even been born. As "Bowden" and "Loriot", Bazot's career had already spanned half a century of circus history; Tati took him out of retirement to give him his last, perfectly-timed turn on screen.[84]

TEN

The Centaur

A mime artist crosses the wall of language
JEAN COCTEAU

Tati's professional life took off in 1936. But he also tried to do something more respectable – to go into business on his own account. He set up a limited company, "Le Cadre lumineux", to manufacture and market a little invention of his own, picture frames with an incorporated spotlight. It seems to have had no success at all;[85] the company remained dormant for many years, though the fact that the glass-roofed shed at Rue de Penthièvre was its legally registered premises in 1936 enabled Tati to get round planning restrictions in the post-war years when he wanted to make what was then his home (after a good deal of reconstruction and remodelling) the registered offices of his film company for a time.[86]

After his success at the Théâtre-Michel, he decided to try to make it in London, and set off there in March 1936. The rough and noisy audience at the Finsbury Park Empire remained forever etched in his mind, and in later life he would often refer to that daunting nightly challenge as his real education as a performer; indeed, it can't have been easy to tame a whistling, jeering crowd with silent mime alone. He also auditioned for other engagements in England, and performed at the London Casino and the Mayfair Hotel;[87] but Tati's memory of humiliating London auditions with coarse-tongued impresarios added to the conventional mistrust that performers have for the managers of the entertainment business.

He came back to Paris with the best job he could have hoped for: a top billing at the A.B.C., with two shows a day, at 3 and 9 pm. The programme of the summer-season revue, which ran from 29 May through to early September, included a fair number of scantily-clad women (bare-breasted tableaux were the conventional attraction of the Parisian music-hall then, as now), a comic acrobat (Raymond Dandy), the young Michel Simon (a sentimental singer before he rose to fame as a cinema star), and the child-prodigy, Gaby Triquet. But the main attractions were the singer Marie Dubas – and Jacques Tati. Marie Dubas, though not nearly so well known today as Edith Piaf, was a quite remarkable singer-performer with a voice that could range from mezzo to the highest notes of a dramatic soprano. She had become a national celebrity with a single song, *Pedro*, and then starred at the Folies-Bergères, in a show entitled *Sex Appeal Paris 32*. She was the first to perform *Mon Légionnaire*, a song now associated with her rival Piaf; she was also a *diseuse*, performing "spoken songs" with musical backing, such as the tear-jerking tale of a repentant prostitute, *Quand La Charlotte prie Notre Dame la Nuit du Réveillon* ("When 'Charlotte' prays to Our Lady on Christmas Eve"); her repertoire included scabrous and inventive acts like *Mais qu'est-ce que j'ai?* ("Just what's got into me?") – the answer being, of course, sex. From the late 1920s until the débâcle of June 1940, she was also a much-recorded artiste, and at least as well known as Piaf, Yvette Guilbert, Mistinguett, Rina Ketty, and Maurice Chevalier. Her main quality, though, in a world not short of gifted entertainers, was her electric and infectious stage presence. She was in great demand for celebrity galas all over France, and spent a good deal of her time on the road, travelling in a magnificent chauffeur-driven Hispano-Suiza limousine. This tireless and good-humoured performer was an international celebrity already when Tati first found himself billed as her principal supporting act.

Tati's act at the A.B.C. was much the same as it had always been, at rugby club reviews or at the functions held by *Le Journal*: a set of "sporting impressions", that is to say, mimed imitations of the goalkeeper, the tennis-player, the angler, the boxer, the cyclist, and his tour de force – of the rider and his horse, or, to be more precise, of the *haute école*, the art of the Viennese manege, the high-stepping circus horses which appear to dance in time with the music. It was neither impersonation nor slapstick, neither ballet nor acrobatics, though it partook of all these genres. In a bravura review vaguely indebted to Paul Valéry's essay on dance, Colette gave a memorable evocation of what was so special about this fabulously well-honed mime act:

> From now on no celebration, no artistic or acrobatic spectacle can do without this amazing performer, who has invented something quite his own ... His act is partly ballet and partly sport, partly satire and partly a charade. He has devised a way of being both the player, the ball and the tennis racquet, of being simultaneously the football and the goalkeeper, the boxer and his opponent, the bicycle and the cyclist. Without any props, he conjures up his accessories and his partners. He has the suggestive power of all great artists. How gratifying it was to see the audience's warm reaction! Tati's success says a lot about the sophistication of the allegedly "uncouth" public, about its taste for novelty and its appreciation of style. Jacques Tati, the horse and rider conjoined, will show all of Paris the living image of that legendary creature, the centaur. [88]

Fig. 23: *Jacques Tati, studio portrait, 1936*

From this point on, Tati was a star with almost equal billing to Marie Dubas at the numerous one-night stands that they did together at provincial venues. After the end of the summer season at the A.B.C., they were at Brides-les-bains in July, at Vittel in August, and then again in Paris, at the Européen (1 to 8 January, 1937); in the spring they appeared together as entertainers at a kind of extension college, l'Université des Annales,[89] then once more at the A.B.C. (5 to 25 March), and at some point appeared together in Rouen.[90] With his charm and ease, Tati usually managed to get a ride to these provincial engagements in Marie Dubas's limousine: a first taste of the grand life of a star.[91] In 1937 and again in 1938, Tati took off for Berlin, where he played for several months at the Scala and also at the famous KadeKo, the "Kaffeehaus der Komiker" (Comedians' Café)[92] recreated in the musical *Cabaret*, and returned to Paris for the 1938 spring show at the Bal Tabarin, one of the most legendary of Parisian restaurant-night-clubs of all time, with its rising stage which allowed spectacular tableaux to come as if from nowhere into the middle of the dance floor. At the Tabarin, Tati's act became sufficiently famous to be included in a documentary film, of which a tiny clip still exists: it shows Tati doing his boxing sketch.[93] Years later, Tati declared, in a quite different documentary film about the final demise of the Tabarin,[94] that "there is no break between the Tati of the Tabarin and the Tati of today." He did not mean that his season at Le Bal Tabarin was when he first really became a star; on the contrary, he meant to declare his fidelity to the discipline of live performance, to the art of mime based on observation and practice, and to popular, rather than intellectual, forms of entertainment.

Engagements followed in quick succession throughout the 1938–39 season at Cannes, the Lido de Paris, Stockholm, and San Remo,[95] and then a booking, for the whole month of September 1939, at the Radio City Music Hall in New York[96] . . . which had to be abandoned, because at precisely that point Germany invaded Poland, war was declared, and, like all men of military age, Tatischeff, Jacques, a reservist of the Sixteenth Dragoons, was instantly called up.

Throughout this dizzy period, Colette's article remained Tati's passport to fame, and he had copies made, in French and in English translation, to distribute to managers and impresarios world-wide. He also adopted the image of the centaur that Colette had given him, and had a publicity photograph made that played on it:

Fig. 24: *Tati-centaur, circa 1937*

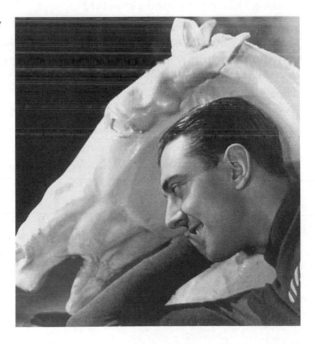

Tati's world, which up to 1936 had been exclusively French, had suddenly become pan-European, and he mixed – in modest hotels, in dressing rooms and in the after-show dinners and drinks – with an international travelling set of first and second-rank entertainers. It must have been during these tours that he picked up a smattering of English to add to what he had forgotten from school, and a few words of Swedish and German too. He did his shopping when and where he could, and ended up with a mixed bag of Swedish socks, Italian shirts, and German underwear – a trivial detail, to be sure, but one of those details on which a whole life can turn.

The milieus in which Tati spent his young manhood – from the picture-framing trade to sports fraternities, from bars and clubs to the professional music-hall scene – were not remotely intellectual ones, nor were they politically self-conscious. In his own terms, Tati had no politics. But his act was based on something that others thought politically significant to a high degree.

Sport as we now know it is not an eternal human activity, and it arose in quite specific historical and social circumstances. As a word, "sport" entered the French language as late as 1878; prior to that, it was barely distinguished from gambling and from those aristocratic pastimes (horse-racing, hunting, shooting, card-playing) on which wagers were made.[97] Rule-governed physical contests between individuals or teams – what we now mean by the word "sport" – arose alongside, and inside, modern industrial cities and the working class in the period 1870–1914.

The Olympic Movement, founded by Pierre de Coubertin in 1898, claimed its roots in the *games* (not the sports) of Ancient Greece, but its aims were fundamentally social and political – to improve the physical qualities of the urban young, and to move national rivalries from the battlefield to a less damaging arena.[98]

Sport really took off after the Great War: by the 1920s, it had become a remarkable social and cultural phenomenon. It cannot be entirely coincidental that Tati's first attested sports mime, on the beach at Saint-Tropez, was performed at the same time as the VIIIth Olympic Games in Paris (the stadium at Colombes, where Tati later played rugby, was built for that occasion),[99] nor that his breakthrough as a sports mime in the professional variety theatre coincided with the notorious Berlin Olympics of 1936. In the intervening years, cycling, football, boxing and wrestling became significant professional and commercial activities. In such circumstances, the social phenomenon of sport rapidly became a subject of political debate: all the main parties had something to say about it, and most had a use for it in their recipes for the regeneration of France. The right-wing PSF put the reorganisation of popular sport at the centre of its political platform; trades

Fig. 25: *Tati in performance at the Scala, Berlin, 1937 or 1938*

unions and newspapers associated with the Communist Party thundered against the commercialisation of sport. The political appropriation of sport came into the mainstream when in 1936 the Popular Front government of Léon Blum created the world's first minister for sports, and appointed Léo Lagrange to the cabinet-ranking post.[100]

The idea that the battle of Waterloo had been won on the playing fields of Eton did not occur to anyone at the time. The moral benefits of collective discipline in competitive team sports, even if they were first promoted by the pedagogues of Britain's leading schools, were not commonly accepted until the early decades of the twentieth century. But once they gained currency, they became self-evident to all authoritarian regimes. Both in Soviet Russia and in Nazi Germany, sport was seen and used as a means of turning out "new men" in the heroic and obedient mould that both ideologies required. By the time Tati made his breakthrough with "Sporting Impressions" in 1936, sport was part of almost every political and social agenda in the Western world.

The representation of sports and sportsmen became a common theme for all the figurative arts, at all levels of sophistication, in the same years. German painters of the *Neue Sachlichkeit* movement (Piscator, Dix, Grosz, for example) as well as Italian Futurists and their French imitators (Marcel Gromaire, Robert Lallemant, Alfred Reth) celebrated the speed and elegance of tennis-players, footballers, rugby-players, swimmers and gymnasts; less avant-garde artists of the 1920s and 1930s – most often associated with the movement restrospectively called "poetic realism" – developed a heroic, pseudo-classical style for representing the idea of sport and individual sportsmen and women in painting, poster-art, sculpture, and newspaper caricatures (see, for example, Georges Sabbagh's *Venus Anadyomede* (Musée des Années Trente, Boulogne-Billancourt) which shows a thick-limbed but still Botticelli-like Venus rising from the waves in a sturdy bathing costume, a red bathing cap, and a green terry towel).[101] Tati's sports-mime career began at exactly the same time as that of the cartoonist Pellos (the inventor of *Les Pieds Nickelés*), who began to publish his drawings of cyclists, table-tennis players and the like in the early 1930s, before becoming for many years the "official" cartoonist of the Tour de France.

Tati's breakthrough is thus a part of a broader context in which sport, having very recently acquired a whole set of national, political and social meanings, was a subject of intense and varied representations and interpretations. Tati's act must have seemed to some to be a celebration of sport, and thus to bolster one or another of the highly exacerbated ideologies of the day which gave sport an important supporting role. But others could well have seen it as gentle mockery of the whole phenomenon. Tati never said what he *meant* by imitating goalkeepers, boxers and so forth; but that does not mean that his appreciative audiences found no meaning in the exaggerated but graceful movements of the mime.

It is more difficult to know how much Tati really accepted the anti-Semitic views that were, lamentably, part of the general atmosphere of 1930s

France, nor what his attitude to Nazi Germany really was before the war. The Racing-Club had many Jewish members (at least two – Broïdo and Schneider – in Tati's regular team), and according to Sauvy's probably rather naive biographer, anti-Semitic remarks made there in abundance were taken in good humour, "just like jibes at people from Normandy or Marseille".[102] In the close-knit society of travelling entertainers, there was an *esprit de corps* that took little account of national or ethnic origins: Marie Dubas, Mitty Goldin, the manager of the A.B.C., the playwright Tristan Bernard, and many others were Jewish, and they do not seem to have suffered profession-ally before 1940 from the rising tide of xenophobia and racial hatred. Whatever superficially anti-Semitic attitudes Tati may have absorbed, they do not seem to have overridden friendships and loyalties established on the rugby pitch and on the stage.

Tati's anti-Semitism only became at all noticeable when it was badly out of date. Returning to the studio where a young assistant was working on the remake of *Jour de fête*, one day in 1961, Tati slumped his great frame into a chair, clearly exhausted and bruised by the session he had just had with a pair of notoriously difficult (and patently crooked) film financiers, who happened to be Jews. "They really shouldn't have shut down the gas chambers," Tati exclaimed, forgetting entirely that his young assistant was also Jewish.[103] But few people ever held it against Tati that he was a man of a particular class and generation; indeed, one of his fondest and longest-standing Jewish friends often greeted him as "my favourite anti-Semite".[104]

In 1936, Tati's act was hailed by Colette and others as original and unprece-dented. On the other hand, dumb-show itself must be as old as human society. In France, it has a specific and quite well-known modern history. Silent theatre on the unlicensed stages of the boulevards was one of the main forms of popular entertainment in Paris from 1815 to 1848, and the undisputed monarch of the Funambules theatre, Jean-Gaspard Deburau, founded a dynasty and a tradition which continued into the twentieth century.[105] Deburau trained his son Charles, who taught Louis Rouffe, from whose troupe came Georges Wague and Séverin. A direct inheritor of the mime-theatre recreated by Marcel Carné in *Les Enfants du Paradis*, Séverin brought mime to the music-hall, for he was one of the regular stars of the Folies-Bergère in the first two decades of the twentieth century. And it was to the Folies-Bergères also that the English impresario and acrobat Fred Karno had brought his mime show, "The Mumming Birds", in 1908. Amongst the "juniors" in Karno's troupe was a rubber-limbed youngster, Charles Spenser, who would soon be known to the French as Charlot, and to the rest of the world as Chaplin.

Tati's trumpeted and no doubt genuine originality did not lie in his doing a mime act in cabaret and music-hall. Nor did he invent the application of mime to popular sports and leisure activities: Harry Tate had been doing imitations of anglers, pool-players, racing-drivers and so forth on the London and Paris stages since the turn of the century.[106] What was new and unprecedented in Tati's *Impression sportives* can only have been the artistry and grace with which the mimes were done, and the accuracy of the observation on which they were based. Short of inventing a stage persona and a narrative thread (like Deburau's Pierrot, Chaplin's "Charlie" figure or Marceau's character, Bip), there are not many ways in which mime can itself aspire to originality in the conventional, literary sense of the word.

The popularity of music-hall mime in the 1920s and 1930s ran parallel to a renewed interest in mime in avant-garde theatre and theatrical research. Jacques Copeau's Ecole du Vieux-Colombier, headed from 1924 by Louis Jouvet and Etienne Decroux, put great emphasis on "corporeal mime" in the training of actors. Breaking with centuries of essentially verbal theatrical practice, Decroux's pupils were made to improvise the body-language of (for instance) a man trying to shoo away a fly, a woman strangling a fortune-teller, or the operation of a machine.[107] Inspired in part by the No theatre of Japan, Decroux aimed to revolutionise acting by creating a style involving few words, no sets, and perfect control of bodily expression. His first real trainee and disciple (from 1931) was Jean-Louis Barrault, who quickly became Jacques Tati's principal public rival, from his debut in the music-hall to the early 1950s. But Decroux also took on cinema roles (he appears in dozens of films made in the 1930s and 1940s, including *Les Enfants du Paradis*) and spread his views and his training exercises amongst a great number of aspiring French actors for screen and stage.

The avant-garde mime group of the 1930s – Decroux, Dullin, Barrault – had "advanced" ideas in every domain: they were mostly vegetarian, many were nudists, some considered themselves surrealist, and they were intellectual socialists to a man. Tati could hardly have been more different – a sports-loving, chain-smoking, meat-eating, apolitical entertainer. He had had no school but his own. He had not been born into an acting family, was not apprenticed to any troupe of travelling players, nor was he ever taken on by a Wague or a Karno, even less by a Copeau, Dullin or Decroux. Thus he naturally thought that he had invented every aspect and detail of his act for himself: and from his point of view, he had done just that, even if, in historical retrospect, we can now see him not only as part of a long tradition, but also as one amongst many instances of the re-emergence of mime as an art form in the 1930s. Tati thus had great difficulty in accepting that anyone else could have the right to perform mimes of the kind that he was doing, and of which he was, in his own view, the only begetter. The ironical thing was that the success of his own act made impresarios look for other mime artistes, and for a while, many other gifted artistes did dumb-shows on the music-hall stage.[108] It was when the now-illustrious Jean-Louis Barrault also began to perform a horse-and-rider act that Tati could hold in his sense of outrage no longer.

> "Sir," he wrote in his most official and haughty tone, "since 1931 I have created a Music-Hall act based on a considerable amount of intellectual creation . . . However, I understand that M. J.-L. Barrault performed at the last Gala des Artistes, and intends to repeat it at the Bal des Petits Lits Blancs, an act entitled *Show Horse* and which is in all respects identical to the one of which I am the author."[109]

He wanted to put a stop to such blatant profiteering from what he, Tati, had discovered, invented, perfected, and made popular, or else be granted payment in compensation. He returned to this grousing theme again and again:

> I'm the one who invented the horse . . . That's right, the horse is mine. Before Barrault and the others . . .[110]

But there is no copyright in ideas, and even less in a mime act that is itself an imitation. Although "intellectual property" is inalienable in French law (thus Tati's insistence on the "intellectual" content of his act), the definition of intellectual property restricts it to what can be reproduced in documentary form. The action against Barrault, based on a fundamental misunderstanding of what can be owned and what cannot, was thus doomed to failure, but it was not to be the last of Tati's Quixotic attempts to defend his "property", that is to say, his own "ideas", without substance except in the act of expressing them. From this initial misconception, perhaps, a misconception which continued to irritate him throughout his life, sprang at least in part the sporadically ungenerous attitude of Tati the film director towards the contributions of many of his more talented collaborators, whom he seems to have suspected of always being about to steal his ideas. The centaur is, as Colette said, a fabulous creature, but it has no patent or copyright. But for all Tati's anxiety about losing control of his creations, he managed in the end to lose all his rights over his film work, which is in principle far better protected than mime.

ELEVEN

Make-Believe

Tati did not abandon his ambition to become a film actor as soon as his music-hall career took off, for 1936 was also the year of his most accomplished short film to date. At its dramatic centre is a sports mime sketch that draws its inspiration, like *On demande une brute*, from Tati's music-hall routines; but it is set in a narrative frame that is considerably more interesting, and in a film that is far more intelligently made.

Soigne ton gauche ("Work on Your Left") may or may not have been the final fruit of the sketch that Tati borrowed from his old rugby captain Alfred Sauvy, but it bears the last trace of the *bande de copains* in a much more visible way, because one of the secondary roles – a sparring partner – is played by Jacques Broïdo, who had become a technical executive in Bernard Nathan's re-invigorated Pathé company.[111] The film also benefited from the talent of its director, who had been Charles Barrois's assistant on *On demande une brute*, a young man by the name of René Clément. Though made on a shoestring – the entire film is shot in one location, a sun-drenched farmyard and the field lying just beyond it; a child's perambulator running between lead pipes was used as a dolly for the few travelling shots – the quality of the images, the framing and placing of the shots, make it a work of far greater standing than anything Tati had been involved in before.[112]

The basic scenario is a familiar one – familiar from Tati's own work already, but also from a dozen Hollywood shorts and a myriad later circus and television comedy acts: a dim-witted lad finds himself taken on as a champion's sparring partner, and, by a series of mishaps and disasters, ends up winning against all reasonable odds. *Soigne ton gauche* is interesting for almost everything in it apart from its basic idea.

The champion is training, implausibly, in a farmyard, where a temporary ring has been constructed. That farmyard still exists, more or less as it was in 1936: La Croix-Saint-Jacques, in the village of La Ville-du-Bois, 20km south-east of Paris.[113] The champion has already disposed of a clutch of sparring partners (including a black with rippling biceps); the mood of the establishing shot is of a lazy, fly-infested, summer afternoon.

The second establishing shot shows a group of children pretending to be newsreel reporters at the closing stage of the Tour de France, with an overgrown child – Jacques Tati – acting out the final sprint, the victory handclasp, and the winner's breathless speech into the toy microphone: a little world of make-believe sporting achievement. The child-reporters were played by local schoolchildren; this is probably Tati's first use of non-professionals in his film work.

Fig. 26: Soigne ton gauche: *Tati's first cycling exploit*

Tati is summoned back to his duties as a farm hand by a short and cylindrical, sharp and angry mother-peasant, and he resumes loading hay-bales from the barn to the cart – or vice versa: the alternation of bales transported a few feet from the outside to the inside and back again is the first (and very accomplished) example of Tati's art of creating entirely ineffectual activity. The street-sweeping scenes in the "old town" of *Mon Oncle* – with a sweeper whose brush-strokes never actually clear anything from the roadway at all – is perhaps the best known version of this vision of "convivial" labour.

Cut to the farmyard ring, where a cycling postman – played by Max Martel – arrives bearing a telegram: the "big match" is on, the tickets are sold out, the boxer has to be in top form. One by one, the sparring partners go back into the ring, throw a few punches, and are knocked out cold. The manager is in a fix: he has run out of training partners for his champion.

Cut to the farm hand, Roger, carefully chalking up his utterly confused tally of bales on the barn wall. (If it was true that Tati could not really do arithmetic, as Fred Orain later claimed, then Tati was certainly prepared to make public fun of that inability.) He also starts to play-act the boxers in the ring, in a perfectly private dumb-show of his own. But the impresario sees him prancing around, and has the bright idea of taking on this light-headed beanstalk as a substitute for the regular sparring partners, who are still out cold.

Fig. 27: Soigne ton gauche: *play-acting in the farmyard*

This set-up for the unequal boxing match is much more interesting than the clumsy dramatic sketch invented for *On demande une brute*, for it sets the play-acting that is to follow as the logical result of child's play. No need for a "wise guy" to sort things, no need for a "story" other than the story of the Tati-figure's own Walter-Mittyish personality. And that person-ality is quite the opposite of a Chaplinesque clown, for it is not the farm hand's ingenuity or jokiness that gets him into the fight. Tati the farm hand is the victim of his own imagination, of the consequences of dumb-show, which is precisely what (as an actor) he now has to perform.

The slapstick fight is also handled with at least a degree of originality. The farm hand notices that the champion has been consulting a boxing manual, left face down on the ring-side stool. So between rounds he snatches a glance at it, and then does his best to apply the positions that he has glimpsed, providing yet a further nested level of imitation. The cycling postman, who has stayed around, also glances at the book, and replaces it incorrectly in a way that shows the back cover, an advertisement for a companion volume on the art of foils. So at the next break, the farmhand-boxer takes a look, and returns to the ring acting out the foot and arm posture of a fencer. The champion can't quite get the measure of this new "style" and throws a punch which goes straight into the postman's mustachioed mouth.

Fig. 28: Soigne ton gauche: *boxing with foils*

Cut to the postman, cycling over a field, where he meets a handful of resting harvesters, and tells them the tale of the brute who punched him. The peasants consider an insult to the postman an insult to them all, and march back to the farmyard, where they mount the ring, and collectively launch into the champion. After a few minutes' mayhem, the temporary ring collapses, the champion is knocked out by a piece of dislodged carpentry, and Tati emerges victorious.

Cut to the farmyard children, who have been "filming" the entire "show" with a box-shaped coffee-grinder mounted on a tripod, with a sapling in a flower-pot serving as a sound boom. Of course they "interview" the new champion, in a final piece of self-representing, self-mirroring play. The

postman cycles off through the farmyard gates, followed at a distance by
a running child cameraman, whose final "view" of the rider is identical
to ours.

Soigne ton gauche, though it is barely over twelve minutes in length,
contains far more cinematic and theatrical invention than both of Tati's
prior films put together. It also introduces topics which Tati will reorganise,
redevelop, repeat and enrich in many of his subsequent films: the countryside setting (the cycling postman in *L'Ecole des facteurs* and *Jour de fête*); the
use of children as viewers of the frame, inside the frame (*Les Vacances de
M. Hulot*); and the "unending labour" gag (*Mon Oncle*, and also *Playtime*). At
the same time, the dreamy screen personality of the character played by
Tati seems to be much closer to an individual creation – and quite plausibly,
to a personal expression – than anything Tati had done before, for it thema-
tises make-believe as the key and as the source of all that happens in the film.

The dialogues of *Soigne ton gauche* are credited to Jean-Marie Huard, about
whom little else is known (he worked as journalist and theatre-reviewer
for the collaborationist *Paris-Midi* during the German Occupation), and the
current copy of the film gives no credit line for the script.[114] Was it invented
by Tati himself? That seems very likely, given the strong links between this
material and Tati's later work; but it is naturally impossible to judge how

Fig. 29: *Closing shot of* Soigne ton gauche

much of the work that has survived springs from the talents of its director, René Clément, and how much from those of its star, Jacques Tati.

The mystery of the film's original production and financing remains almost complete. *Soigne ton gauche* seems to have been released and to have been distributed in Germany, which is where Tati found a copy after the Second World War: but we have no record of reactions to the work, nor any material details of its early career. The film marks the culmination of Tati's "Sporting Impressions", and their effective dissolution. Though a mimed boxing match is the centrepiece of the movie's plot, all the interest of the work is in what is added to the comic fight – its pictorial and narrative surround, its fictionalised context, and especially the make-believe of the children and of the character of the unintentional sparring partner.

Tati was involved in one more film before war brought things to a halt, but all physical trace of it has been lost; it is not certain that it was ever completed, or even shot. The title – *Retour à la terre* – suggests a development of the rural setting of *Soigne ton gauche* and perhaps also the conservative theme of *Jour de fête* (at the end, the postman who had tried to rival the US Postal Service does indeed "return to the land"). Had it not been for the outbreak of war, Tati would no doubt have gone on developing his art as a performer in comedy films, and – who knows? – maybe he would even have got to make a film of his own. For the only documentary trace remaining of *Retour à la terre* gives Tati's name not as actor, but as author and director.

TWELVE

Tati's War

I don't know si vous vous rappelez
les Ardennes en temps de guerre?
LES VACANCES DE M. HULOT

"Have you ever been lost?" a journalist asked Tati in 1953.

> Yes, in July 1940. I was on my own, I didn't recognise anything, I
> had no idea where I was. I was really lost.[115]

On his way back to Paris from a conference in Prague in late 1938, Alfred
Sauvy had to change trains in Nuremberg. What he saw in a few hours in that
Nazi-run city left him in no doubt about the coming disaster. As soon as he got
home, he took out a long booking on an entire hotel in the French Alps, and
summoned all his friends for a last skiing holiday before the inevitable war. Tati
could not make it for the team reunion; he was otherwise engaged, in Berlin.[116]

Tati never said a great deal about his life in the period from 1939 to 1945.
Like all men of his age, he was called up in September 1939. During the
phoney war, which lasted through to the following spring, he seems to
have been stationed near Cambrai, in north-eastern France, near the Belgian
border.[117] Although there was no enemy action, Tati suffered the fright of
his life during this time. The quartermaster of his unit had had difficulty
finding a uniform to fit him; the one issued in the end was just about
adequate in the upper half, but far too short in the leg. One night, after dark,
he was stopped by a military policeman, intrigued by this giant of a man in
ill-fitting, brand-new clothes that seemed not to be his.

Name?

Tatischeff.

Now, that sounds like a foreign name to me! And you say you're in the
French Army? Where's your ID?

Tati had forgotten his passbook at the barracks. It was a dangerous
situation: in the military zone, there was generalised paranoia, fanned by
government scare-mongering on the radio and in the press, about a "fifth
column" inside France that was set on sabotaging national defence. Tatischeff
was arrested and marched off to the command post, for interrogation. He
gave his rank, his unit, and his serial number; but the military police could

not get through on the field telephone to Tati's CO to confirm that this foreign-sounding, oddly clad giant was indeed a French soldier. He was made to strip. His underwear provided almost conclusive evidence: socks from Stockholm, a vest from Fascist Italy, and worst of all, underpants made in Berlin . . . Tati was clapped into a cell for the night. He fully expected to be shot the next day as a spy.[118] It was the longest night of his life, so Tati said in later reminiscences. But when morning came, he was told he was free to go: confirmation of identity had arrived some time in the night. Tati dressed, and turned to the mirror to comb his jet-black hair: except that it was no longer black, but quite, quite white.

Fig. 30: *Tati in uniform, probably 1940, probably with his sister, Nathalie*

The punch-line of the story as Tati told it so often is patently invented: Tati's hair is still jet black in his wedding photographs in 1944, and the location photographs of *Jour de fête*, from summer 1947, show him with greying temples, at the worst. But the anecdote – often repeated in public and private[119] –is perhaps a metaphorical declaration about Tati's war, which was also, lamentably, a war between Frenchmen.

In *Jour de fête*, the film closest in time to Tati's war, François the postman tries to weave through the stalls of the village fair on his bicycle, and falls off into the open back door of a booth. He stands up, and finds himself right in front of the target of the airgun shooting range. For a split second we see Tati in his postman's uniform and kepi – so much like military gear – with his hands up in horror, facing his own mock execution. There are several location photographs of rehearsals for this scene, with Tati, half-naked in the summer heat, miming his hands-up shock routine. Not all comedy can be reduced to the abreaction of anxiety, but this episode most certainly is a conscious recreation in comic vein of the worst episode in Tati's war.

Regimental and divisional arrangements were changed several times during the winter of 1939-40, and Tati could have been transferred into almost any of the new units that were being formed. Officially, Tati's old regiment, the Sixteenth Dragoons, was disbanded and incorporated into the 3rd *Division Légère de Cavalerie* (DLC), which took part in the Battle of the Meuse, in May 1940, when the German Army swept through the Ardennes into northern France. Tati never spoke about the details or the dates, but he alluded now and again to having seen military action during the Blitzkrieg. The experience of warfare is also explicitly invoked in *Les Vacances de M. Hulot*: when the fireworks intended for the last-night festivities are accidentally ignited en masse, the sound track consists of machine-gun and mortar fire.

Some shadow or perhaps a direct reminiscence of the German invasion can be seen in a film script Tati wrote for Swedish television in the early 1970s (the English is perhaps his own, perhaps that of a Scandinavian translator). It is the only explicit description of war – and also, the only formal flash-back – in all of Tati's work. Hulot is in a television studio, and the monitor is showing a news flash from some war-torn part of the world.

> This war scene reminds the Director of his experience in 1939–40,
>   when Hulot distinguished himself in his own particular way
> EXT. DAY   FLASH-BACK
>   War field: During the bombardment of a field which is being
>   fought over, Hulot finds himself practically abandoned by his unit.
>   Under cover in a shelled hole, the bombs fall hard as the enemy

approaches. On the outlook for a way to escape, Hulot sees a lone bicycle against a wall near a pathway. He suddenly leaps out of his hole, dashes, jumps, zigzags among the explosions, plunges headlong under machine-gun fire, gets up and dashes forward, jumps on to the bicycle, pedalling with great vitality. Unfortunately, he can make no ground as the bicycle has been abandoned for lack of a chain. Hulot leaves the bicycle and plunges into a ditch, just as a shell explodes nearby.[120]

The 3rd DLC retreated from the Meuse across most of France, and reached Mussidan, in the Dordogne, not far from Périgueux, by the time the Armistice was declared on 22 June 1940.[121] For almost all French soldiers on or near the north-eastern borders of France, the war of May–June 1940 was a confusing and completely demoralising rout:[122] large parts of the army were surrounded and taken prisoner, other units were quickly pushed back towards the Channel, and others retreated towards Paris but were not able – indeed, were not allowed – to defend the city, into which the German Army marched in mid-June. Tati was not taken prisoner, nor was he part of the small band that fought a difficult retreat into Normandy and then crossed to Britain to carry on the fight. Like hundreds of thousands of others, he made his way south, a few miles ahead of the advancing German columns. After the success of *Jour de fête*, in which he played the role of a rural postman on a bicycle, Tati was asked if he had ever done any real cycling, that is to say, time-trials or road races. His reply was not quite what the interviewer expected:

> In 1940 I did Liège-Périgueux on a bicycle, with the Germans on my tail. It was a good performance. But I think Anquetil or Poulidor would have made a higher average.[123]

France was henceforth divided into two zones, the "Non-Occupied Zone", south of the Loire, ruled from the obscure spa town of Vichy by a National Government headed by the aged Marshal Pétain, and the Occupied Zone to the north of the Loire, and including a broad strip of land along the Atlantic coastline, down to the Spanish border. Périgueux – if that was where Tati really ended up – was in the Non-Occupied Zone, but, since he was neither a Jew, nor a Communist, nor a trade-union organiser, he had no particular reason to see the "Zone Nono" as a refuge; like millions of other Parisians who had been displaced by war or who had fled the city in fear of the German attack, including most members of the French Armed Forces, who were demobilised, Tati returned to the capital once the dust of the armistice arrangements had settled. And he returned to his trade as a music-hall entertainer.

Much of the Paris entertainment scene had gone dark. The anti-Semitic laws passed by Vichy as early as October 1940 drove many owners, impresarios and performers into exile, or underground: and it was some time before "Aryan" managers could be put into place to resurrect the legendary capital of European night-life as a rest-and-recreation facility for German troops. But despite shortages of almost everything, from electricity to sequins, from staff to salt biscuits to go with the champagne, Parisian night-life was reconstituted, and a reduced number of music-halls, cabarets and theatres ran to packed houses for the remaining four years of the war.

In March 1941, Tati performed his *Impressions sportives* at the Lido de Paris. It had been requisitioned, and only German military personnel were allowed in.[124] In the eyes of some, doing an act at the Lido was equivalent to collaborating with the enemy. It is an episode about which Tati was entirely silent after the war; but he never thought to remove the reviews from the press-cuttings book into which he pasted them at the time. In the summer of 1943, Tati did a season at his old haunt, the A.B.C.[125] (Its resident orchestra was conducted by Jean Yatové, who also composed most of the accompanying scores.) The main review of this show appeared in the notoriously anti-Semitic *Je suis partout*; another reviewer gave a xenophobic twist to his remarks: "excellent act, unblemished by foreign formulae or Anglo-Saxon humour, is half-way between fantasy and poetry".[126] In between these documented engagements (and perhaps others not reviewed in the press), Jacques Tati went to Germany, and performed once again in Berlin, alongside another French comic, Henri Marquet, who became a life-long friend.

Under the Occupation, Tati made no films that we know of, and that is not easy to explain. The Germans banned all film imports, leaving French screens available for German and home-grown productions alone. Despite the well-funded activities of Continental Film, a stooge-company for German and Nazi interests, it was rapidly granted that the French were not interested in German movies, and so French film production increased at a rapid pace. At last, it had a captive audience: regrettably, in more senses than one. Opportunities abounded for film people of all kinds, for the number of films in production increased, whilst a host of technicians, creators and performers vanished from the scene. It should have been easy for Tati to find a way up in the film industry at that time: the fact that he did not suggests that Tati did not seek an easy entry into the cinema under the Occupation regime. In this respect he acted quite differently from nearly all the actors, screen-writers and directors who would emerge as the leaders of the post-war renaissance of French film (Clément, Carné, Bresson, Autant-Lara all made films during the war). And most of those last mentioned were guests of honour at a "lunch" held at the Hôtel de Ville on 23 April 1943, in

Fig. 31: *Tati at the A.B.C., 1943*

the presence of Fernand de Brinon, Pétain's "ambassador" in Occupied Paris, to salute the première of a propaganda film, *Portrait de la France*. All the top brass of the Paris city hall, of the *Propagandaabteilung* and the *Filmprüfstelle* (the censorship office) were there, clinking glasses with Jean Giraudoux, Marcel Carné, Claude Berry, Abel Gance, Jean Grémillon, Sacha Guitry, Serge Lifar, and Marcel L'Herbier. Tati was not on the guest list; but there was someone – and who could he have been? – called François Hulot.[127]

To simplify what was without doubt a confused and dangerous period of his life, Tati said in post-war interviews that he was sent to Berlin by the "STO". The *Service du travail obligatoire* was introduced in February 1943, ostensibly to replace military service for Frenchmen of military age who had no army to serve in, but in fact to provide German industry with cheap labour. A second device for obtaining labour from France was "la relève", a scheme by which (in theory) for every three men who volunteered for work in the Reich, a French prisoner-of-war was returned home to France. Both schemes were deeply unpopular in France, and in the post-war period the "relève" and the STO were often retrospectively assimilated to deportation, making heroes out of all who had gone to Germany during the war. But Tati could not possibly have been a regular STO conscript: he was long past the age at which the scheme could have applied to him, and he was in any case a demobilised soldier with an active service record.[128] That is not necessarily to say that his engagements in Berlin were voluntary. From 1943, every Frenchman exercising a profession (except railwaymen) was required to carry at all times a certificate issued by an employer; and such a thing must have been difficult to get for a freelance music-hall artiste. There were many forms of administrative pressure available to the Germans apart from the notorious STO. But the main motive for most Frenchmen who went to work in Germany at that time was the plain fact that there was work to be had, and a better chance of staving off hunger.

Tati was a successful performer on the Paris music-hall stage, and his audience necessarily included German officials and officers (indeed, at the Lido, it consisted exclusively of such). He had also performed at the Berlin Scala and the KadeKo only a few years earlier, and it is not difficult to imagine him being called back – by an impresario, a theatre director, an agent or through the mediation of one of his German fans posted to Paris – to help maintain an element of normal life in a city with a labour shortage all its own. His act, after all, was one of the few unimpeded by the language barrier. It might well have been foolish to refuse.

Nearly all French music-hall stars of greater or lesser renown did tours of Germany during the war, and many of them were called to account after the Liberation. Tati seems to have escaped the interrogations (both in public and in front of a tribunal) that plagued Maurice Chevalier and Edith Piaf (for instance) in the immediate aftermath of the war. For that reason he does not seem to have needed to lie, as Chevalier did quite blatantly, maintaining that he had only gone to Germany to perform in French POW camps; and maybe that is also why he did not need to say much about it at all.

Like Tati, Sauvy stayed on in Paris during the Occupation and published his most important books in that period: La Population (1943); Richesse et Population (1943); La Prévision économique (1944). Prior to the war, Sauvy had been very favourable towards an "open-doors" immigration policy; but that aspect of his thought, together with the entire current political situation of Occupied France, is well hidden in the books that he published under Vichy. He also learned to cope with the shortages of Occupied Paris: having a weekend house in the country, he implemented Pétain's call for a "return to the land" by growing all his own food in the backyard, from vegetables to rabbits, chickens and ducks.

Broïdo, who was Jewish, but protected (up to a point) by his Swiss passport, holed up in the Pathé labs at Joinville-le-pont where he worked on the "Ciné-mitrailleuse", a tiny movie camera that could be installed in the nose of fighter planes. (Its first operational use was on the planes of the famous Normandie-Niémen squadron, based in RAF fields in Kent). Schneider, also Jewish, but protected for a time by his US citizenship, was very nearly captured by the Gestapo one night when he was with Tati and Broïdo: he saved his life by hiding underneath the street-side balcony, clinging on by hands and toes. At the Liberation he joined the US Army and took part in the final stages of the war, winning distinguished service medals from both the USA and France. He was in the unit that liberated Dachau, and he came back to Paris (and in due course to a prestigious job at UNESCO) with some of the very first photographs of concentration camp scenes.

Tati's war-time survival tactics did not endear him to such friends, nor – most especially – to their wives. Mme Broïdo, for example, vetoed her husband's wish for Tati to be godfather to their second son, born in 1945. Despite their continuing friendship (Broïdo was one of the very small crowd that attended Tati's funeral in 1982), there were topics and times that were simply never mentioned between them after the war.[129]

Berlin's labour shortage was simple to explain – all the men had been drafted to the front, and there were only children, the aged, women and bureaucrats left in town. To staff the restaurants, theatres, hairdressing salons, hotels, shops, trams, and more or less every other aspect of normal city life, the Germans had had to import "foreign specialists" (not yet dignified by the term of "guest worker") from all those continental countries whose armies they had destroyed or demobilised.[130] The French were considered to have the best chefs, waiters, hairdressers and entertainers in Europe: and so Tati found himself in "occupied Berlin" in an almost entirely French-speaking environment, amongst artful dodgers and titis de Paris who could always find a few slices of garlic sausage for a compatriot even when German shelves were entirely bare. Some years later, he thought of making a comedy film about "The Occupation of Berlin", but the project (thought up around the time of the launch of Les Vacances de M. Hulot) was dismissed by produc-ers as being in thoroughly bad taste – which it was, at that time. It is a great pity that nothing much has survived of a project that would now have considerable historical interest.

In his autobiographical interviews Tati described his war-time stint in Berlin as intolerable: he could not bear trying to make Nazi officers laugh. So he took leave from his engagement, and ran away, together with his chum Henri Marquet, and ended up in deep cover in the very heart of rural France, near the small town of Sainte-Sévère-sur-Indre. This story eventually became the self-explanatory basis of Tati's post-war career. As he said in 1961:

> Everyone knows that I made *Jour de fête* in the village where I holed up with a few pals during the war, to avoid the STO. [131]

Or again in 1977:

> I had been commandeered by the Germans in '43 and I escaped and holed up at Le Marembert.[132]

It is certainly true that Tati and Henri Marquet turned up one day in Sainte-Sévère-sur-Indre; but it is not certain that they travelled there from Berlin. In the memory of André Delpierre, a music-hall artiste who had taken refuge during the exodus and débâcle in his grandparents' farmhouse at Le Marembert, ten km south of Sainte-Sévère, the two wandering clowns turned up in *military uniforms*, which clearly would not have been possible after the armistice of 22 June 1940 and the demobilisation of all French forces under Pétain's control:

> They came to Le Marembert. They were sort of "deserters". The great collapse, remember? He came with Riquet [Henri Marquet], they were dressed as soldiers. They took a side road, saying, we're bound to find something around here . . . [133]

Delpierre's vocabulary (*désertage, débâcle, troufions*) if not his syntax makes this reminiscence an accusation – that Tati and Marquet took refuge in Sainte-Sévère not when running away from more or less forced service in German cabaret, but in the summer of 1940, during or shortly after the retreat of their unit from the Belgian border to south-central France. Delpierre's memory was perhaps failing by 1994 (François Ede noticed at least one retrospective illusion in the account that he gave of the shooting of *Jour de fête*); but his version of Tati's arrival in Sainte-Sévère makes just as much historical, political and geographical sense as the more widely publicised version.

In some interviews, Tati gave the impression that he spent most of the Occupation period in this rural hide-away, for fear of being arrested as a deserter from the Labour Service.[134] In fact, according to the lady whose lodger he was, Mme Vialatte, he spent no more than four months in the region of Sainte-Sévère. Of course, it might have seemed like four years: people still alive today recall that Tati was so bored and frustrated with sleepy country life that he volunteered to help with the work in the fields, just to have something to do.[135] Tati was certainly grateful to the peasants who housed and fed him, at a time when life in Paris (and Berlin) was difficult and unpleasant in the extreme; but he did not overstay his welcome, and was back in the city fairly soon.

At the start of the war, Tati had been a successful young touring entertainer with a single subtle mime act and three forgotten short comedy films to his name. By the time it began to end, five years later, Tati was no further on with a career; he had trodden water, professionally speaking, just kept himself afloat for the duration. He had seen action; he had seen defeat; he had encountered the fear of death. His hair had not actually turned white, but he had aged. His youthful good looks were no longer quite those of an overgrown child. And he decided to settle down.

Tati owed his encounter with Micheline Winter to his sister Nathalie, a high-class *lingère* whose pre-war customers included members of royalty. Nathalie had noticed the striking, modest beauty of the daughter of a business acquaintance, Mme Oudin, and, at a tea-party she organised for this purpose, she made sure that her younger – but now not so young – bachelor brother got to meet the eighteen-year-old Micheline. It turned out rather better than do Mme Arpel's efforts, in *Mon Oncle*, to foster her brother Hulot's acquaintance with a marriageable neighbour. Micheline was entranced by the shy and funny giant; and Tati – whose youthful affairs, if they ever existed, seem to have left no mark on him, and certainly no trace of a documentary kind – was just as entranced with Micheline.

Micheline Winter – whom Tati called Michou, or (more affectionately, and also more obscurely) "patounette" – was the daughter of a well-established ENT specialist (the family name, though pronounced in the English manner, came from the east of France) who was also a keen sportsman and a keep-fit fanatic; Micheline was also very athletic and played a lot of basketball. Though Tati was nearly thirty-seven, he did not seem too old for his young bride, and the wedding was fixed, with some haste, for March 1944. The main difficulty of the whole affair was its celebration. Micheline's mother Germaine Oudin (who had been divorced from Winter many years before) insisted on a church service; Winter himself was an atheist of the French, anti-clerical variety, and refused to set foot inside a church, so did not attend. Tati, for his part, wanted a very simple ceremony, without crowds, without any metaphorical and certainly without literal frills. That is why he looks inordinately grumpy on his wedding photographs, for "la tante Germaine", Micheline's mother, far from keeping her word, had laid on a highly elaborate, full-scale wedding with all the trimmings available in those impoverished times. Micheline must have been torn in two; Tati was in high dudgeon, and played up in every way.

Tati expressed his disdain for pomp and circumstance by walking up to the

Fig. 32: *Micheline Winter as a young woman*

altar with a comic stride, and by acting the part of the groom with exaggerated, ballet-like movements. For those of Michou's friends whose memories of the scene have been recorded, it was one of Tati's greatest and most pointed performances in mime.[136] It must have added some humour to an afternoon which – to judge by the photographs – seems to have been otherwise fairly grim.

Auschwitz would not be liberated for another thirteen months; the Americans, fighting their way up through the toe of Italy, were bogged down on the Gustav Line. Did anyone at that very middle-class gathering at the Eglise Saint-Augustin even guess that preparations for the Normandy landings were well under way, or imagine that the German Occupation of Paris would end within five months? Did they expect to carry on living in a pauperised, Nazi-run half-state? How many of them joined the huge crowds that greeted Pétain on his visit to Paris just four weeks later? And how many

Fig. 33: *Tati and Micheline at their wedding, Eglise Saint-Augustin, March 1944*

of them were in the crowds that welcomed Charles de Gaulle barely three months after that? Which side were any of them on – if any of them considered themselves to be on a "side" at all? Perhaps only the very far-sighted had a conception that the future might arrive very soon, and would put many of them at odds with history. Their main individual and collective aims must have been just to carry on.

No one from Tati's own circle seems to have been at the wedding. They were after all mostly circus clowns, acrobats, singers and Bohemians of a barely respectable kind – except those that were really famous, like Marie Dubas (but she was a Jewess, in hiding, in the south of France). Though the guest list has not survived, the names absent from it must have told their own tale of middle-class French attitudes in the last weeks and months of the Vichy regime.

As far as can be told, Jacques Tati was neither a war hero, nor a member of the Resistance, nor an active collaborator. He had carried on with his trade, in so far as it was possible, in those places where he could get engagements; otherwise, as far as we know, he kept a very low profile (and may even have gone back to work for his father in the framing trade for a while.) In other words, he behaved like most French men and women. After the Liberation, some of them hurried to grant themselves a degree of retrospective glory, often at odds with historical fact, or else carefully covered their tracks. Tati never said anything much about how he survived from 1939 to 1945 and, save for the punch-line of the anecdote about how he got his white hair, cannot be accused of embellishing his own war-time story at all.

On the surface, Tati's major work in film from 1945 on seems entirely unrelated to the issues or the experiences, traumas, anguish, and confusion of the period immediately preceding it. Like the official history of France as it was written in the 1950s, Tati's work seems to bracket out the entire period of the war and occupation. Save for the small traces noted above – in a sequence of *Jour de fête*, in the sound track of *Les Vacances*, and in the script of an abandoned film project – Tati's oeuvre does indeed reproduce the historical amnesia that characterises the first decades of post-war France.

THIRTEEN

The Way Back

Tati's first family – his parents, his grandmother, his sister – survived the war, as did all of Micheline's complicated tribe; most of Tati's rugby-club chums – Gorodiche, Broido, and Schneider, at least – also came through in good shape. Sauvy did even better: he switched from running the Economic Forecasting Unit to a junior ministerial post in de Gaulle's first provisional government, as Secretary of State for Population and Family Policy.

Such relative good fortune did not exactly leave Tati with a clear path ahead. He was approaching forty, and would not be able to keep up his strenuous music-hall routine for much longer; in any case, the life of a travelling performer would be difficult to square with his new role as a husband and (very quickly) as the father of a young family (a daughter, Sophie, was born in 1946, and a second child, Pierre, came along in 1949). Tati looked to the cinema to find his mature career; but as he was not part of the crowd that had clambered up the slippery pole when it was easy, under the Occupation, he had (once again) to start at the bottom, just at a time when the industry was going through yet another major convulsion.

He seems to have owed his second start in life to his war-time music-hall performances, all the same. In 1943, the director Marcel Carné was planning to shoot Les Enfants du Paradis – a historical costume drama centred on the life of Deburau, the legendary father of French mime – at the Victorine studios in Nice. He had hired Jean-Louis Barrault for the role of Baptiste, but, on hearing that Barrault also had commitments at the Comédie française, he was doubtful that his young star would be able to keep his film engagement. Carné went up to Paris, and, whilst there, dropped in to the A.B.C.

> An actor was performing a series of sketches in which he mimed sportsmen with great wit and a stunning sense of observation – the rugby player, the tennis player, the boxer, the goalie, and so on. In my fear of not being able to get Barrault, I saw the performer as a possible stand-in for the role. What's more, he was tall and slim . . .

and in profile he looked more like the contemporary prints of Deburau than did Barrault, who was smaller. But given the importance of the part, it seemed a big risk to take . . . [137]

In fact, the "Tati option" for Les Enfants du Paradis was set aside after Carné discussed it, back in Nice, with his director of production, Fred Orain; but the name of the music-hall mime must have stuck in Orain's memory. For when he found himself director of production once again for a costume drama directed by Claude Autant-Lara, in the very last months of the war, and again in need of a non-speaking actor with screen presence to play the role of a ghost, he got hold of Tati and told him to come down.

Fred Orain, whose role in the launching of Jacques Tati's career can hardly be underestimated, had graduated with top marks from the electrical engineering school (Supelec) in 1931, and went to work as a sound specialist in the Paramount studios at Saint-Maurice. In 1940, after spending some time on newsreel production, he was offered the post of chief technical officer at the Saint-Maurice studio complex. The producer André Paulvé promptly offered to double Orain's salary if he would take charge of the Victorine studios in Nice. The young engineer thus became the director of the only major film facility in the Non-Occupied Zone of France, and thus the executive producer of the finest and greatest film ever made there, Les Enfants du Paradis.[138]

Orain got to know Tati during the making of Autant-Lara's Sylvie et le fantôme, in the summer of 1945, at the Studios Saint-Maurice.[139] The main interest of this adaptation of a play by the actor-writer Antoine Adam is the use of a laborious device for creating the effect of a diaphanous ghost. Autant-Lara explained later, when already a member of the European Parliament, representing Jean-Marie Le Pen's National Front, in his typically hyperbolic and vulgar tone:

> It's the one and only special effects film in the history of French cinema! It was an insane idea! One hundred and three takes with special effects, and we had absolutely no gear! We used an optical glass, just like when in a railway carriage you can see in the window both the scenery on the other side and a reflection of the people inside. You look at the set through the optical glass, and on the left, placed at exactly ninety degrees to it, the same identical set covered in black velours. Imagine the size of the whole thing! Two sets instead of one! And it was all shut in, it was like an oven in there! The slightest movements of old Tati had to be mapped out on both sets . . . we were stuck in the studio for four months, we got about three hours' sleep a night, whilst that producer wrote me letters saying I was a scoundrel and a thief! [140]

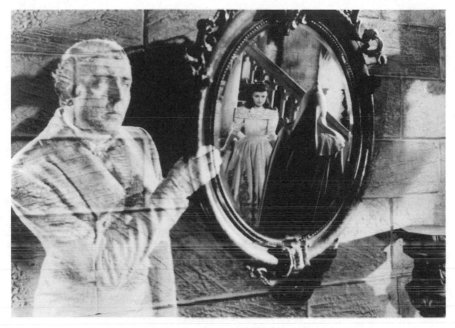

Fig. 34: *Tati reflected on to the set of* Sylvie et le fantôme

Four months' work as a silent reflection may have paid the rent at Rue de Penthièvre, but Tati must have been engaged in other gainful activity in the first couple of years after the end of the war. Perhaps as a music-hall performer (though there are no press-cuttings or programmes to confirm it), perhaps in the kinds of "grey market" deals that nearly everyone was engaged in during the long period of rationing. But with the new contact with the world of professional film that Orain gave him, Tati was soon planning a real career on the screen, and a new kind of comedy film.

Fred Orain, who had learned all he needed to know about production from his time at Victorine, was eager to set up on his own. He liked Tati's idea for a new series of comedy shorts; it was a genre in which, in the past, a lot of money had been made (though Méliès, Linder, and Keaton had also then lost it all again); it was a good enough place to start.

Tati's idea had something in common with his own pre-war shorts: it was to be set in a sleepy French village, as was *Soigne ton gauche*; the drama and comedy would arise from the arrival of some aspect of the new urban world of efficiency and speed. Not a great deal has survived from those early discussions, projects, and plans; but what has survived suggests that *L'Ecole des facteurs*, the first film of the Tati-Orain team, was conceived of from the start as a trial run for something much more ambitious.[141]

Cady-Films, named after Orain's pet dog (so he says), was incorporated in early 1946, and the shares were divided between Tati, who put his services as scriptwriter and actor into the common pot, and Orain, who also put in his services and a significant lump of capital. In the meantime, Tati took a small role in another one of Autant-Lara's films, also produced by Orain, an adaptation of Radiguet's famous novel of adolescent passion, *Diable au corps,* starring Gérard Philippe; and he lined up his old friend René Clément to direct *L'Ecole des facteurs.*

Apart from the formal date of registration of the company, the chronology of this period is rather confused. *Diable au corps* was shot near Aix-en-Provence in the summer of 1946;[142] but in business correspondence with government agencies, Orain referred to *L'Ecole des facteurs* as a film made in 1945. There are moreover photographs of Tati dressed as for the role of a peasant or bumpkin dated "Aix 1945". All that can be said with any degree of certainty is that between the fall of Berlin in May 1945 and the end of the following year, Tati had two film roles in works by Autant-Lara, founded a film company with Fred Orain, and shot his first real short. It does seem that he had a clearer vision of where he was going, and more of the means to travel along his chosen path, than at any time before.

Fig. 35: *Jacques Tati, Aix-en-Provence, October 1945*

L'Ecole des facteurs is in part a development of the "cycling postman" act played by Max Martel in *Soigne ton gauche*.[143] It opens at the post office where a martinet of a postmaster – played by Paul Demange, who also acts in *Sylvie et le fantôme*[144] – in a quasi-military uniform, is instructing his team of three cycling deliverymen in new methods of mounting, riding, and handing out the mail: for their round must be cut from its previous duration of two hours and fifty minutes to two hours and twenty-five, to allow them to connect with the brand-new airmail service from the local airstrip.

Two of the postmen are short and tubby, and the third, in the centre, is extremely, absurdly tall: for it is Tati. With the bicycles set on rollers, the pared-down, fundamentally idiotic new movements can be rehearsed, repeated, perfected, without the camera needing to move at all. But the big man always makes one mistake. When he stretches out his arm to deliver imaginary letters, in the efficiency ballet conducted by the falsetto-voiced postmaster, he returns his hand not to his satchel, but to his mouth, as if to down the glass of wine that his peasant customers no doubt normally provided. It is effectively a music-hall mime act, and was later performed as such on the stage of the Olympia; but in *L'Ecole des facteurs* it is the "set-up" for the film's main action, a mad postman's manic round of a still mediaeval French village, with each call providing the frame for another simple, unsophisticated gag.

The gags are not bad: one letter stuffed beneath a horse's tail because the blacksmith expects the postman to linger, but he can't, because of his shortened round; a parcel delivered hastily straight on to a butcher's cutting table, right under the knife, which slices straight through a new pair of shoes ("at least they won't pinch your toes", says Tati); a letter delivered to a bell-ringing curé, who gives the rope to the postman, who promptly disappears into the belfry; the bicycle left leaning against a car, which then drives off, taking the bicycle with it; an almost-standard level-crossing gag; and so forth. The most striking and inventive are those which involve Tati hooking his handlebars on to the back platform of a truck, and using the platform to sort and frank the mail whilst in movement (a special effect created by the already well-known device of rear projection); and the sight of Tati's giant frame on his boneshaker bicycle overtaking a squad of racing cyclists. He makes it to the airstrip just in time to see the airmail biplane taxiing towards take-off; he manages to deliver his satchel of mail in the nick of time, and in a gentle parody of the Western, by lassoing it to the moving tailfin.

There is not a visually dull moment in *L'Ecole des facteurs*, and its quality derives in large part from its extreme economy of means. But without the peculiar effect of Tati's size, of his antiquated, half-military uniform, and of his comic clumsiness so well-honed that it acquires a kind of grace, the film would not be anything very much. It was intended as a launch-vehicle for Tati as a new comic cinema personality. It is not a masterpiece; but it is a very promising start, far ahead of anything Tati had done before the war.

In the event, *L'Ecole des facteurs* was not directed by René Clément, who was far too busy directing and editing his hymn to working-class resistance, *La Bataille du rail*.[145] Instead of contracting another director to replace him, Tati stepped straight into his shoes. It was a role Tati had been striving towards for more than ten years; and it seems to have fitted him like a glove. His control over the film was unusually complete: he was a director of the production company (and would thus get a share of the profits), he was the scriptwriter (and thus would get a notional fee), he was the star, and also the director – almost a whole industry wrapped up in one (albeit large) man. Not until he was bankrupt and forced into compromise, in the 1970s, did Tati ever make a film in any other way, that is to say, as sole proprietor of all aspects of the creative process (story, image, sound, and performance). Few other film-makers since Chaplin have managed to combine all those roles – certainly not any of those who spoke most vehemently in defence of the *cinéma d'auteur*. Tati, from *L'Ecole des facteurs* to *Playtime,* is the epitome of what an *auteur* is (in film theory) supposed to be: the controlling mind behind a vision of the world on film.

The vision that we share through *L'Ecole des facteurs* is a satirical one: through exaggeration and ridicule, it prompts a negative view of those things that Tati disliked – work, efficiency, hurry, organisation – and no less surely suggests that men in peaked caps are arrant fools. These are hardly original targets of satire: Dickens's critiques of bureaucracy and the cult of efficiency are more sentimental, and also more courageous; but Tati's filmic reference must surely be the Chaplin of *Modern Times*. The difference is that Tati shows an efficiency-clown in a setting that is not modern at all, but the very image of *la France profonde*, the allegedly unchanging rural heart of the country. A cleric, a butcher, a blacksmith, a farmer and a farmer's wife – all the cardboard cut-out characters of a model village are there as the comic butts of François's accelerated round. Now that the village square has probably become a parking lot, the church is only open every third Sunday of the month and the blacksmith's son the struggling operator of a Kwikfit franchise, the human decor of *L'Ecole des facteurs* has turned into a historical document. In the immediate aftermath of the war, however, and shortly after the end of the Vichy state – with its emphasis on conservative, rural values and the maintenance of national traditions – Tati's short was much more ambiguous. Its main point, to be sure, is to allow us to watch some very well-executed comic acrobatics by a large man with a bicycle. But the story, such as it is, shows a rural postman *succeeding* in implementing the first steps in the modernisation of France, which is also the superficial target of the satire. Far from being a film of "resistance" or even a gentle critique, *L'Ecole des facteurs* is a work of acceptance and reconciliation. Unless of course the entire set-up and execution is to be taken, at a higher level of self-designating tomfoolery, as a send-up of both the old world and the new.

FOURTEEN

Mr Byrnes and M. Blum

At the Liberation of France the provisional government of General de Gaulle declared the Vichy regime null and void, and until very recently Pétain's war-time *Etat français* was held to be not part of the history of the legitimate French state. Legitimacy had resided during those years in London, in the person of de Gaulle; and so the laws of France, as from August 1944, were those that had been in force up to June 1940. None of Vichy's legislation – including its infamous racial laws – needed to be repealed, by decree or by new legislation: it simply did not exist.

Almost unique in this respect, the cinema industry did not return to the *status quo ante*: French post-war cinema was built on the structures, the systems, the personnel, and the staff that had arisen or taken their place under Vichy France. How could this have happened in a country that had officially wiped the slate clean of all that happened in those four dark years?

The structural legislation on the cinema industry introduced in October 1940 had actually been designed in the late 1930s to bring some order to the chaotic free-for-all of the early years of sound, which had led to the "scandalous" bankruptcies of two major French film production companies, Gaumont and Pathé (liquidated in 1934 and 1936 respectively). So although the new structures had been used by an authoritarian, paternalistic, and manipulative regime, they also expressed a longer-standing wish to clean up an industry still smarting from a defeat (the sound revolution under American hegemony) that was seen as the effect of internal disorganisation.

The film laws of October 1940 made production, distribution and per-formance of film works subject to prior authorisation from a new, central body, the *Comité d'organisation de l'industrie cinématographique*, or COIC. Such permission could only be requested by holders of the new "professional card", issued by the COIC, on behalf of a new government department, the *Direction générale du cinéma*. The old unions and employers' cartels were dissolved; and the new corporatist structures were of course themselves subject to racial laws, which they were required to implement, so as to free French cinema from the mythical grip of Jews, Masons, and Bolsheviks.[146]

Coincidentally, so to speak, French screens were closed to foreign films: because of the military situation, the new regime of the COIC coincided with the convenient absence of British and American competition for cinema audiences. So despite the shortages of raw materials (electricity, film stock, and, in the later stages, even food to put on tables in restaurant scenes), despite the constant involvement of propaganda and censorship, and despite the persecution of a significant proportion of the personnel of the French cinema industry, the Vichy years were, structurally at least, a golden age for French film.

At the Liberation, the COIC was rapidly replaced by the *Centre National de la cinématographie* (CNC), and the racial laws of course disappeared overnight; but the main structures of the Vichy regime's reorganisation of the industry were retained. The CNC continued to control the issue of professional cards and the rule of "prior authorisation" was maintained. This ensured that films were made by qualified staff, and that national norms could be established and imposed on a whole variety of issues, from financing to staffing, from safety at work to overtime rates. The involvement of the French state in the cinema industry was also maintained through the Crédit national, a publicly-owned bank which had special responsibility for making loans to businesses involved in film production.[147]

But the CNC had to confront an entirely different situation, for there was no longer a blanket ban on film imports: the old law of 1936, setting a quota of 188 foreign films per year, came back into force, but in a context that it had never been designed to deal with. There was a back-log of over two thousand US movies made since 1939 that had never been seen; liberated France was hungry for new films, and most especially for all those Hollywood movies it had missed.

At the same time, the country was virtually bankrupt. It had been plundered by the Germans, much of its industrial plant had been wrecked, and its gold reserves were virtually zero. The shortages of the war actually grew worse in the first years of the Liberation; food was rationed, harvests were meagre, there was an acute shortage of skilled labour, and huge war debts to settle. Relief could only come from the US.

Léon Blum, the former socialist Prime Minister, was appointed chief French negotiator, and sent to Washington to raise American aid. The deal he made (a forerunner of the more broadly-based Marshall Aid Plan of 1948) was not ungenerous: all France's war debts were cancelled, and a major line of credit was opened for the purchase of basic foodstuffs and agricultural equipment. But Mr Byrnes, the American negotiator, insisted on a number of French concessions, including the abrogation of import restrictions on American films. It was a highly sensitive political issue in France: the film industry feared American movie power; the Communist Party feared it too, for its ideological effect; the film industry and the CP both had wide support in France.[148]

Blum was more concerned with saving the French from starvation than with protecting them from Hollywood B movies, and agreed a compromise with Byrnes: instead of a numerical quota on imports, a screen-time minimum was fixed for home-made productions. In each thirteen-week quarter, French cinemas would be obliged to programme a French film for four of those weeks, and could show whatever they liked for the other nine. This clause in the treaty was kept secret for a few weeks, and announced well after the otherwise generous terms of the accord had made their political impact. As a result, the film clauses of the "Blum-Byrnes Agreement" of April–May 1946 were treated by the professional film press, and then by the national press, as a scandal. The anger seems in retrospect misplaced, the tool of a probably cynical piece of internal politicking; but at the time, alarm over the effect of the Blum-Byrnes Agreement on the prospects for the renaissance of French film was a major public issue, and the industry was virtually unanimous in denouncing it.

Nowhere was competition with American film likely to be more keen than in the genre of comedy. Chaplin, Sennett, Keaton and the others had long since set the standards by which film comedy was judged. What could France do that would equal if not surpass the attraction of the American comedy films that would be pouring in under the terms of Blum-Byrnes? Since the death of Max Linder, its own comic works had relied heavily on verbal wit, on "filmed theatre", on the art of the double-entendre and the exchange of sophisticated banter. Comedies of that kind were hardly likely to stand up against slapstick in the domestic market, and even less likely to win audiences abroad.

"Have we lost our ability to laugh?" Maurice Henry asked in July 1946, reviewing a pair of lamentably unfunny shorts (*Couple idéal* and *Leçon de conduite*). "The art of making people laugh is the hardest of all," he sermonised; and then, with a prescience that was perhaps not entirely unprompted, he declared:

> But we are not short of comic actors who could be made famous by
> a few good films. At the moment they are playing walk-on parts or
> earning a living in the music-hall. [149]

This little comment may have been the fruit of inside knowledge about various films in the pipe-line at that time – *Farrebique*, for example, or Prévert's *Voyage-Surprise*. But it sounds very much as if – thanks perhaps to Fred Orain's rapidly expanding ambitions for Cady-Films – Maurice Henry was holding the door open for Jacques Tati.

Part Two

Years of Achievement

1946–1960

FIFTEEN

Local Colour

> Estelle: *People talk about them all the time ...*
> *but we never actually see colour films*
> (*LE CRIME DE MONSIEUR LANGE*, 1936)

Thomsoncolor

Jour de fête, Tati's first feature film, was written and rewritten several times. starting most probably as early as 1945. Called *Fête au village* in one version, *Mon Village* in another, all surviving drafts are assemblages of two separate narratives – the depiction of the visit of a travelling fair to Follainville, in the heart of rural France, and the story of a dim-witted postman's accelerated cycling round, already used as the material of *L'Ecole des facteurs*.[150]

There are several real places called Follainville: but it is most unlikely that Tati had any of them in mind. "Follainville" is a suggestively comic name, "fol-" being cognate with words like *fou*, *folie*, *folichon* ("mad", "madness", "silly") and so forth, and it is no doubt for this reason that it was used

It may well be that the "village fair" material came initially from Henri Marquet, credited as co-author of the film finally made; various ways of blending the two stories in the different drafts may be the work of René Wheeler, a professional script-doctor called in to help; but it seems pretty certain that the cycling motifs, manifestly designed to allow Tati's talent as a mime to come to the fore, were imagined and constructed by the performer himself. They fill only a very small part of the written drafts, no doubt because Tati had them all in his head.

In all the surviving versions, the cycling stunts are prompted by the dimwit postman's exposure to a documentary film about the US Postal Service. In one version, the accelerated round is the village postman's dream; in another, as in the film, it is a reality, which alone allows a lesson to be drawn.

Fred Orain was instrumental in encouraging Tati's ambitions to make this film. He also helped to raise the finance for it. He put up significant cash of his own – two million francs, partly raised by selling his country seat;[151] he set up a company – Cady-Films – to produce it; and it was either he or Tati who persuaded a private bank, Dubail, to invest the first five million francs in Cady-Films, secured in part by the as-yet unreleased *L'Ecole des facteurs* (valued at two million francs) and by Tati's exclusive service contract with the company (similarly valued at two million).[152]

But Orain did much more than that to launch Tati, Cady-Films, and *Jour de fête*. In 1945, Jean Painlevé, the head of the CNC, had asked Orain to work out a plan for the reconstruction and modernisation of French film plant. Orain set up a standing committee of experts from all the technical branches of the industry, which was eventually officialised as the *Conseil supérieur technique* (CST). Tati's sole business partner thus had access to information on all the resources of French film studios, and he had his own ideas about how they could be improved. So when Orain heard of a new colour process under development by a major French company, he jumped at the chance of combining his new career as an independent producer with the renaissance of French industrial might. *Jour de fête* would be a colour film. More than that: it would be the first film shot in local Thomsoncolor. "I, and I alone, am responsible for the whole adventure," Orain claimed in 1987,[153] and there is no reason to doubt him.

It is something of a miracle that *Jour de fête* survived the Thomsoncolor episode, which was actually more of a scam than a gamble. For Orain, for the CST, for Tati as well, the stakes were high. Like sound, colour had been an implicit part of the technical agenda of photography and film since the very start; and, like sound, it had had numerous early realisations, each of which had been abandoned for financial or practical reasons. Just to list all the patent names for the regular breakthroughs in colour technology which accompany film history from the late nineteenth to the mid-twentieth century is rather like reciting the marques of all those improbable flying machines which ended their short lives as scrap: Dufaycolor, Coloris (used on most Pathé films made in the period 1900-1914), Francita, Chromacrome, Gevacolor, Rouxcolor ... None of them really worked very well, or for very long (all Gevacolor stock, for instance, faded within a couple of decades to black and white). In Germany, however, Agfa developed effective colour during the Third Reich, whilst in America, the cumbersome additive method of Technicolor produced such beautiful results – the classic example being the film version of Margaret Mitchell's *Gone with the Wind* (1939) – that it swept all before it. The Soviet Union appeared to have invented its own method, Sovcolor, but it later turned out that the film stock used had all been taken from the Agfa works at Wolfen (indeed, the name "Orwocolor" used by some Eastern European film industries in the 1940s is a give-away abbreviation of "Origin – Wolfen".[154]

There was no French-made colour process in operation in 1945, and that was a blow to national pride. There were US colour movies on show shortly after the Liberation, and many more waiting to be screened. Unless a home-grown process could be developed soon, French cinema would have yet another handicap in its fight to survive.

French film-makers could not purchase colour stock from the Eastman-Kodak labs in Rochester, NY, or from Britain; in any case, Technicolor required three separate reels, extremely intense lighting (and hence a reliable and powerful supply of electricity, which was simply not to be had on location in France) as well as the uninterrupted presence of a Technicolor Consultant – far beyond the financial means of any French production company at that time. On the other hand, post-war legislation allowed French-registered companies to appropriate the patents of German industrial processes used by them under the Occupation; the colour used by Pagnol in his Marseille studios in the later 1940s was recuperated from Agfa in just that way.

Orain seems to have acquired at least a brief experience of colour film before launching Jour de fête. Couleurs de Venise, directed by Jean Faurez and Jacques Mercanton for André Paulvé, Orain's old boss, came out in 1946. According to the summary given in Chirat and Romer's monumental catalogue of French short films, this twenty-five-minute fantasy tells of a girl dreaming, in a grey, drab Paris winter, of travelling to Venice, where the ghost of Casanova shows her the gaily-coloured sights of the town.[155] Although no copy of this film seems to have survived, Couleurs de Venise may well play a role in the pre-history of Jour de fête, since Orain hired Mercanton to direct the photography of Jacques Tati's first film.

Thomsoncolor was not actually a new process, but a very old one, based on patents originally taken out in 1908, and developed step by step over the following forty years. Its basic idea was to capture the colours of the world on an embossed film, using a "honeycomb" photosensitive surface composed of literally thousands of tiny prisms per square centimetre. The negative looks like black and white; only when the light is projected through it at the correct angle does an embossed film show its true colours.[156] When Orain signed up with Thomson-Houston in 1946, the process seemed near to perfection. He had seen sample reels on screen, and had been impressed; and he had no doubt that the remaining technical hurdles to be overcome, and which Thomson had probably made little of in the discussions, would be solved in good time. "The CST was entirely confident that the Thomsoncolor system would work," Orain said in an interview recorded in 1987.[157] Indeed, Thomson was investing large sums in the process, and was building a brand-new factory right next to the Pathé labs at Joinville-le-pont, where Tati's long-standing friend Jacques Broïdo was now directeur-général des usines.[158]

Local colour

According to a widely held belief in the small town of Sainte-Sévère, when Tatischeff (Jacques) took his leave in 1943[159] and thanked the locals who had provided him with food and shelter for a while during the war, he made a half-solemn, half-joking promise: that he would return there one day, and make them all famous on film. So when Tati turned up in his jeep in May 1947, with his cast, his cameras and his crew following behind, he was coming to make good on his promise. It is hard to believe that there is no truth at all in this version of local history, because *Jour de fête* is (amongst other things) a humorous but loving portrait of that particular place, and, in some respects, an ethnographic document on the life of *la France profonde*. In the film itself, the fictional name of Follainville is not used once (it found its way into some of the newspaper reviews from the press-releases put out by Cady-Films); but "Sainte-Sévère" is clearly displayed as the name of the place on a road sign seen to the right of the screen when the camera tracks an intrusive and shiny black saloon entering town.

   The realisation does not necessarily match the intention, of course, and the Sévérois may simply be under a kind of retrospective illusion. Jacques Mercanton, the director of photography, tells a story that seems to clash with the film's supposedly local roots:

> *Jour de fête* was developed from a black-and-white short, *L'Ecole des Facteurs*, which Tati had acted and directed in 1946, and in which I participated.[160] We looked for locations far and wide, as far south as Provence, since we were looking for sunny places for a film with a lot of out-door takes. But the atmosphere of the Midi and the cast of the scenery did not appeal to Tati, and we fell back on an area that he knew. He had lived at Le Marembert, about ten km from Sainte-Sévère. In the evening I went for a walk in the town and was charmed by its picturesque appearance. I told Tati how enthusiastic I was about the place . . .[161]

From this account, it would seem to have been Mercanton who picked Sainte-Sévère, for its picturesque and filmable qualities; by the merest coincidence, it was a place Tati already knew and liked. But Tati was not a very talkative man, and he was quite capable of silent manipulation. Maybe he wanted his director of photography to feel that he had selected the location. It does not necessarily follow from Mercanton's account that Tati had not intended to shoot at Sainte-Sévère all along; local beliefs aside, however, there is no actual evidence of Tati's war-time promise, or of any formulated plan to use that particular village square.

Colour theory

Tati had a colour theory that was all his own. To test it, years later, he carried out an experiment on friends who were frequent travellers through Orly airport. "What colour are the seats in the departure lounge?" he asked each one separately; and he claimed that he heard as many different replies as he had respondents to this amateur colour-blindness test. In Tati's view, the varied answers proved that colour was not part of what people see unless it has some function or meaning. We recall significant colours, but for the rest, our memories are mostly monochrome. [162]

Tati thus regarded decorative colour in film as somehow untruthful, at odds with the way the world really looks. He preferred to use *touches* of colour, to highlight specific objects and to endow them with meaning. Had he been able to use colour for *Les Vacances de M. Hulot*, for example, he would have shown up the varying tans acquired by the different holiday-makers during their week by the sea, and he would have made comic colour contrasts between the horizontal stripes on sailor-vests and the vertical stripes on canvas beach-tents and wind-breaks. But he would have left back-grounds, buildings, sea and sand in dull and unobtrusive hues, if not quite in monochrome.

Tati had exactly the same reservations about colour when he finally shot his first colour film, *Mon Oncle*.

> I am afraid that over-strong colour spots will distract the viewer's attention from the intended gag or from amusing details .... I went so far as to have the brown shop front of a little café repainted grey. Only the sequences that take place in Hulot's brother-in-law's villa and in the factory will be shot in tones that are – just a little – brighter ... [163]

Similarly, in *Playtime*, many scenes are chromatically plain, or else use a single dominant hue as a wash over the entire depicted set (green for the drug-store snack-bar, blue for the night view of the "fishbowl" flats). Perceptible colour, in Tati's cinema, always speaks of something: where there is nothing to say with colour in a given sequence, it is filtered down to be as near to monochrome as you can reasonably get.

For *Jour de fête*, Tati made thorough-going alterations to the natural colours of his location decor. He had much of the main square of Sainte-Sévère painted grey; curtains, window-boxes, and shop-lettering were removed; then touches of local colour were inserted, to highlight significant aspects of the story he had to tell. Colour was to be the sign and the meaning of the travelling fair, not of village life:

Fig. 36: *The "Drugstore" in* Playtime. *This shot is suffused with a
greenish glow from the chemists' neon sign*

> I had the peasants and especially the women dressed in black so that
> there should be almost no colour on the village square, and so that
> the travelling showmen and their accessories should bring colour
> to the place . . . [164]

This is a dramatic theory of colour: colour not as fidelity to the real or as a
decorative improvement, but colour endowed with meaning in the world
shown on film. Tati's projected use of colour in *Jour de fête* was also naive
and, to a degree, sentimental, as it was intended to attribute heightened
value to the transient fun of the fair. The drabness of everyday life in a rural
backwater would be signified by its monochrome hue.

This approach to colour stands in complete contrast to what was generally
done with colour technology in the first decades of its commercial exploitation. Most early colour films have plots that are medium-driven: they are
set in Venice, or Bruges, or parade lavish costumes, or display exotic landscape scenery, to show off what the technology can do. Stanley Donen and
Gene Kelly's *On The Town*, for example, shot in Technicolor just when *Jour
de fête* was finally released in black and white, has its leading ladies dressed
respectively in a lush peach stiff gauze skirt, in a mauve satin gown and in a
lime-green silk sheath. This is obviously not because New York office girls
might actually wear such things on a night out with three sailor-boys in

sparkling navy whites. The roof-top dance scenes, set against a blue-grey city skyline, demonstrate the technical quality of the medium used by showing these brilliant colours whirling about without the slightest loss of definition, even when mauve passes across peach and when peach comes up against lime. Gorgeous as it is, *On The Town* is a fair example of the medium-driven, decorative use of colour that Tati deplored, not simply when he lacked the means to rival it, but throughout his work in film. All the same, his intended use of Thomsoncolor in *Jour de fête* seems contrary to the industrial and commercial purpose of the film – to launch Jacques Tati on the back of a new colour process, and to launch the colour process on the back of Tati's mimes. In the end, it did not matter one jot: Thomsoncolor did not really exist, and Tati and Orain discovered that they had been taken for a ride. Although the negative film stock certainly existed, and filmed the shots in the normal manner, no means was ever found of printing positive copies from it. Even whilst Tati was still shooting *Jour de fête*, Thomson-Houston decided to close down its colour laboratories, and abandoned its only half-finished factory building at Joinville. By providential foresight, *Jour de fête* had also been shot in black and white. Without that miraculous back-up, Tati's career as a director might never have got off the ground.

SIXTEEN

Sounds and Words

Anyone who has seen any of Tati's films knows that he handles sound in quite peculiar ways. But then sound is an altogether peculiar thing. If you hold out a microphone and record the sounds around you, and then play the tape back, most likely you will get just a meaningless jumble of noise; whereas what you heard was not meaningless at all, but an aural tapestry in which (let us say) birdsong, distant car engines, autumn leaves scrunched by a passing squirrel, and the whirr of a computer fan are recognisable threads. To reproduce the sound of that ambient noise on tape or film, you have to reconstruct it thread by thread, and then weave the threads together, in a process called mixing. But to take a snap of the view from your window, you just point the camera and press the button. You may not get a good picture, but at least it will look something like what you saw through the viewfinder. Sound is very different from sight, and a few mildly technical terms and notions are needed in order to understand how Tati used it in his first feature film.

Noise versus sound

The ear is a blunt instrument when it comes to making blind discriminations between the sounds of different things. Set up primarily to transform the river of noise from the world around into separate and meaningful streams, hearing takes "prompts" from the eye. To interpret a sound as being a loud one from far away or a soft one coming from much nearer, for example, or the words spoken by a mouth turned towards us as opposed to those floating over from conversations in which we are not directly involved, our ears are often prompted by the evidence of what we can see. Other senses, too, help us to unbundle noise into sounds – the feel of the wind on our cheek, or the smell of burnt fuel, may serve as instant clues to determine the right sense to give to a sibilant hiss, or to a thunderous growl. But the ear possesses not only a sensitivity to volume, timbre, pitch and the other acoustic formants of sound: from earliest infancy, it has a life-preserving ability to perceive orientation. In general, in the absence of all other clues, we can tell blindfold where a sound is coming from more instinctively and more accurately than we can tell what it is.

Radio sound is the purest of the artificial contexts of sound, for it is supported by no information at all from any of the other senses; prior to the introduction of stereophonic broadcasting in the mid-1960s, it had no orientation either. Cinema sound derives in part from the techniques of radio dramatists, but also has its own conventions and rules, designed to create the illusion of "real sound" in a medium missing most of the clues that we usually exploit for dealing with the real noise of the world.

Synchronicity

Synchronising picture and sound was the holy grail of early talking-picture technology. Once that had been achieved by optical-recording devices, film-makers found that the magic of synchronism could cover up a multitude of sins and simulations, many of them borrowed from radio practice, and even from the music-hall.[165]

The importance of synchronising sound and picture in the cinema is rather paradoxical. In real life, large distant events – volcanoes exploding, buildings collapsing, fighter aircraft firing, etc. – are heard a split second, or even as much as half a minute, after they are seen, because of the different speeds of light and sound. But in the classical sound cinema, everything that is seen is heard simultaneously. The expectation of synchronicity is so strong that acoustically accurate sound-lags on screen seem artificial. (In some cases, of course, the strangeness of asynchronous sound may serve a dramatic purpose.)

Given the relative poverty of information accompanying the sound-streams in the cinema (no smell, no feel, no orientation), synchronicity alone tells us what the sound is coming from. The reciprocal result is that as long as a sound is synchronised with an action on screen, it is interpreted, irresistibly, as the sound of that action, irrespective of the acoustic quality of the sound. The recorded sound of a running bath-tap synchronised perfectly with a clip of a moving railway train will almost certainly be heard as the special noise of that particular train, and not as a bath-tap running somewhere off screen. It follows that a great deal of care and artistry is needed to allow or to oblige a spectator to hear a fully synchronised sound as wrong, or ridiculous, or even just comic. The percussive noises of everyday objects coming into physical contact – a door banging shut, a letter-box lid being closed, a bicycle thrown to the ground – can be "figured" in sound cinema by almost any random noise, for the ear will take the noise as the sound of what it can see happening on screen. Only highly-trained and attentive listeners could possibly distinguish the sound of a ping-pong ball on a tile floor from that of shoe-leather on a wooden stair-tread. This is not to say that anything goes in cinema sound. Jean-Claude Carrière recalls following Tati into a sound-recording studio and "watching with astonishment as he broke glasses, one after the other, for hours, with utmost seriousness, in order to obtain the best possible sound".[166] But when the illusion of real sound without comic effect is sought, there really is no point in being too precise, since the ear's power to discriminate in real time is not very great. Synchronisation is so powerful in prompting us to attribute a sound to a thing seen that once we have done so – once we have "heard" the clacking as the noise of the footsteps on the stairs, we no longer hear the clack (the acoustic specificity of the sound recorded) but the step. Something else – something rather tricky – would have to be done to force us to pay attention to the sound itself. Tati became the absolute master of such tricks. And his work on deconstructing cinema sound began in *Jour de fête*.

Perspective

In mono sound, all noise comes from the same stationary source, the loud-speaker above or beside the screen. But as we are accustomed to using our ears to interpret the location of sound sources, something else has to stand in for those missing orientation cues. In radio and cinema, the directionality of natural sound is simulated by volume control, and the rules governing its use are called sound perspective. Simply stated, sound perspective means that something seen happening in the foreground of the shot must make a louder noise than something seen to be further away. Most failures to respect the rule are instinctively heard as "bad sound", as imperfect or amateur use of recording technology. Which is why the non-perspectival sound of some of Jean-Luc Godard's more avant-garde movies is taken by some to be intellectually refreshing, and by others to be just awfully bad.

Synchronicity and perspective apply to things seen on screen: noises of things not seen have to be removed, or put in quite specifically as "background noise". Sound cinema in its classical form follows the rule that if the clucking of a chicken is to be heard, then a chicken must be shown at least once, for the spectator to be able to attribute any further instances of it to the stream of "farmyard noise". Noises for which no visual attachment has been provided cannot be used, save for conventionally unseen sound-sources, such as an owl hooting in the night, when the visual context (night, exterior, countryside) allows such an attachment to be made.

Streams and tracks

In the bundle of noise heard, the ear attributes different formants to separate streams of sound; the talking pictures simulate that instinctive unscrambling by recording three separate tracks, which are then mixed into a humanly appropriate muddle. The three tracks normally distinguished are those of musical accompaniment, sound effects (background noise), and dialogue.

Musical accompaniment in film work of all kinds is a curious paradox, since it runs counter to the illusionist aesthetics of most kinds of film art. Outside of American shopping malls and hotel lobbies, real-life sound does not have a musical backing. Traditional accounts of this curious device state that film music (scores played by live orchestras in the early days of silent film) sprang from the dire need of something to mask the noise made by the projector[167] and, in open-air performances, by distracting audience noises and sounds off – owls, cicadas, maybe even howling prairie dogs. But it is also surely an inheritance from the traditions of popular entertainment: music has always been used to create conviviality in bars and dives, and to back up mime, acrobatics, circus stunts and such like. Amongst the forms of live art, only theatre is devoid of a musical track. The sound of background music as the credits roll at the start of a film tells us first of all that we are not about to watch a classical tragedy by Racine.[168] We are out to have a good time.

Conventionally, the music track in fiction film is non-diegetic, that is to say it is not part of the story seen on screen, but designed to create atmosphere, ambience, to raise tension or to diffuse it, in rough parallel to the story as it unfolds.[169] Diegetic music is also a feature of many films – those that have musical subjects, as did many of the early sound films, but also fiction films where a band plays, or where we set eyes on a fairground hurdy-gurdy, or follow a chap whistling as he walks down the lane. But in such cases, a boundary between non-diegetic and diegetic music is marked clearly enough for it to be understood. Most of the instances where the rule is broken – in Lang's *M*, for example, where a Grieg melody serves both for the background track and for the whistling murderer's give-away – are very carefully calculated indeed.

Speech is acoustically more complex than music, and the relatively poor quality of early sound technology meant that dialogue had to be handled with great care. To ensure that what was said was understood even by spectators not fully at home in English, and by those huge numbers for whom it was a foreign tongue, things said are always said by someone who can be seen saying it on screen. In the grammar of classical sound, the speech track carries the story, and is thus always the loudest, clearest track. Sound perspective thus requires speaking characters to be seen in close or medium close shots, since the implied distance of a long shot would make the words too faint for easy understanding. Rather like live actors' technique of "stage whisper", Hollywood sound has characters in close-up heard at a high volume, even when mouthing sweet nothings into each others' ears.

These conventions may seem highly artificial in such a description, but they produce what everyone quickly came to accept as "natural sound". Tati, by contrast, sought to use sound as a comic device; and that required him to unravel the rules of natural sound, and to turn them upside down.

Bleeding

The sound-effect and dialogue tracks (unlike background music) are normally cut, in standard sound cinema, at exactly the place where the image is also cut. This rule seems to be merely a natural consequence of the basic principle of synchronicity. In fact, the sound/image edit rule is often broken, usually in the service of the *perception* of synchronicity. Given the slower speed of the ear compared to the eye, as well as its relative obtuseness, it often helps comprehension to have the sound of the next sequence beginning a second or two before the edit, so that the new sound-stream will be fully perceived in tandem with the new scene. "Bleeding" or "overlapping" usually works in this forward-oriented way, leading the viewer/hearer to pay more attention to those features of the following sequence which the sound bridge identifies. In *Jour de fête*, for example, the shot is still on Roger unloading the roundabout horses from the back of his trailer when the village-crier's drumroll begins, and the sound bridges over the cut to a shot of the crier, announcing the *grrrande séance de cinéma*. Whilst the crier is still on screen, the sound of dialogue from the test run of *Les Rivaux de l'Arizona* begins to be heard, and bleeds over the cut to the next sequence, where we see Jeannette wheeling laundry towards the front of the cinema marquee. Such sound bridges speed up the narrative unfolding; but backward overlaps also have their uses, as when a sentence trails over the edit from the previous scene, to place the following shot in its appropri-ate narrative context. There are no such reverse bleeds of sound in *Jour de fête*: with its very thin narrative line, it needs to move attention forward all the time, to maintain the expectation that something is about to happen.

Tati's grammar lessons

Contrary to the general impression given by many of his most sympathetic commentators, Tati does not break all the rules of natural sound all the time in all of his films. *Jour de fête* shows that he knew what the rules were – and also that he was learning how to play games with them.

Tati had used sound before, of course. In his music-hall act he must have made use of cues from the string and timpani sections of the resident band: make-believe punches in the boxing sketch, for example, would have been marked by a clash of cymbals, the saves of his football goalie by a muffled beat on a drum, and the twangs of racquet on ball by plucks of a tuned-down cello string. As for the horse-and-rider turn, it must have had orchestral backing, to show that the prancing beast was keeping to time (in fact, of course, the orchestra follows the horse, even when its hooves are figured by the feet of Jacques Tati). Even the angling sketch must have needed some sound effects – a whizzing noise (kazoo? penny whistle?) for the line being thrown, and a less discreet "plop" (from which instrument?) for the one that got away . . . These tricks of the dumb-show – which is not a *silent* medium, but a *speechless* one – are no different in principle from what is done in radio drama; but on stage, they depend absolutely on timing, just like the sound effects of film.

Comic sound

The cello-twang signifying racquet-and-ball in a music hall act is not meant to reproduce the sound as it would be heard by the spectator if he or she were indeed sitting at roughly that distance from a real tennis-player: the twang mimics the sound-sensation heard or felt by the player. Tati uses sound in this music-hall way in all his mature films: in *Playtime*, for instance, when Giffard, the manager of the office complex, walks into an impeccably clean glass door, the comic-strip "scrunch" that marks the contact of nose and glass for the ear is not remotely like the noise that would be heard were we located at the same distance from the glass door as the camera. It represents the noise of the *feeling* of a glass door on your nose. Comic sound effects, even though they rely on synchronicity, are most often examples of non-realistic, *subjective* sound.

The comic potential of sound-synchronisation is exploited in a different way in *Jour de fête* when François, having slept in a freight car, clocks in at the post office for work, and then exits the frame to wash his face.[170] The postmaster and his mate remain seated at their desks, franking mail at the infuriatingly slow, post-office regulation pace. They stop and look up; then resume franking. They stop and look up a second time; then resume franking. Without sound, the sequence would be incomprehensible. But because the sounds synchronised with the head movements of the post-office workers are hammer-blows, cascades, burps, and gurgles, they are heard as exaggerated plumbing faults – comical to those who have had to live with historical pipework, but probably less and less comprehensible to generations unaccustomed to air-locked hot-water systems. In principle, this sound sequence is no different from many a music-hall gag. It is more obvious and vulgar than most of the sound humour in Tati's later films; but it tells us that the maker of *Jour de fête* had learned the basic grammar of film sound.

In his pre-war shorts, at least in the form in which we possess them nowadays,[171] Tati used fairly primitive sound in standard ways with no great artistry or success. Probably because of poor equipment and lack of recording time, sound perspective is virtually nil in *On demande une brute*, *Gai dimanche* and *Soigne ton gauche*, and the dialogue is not easy to make out. This is particularly unfortunate for the first of the shorts, where the entire motivation for the mimed wrestling match is constructed theatrically, through conversation (with Rhum, with Roger's wife, with the impresario, in interview and on the telephone). It matters less in *Gai dimanche*, because most of the comic action is comprehensible as a dumb-show; and it is least important of all in *Soigne ton gauche*, which, like Tati's post-war work, relies very little on the meaning of what is said by characters to each other. In *L'Ecole des facteurs*, the division between "theatre" and "mime" is clearly marked: the set-up scene, where Paul Demange explains in his comic falsetto the reasons for the accelerated bicycle round, is the only part in which language plays a directly informative role. Conversely, the music track (the same Yatové jingle used for the "cycling theme" of *Jour de fête*) is much more evocative, and creates a good part of the lunatic atmosphere of the cycling scenario. For that reason there is almost no sound-effect track: the music is too constant and loud.

Most viewers recall *Jour de fête* as a virtually wordless movie. That is partly because the original versions (1949, most especially, but to some extent the 1961 remake too) have sound tracks with poor acoustic definition, and it is hard to catch just what the characters say. But if we listen to the 1995 restored colour version, with a sound track entirely re-recorded by Sophie Tatischeff to implement what she reasonably believes to have been her father's intention for the film, we hear quite a lot of language – but still we do not really grasp all that is said. Spoken language does not fulfil the functions that speech is normally called on to play in a fiction film. In a quite peculiar way, Tati treats the dialogue track as if it consisted of background noise, and sets the background noise in forward perspective, as if that were where the story really lay.

Farmyard symphony

The most striking feature of the sound track of *Jour de fête* is the constant presence of countryside ambience noises. From the opening of the film to its closing shots, we hear a thousand cocks crowing, hens clucking, horses neighing, geese cackling, dogs barking (no cats meowing), cows mooing (no sheep bleating), as well as an owl hooting, a swarm of cicadas, and, on three separate occasions, a loudly buzzing bee. Almost all these animal and insect noises come over at fixed volume, without variation of intensity that could be attributed to proximity and distance. The most nearly comparable ambience track is the enervatingly loud and constant road noise of *Trafic*. In the latter case, clearly, the refusal of sound perspective by an established master of the medium underlines one of the meanings of the film. The novice director of *Jour de fête*, however, might just have been making what Tati called his "spelling mistakes" in the editing and mixing of the film. To show that the refusal of perspective is not just a blemish in *Jour de fête*, but a voluntary effect, Tati included a standard sound-perspective exercise in the film.

When Roger's assistant starts the hurdy-gurdy on the merry-go-round, signalling the opening of the fair, the film cuts to several shots of the consequences in the village square – a boy rushes out of a front door, before being collared by a parent, and from a different doorway a member of the marching band looks out, downing his last glass before he sets off to join his mates. In these "consequence" shots, the volume of the hurdy-gurdy remains stable, for we are still close to the noisy merry-go-round in the square. The film then cuts to the bandsman on his way, rushing down a back street: and at the edit, very precisely, the volume of the hurdy-gurdy goes down by half, signifying that the position on screen is further away from the source of the noise. As if Tati were saying: sound perspective is as easy as that.

We first hear Yatové's musical "mad cyclist" theme over the image of a letter-box (in which Roger has posted a letter) held in close-up, centre-screen, for a couple of seconds, to help us make the metonymic jump from "letter-box" to "postman". The jerky penny-whistle theme bleeds over the edit to François's first appearance, cycling down a country lane, and from the music emerge two sounds that will turn out to belong to the narrative (though we do not yet know that) – the tinkling of a bell, and a buzz. From the top of a grassy slope overlooking the lane, the camera tracks the cyclist in long shot; as he begins to flap his arms, as if trying to disentangle himself from some imaginary reel of sticky paper, the music falls back to leave the buzz and the bell as the dominant sounds. The buzz, contrary to most people's memory of the sequence, actually remains at the same intensity over the cut to the next, medium close shot, where François, seen front on, dismounts and dances a frantic ballet with the pestering bee. (How close is this demonstration mime to Decroux's training exercise of "man pestered by a fly"? How near to a parody of what Tati must have heard about, if not actually seen, from the many actors who had been through Decroux's school?) The music comes to its final bar at the precise moment when François gets off his bicycle (and thus declares itself to be the theme of François-the-cyclist, not of François on foot). From this point on, we hear only the unrelenting buzz, and the bell (sounding much more like an Alpine cow-bell, or one of those bells-on-sticks carried by Shakespearean fools, than a regular bicycle bell) which is synchronised with the more abrupt jerks of the postman and his metal steed. The buzzing and the bell also bleed over the next edit, to the famous long shot from the top of the grassy slope where we now see, from behind, a peasant scything the hay, looking down on the scene that we see. Though the sound track is now enriched with the satisfying hiss and rip of the scythe (and a generous helping of chicken and geese), the intensity of the bee-noise (a kazoo? paper-and-comb?) hardly alters as the cyclist in the distance calms down, and the peasant in his turn begins to flap his arms about his head. Yet everyone who has seen *Jour de fête* remembers the bee *moving* from François to the peasant: that is after all the whole joke. Technically, acoustically, the sound perspective is virtually zero. What we understand of the narrative is created by our eyes alone, as in a music-hall mime; our grasp of the situation *depicted* overrides and rubs out the truth of the sound. Even if Tati struck on this gag by accident, or by a technical incapacity to implement the rules of cinema sound, its implications run deep for the development of his sound work in film. Rules of sound perspective can be broken when the images are powerful enough to provide meaning by themselves.

It is certainly with a sound gag of the same sort that Tati starts us off on the aural adventures of *Les Vacances de M. Hulot*. Sputtering explosions begin just before Hulot's Amilcar appears on screen; but the noises do not grow louder or softer as the vehicle moves nearer or further away, and the loudest back-fire comes after the car has stopped. None of the sound of *Les Vacances* can be attributed to incompetence or to poor equipment, as might be the case in *Jour de fête*: Tati had the means to do exactly what he intended in his second film. The refusal of perspective in the opening "Amilcar" sequence sets the "sound style" that is the hallmark of Tati's whole oeuvre.

In the first shot of the "bee gag sequence" in *Jour de fête*, Tati gives a slight twist to the rules that would keep diegetic and non-diegetic music distinct, since the buzz and the bell begin when the theme tune is in full swing, and seem at first to be part of it. He plays many other tricks on the music track, not all of them very pleasant to the ear. The worst cacophony

Fig. 37 & 38: Jour de fête: *the buzzing bee*

arises when the marching band comes into the main square, and effectively mounts a contest for aural supremacy with the hurdy-gurdy on the merry-go-round. It becomes impossible to tell what is background and what is diegetic sound: in effect, the whole aural bloodbath *is* the story that is being told. Just as crafty is the cross-over of the bar-room pianola, whose polka appears to be the background music when we cut to Tati entering the room, but reveals itself as diegetic in the same shot when the pianola breaks down, and the music stops.

Another game with sound synchronisation, perspective and source comes when Roger meets Jeannette in front of the marquee where the projectionist is doing a test-run of *Les Rivaux de l'Arizona*, in preparation for the main show of the fair. Roger and Jeannette say nothing to each other; but their physical movements (body, eye, smiles and retractions) are cued in to the extracts that we hear from a "boy-meets-girl" episode in the American film. In the 1949 version, the US movie speaks a pathetically formal kind of French, and the sound is caricaturally loud and clear (we have to imagine the scene as a close-up); in the 1961 remake as in the 1995 version, the US movie is heard in equally stilted and overloud American English. But the language does not matter very much, because the point of the invented *Arizona* dialogue is not to say anything in particular, but to *sound like* a romantic interlude in Hollywood sound, as if, in a cultural reference Tati probably could not himself easily conceive, the Agricultural Fair episode of *Madame Bovary* required a modern, and more explicitly comic setting. (In this famous chapter of Flaubert's novel, a seduction is enacted in dialogue set on the balcony, whilst speeches are made on the village square, and the two "language streams" provide ironic commentaries on each other.) So what we see in Tati's version of this set piece is like a deconstruction of the principle of dubbing. Whatever Jeannette and Roger might have wanted to say to each other, it is said by someone else.

Perhaps the most extraordinary sound gag in the whole of *Jour de fête* is the "*ciné-poste*" sequence. Alongside the *Arizona* feature movie, the fairground has also brought along a documentary entitled (on posters clearly seen outside the marquee) *La Poste en Amérique*. François is enticed to watch it by locals who think it should be part of his education as a modern postman. Although still preoccupied by trying to mend a puncture in his front tyre, François has his head shoved through a gap in the awning to watch this paean of praise to the valour, skill and technology of the US Postal Service. He sees it in fragments; sound perspective is obeyed entirely by making major shifts in volume at the cuts between shots of the documentary itself, with François's head seen in the bottom right-hand corner of our screen, and medium close shots of François from outside the tent (we see him from behind, and also moving away to attend to his puncture). As a result, we hear clearly only disjointed fragments of the commentary, which makes it barely coherent. What we see of the documentary are also disjointed fragments – sorting machinery, then helicopter training exercises, then motorcycle stunts, and a clip from the Mr Universe contest.

The meaning of the *ciné-poste* sequence is created not by any of its elements but only by their combination: it is an exercise in classical montage, like a parody of Eisenstein's famous cuts from beaming peasant to gleaming dairy machinery in *The Old and The New*. The raucous musical track is also a parody of newsreel excitement, and sets the general tone of the documentary. The voice-sound, switching abruptly from high to low volume at the edits, gives aural prominence to a few key terms – "postman Yankee", "US Postal Service", *rapidité, régularité, efficacité* ("speed, regularity, efficiency") – and drowns the rest beneath music and rapid tremolo diction. Just enough narrative sense can be extracted from these sound elements to link the visual fragments together. François – whose attention is any case divided – is taken in by the montage; the spectator of the film can see what it is that seduces François into seeking to rival the American postman, and can also see that he has been fooled.

Tati's parody of the way sound is used in newsreel commentary to cover up stock shots is only one level of the comedy of this sequence. What also stands out is the way voice-sound is used in almost exactly the same way as background noise. For the sentences actually spoken are not really what is heard, either by François or by the spectator: what is registered by the ear is an overall impression of hype, exaggeration, false praise – just as the clucking, cackling, mooing and crowing of the more general background track leave an impression of human life irremediably drowned in the animal world.

Speech

Jour de fête uses no dialogue at all to establish the setting and the narrative. The arrival of the travelling fair is shown, not stated, and the nature of the location is explained by the rich farmyard noises of the background track. The caravan winds its way into Sainte-Sévère and comes to a halt in the square; the showman opens the door of his trailer, comes out, and sets off; only at this point – nearly five minutes into the film – do we hear any articulated language, when the showman's sour wife says, "Roger, get me some water." For the rest of the film, most of the fragments of speech that are heard are just as inconsequential, in strictly narrative terms.

Of course, the smart-Alec showmen manipulate the postman into putting up the maypole by talking up his strength, his ability to lead, his intelligence and so on; but these dialogue snippets are, similarly, more like *gestures* than conversational interaction. When François tries to control his team of helpers by uttering verbal commands, all he can manage are ritual tautologies: *Ceux qui tirent sur la gauche, sur la gauche; ceux qui tirent sur la droite, sur la droite* ("Those on the left, pull left! Those on the right, pull right!") When he tries later on to explain to people he meets on his round how he managed nonetheless to raise the flag, all we hear are perspectivally-distanced fragments of the same mumbled sounds.

An early instance of "language as gesture" can be found in *Soigne ton gauche*: the children's make-believe newsreel report of the farmyard cyclist's great exploit simulates the tone, the diction, the speed of a real reporter's sports commentary (save for the unbroken boy's voice in which it is reeled off), but nobody is meant to listen to what the children actually say. What counts, for the narrative of the film, is the nature of the discourse, its status and overall sound. What we hear is not a speech as such, but the sound of a speech being made.

Lots of people make such "language noises" in *Jour de fête* – Bondu the barman, his wife Marie, Roger and Jeannette in the lucky-dip booth, villagers keen to have François see the documentary on the post office, the showmen, even the gendarmes who pass by the farm where François has delivered a cake: but none of them say anything much that could be allocated to the diegetic (or strictly narrative) dimension of the film. Language, in *Jour de fête*, is really just human background noise, just as the clucking of hens and the crowing of cocks are animal background sounds.

Animal language

The cross-over between the animal and human worlds of Sainte-Sévère is made quite explicit by the sound track of a sequence already discussed, when François returns to the post office after his rough night in the freight yard. The showmen who had got him drunk the night before made him look down a trick conch-shell that left a circle of black ink around his eye. So when François opens his locker and looks at himself in the mirror, he sees his "oeil de lynx" and is for an instant bemused. Like a child, he looks away and then switches his glance back again, to check that the black mark is really there. The head movements are jagged, like a chicken's darting pecks: Tati dubbed chicken noises over François's attempts to make the black eye go away. So the sequence becomes a mime act of a man behaving like a fowl, and the most explicit notation of the equivalence, in a French country town, between human and animal life.

Tati was fascinated by parallels between humans and animals. In *Gai dimanche* he has tourists turn into hedge-jumping horses as they try to catch a chicken for lunch. In *Soigne ton gauche*, the camera closes up on two roosters squabbling in the farmyard; Roger the peasant imitates them by puffing up his chest; the camera then cuts to the boxing champion undoing his jacket zipper by pectoral pressure alone, quite unaware that he is only following the style of the free-range poultry parade. On stage (as the horse and rider) and on screen in a dozen different scenes in his post-war films, Tati obliterates the distinction between the human and animal worlds. The repetition and intensity of this theme make it more than just a series of jokes.

An argument with language?

Les Vacances de M. Hulot opens with a justly famous sight-and-sound gag. A station platform is seen in a long crane shot that manages to include the public-address loudspeaker in the top right-hand corner of the frame. People rush from platform A, down the subway stairs, and emerge on platform B, just as a train passes through without stopping on track C. People rush back to the subway stairs and re-emerge on platform C as another train draws in to platform B. The voice track over this scene consists of incomprehensible squawking, half-way between the distorted sound of actual PA systems, and a muted trumpet, with shades of the farmyard added in. It is of course a satire of the real difficulties we all have in understanding station announcers, an exaggeration of a real-life problem. But it is something more than just a comic vision of holidaymakers in disarray at the most stressful point of their journey. Tati offers us also a vision of humankind rushing back and forth in response to incomprehensible injunctions, as if language served most of all to put people on the wrong track.

Tati's argument with language begins in *Jour de fête*, which is far from being the silent comedy with noises attached that many critics make it out to be. It is not just because it is a comedy film that it treats language as gesture, as sound effect, as an element of the aural environment. Indeed, most French comedy films – for example, Prévert's *Voyage-Surprise*, shot the same year – do the exact opposite, and draw most of their laughs from witty dialogue. Tati's ambition, no doubt fed by Orain, for the world mantle of Mack Sennett and the classical comedians of the silent screen must also be counted as a marginal reason for the downgrading of coherent speech in *Jour de fête*. Through its quite peculiar sound track, Tati's first film expresses

Fig. 39: *Shooting* Jour de fête *with two cameras*

its maker's own relation to language. Tati was not good with words; some acquaintances found him inarticulate, even obtuse. But he was also endowed with a different kind of intelligence. The language-sounds of *Jour de fête* are not what we would like to hear, or what we like to imagine we hear when we recall the already-interpreted scenes of our lives. But they are quite close to what we *actually* hear – broken fragments of sentences, phatic utterances disconnected from part of their context, stock phrases, the flotsam and jetsam of a confused and confusing aural environment. The riddle is to understand how someone who presumably did hear the world in that way, whose ear was probably not fast enough to invent the missing links that give coherence to the bits of language that we take in, nonetheless had the genius to reproduce exactly that state in a sound track, and, in so doing, to invent a new kind of aural realism in comedy film.

SEVENTEEN

Back-Up

In the same way that the French adapt foreign words to their
pronunciation, they adapt feelings, thoughts, even objects; for every
foreign fruit there must be a substitute grown in their own soil
JOHANN WOLFGANG VON GOETHE, 1819

Tati did not make *Jour de fête* on his own, nor was he, in principle, coming just to make a comedy film when he arrived in Sainte Sévère sur Indre in May 1947. He was in joint command of an important industrial adventure – the first application of a new French colour process which, if successful, would change the prospects of French cinema at a stroke.[172] This had no direct financial implications for the film, since Thomson-Houston provided the extra camera, the colour film stock and an on-site technician for free. Indirectly, though, it slowed down the shoot, and made it more expensive than it would otherwise have been. Orain and Mercanton both decided that it would be safer to shoot a "back-up" version in black and white; but as the colour and monochrome film stock needed different intensities of lighting, and also could not be set up at exactly the same angle for each shot, nearly everything in the film was done twice over – not counting bad takes. Fig. 39 shows the two cameras side by side: from these positions, they obviously could not have registered exactly the same frames. Since Tati never edited the colour negatives, it cannot be known which of the takes he would have used; nor whether the black-and-white version released in 1949 corresponds take-for-take to Tati's intentions when he was shooting the film. All that François Ede and Sophie Tatischeff could do when restoring the colour version in the early 1990s was to take those elements in the cans that corresponded most nearly to the film that was released in 1949, without any certainty that Tati would have used these and not other takes had he been able to edit the colour version himself.

Even without the complication of the double shoot, Cady-Films was short of cash: Orain had been able to raise only eighteen million francs, about half the current cost of a "normal" feature film, and he and Tati had to make do with that. As a result, *Jour de fête* was financed in large part on tick. Tati, Orain, the technicians and most of the members of the cast took no fees for their work; instead they got percentage shares in the future receipts of the film.[173] Tati often let it be understood that his first film had been made by a workers' co-operative; but it was not to make a political point that *Jour de fête* was financed in that way, only because money was tight. Tati would manifestly have preferred to own the whole show. One of the first things he did when money at last began to roll in was to buy back as many of the smaller stakes as he could. Some of the crew sold out to him, and then came to feel that they had been robbed. In the 1950s, Henri Marquet was often heard snarling that it was *he* who had really made *Jour de fête*, and that he had been tricked by Tati into parting with his rights.

The myth of the "workers' co-operative" goes hand-in-hand with the belief that the cast and crew of *Jour de fête* consisted primarily of Tati's chums, and that the good humour of the finished film replicated the convivial relations between the director and his *bande de copains*. Maine Vallée, for example (Jeannette in the film), was an old friend of Tati's wife Michou, and a frequent caller at Rue de Penthièvre (she was also the daughter of a well-known supporting film actor, Marcel Vallée). However, the main roles went to regular professionals, in spite of the enduring myth of this being an "amateur" film: Guy Decomble (Roger) had acted in *Le Crime de Monsieur Lange*, *La Bête humaine*, and other outstanding films by Renoir and Carné (later on, he played the schoolmaster in the even more famous film that launched the New Wave in 1959, Truffaut's *Quatre Cents Coups*); the role of the bar-owner, Bondu, was given to Beauvais, who had not stopped being a busy character actor since playing in *Forces Occultes* (Nova-Film, 1942), a Nazi propaganda movie denouncing Jews, Freemasons, and foreign spies;[174] Paul Frankeur, who plays Roger's partner in the travelling fair, had also graduated from music-hall to bit-part film acting under the Occupation, and would go on later to be Jean Gabin's regular opposite number in more than a dozen films;[175] Santa Relli (Roger's jealous and nagging wife) was similarly a professional actress with a long list of war-time and post-war credits to her name.

None of the cast was a star, obviously enough, since the star was to be Tati. The supporting actors chosen represent a fairly ordinary cross-section of the second rank of the entertainment world: there really was nothing special or suspicious about a group that had got on with their working lives during the Occupation.

Tati brought in his war-time music-hall chums not as actors, but as members of the technical crew, as "fixers" and as local support. Of these, André Delpierre, with his home base down the road at Le Marembert, must have been especially precious; but Marquet, who had cooked up a good part of the script and had directorial ambitions of his own, also served as a cross between assistant director and "technical adviser"; and Jacques Cottin – who was nearly as tall as Tati and would become M. Hulot's permanent double in later years – was put in charge of props and technical stunts. There was thus a real cohort of *copains* in the "support" team, if not in the cast; and there were also a few hangers-on, like Philippe Dubail, the financial backer's teenage son, who helped out with the maintenance and driving of the few motor vehicles needed on and around the set.

Fig. 40. *Jacques Tati and Henri Marquet at Sainte-Sévère, 1947*

The most delicate part of the back-up for *Jour de fête* were the townsfolk themselves. It was far from obvious that the mayor, the local notables, the farmers and their wives would welcome an invasion of Parisians; moreover, the strangers wanted to occupy the main square – the only market and meeting place for miles around – the whole summer long. It is quite possible that we owe some of the documentary and ethnographic features of *Jour de fête* to the negotiations that Tati seems to have pulled off with great grace. "Believe me," Orain reported to Wagner, his correspondent at the Maison Dubail,

> the good humour that prevails between the crew and the inhabitants of Sainte-Sévère did not happen just by itself . . . The locals' goodwill towards us all is the fruit of a great deal of tact and diplomacy.[176]

The "tact" may have involved promising locals that they would indeed be seen on film, and that the film would in some sense be the story of their town. That may be why the Sainte-Sévère road sign is included, in contradiction to the script's setting of the action in an anytown that is just as much "mon village" as "Follainville". It may also be why there are some delightful sequences – a farmer finding out how to get back in the driving seat of his cart without soiling his daughter's silk blouse, families making their way to the fair, girls with sore feet wending their way home from the dance – that could be seen (and were indeed criticised by reviewers) as irrelevant to the film's comedy plot. Nearly all the inhabitants of Sainte-Sévère appear in the film,[177] and certainly the totality of the town's under-tens. Many appear simply as themselves: the bowler-hatted mallet-wielder in the maypole scene, for example, was a local farmer who really did have a bad squint. Others were made to act familiar roles: Tati got his former landlord at Le Marembert to fill in for the mayor, for example, who did not want to represent his own office in a fiction film. The only locals who had to be asked firmly to stay out of the way were the real village postmen, twelve in all, who used bicycles somewhat less antique than the fixed-wheel Peugeot that François rides. How Tati soothed their susceptibilities is a mystery, for they are the only Sévérois who have no role at all in the film; but he established an excellent rapport with these unseen "technical advisers", who made Tati "honorary postman" during the shoot, and had his framed photograph hung on the post-office wall. . . [178]

Getting hold of props was also a tricky business. The biggest single item was the actual fair. Tati did not need a real marquee – it is never seen in its entirety, so only a few pieces of canvas awning were needed. But he did need a whole merry-go-round, and one that actually worked. And he also needed the showmen's caravan – a living trailer, and an open-top truck-trailer for the wooden horses. Presumably all this could be wheeled out of Tati's circus contacts – but what could not be got by normal means was a vehicle to haul it all along. In 1947 you could not simply go and buy a car, truck or tractor: there were waiting lists of several years for all motor vehicles, and prices were such that a black-market purchase would have dwarfed all the other costs of making the film. (The only moving car seen in the film is Fred Orain's own saloon.) Tati, or his technical assistants, scoured the countryside for something they could borrow. It soon turned out that there was only one vehicle for miles around that would be at all suitable: a brand-new Farmall tractor delivered just that spring to a local farmer, under the Lend-Lease programme (one of the fruits of Blum's mission to Washington, and a forerunner of the more substantial Marshall Aid Plan). Such a treasure was not a toy. And no, you couldn't have clumsy actors driving it around. Anyway, it was needed pretty much every day for work in the fields. How much Tati paid the farmer to let him use the precious tractor is not known; but he did not get permission to drive it, nor to let anyone other than its anxious owner turn on the ignition. For that reason, the tractor is seen only in long shot when moving, for it is being driven not by Paul Frankeur, but by its proprietor; the tractor is actually stationary in those few shots where we see Frankeur in the driving seat, but the editing of vision and above all of sound masks this very effectively.

Problems like these must have abounded, given the terrible poverty of rural France in 1947. The previous winter had been extremely severe throughout northern Europe, and food stocks had nearly run out; in Germany, there was real starvation, and France was not that much better off. Sainte-Sévère had only two working telephones (one in the post office, and one in the café-bar, which was not actually located where we see Bondu's café, a set constructed specifically for the film). Few of the houses had electricity, and mains sewage had not even been imagined. The shot of a lady emptying her chamber-pot in the gutter should not be seen as a scatological joke, but as a document of village life as it was. Those "technical advisers" – Cottin, Marquet and Delpierre – no doubt spent some of their time just making sure there was enough fuel, enough food and enough power for the shoot to continue. And for that, quite a lot of ingenuity must have been required every day.

Tati's happy relations with the Sévérois were by no means replicated every day on the set. For all sorts of reasons, most of which he bottled up, Tati could spend whole days with a grumpy scowl on his face. "The mood was sometimes quite stormy," Maine Vallée recalled in later years. "Tati could be dreadfully gloomy. When he was, he clammed up completely."[179] But at the collective dinner table, after the day's work, he usually found a way of lightening the mood, with a gesture, a mime, or a joke. And some of the time was just spent larking around.

Meanwhile, Fred Orain, who drove the exhausting two hundred miles up to Paris every couple of weeks, got on with the business of launching Tati and Cady-Films. L'Ecole des facteurs had had a very successful trial screening at the Colisée a few months before the shoot of Cady-Films's first feature began, but, mortgaged as it was against the advance from Dubail, it had not yet been released for commercial showing in France (its value was much higher as an unreleased film). A copy of Soigne ton gauche had been found (in Germany, so it seems, though the information comes from only one, not necessarily reliable source). Orain had a new Cady-Films credit sequence made for it, with a sound track using the same wild jingle that Yatové had provided for L'Ecole des facteurs, and which would be used again for Jour de fête, and seemed all set to become the "theme tune" of the new comic

Fig. 41: (*left to right*) *Lydie Noël, the script-girl, Marcel Franchi, the cameraman, Jacques Mercanton and Jacques Tati taking time out in Sainte-Sévère, summer 1947*

star and the series he would no doubt go on to make. While Tati was still shooting at Sainte-Sévère, the two shorts were released for the export market through the recently-established state-sponsored Unifrance-Film. (*L'Ecole des facteurs* must have been shown again in France before *Jour de fête* was finished, since it won the 1947 Max Linder prize for the best comedy short made in France that year.[180] On that occasion Tati met Maud, Linder's daughter, and an expert on her father's career. Linder too had been a sportsman as well as the "King of Kinema", and, like Tati, had never managed to learn the piano.[181] These were all sensible steps to take to generate a flow of cash to Cady-Films, and to pave the way for a feature film that should have come out the following spring. Meanwhile, Orain leaked news of the project and its industrial stake to the professional press. "A New French

Colour Process", trumpeted *L'Ecran français*. Thomsoncolor would give "a finer grain, more body, and more gradations of colour" than Technicolor and Agfacolor. But the producer had still not been able to see any real prints: only "test strips", developed by hand, had yet come out of the unfinished laboratory at Joinville-le-pont. To cover himself against the risk of an as-yet unproven system, the newspaper reported, Orain was making a black-and-white version as well.[182]

These business and publicity moves turned out to be premature. Tati's pace was not exactly fast, and with his lumbering gait and often gloomy face, he did not inspire others to rush around on his behalf. What was supposed to be done in three months actually took more than six.

Jour de fête fell behind schedule at the start, since Tati was off sick for ten days in early May (for what reason, we do not know). According to Orain's rather self-serving letters to the financier, Wagner, it fell behind further because of poor weather. That must be taken with a pinch of salt: historically, the French summer of 1947 was one of the hottest and driest on record, producing conditions that must have been near ideal for sun-drenched shots of life in the fields, even if the drought threatened the harvest on which so many hopes were pinned.

Indeed, the film fell so much behind schedule that the summer season was over in Sainte-Sévère before the main comic episodes had been made – the exploits of François on his manically accelerated delivery round. Tati later teased gullible journalists by claiming that he had the local children glue the leaves back on the trees for the last completion shots. In fact, the shoot moved further south, where the season was less advanced, to film some of the road sequences in a country location near Aix-en-Provence, where *L'Ecole des facteurs* had been made. That is why there is a curious visual overlap between the short and the long film, making it seem as if some takes in *Jour de fête* are pieces of the original short. But the colour camera went south too, and since those takes also exist in the colour negatives, Tati must have re-enacted even the swerves and turns that look identical to their earlier realisations in *L'Ecole des facteurs*. Like any good music-hall artiste, Tati could do his number over and over again. But that does not necessarily mean that the black-and-white version – a back-up, and, by the time Tati started editing in the winter of 1947–48, a let-down and a desperate last resort – does not actually use some of the earlier stock.

EIGHTEEN

US Go Home!

The gullible postman's high-speed round forms the cadenza of *Jour de fête*, but almost the whole of *L'Ecole des facteurs*. In the short, the cycling scenario is prompted by the French Post Office's own efficiency drive; in *Jour de fête*, it is prompted by François's naive ambition to rival the US Postal Service. In the circumstances of 1947 – midway between the Blum-Byrnes agreement and the start of Marshall Aid – that can hardly be considered an insignificant change. *Jour de fête* is not exactly an anti-American film; but the way it uses the idea of America is certainly part of its historical meaning as a French film. A closer comparison with *L'Ecole des facteurs* reveals some fascinating variations.

Most of the material first imagined for the short is replicated in *Jour de fête*. In both films, François hooks his bicycle to the back of a lorry and uses the rear platform as a sorting-franking office; he delivers a pair of shoes to a butcher, who slices straight through them; he drops in at the church where the priest flies aloft on his bell-rope; he causes a car smash by turning in the opposite direction from the hand-signal he gives at a junction, and he ends up overtaking a cycle-racing squad. Indeed, given the thinness of the narrative material of *Jour de fête*, Tati could hardly leave anything much out. There are of course a few cycling gags added in the longer film; but more significant are the snippets of *L'Ecole des facteurs* that were dropped.

The main omission is the whole set-up scene in the post office, where Paul Demange explains why the cycling postmen have to be trained to do their deliveries at a higher speed. That motivating sequence is replaced in the longer film by the mock documentary on *La Poste en Amérique*. By the same token the concluding shots of *L'Ecole des facteurs* – François's breathless arrival at the airstrip and his successful attachment of the mailbag to the tailfin of the airmail plane – also have to go. The first François meets the challenge of French modernisation; the second one fails to turn himself into an American clone.

In both versions of the scenario, François's bicycle is let loose on the streets, and appears to steer itself to its habitual parking lot, not at the post office but at the bar. In the short, Tati catches up with his steed, and drops in for a restorative glass. The interior of the café is barely furnished, but in the back room a few couples are dancing to recorded music. Tati joins in the jitterbug and does a few turns as a comic swinger. The dance scene has its equivalent in *Jour de fête*, though it is introduced rather differently, and is a much more extensive affair – Tati has a larger cast of party-goers available (indeed, he has a whole village) and it is also logical to have a much more crowded floor, since it is the evening of the fair.

What is really different, though, is that the male dancers in *L'Ecole des facteurs* are American GIs. (One of the women, incidentally, is Micheline Tati.) In 1945–46, Americans can be shown as part of a convivial French scene, in a short that has no axe to grind about the forces that had just liberated France. In *Jour de fête*, by contrast, the image of America is ever present, but there are no convivial Americans to be seen – not in the bar, nor at the fair, nor around town. That is actually rather unrealistic: Sainte-Sévère is about twenty miles from the huge US airfield and army base at Châteauroux, and in 1947 American soldiers were certainly not confined to base. Like the real postmen of Sainte-Sévère, the local GIs were kept off the set, even though the famous jeep that Tati and Marquet got around in (Fig. 40) can only have come from a US surplus store.

Fig. 42: L'Ecole des facteurs: *GIs in the bar of the original Follainville*

We see the selfsame jeep in the film, dolled up with white paint and stencilled "MP" markings. François has been ordered by the irate Bondu to take his broken telephone back to the post office to be mended.[183] He pedals off with the mahogany, wind-up device on his handlebar rack, and, in a make-believe play similar to the ones devised for *Soigne ton gauche*, pretends to himself that he has a walkie-talkie radio telephone as the military police jeep comes into view.

Two white-helmeted US soldiers are draped against the bonnet, in a mime posture signifying indolence and stupidity. Amazed to see a mere French postman with a mobile communications device, the Americans stare hard at this apparition. François acts up to the situation, audibly calling "*Allo, Paris?*" and "*Passez-moi New York!*" as he pedals past. The soldiers clamber back into their jeep (doing the usual slapstick routine of bumping into each other as they try to go round the rear of the vehicle) and start to chase. But their eyes are on the outsize cyclist, and they drive off the road into the ditch. "Everything OK? Everything OK!" the postman cheerily yells as he pedals off out of the frame.

This additional gag, taken with the ones cut away, transform the meanings we might attach to the cycling motif in *L'Ecole des facteurs*. *Jour de fête* offers a critique of American film styles (the parody of Hollywood sound in the mimed encounter of Roger and Jeannette against the cooked-up dialogue

Fig. 43: Jour de fête: *The Ugly Americans*

from *Les Rivaux de l'Arizona*) as well as a parody of American newsreel propaganda; its closing moral, given by the old lady who has acted as commentator and chorus throughout, is that faster mail won't make the crops grow any faster, and that good news doesn't go bad if it comes a little late. Just to rub in its consoling message a little deeper, it also shows a pair of ugly Americans taken in by an easy trick. Tati may have asserted that he had no political points to make; but, like it or not, he certainly made some historically significant jibes in *Jour de fête*.[184]

The view of America that emerges from *Jour de fête* could be seen as a by-product or consequence of the film's original purpose – to compete with US colour technology, and to win Thomson-Houston a slice of the terrain occupied by Eastman-Kodak. It also articulates the peculiarly sour attitudes of the French film industry (and of many other parts of French cultural life at that time) towards the liberating forces, whose sheer power and wealth, unlike the thieving brutality of the Germans, seemed to threaten the survival of a specifically French way of life. But a film does not just express attitudes, it also affects them, especially if it is enjoyed by large numbers of people. The comic thrust of *Jour de fête* contributes to many of the themes of anti-American propaganda of the late 1940s. In doing so, it contributed its own weight to the bizarre cultural politics of post-war France, where people did indeed rush to watch Hollywood movies in large numbers, but also marched down the streets chanting "*US go home!*"

Tati never freed himself of his suspicion of America, even though he came to enjoy his visits to New York, and was more than satisfied when he won the Oscar for the Best Foreign Film of 1958. His reasons for turning down opportunities to work in Hollywood, for his refusal of television as a medium, and for the many other superficially anti-modern positions that he took up, are quite complex and will be discussed in due course. But *Jour de fête* is all the same a striking example of political deflection, for it heaps ridicule on America barely two years after the final defeat of the greatest evil France and Europe had ever known. Who could guess from watching this film that less than three years before the shoot began the Gestapo still had an office on the main square of Sainte-Sévère?

NINETEEN

Deepest France

The character created by Tati for his role in *Jour de fête* is a mumbling dreamer, a sympathetic butt of the clever-dicks who cross his path, and not far short of being the village idiot. The name of Roger, used for the gormless characters Tati had created in his pre-war shorts, is transferred to the showman with the roving eye for the girls; his wife even snaps and snarls like the martinet married to the Roger of *On demande une brute*. The François of *Jour de fête* has no wife, no family name, and as far we can tell no home of his own. He is taunted by children, who put a mock-letter in the post-box just before he is due to pick up the mail. Knowing he is being watched by the brats, François puts on a stern face and cycles off with simulated dignity. But the authority role is patently out of place: the children break cover and jeer at him from behind his back.

The two showmen pick on François as fall-guy as soon as he appears in the village square. Bondu has already suggested to Roger that the local postman is a bit peculiar, and the sight of him, bolt upright on his primitive bicycle, confirms the idea that he can easily be ragged. François laps up their condescending praise for his size, his strength, his sense of leadership, and he walks straight into the trap. He soon finds himself in charge of raising the maypole – and holding the whole thing up, when his helpers abandon the great trunk as it begins to sway and lurch.

Tati constructs the image of François as a rural idiot in part by facial make-up (puffed-out cheeks, like a baby's, and a three-day growth of beard) and partly by diction – a slobbering mumble in an exaggerated countryside accent, something like a French version of Mummerset, the artificial actors' diction for village idiots on the British stage. In Bondu's bar, François is engaged by local boozers in a drinking contest: they substitute cognac for the *petit vin blanc* that François had expected to down, and trick him into getting really drunk. At the end of the evening, the showmen make him look down a conch-shell that leaves a black ink circle around his right eye. The bar closes and the lonely, inebriated fool sets off into the night. Stranded in the ditch

Fig. 44: *The Village Idiot*

and a little unsteady, he tries to remount his bicycle by keeping it still against a wooden railing, but gets his leg caught in the fence. Like most of Tati's physical gags, it is done twice: François moves his bicycle past an opening which allows him to come round to the other side, and then tries again – but just bestrides the same fence from the opposite side. Once mounted, he cycles straight into the trunk of an apple tree, which rains fruit down upon him (the falling apples sound more like a gross of cricket balls). The collision has knocked his handlebars out of true: when he puts them in line to remount, the front wheel is turned to the side. After three attempts at finding a way round the problem, he performs an extraordinarily elegant rotation of the machine underneath him, which magically seems to lever the handlebars back into position as it levers the rider into the saddle. François then pedals himself straight into a high hedge that looks and sounds like holly.

Acting drunk is just about the most banal form of mime that exists, and it is a turn that Tati had done ever since his jolly days with the rugby crowd. The drunk-by-night sequence in *Jour de fête*, however, is comic only as long as the spectator does not see it as pain. Pedalling on a wooden fence must be pretty hard on the crotch, and having your head stuck deep inside holly cannot be too pleasant either. Keaton, it is true, had invented even more dangerous fixes for his comic-victim role; his and others' Hollywood burlesques had taught audiences world-wide to laugh at pain-and-punishment routines that seem quite unappealing nowadays. If any part of *Jour de fête* really is a bid for the mantle of Mack Sennett – a "completely unseemly" one, in the view of the *New York Times*[185] – then it is in the nocturnal cycling sequence, an eerie solo mime performance without let-up or con-clusion (we never see how the postman gets out of the bush) which takes slapstick to the edge of sacrifice. Tati's rural fool is perhaps not a saint; but what he suffers in this episode is not far short of martyrdom. Let us not forget that François's inebriated state is explicitly the fault of others.

For most of the sequences in which he appears, the cycling postman is a combination of village idiot and local hero. In his uniform and peaked cap, with his long legs and little moustache, he has an uncanny overall resem-blance to the leader of Free France, Charles de Gaulle, who had resigned in a huff from the presidency of the Provisional Government in January 1946 and retired to Colombey-les-deux-églises. In private, Tati could do startlingly life-like impersonations of *le général*, and there is one recorded instance of him doing it on stage (not in France, though: in London, at the British Film Institute). In the intensely polarised French political context of 1947, it must have been tricky to decide how to deal with a resemblance that could hardly be expected to pass unnoticed.

Like de Gaulle, François takes on responsibility for raising the flag: the maypole is the means by which the tricolour can float over the village fair. His words of instruction to the rag-taggle team of pole-haulers is just nonsense, of course, but it is also Gaullist doctrine – a national movement claiming to be above party politics and to represent both Left and Right: "Those on the left, pull left! Those on the right, pull right!"

When François cycles into the village square later on and hears what he thinks is the creaking of the pole (though the preceding shot and sound-effect track has allowed the audience to see that it is nothing of the sort), he steers himself straight into Bondu's bar, and appears once again (as after his first appearance in the square, when he was indeed nearly crushed by the falling pole) at the first-floor balcony. A very curious sequence follows. The film cuts to a high-angle shot looking down on the square, as seen from François's point of view on the balcony, with the postman's huge back filling

Fig. 15 Raising the maypole

the right half of the frame. It is the moment when the aural contest between hurdy-gurdy and marching band reaches its resolution, for the band now enters the square and draws to a halt. The bandleader in the far depth of the field (you only see him because he is in the implicit line of François's sight) gives a bow-legged bow, almost a curtsey, and a military salute on the last beat of the last bar. As if by reflex, the idiot-postman takes the salute and responds in kind – but then realises that he is not on a state visit, and pretends he was trying to reach a tickle on the back of his neck.

Jérôme Deschamps sees the very raising of the maypole with its tricolour flag as a symbol of France rising once again from its war-time defeat.[186] In the same line of thinking, the balcony scene could be interpreted as a homage to the incarnation of Free France. But it would be tricky to have people laugh at de Gaulle – from behind his back, what is more – if Gaullism was intended to be the general "colour" of the film. And there is a great deal else

Fig. 46: *François takes the salute*

in *Jour de fête* that seems to correspond to a very different political vision, even if it was one that could not be openly declared.

Let us return to the establishing sequence: a tractor-drawn fairground trailer seen in various long and medium shots moving along a sinuous road through fields where horses graze and others where jolly labourers mow the hay. *Labourage et pâturage sont les deux mamelles de la France* ("Arable and livestock farming are France's two breasts"), Sully said to Henri IV in the sixteenth century, and Pétain's propagandists picked up the observation and made it into one of the slogans of the "National Revolution" of 1940–44. Along with the child running down the slope to meet the travelling fair and hop-skipping along behind the fairground trailer, the horses in the field, the geese in the road, the chickens in the coop, the dog at the gate, the hearty welcome from the tillers of the soil dubbed over the bright and lyrical musical track state as clearly as can be imagined that the agricultural heart of France is a happy and contented one.[187]

Now let us look at the ending: the supersized postman overtakes the Tour de France (in the summer of 1947, it was raced for the first time since the outbreak of war), takes a bend too fast before a hump-backed bridge, comes off the road and plunges into the river below. Drenched and repentant, he hitches a lift back into town with the hunch-backed peasant who has acted as chorus and commentator throughout. "The Americans won't make all that grow any faster," she says to comfort the bedraggled village fool. "And as for good news, it doesn't go bad for waiting a little while." They pass the haymakers in the field that had been seen at the start. François leaves the cart and joins in the work in the meadow; young Gaston dons the postman's hat and skips off behind the departing fairground caravan, to complete the postman's round for him.

This bucolic conclusion reunites François with the traditional, agricultural life of his community, where common sense and the national values of the film clearly lie. It is a comic conclusion in one conventional sense – a "happy end" to the conflict between the values of the real Sainte-Sévère and the imaginary US Post Office. But it is not a *funny* ending. It can only be called a moral ending, if not an explicitly political one. If we take its narrative surround at face value, *Jour de fête* tells us that France should retain its slow-paced and convivial agricultural heart, and keep it safe from corrupting and inappropriate foreign ideals of speed, efficiency and so forth. Contextual elements make it impossible to think of *Jour de fête* as a film that might have been made under the Vichy regime (there could have been no *Arizona Rivals* nor the *ciné-poste* documentary on show in war-time France), but in all other respects, it expresses – albeit in light-hearted, comic vein – some of the main tenets of the Vichy regime.

Fig. 47: *François returns to the land*

That is not to say that *Jour de fête* should be taken at face value, as propaganda on behalf of a discredited and shameful regime. It suggests just as much that the nostalgic, backward-looking and xenophobic strands in Vichy's political platform corresponded to attitudes that were unreflectingly held by a broad section of the public, and that such attitudes did not disappear overnight when the regime that had exploited them to disastrous effect came to its well-deserved end. *Jour de fête* gives voice to that strong undertow in twentieth-century French life which would have the world stand still. This old and everlasting France is a land where there is time to watch the grass grow, where the postman can stop for a drink now and then, and where the seasons' round is marked by the annual visit of the travelling fair. It is not so different from some of the "laid-back", ecological strands that came to the fore after May '68, articulated for example in Jacques Doillon's first film, *An 01: Tout s'arrête*. These themes had no left-wing, anarchical or subversive echo at all in 1947. Vichy, with its appeal to home-grown values, was still far too close.

Comedy is always a double-edged sword. Unlike Georges Rouquier's recreation of traditional rural society in *Farrebique* (also 1947), Tati's constantly mooing, neighing, clucking, and cackling Sainte-Sévère can also be taken as a string of city-dweller's jokes about country life. With hens in the barber's and a goat in the lounge, a corpse in a front room and a man lost down a well, with a cesspit covered by a lid that won't take a man's weight and ladies having to empty their husband's night-soil in the square, the "deep France" of *Jour de fête* is presented as a most insanitary and exceedingly pungent place. It is also a lamentable muddle: telegrams are delivered to the wrong people, withheld because they contain bad news, or consumed by a peckish billy-goat. Tati's only feature film about country life is pretty delicately balanced between celebrating its conviviality, and making fun of its smelly awfulness.

The Sévérois themselves saw Tati's portrayal of their way of life as a celebration and nothing else, and over the last fifty years have come to define their town almost exclusively as the home of *Jour de fête*. The process of memorialisation was begun by Tati himself. Once the film was commercially released in Paris, he arranged with the mayor – who had become a good friend, and would remain one for many years – for a gala screening in the main square of Sainte-Sévère, precisely where most of the footage had been shot. The whole cast, the crew, the producer, and many of the families and children of those involved, assembled, on 19 June 1949, a mile or two down the road, and re-entered the village like a travelling fair, in a jeep (for Tati), a car (Oram) and a bus (for all the rest) decorated in bunting and bright colours. A local brass band – L'Harmonie de La Châtre – played the *March of the Red Devils* as the parade came into the square, where a newsreel camera was all set up to film the film-makers' triumphant return.[188] The soundless clip shows the mayor reading out a great speech and handing Tati the keys of Sainte-Sévère before unveiling a peculiarly ugly, twice-life-size plaster bust of *François le facteur*, the first item of Sainte-Sévère's now substantial collection of Tatitrash.

Ever since, Sainte-Sévère has been seriously afflicted with Tatimania. *Jour de fête* is the local foundation myth, the proof that such a small and unremarkable town really exists. For round-date anniversaries of the shoot, the town centre is decorated in bunting, shop windows are adorned with images of the cycling postman, and the souvenir stalls stock up with models, key-rings, postcards, musical toys and fluffy dolls in the image of the film. Yet there is no powerful marketing organisation behind the Sainte-Sévère spin-off business: the theme-park mentality seems to be generated by the townsfolk themselves. It is true that with the decline of small-holder farming, there is not much else of note in Sainte-Sévère. But the greatest irony of *Jour de fête* as a satire of American cultural influence on French life is what can now be seen as the Disneyfication of the Sévérois themselves. In the film, François is a loveable, gullible fool; in the longer-term history of the film, however, it is not entirely clear who has been taken in.

TWENTY

Windows and Frames

In most fiction films, the illusion of "real presence" is created by placing the spectator right inside the scene. By a visual convention to which we have become totally blind, the unframed frame on the screen is interpreted as what we would see if we were *there*, as in a dream. In *Jour de fête* Tati does not allow his audience to make this easy elision of the mind's eye with the viewfinder's frame. He shows us at the start, and reminds us all along, that what we are looking at are *pictures* of Sainte-Sévère, as in his grandfather's gallery, not in a Spielbergian dream.

The true opening of the film, which precedes the most often remembered shots of the travelling fair, fades a flapping gauze curtain from the stencilled credits to a casement window, at which a boy appears, eating bread and jam. We see him from inside the room, looking out. The shots that follow – the tractor, the trailers, and the idyllic hay-raking scene – are thus interpreted as what Gaston has seen, and towards which he rushes, in other intercalated shots, across the field and the stream.

Tati is hardly the first film-maker to use an open window to figure the opening of the world to be seen on screen. Renoir, for example, used it hamfistedly in his adaptation of Flaubert's *Madame Bovary* (where it also corresponds to a recurrent, claustrophobic theme of the book). But in *Jour de fête*, the boy at the window is only the first of many shots that include a person viewing what the spectator can see, or soon will: the scything peasant in the bee-gag sequence, for instance, or François looking at the *ciné-poste* documentary, and again looking down from the balcony at the saluting bandmaster; and even more often, there is a hunchback peasant woman with a nanny-goat and crook, croaking folksy comments in Berrichon patois on what can be seen in the same scene.

The inclusion of a seeing eye inside so many frames is a striking feature of Tati's early film style. It first occurs in *Soigne ton gauche*, where the make-believe film-makers snap the postman leaving the last frame. It is developed massively in *Jour de fête*, and, had Tati not had second thoughts, would have

structured the whole narrative of *Les Vacances de M. Hulot* (1953). In the
original script, a painter arrives at the seaside resort and repeatedly picks up
picture postcards at the stall: these fixed frames of holiday scenes would each
have been faded into Hulot's next escapade. The idea of a tour guided by a
painterly eye was abandoned for the first Hulot film, but resurrected and
recycled eight years later, for the remake of *Jour de fête*. For this second
version, in which Tati was able to add at least touches of the colours he
had originally wanted (see pp. 232, 235 below), he returned to Sainte-Sévère
and shot a whole new dimension to the tale: a Dutch painter (played by
Alexandre Wirtz, who really was a Dutch artist spending time in Paris) visits
a slumbering village to paint its picturesque sights; we see him sketching
the market hall, the maypole, the café, each sketch melting into the
appropriate and now-colourised sequences of the original film.

Fig. 48: *Tati directing Alexandre Wirtz during the retakes for* Jour de fête,
Sainte-Sévère, September 1961

The addition of a painter-guide to the remake of *Jour de fête* (a version
usually labelled in video listings as the "original" film, to distinguish it from
the rediscovered and recomposed colour version released in 1995) makes
the hunchback chorus-lady redundant, and it is perhaps a pity that Tati
did not edit out the scenes where she appears. (It also creates continuity
problems – Wirtz wears jeans of a style that did not exist in 1947,[189] yet

François plays around with a kind of telephone that had disappeared entirely, even from rural France, by 1961, as had the steam shunters in the station yard, and much else besides.) But the question is more interesting when put the other way round: given that the original *Jour de fête* already has a guide and chorus figure to lead us around, why did Tati feel the need to add another one?

The presence in a shot of a figure from whose (literal) point of view the shot can be seen makes it quite clear to the viewer of the film that s/he is not a participant, but a spectator of the scene. In short, it is a distancing device, creating fairly exactly what Brecht meant by *Verfremdung* (alienation) in the theatre. It makes us see the fiction as fiction, and not as a false truth. Strange as it may at first seem, Tati's camera style in the easily accessible comedy of *Jour de fête* is a highly intellectual one, for it asks us to take on the role of *observers*, and not to get too involved with the characters and actions on screen.

Tati's preference for the long shot is entirely consistent with this general appeal to the eye as the tool of the mind. Long shots, first of all, show us actions in a wider context, and oblige us to look a little harder to locate and interpret the action going on. And very often, the significant detail is not a "big thing" in the middle, but a sub-action in some non-centred part of the frame. In the maypole-raising episode, for instance, there is one medium long shot of Bondu putting up the bunting on the awning of his café terrace, stepping from one chair to another to pin it right along. François enters stage right, notices that one of the chairs is out of place and that Bondu risks falling into the gap, and he quickly puts the chair back in the row. But we hardly see this, because the shot is centred on François as he rushes around trying to keep the pole-haulers on the right track. Cut to a different shot of François as he commands the raising of the pole; then cut back to François rushing to get out of the way, and pulling a chair from the row to make space. Only in the next sequence does Bondu step into the reopened gap and come crashing down with the bunting. The gag has been doubly prepared, but only viewers who watch carefully all of what is going on in all of those shots understand why it is not just a painful fall, but a funny one.

Tati's camera asks us to see the world as comedy, but in order to do so we must see it from a certain distance, not in close-up. There are only three close shots in the whole film: the squinting eyes of the peasant, almost as painful to watch as the eye in Buñuel's *Chien Andalou*; the post-box, a moment of pause and a figurative transition from fairground to postman theme; and François examining his black-circled eye in his locker mirror at the post office. Medium close shots (which the French call *le plan américain*) are used for the parody of Hollywood shot/counter-shot style when Roger and Jeannette make eyes at each other in front of the marquee, and for some of the gags – François franking mail on the back platform of a moving truck, or talking to the hunchback when she gives him a ride in her cart, as well as for a number of interior scenes (at the barber's, for instance). But for the rest, the film is made in long view, with a depth of field that is sometimes quite huge (the travelling fair seen coming round the bend from far away, the marching band arriving in the square) and sometimes only appropriate to Tati's large frame.

In the circus and the music-hall traditions, the audience always has a representative on stage, a ringmaster or *compère* who introduces each act and provides a kind of continuity script. The hunchback commentator of *Jour de fête* (played by a male music-hall artiste, Delcassan) plays that kind of role, familiar also from children's-story style. The painter-guide device, transferred from *Les Vacances* to the remake of *Jour de fête*, seems to me an idea that comes from somewhere else: perhaps from Tati's friendship with the painter Lagrange, who did indeed collect postcards of the seaside resorts that he visited when scouting for locations for the first Hulot film; but it comes perhaps from much further back, when Tati spent his time framing still lifes and landscape scenes in the workshop of Cadres Van Hoof. As if he wanted to say, in this modulated and indirect way, that even if he could not paint with a brush, he too could see the world through painterly eyes.

TWENTY-ONE

A Slow Release

Jour de fête was finished around the end of the year 1947, and was shown to distributors, none of whom wanted it. Was it because it was too politically sensitive, with its fleeting but recognisable allusions to de Gaulle? Or because of its potentially Vichyist moral ending? Or simply because the distributors did not find it very funny? At all events, the film's first showings fell completely flat, and Tati was nearly ready to give up. Cady-Films, though, had no intention of folding: Orain carried on financing and producing shorts by other people, including Tati's close friends Henri Marquet[190] and Borrah Minevich.[191] To earn a living somehow or other (for he now had daughter Sophie as well as Micheline to support), Tati packed his bags and went back on tour as a music-hall mime.

Many of Tati's acquaintances – Edith Piaf and Billy Bourbon, for instance – had had lucrative engagements in Stockholm, at the old-established China Variety Theatre, which ran music-hall shows twice nightly from April through to October each year. Tati got a one-month engagement there in July 1948, to do his *Impressions sportives* once again, at 7.15 and 9.30 pm six nights a week. It would have still been light even when he left the theatre to wander back to the tiny flat that Eskil Eckert-Lundin, the manager of the China, had let him have, through the streets of that beautiful, and at that time almost uniquely prosperous city. In a variety programme that included topless dancers ("The Blue Bell Girls"), jugglers, acrobats, stand-up comedians and singers, Jacques Tati – *"fransk imitatör"* – was given relatively modest billing in the programme[192] with a half-page Studio Harcourt photograph of him in tennis whites and tweeds.[193]

It was during this stay that he got to know the Swedish table-tennis champion, Bengt Grive, who had turned his sporting talents into a comic stage act. The two of them got on famously, and went one afternoon to the stadium to see Sweden's star centre-forward, Hasse Jeppsson, play at home for the Djurgården team. Tati had a brilliant business idea: he would arrange a transfer for the Swedish amateur to the professional French team at Le Stade

Français, for which Jeppsson could expect a handsome fee. Was this scheme just a practical joke? Probably not: from Le Cadre lumineux in 1936 through to his brief experience as a cinema manager in the 1960s, Tati was frequently on the brink of launching some business idea or other. Given the talent for financial management that Tati was to show in his later film career, Jeppsson was wise not to sign up with the improvised sports manager.

One night, Tati dropped his wallet in the street. During the show at the China next day, a young lady with blue eyes came and gave it back to him. Tati was overwhelmed by what he took to be Swedish honesty, and at the end of his act he made a little speech, in French and then in English, to thank the young woman who, he said, was the very spirit of Sweden. Blue eyes, he said, were like an open book: through them you could see that all Swedes had honest souls. The young lady then stood up and, in a language Tati could not understand, explained that she was a tourist from Oslo. It was only twenty-five years later, when Tati was in Stockholm again, that Bengt told him the truth.

Bengt Grive claims in his memoirs that it was the Swedish music-hall that gave Tati enough money to finish filming *Jour de fête*, but in this he is surely mistaken. Star acts at the China were probably very well paid by French standards of the day, but a one-month engagement can hardly have supplied the kind of sums involved in film production. In any case, *Jour de fête* was already finished. Although it still had no French distributor and had yet to be released, export deals were nearly tied up, and the advances from Belgian, Swiss and Argentinian distributors would soon recoup about half of the film's total cost to date.

Bengt Grive was in Paris a little later that summer, for the table-tennis championships being held at the Salle Wagram. He recalls visiting the Tatis' flat in Rue de Penthièvre, where he was instantly assailed by a powerful smell of coffee beans. The flat was packed full with sacks of the stuff;[194] as a result, Tati and Michou could not countenance drinking anything other than tea. Grive got the impression that Tati was into yet another part-time business (one which the Swede assumed to be "grey" if not actually part of the black market); alternatively, he may just have been letting some friend or other use his flat as a depot. At all events, Tati got Bengt Grive another sports fixture at Le Havre. The fee arrangements show the kind of unofficial economy in which everyone worked before the start of Marshall Aid: fifty Swedish kronor in banknotes, plus five cartons of contraband Camel cigarettes. On the black market, the only one which actually worked, the cartons were worth about three times the declared fee.[195]

Tati liked Sweden a lot, and he went back to Stockholm many times. He never missed attending Swedish premières in person, and at one time he looked carefully at Stockholm's brand-new Arlanda airport buildings as a possible location for *Playtime*.[196] Sweden paid back Tati's fidelity a hundredfold. His films were immensely popular there, and Swedish critics treated his work with great respect (it must have made a pleasant change from writing up the latest Bergman); and, largely because of his huge standing in the country, Swedish money, Swedish technicians and even airfreighted cans of film from Stockholm came to the rescue of Tati's last fiction film, *Trafic*, when it was stranded in a ghastly mess on a dock outside Amsterdam.

The Stockholm season was not the last of Tati's returns to the music-hall: he was on the bill in Biarritz in August 1949, and then at Lausanne, and starred again at the "Gala du feu" in Lyon in 1951.[197] But it was also a sad occupation for a man in middle age, and it is the pathos of decline and failure that informs a long film-script that Tati wrote at some point in the early 1950s under the title of *L'Illusionniste*, "The Conjuror".[198] From dingy London music-halls to cafés in Berlin, the conjuror slides down the ladder of international engagements to end up amusing Ruritanian peasants in bar-rooms somewhere in the back of beyond. There, at last, he finds an admirer for his disappearing rabbits, his doves, his silk handkerchiefs that knot and unknot – a wide-eyed, teen-age girl who really believes in the magic that she sees on stage. She follows the entertainer as his career begins to take off again and comes with him to the Great City (thus the script's alternative title, *La Grande Ville*, which was also used at an early stage for the quite different ideas that became *Playtime*). There she falls for a student – an intellectual who makes her realise that the conjuror has no special powers, just a quick turn of the hand – and runs off with him. The sad conjuror accepts his fate, losing his suitcase and his gear as he catches the train out to his next fixture, in some other unidentified town.[199]

It is probably just as well Tati never actually made this film, with its complicated, sentimental, and obviously autobiographical plot. The drafted text expresses feelings about the music-hall trade that are hardly cheerful or positive. In the film work that he took beyond the drafting stage, Tati would always seek to use as few of the cinema's illusions and conjuring tricks as he could; his broader aim was to offer a new kind of comic realism on screen.

However, in the later 1940s, whatever expedients Tati used to pay the bills at Rue de Penthièvre – sports promotion, black market, and, no doubt more reliably, mime – his frustration with the cinema business must have been growing with every day that passed. He had a film, a film he believed in, and that would entertain the public at least as much as his music-hall act – if only the public had a chance of seeing it. To break the deadlock, and in association with Orain, who had now taken full control of Cady-Films, Tati persuaded the manager of Le Régent at Neuilly to show *Jour de fête* in lieu of the advertised film.[200] And he made sure that other managers, as well as critics and friends, were among the audience, most of whom did not know at all what lay in store. It was a risk; it was not exactly a proper thing to do, even if it was not strictly illegal; but then, it really was a last throw. Tati's nerves before the first appearance on screen of the cycling postman must have been in a dreadful state, for off-stage he was a shy and often anxious man. But the audience laughed at the very first gag, and went on laughing to the end of the film, and even after, as they gathered in the foyer. It was a triumph, and it overcame the distributors' reluctance to proceed with the film (a reluctance that in retrospect seems barely comprehensible). *Jour de fête* was at last accepted for a season at a small chain of four Paris movie theatres – Balzac, Helder, Scala, Vivienne – from early May 1949.

Most of this story, often repeated by Tati and backed up by Orain, must be true, but there are aspects of *Jour de fête*'s public history that do not quite fit. From correspondence in the archives of the Crédit national we know that foreign rights – for Argentina, Belgium, Switzerland and French Africa – had been sold for a good price in 1948, recouping about half the film's total cost; that year, Tati had enough money available to record a new sound track for the English-speaking world – not a dubbed version, but one with "easier" French (*bicyclette* replaces *bécane* and *vélo*, for example) and with special "French ambience noises" held to be more recognisable abroad. That international version of *Jour de fête* was shown in London in March 1949, got good reviews, and went on general UK release. Tati travelled over for the première, and did a stage act before the curtain went up (the safety-pin holding up his hired and ill-fitting dinner-suit trousers came adrift, and he had to improvise mimes that allowed him to keep one supporting hand in his pocket).[201] French distributors must have got to hear of a low-budget film that was making money abroad (only a few French films have ever really done that); the release of *Jour de fête* in France came just a few weeks later, and even if its contraband showing in Neuilly clinched the deal, the news from London must have been close behind.

All of Tati's subsequent films were also made or broken by their overseas careers; and the odd way in which *Jour de fête* finally reached its French public surely accounts for the distinctly international turn that Tati took in his subsequent scripts and projects. On the other hand, Tati was never seriously tempted to work abroad; he clung on to his home base – not simply his real home, at Rue de Penthièvre, and later on at Saint-Germain, but his "home" amongst Parisian chums, collaborators and technical plant – as a resolutely rooted French film-maker who happened to make money abroad. Until the release of *Playtime*, that is. The whole project, conducted at monumental expense from 1964 to 1967, had been predicated on massive returns from the American market, and when no US distributor showed any interest, Tati's house of cards collapsed.

Jour de fête might have had an easier run in France had it come out on time, in late '47 or spring '48. By May 1949, it had been overtaken, so to speak, by films like Prévert's *Voyage-Surprise* and Rouquier's *Farrebique*, for despite their differences, these comic and quasi-ethnographic treatments of French country life occupied some of the same terrain as *Jour de fête*. Moreover, *Jour de fête* seemed almost amateur by comparison with these and other more routine French films. Art Buchwald, writing from Paris for the *New York Herald Tribune*, reflected the generally luke-warm feelings of the French critical establishment, and also the very narrow definition of the genre of the film when he called it "a fairly good slapstick comedy".[202] Even generally favourable newspaper critics – Louis Chauvet,[203] Jean Pierre Vivet, and the influential "Jeander", in *Libération*[204] – thought it lacked the appropriate rhythm for a comedy film. André Lang, too, disliked the long-drawn-out set-up of the visit of the travelling fair;[205] for him as for most other reviewers, the cycling stunts were too long delayed, but made the film, overall, worthwhile. Tati, most critics agreed, had created a hilarious new comedy act, and had proved himself a world-class mime. But he wasn't much of a director, in the general view of 1949. Tati should hire a decent dialogue-writer and take lessons in basic film structure, *Le Monde* sermonised, if he wanted to produce more than a puffed-out comic short. *L'Aurore* went even further: "*Jour de fête* is supposed to be a comic film. In our view, it does not deserve to be called comic, nor to be called a film."[206]

Jour de fête is indeed in one sense a "puffed-out comic short", and what disappointed its first professional audience was that it had not been puffed out with more of the same: "Every fifteen minutes or so, Tati shows us his indisputable good humour; but why didn't he cram more gags into the film?" asked Henry Magnan;[207] and Vivet reckoned that what made the film so unsatisfactory was "a structural mistake which divides our attention between the fair at Sainte-Sévère and the postman's cycling stunts". Even worse, in Chauvet's words which echo those of most other critics, "Caricature is displaced by observation, sometimes even by mere poetic notations." All that was not screwball, slapstick, mime or caricature, seemed out of place in a new comedy film. *Jour de fête* did not conform to the boundaries of its genre, and was thus only a half-successful comedy film.

"Jeander" was nonetheless optimistic about the prospects for the film and its star, perhaps because he knew about its snowballing reputation abroad. Unlike any French comic artiste before him, Tati did not rely on verbal wit or specifically French cultural reference to create his effects; *Jour de fête* shows that it is possible to speak an "authentically universal language of comedy", just as Chaplin and Keaton had done years before. But as for Tati's gifts as a director, "Jeander" was no more complimentary than *Le Monde*.

Only the satirical weekly, *Le Canard enchaîné*, gave *Jour de fête* an unequivocal welcome.[208] Its anonymous reviewer, who was probably Jean Queval, a close friend of Queneau and Vian, liked the film for its utter lack of intellectual pretension and for its obvious intention to amuse without unnecessary words. Could it be that the first real grasp of Tati's new art of comic film came from a writer who would be one of the twelve founding brethren of the OuLiPo, that irreverent literary group that gave Georges Perec an intellectual and literary home? It would be perfectly logical. For there is a family resemblance between the half-serious and profoundly original games that Oulipians played with words, and the formal restrictions and the good humour of Tati's art of film.

TWENTY-TWO

Declarations of Independence

The tepid reception of the film in the Paris press had little impact on cinema audiences, who loved *Jour de fête*. Nevertheless Tati could not but be hurt and perplexed by the blindness of the film-art establishment to what he had tried to do. Later on, he granted that in his directorial debut, which was almost a training exercise, he had made "spelling mistakes" – as unimportant, in his view, as the spelling mistakes he made whenever he tried to write things down. What the critics had sniped at, though, were not surface blemishes, but the fundamental structure of the film. Tati took those strictures to heart in a quite particular way: his next film would have even less narrative tension and an even less conventional rhythm, to show that what he had done was not a mistake, but his own view of how films should be made.

As *Jour de fête* pursued its career, paid back its costs, and began to produce a real income for Cady-Films,[209] Jacques Tati chased it around the world, often appearing in person at national and sometimes regional premières, where he would always do a mime act on stage before the curtain rose. In France, too, *Jour de fête* slowly gained recognition. In 1949, it won the prize for best scenario at the Venice Film Festival, and in May 1950, Tati's first film was awarded the *Grand Prix du cinéma français* – a prize less grand than its name suggests,[210] but an agreeable salute all the same. But Tati turned down all proposals to make sequels under titles like *François in Love*, *François Goes West*, or *François and the Airmail Plane*. A producer tried in vain to lure him into a duo with another gangling, sad-faced clown, the Italian Totò – under a jingling joint name of *Toto e Tati*. All Tati's friends thought he should make more of François; but the director was adamant that he would only make his own films, not those that others wanted him to make for them.

Tati was determined to remain his own man and he only knew one way to do that. He was afraid of having smart Alecs in studios running rings around him, like the showmen who manipulate François in *Jour de fête*. Family background came into it as well. Tati came from a small business culture, not from a line of corporate pilots and organisation men. Independence was his goal, perhaps before all else. Anyway, *Jour de fête* was now earning the first significant money that Tati had ever had, and there were plenty of other things to get on with in life. He didn't need to work just for the sake of it. He was perfectly able to enjoy doing nothing much for a while.

Tati was a proud father of two children, Sophie, born 1946, and Pierre, born in 1949; the flat at Rue de Penthièvre had to be extended and remodelled to make room for them, and for Tati's own office-study. It was there that he spent hours with his painter-friend Jacques Lagrange, chatting, musing, and drafting ideas for his future films.

Tati's first meeting with Lagrange must have gone back to the Occupation period, or perhaps even pre-war days (according to Lagrange, Tati was still working in the picture-framing trade when they first made acquaintance). Lagrange, in a smart suit and a tram-driver's peaked cap, made an immediate and lasting impression on the mime. When the two met again in 1946, after the painter's release from several years in a POW camp, Tati was delighted to help his old friend find a studio, and to steer him towards an ideal place in his own courtyard, at 30, Rue de Penthièvre. For the following ten years, the two Jacques were neighbours, and became close chums.

A man-about-town and a *bon-vivant*, Lagrange was the son of the Citroën firm's regular architect, and the son-in-law of Gustave Perret, the architect member of the firm that had built many of the major public buildings put up in the 1920s and 1930s – the Musée des Travaux Publics, the Mobilier National, the Théâtre des Champs-Elysées, and much else besides.[211] In his personal life, though, Lagrange was just about as Bohemian as you could get. Tati loved the combination, which mirrored his own half-bourgeois and half-artistic existence, whilst taking it to a greater extreme. Lagrange, like other painters in the Ecole de Paris, found himself rather successful in the ten years after the war, when contemporary French art was easy to sell; and Tati was impressed – envious is perhaps not too strong a word – when he saw his well-connected, anarchical chum off to *vernissages* on first-class Air France tickets.

Around this time too, Borrah Minevich returned to France, and settled down with his second wife Lucile in a quaint mill at Méréville, near Etampes. Most weekends, Tati would drive from Rue de Penthièvre to Le Pecq to lunch with his parents, still living in the same house in Rue de L'Ermitage, and then on down to Etampes, to spend the rest of the day (and often much of the night) larking about with his American-Russian pal. With the million dollars that Hohner had paid him for the rights to the chromatic harmonica when he was just twenty-one, Minevich had done a *mitzvah* – he built a

Fig. 49: *Jacques Lagrange at Saint-Marc-sur-mer, 1952*

synagogue for his mother in Boston, MA – but for the rest, he had devoted his life to having fun. He had become an irresistible typhoon of a man, sleeping no more than four hours a night, and dissipating his vast energy in a whole number of different trades. Simultaneously music-hall performer, comedy film star, impresario, distributor and financier, he had cooked up a simple scheme to achieve ubiquity: he licensed out his name to several other harmonica-playing comedians, who became "Borrah Minevich" franchisees. He tried to persuade Tati to do the same with his cycling postman act; the Hulot idea, in his view, was too much of a risk – and why bother, when you have a gold mine already? Minevich, accustomed since youth to being a millionaire, had learned to live in a big-handed style, picking up the bills in bars and restaurants, just like the tubby American *bon vivant* in the Royal Garden sequence of *Playtime*. And he knew everybody there was to know. Charlie Chaplin? An old friend! And the Pope? Yes, a private audience! At Méréville, Tati was only one amongst many famous house-guests – Marlon Brando, Daniel Gelin, Boris Vian and perhaps, once or twice, Raymond Queneau – but he was all the same a special Russian friend of the Boston Jew.

One day, Minevich was driving Tati down the Champs-Elysées in his open-top Ford (the two wives, Micheline and Lucile, were in the back). "Would you look good in a real kepi?" Borrah asked Tati. "Sure I would. My grandfather, I'll have you know, was a military attaché and looked terrific in uniform." "Your word is my command," said Borrah. As they passed a traffic policeman, he stretched out his arm and lifted off the man's kepi, placing it in one swooping movement on Tati's wind-ruffled head. He accelerated away, and then did a *tour de piste* up and down the Champs-Elysées, with a very tall "policeman" sitting bolt upright in the front seat. The ladies, especially Micheline, were outraged, and they nagged Borrah and Jacques to stop behaving like boys. "OK, OK," Borrah said, and did a U-turn so as to coast up to the now explosively red-faced gendarme. "Thanks for the loan, my friend. Can I do you a favour in return? Do you have a lady wife? You do? And children too? Well that's nice! Would you like to have a car so you can take the family out, for a ride? You would? Well, that's great!" Which is how Minevich and Tati did not get booked for insulting a policeman, but had to do without the Ford for a couple of days.[212]

Minevich did Tati more of a real favour in 1952 when he arranged for the launch of a dubbed version of *Jour de fête* at the 55th Street Playhouse in New York, under the title *The Big Day*. The editor of *Variety* was another of Borrah's pals (it was with him, in fact, that he had been to see the Pope) and gave the jolly scoundrel a handsome and scarcely merited accolade in return:[213]

> This pic is an education. It took an American showman to demonstrate to the French, on their home plate, that a picture could be made here on a $30,000 budget and gross $12,000 in its first week's simultaneous release in four small Paris first-run houses headed by the Champs-Elysées' Balzac. This is a constructive answer to local producers' gripes that Hollywood opposition kills their industry. Borrah Minevich, who has been in Paris a couple of years, put together the money, story, star and, above all, the know-how.[214]

Of course Borrah had done nothing of the sort; but it was probably advantageous to Tati as well to have an "American alibi" for a film which could easily have been taken in New York for yet another expression of the

paradoxical and irritating ingratitude that the French seemed to feel for their main ally.

As with Broïdo at one time and with Rhum at another, Tati and Minevich played up to each other – Minevich as the madcap, Tati as the anxious partner in screwball crime. At evenings at Méréville, and also in Paris bars and restaurants, Tati and Minevich often resurrected the clumsy-waiter act which had got Tati's professional life started twenty years earlier. It seems that they meant a lot to each other for several years, and that Michou too came to treat Borrah as her husband's best chum, one who could listen to her side of things when the need arose to have a confidant. But one day in 1956, when cruising down Avenue Foch in his open-top limousine, reciting Lincoln's Gettysburg Address at the top of his voice, in his own Yiddish translation, Borrah Minevich suffered a stroke. He came round in hospital, and told the nurse that things weren't too bad, as it was only his right arm that wouldn't move. To prove it, he drummed out a cha–cha–cha on the bed-post with his left fist, rolled over, and died.

It was during the period of his friendship with Borrah that Tati heard a pianist playing in the restaurant more or less opposite where he lived, in Rue de Penthièvre. Alain Romains had been executed by the Germans during the war. But the bullet had missed the vital organs, and, left for dead like Balzac's Colonel Chabert, Romains had survived and put his life back together. Tati asked him if he composed. Yes, he did.

Tati had a lazy eye out all the time for performers, creators and technicians who might contribute to his future films. He often went to cabarets and night-clubs, and kept a mental note of acts that he liked; people also approached him, for help and support, and he was sometimes quite glad to give it: to Michèle Brabo, for example, who did an act at Le Boeuf sur le Toit. But quite how he got to know Marguerite Duras – long before she was "into film", and was still a leading member of a left-wing coterie just recently expelled from the Communist Party – remains unknown. At all events, Marguerite was around at Rue de Penthièvre as often as Edith Piaf, and dandled the two Tatischeff children on her knee.

These must have been relatively, and perhaps absolutely, happy days. Tati was a doting father. He allowed Michou to give the children a Catholic education, though he did not give a fig for the Church himself; he was keener to make sure that Sophie and Pierre had proper holidays, and took them off most summers to La Baule, on the south-facing coast of Brittany. They usually stayed with one or another of Michou's old schoolfriends: Ira Bergeron and her husband, a senior manager with Shell, and Nicole Arène, who had married an art-dealer and auctioneer, both had summer homes at La Baule. Tati was quite at ease with the professional bourgeoisie, to which, in one sense, he now belonged; but he was just as much in his element with his Bohemian, music-hall and circus chums. Lagrange was perhaps unique, as he belonged to both worlds at once.

Michou was a shy and retiring woman. For a while Tati wondered if she might not handle his PR, but Michou was reluctant even to make a telephone call herself (Tati often dialled for her, even to call close friends). At one point – around 1950 – Michou was coaxed into starting a business with her friend Ira, to market an old idea of Tati's own – "cadres lumineux", picture frames with incorporated lighting; but what they actually sold were frameless mounts made of Plexiglas, a brand-new material at that time. A maker of synthetic suede, Néodaim, put in an order for five hundred of the new frames; but that was all the business the partnership ever did. Thereafter Michou was happy to be plain Madame Tati, in an unseen and private supporting role. Although she travelled with her husband on many of his grander visits abroad, she kept as far as possible out of news photographers' views. Only in exceptional circumstances did Tati even allow photographs to be taken of Michou in his company. Unlike so many celebrities of the screen, Tati succeeded in keeping his private life out of public view.

The social life of the Tatischeff family was thus quite distinct from the professional life of the director, on the one hand, and from the contacts that Tati maintained both with his old rugby-club chums and with his friends from the music-hall stage. Through his parents, through his wife and her friends, as well as through Lagrange, Tati had a wide circle of acquaintances in commerce, industry and the liberal professions, and some of his more Bohemian friends found his mixing with bankers, art-dealers, architects and medical consultants quite strange. Through his pre-war career he had links with acrobats, clowns and fairly down-at-heel variety artistes, which his middle-class acquaintances thought quite peculiar. Through his own adventures and the flow of Parisian life, he was in touch with a surprising number of intellectuals in the high cultural sphere, which is no less odd for a man who read nothing much, and certainly not a word of Queneau, Duras or Vian. But perhaps the most important aspect of Tati's varied social life in the 1950s is what it left out. He did not mix with film actors. He was never a personal friend of his own producer, Orain, or of any other money-men behind the screen. And he gave a wide berth to all other film directors. In brief, he was not part of the French cinema scene. For such independence, there is always a price to pay.

TWENTY-THREE

Waiting for Hulot

The real revolutionary issue is the problem of leisure

GUY DEBORD, 1954

Like the first draft of *Jour de fête*, the script initially headed just "Film Tati N° 2" has a bald, not to say banal, narrative frame: a week's holiday in a seaside hotel, from arrival to departure. There are innumerable precedents in literature for stories set in holiday resorts (Chekhov's *Lady with the Little Dog*, for instance). In painting, the subject of holidays-by-the-sea goes back to the time when General Tatischeff first arrived in France, in the canvases of Eugène Boudin. But as a new phenomenon and a fashionable preoccupation, seaside holidays also figured as the half-comic, half-enviable subject of many newspaper cartoonists in the period 1870–1900 (see, for example, the long-running series "Le Long des Plages" by "Mars" in *Le Journal Amusant*).[215] But the prehistory of the cinema itself provides perhaps the most famous antecedent for the subject of *Les Vacances de M. Hulot*: a single fifteen-minute show devised by Emile Reynaud for his "Praxinoscope", entitled *Autour d'une cabine* ("Around a Beach-Hut"), which was seen by many millions of Parisians around the turn of the century – and again, in 1946, when Tati most likely went to watch Reynaud's animated characters at play.

The Praxinoscope projects an image from a moving celluloid strip on to a screen; some of the images – background, fixed features – may be derived from photographs, but the moving figures are painted on to the frames by hand, their movements assembled by the artist's intuition, not by rapid-sequence photography. Its inventor and sole practitioner, Emile Reynaud, was an employee of the waxworks museum, the Musée Grévin, which held all rights to the device, and used it as an exclusive attraction. As a result, the Praxinoscope was never seen outside Paris. But its fame spread far and wide, and people came to see it from the furthest corners of France just a few years before the Lumières' *cinématographe* began to spread. Long forgotten, the device was hauled out of storage and presented as one of the main attractions of the French celebrations of the fiftieth anniversary of the invention of the cinema, deferred by one year from 1945 to 1946 for obvious practical reasons.[216] It is thus a moral certainty that Tati saw *Autour d'une cabine* just before he started shooting *Jour de fête*. And that the images and episodes of the world's first beach movie came back to him a few years later, when he got down to devising "Tati N° 2".

The published résumé of this fifteen-minute, hand-painted show is worth quoting in full:

Background: Beach, sea, cliffs. A diving board. Foreground: a beach-hut.

Pers. dram.: Three bathers. A bald and paunchy bather. A young bather. Seagulls. The Parisian and the Parisienne. A little dog. A boatman. Jack-a-dandy.

A bather comes on and jumps off the diving board. Another follows behind and also jumps in. The third bather does a somersault. A bald and paunchy gentleman hesitates. A young man jumps on to his shoulders and pushes him into the water. They splash each other in the water and then swim off, one doing a crawl, the other on his back.

Seagulls appear, move gracefully over the beach, then fly off.

A Parisian couple come on. Both elegantly dressed, the young wife also carries a small dog in her arm. The newcomers agree about beach-huts, then the husband exits towards his, which is off screen.

Jack-a-dandy, dressed up to the nines and wearing a monocle, stops in front of the wife and looks at her with interest. The dog jumps out of its mistress's arms and runs into Jack-a-dandy's legs. He wobbles and nearly falls over, knocking the woman over. He helps her up, doffs his hat to her, apologises profusely, whilst she looks irritated and keeps her glance down.

Jack-a-dandy makes a proposal, which the Parisienne rejects, and shuts herself into her hut. She slams the door in Jack-a-dandy's face. He puts his eye to the key-hole and is obviously delighted with what he can see.

The lady's husband now arrives, dressed in his bathing costume. He gets angry and kicks Jack-a-dandy in the you-know-what. Jack-a-dandy is taken aback but given the husband's anger he goes off, looking crestfallen.

The lady comes out of her hut in her beach-robe. Takes it off and appears in her bathing suit. The two step gingerly into the water, wet themselves, and then swim off.

Jack-a-dandy returns, sees the hut door open, goes in and hides. He shuts the blind on the porthole. A few moments later, the dog reappears, goes round the hut, smells that someone is there,

begins to bark and to jump up against the wall. Jack-a-dandy
opens the porthole, puts his arm through, and tries to shoo away
the dog. Then he tries to hit the dog with his hat, but the dog
snatches it with his teeth and runs off.

The husband and wife swim back into view and come out of the
water whilst Jack-a-dandy shuts himself into the hut once again.
The lady opens the door, then shuts it again fast, and tells her
husband that there is someone inside. The furious husband goes in
and comes out holding the bold fellow by the ear. He shakes him
a few times, and then throws him into the water. Jack-a-dandy
struggles to stand up again and leaves, with his clothes dripping.
The dog returns, chases Jack-a-dandy, and bites his ankle.

A boat appears, with the boatman rowing vigorously. He stops, and
raises a sail on which these words are written: The Performance
Is Over.[217]

Though the comic foil, Jack-a-dandy (*Copurchic* in French) is a very
different character from M. Hulot, the situations invented or observed by
Reynaud, who went to sketch the scenes by the seaside at Trouville in 1892,
are all picked up again, one way or another, by Tati: the voyeur given a kick
up the backside as he peeks (or appears to peek) through the spy-hole of
a changing hut, the tumble into the water, the difficulty with animals, even
the interlude of seagulls in the sky. These are all things that can happen on a
beach in any case, so there may be no need to suppose any direct connection
between the material of the world's first animated film and its most mysterious and magical comedy. But that would be to take scepticism too far, in
our view. *Les Vacances de M. Hulot* is infinitely richer and more subtle
than *Autour d'une cabine*; but it is also, without reasonable doubt, a homage
to Emile Reynaud, a celebration of the most painterly form of early moving-
image technology, and thus a re-appropriation of the moving picture as a
specifically French form of art.

Les Vacances de M. Hulot is also profoundly different from *Jour de fête*, but
overlaps with it in curious ways. The summer spent shooting the latter was
the first in which holidays had once again become possible for the French
middle classes: even the staid *Le Monde* ran an editorial about the return
of "holiday panic", the difficulty of finding accommodation by the sea, the
unending hassle and chaos of travel in a country that had barely begun
to rebuild its roads and railways – such that holidays were truly needed to
allow travellers to get over their exhausting preparatory labours.[218] However,
beyond the fact that both films deal with different kinds of time off, the
connecting thread between them is Henri Marquet, credited as co-author of

both scripts. Marquet was not an intellectual prop for Jacques Tati, since he had had even less education, and boasted a culture derived exclusively from music-hall and circus acts. By all accounts, his sense of humour, like his "Parigot" accent, was a good deal more vulgar than Tati's. He may well have thought up some of the sight and sound gags in the script of *Les Vacances* (it contains rather more material than the film) but it is hard to imagine that the idea, the persona, the very conception of Hulot came from anyone but Jacques Tati.

As Tati was inventing Hulot, Samuel Beckett was writing *Waiting for Godot*, which had its Paris première a few months before Tati's film. Both works do without anything resembling a conventional plot; and if we never learn just what it is that is awaited in *Godot*, so in *Les Vacances* we never learn anything much about M. Hulot.

The formal credits of the finished film acknowledge the collaboration of Pierre Aubert and Jacques Lagrange, but the shooting script, registered with the CNC in 1951, does not. Pierre Aubert was a recent graduate of IDHEC, the film school founded by Marcel L'Herbier. His very first job was as assistant director to Tati, and his credit must presumably be the result of changes made during the shooting of the film. Lagrange's role, on the other hand, was much more fundamental. Tati used his friend and neighbour as a sounding board for his ideas during the whole process of inventing *Les Vacances*, and the painter certainly came to play a key role in the design of the sets and props; which is why he added "avec la collaboration de Jacques Lagrange" in his own, firm hand to his roneo copy of the script.[219]

Lagrange was not just a successful painter (and, later on, a distinguished designer of tapestries and mosaics) but a gifted draftsman and cartoonist too: he could turn an idea into a drawing almost as it was being said. Tati half-resented his own incapacity as a draftsman and his dependency on Lagrange and others like him. Many years later, when his film career had effectively run out of steam, Tati often looked on as his friend Sempé, the cartoonist, worked at his drawing board. He could be heard muttering, with his hand characteristically in front of his mouth: "I wish I had learned to draw like that."[220]

However, with or without Lagrange, Aubert and Marquet, Tati invented a completely original screen character to link and to justify the material of "Film Tati N° 2". Indeed, we can hardly imagine what *Les Vacances* would be like without Hulot. But he is far less easy to describe, to approach and to pin down than almost any other figure of equal fame. More like an idea than a character – and in this, quite like Beckett's Godot – Hulot is a mysterious assemblage of signs.

In the film, the idea that is Hulot is expressed first of all by a posture:

Fig. 51: *Lagrange's preparatory sketches of beach furniture for* Les Vacances de M. Hulot

straight-backed, but leaning forward from the ankles, in defiance of gravity; head held low, like a bird's, bending from the neck, exaggerating the sense of impending disequilibrium; a jutting pipe underlines the forward tilt; elbows splayed backwards, making a gawky, eloquent and comically elongated silhouette. It is a kind of "corporeal sculpture" vaguely reminiscent of Giacometti's spidery lines; it seems to express something, but we can't be quite sure what, apart from an apologetic eagerness to please.

Hulot's stationary posture largely determines his deportment when he moves: almost but not quite on tiptoe, as if he hoped not to put too much weight on the surface of the world. His elasticated bounce of a step seems reluctant to make its full presence felt on floorboards, beach or road. One critic has referred to it as *la discrétion absolue*, "discretion made perfect". And yet . . . it is also a comic routine.

Hulot's facial expression is quite inscrutable or, in Michel Chion's words, "indefinable, somewhere between worry, stupidity and polite neutrality".[221] It is often more than half-hidden – by the hat, the pipe, or simply by its distance from the camera and Tati's constant movement across the screen – but it could hardly be more different from the dim-witted rusticity of Postman François. Hulot is clearly some sort of a gentleman, and is always called *Monsieur* Hulot.

The skills needed to carry out the act of being Hulot come from Tati's long practice of mime, but the Hulot-act is not mime in the ordinary sense,

Fig. 52: *Hulot at the doorway of the Hôtel de la Plage*

as it mimics no designated model, activity or role. Tati claimed that all his art was based on observation, and in defence of that aesthetic, he said he had seen people walk with Hulot's peculiar stride (just as he knew a man called Hulot, with whose permission he had borrowed the name).[222] Be that as it may, the combination of posture and stride in the Hulot act is unique to Tati, and no one has ever thought to reproduce it – not even John Cleese.

Hulot can also be seen as a *negative* construction, an act designed in the mind to invert a whole set of existing bodily signs of film and stage comedy. Hulot's forward tilt is the reverse of Chaplin's iconic posture – the clever wee fellow rocks *back* on his heels, and in the trade-mark iris [223] at the end of his shorts, he struts off into the distance with knees and ankles, not elbows, jutting out to the side; the jerky, marionette-like deportment of Charlot is the obvious antipodes of the springy glide of Hulot.

Hulot's dress is also an assemblage that must have been carefully thought out in film terms. He is seen in several outfits (fancy dress, tennis whites, tweed blazer . . .), but the clothes that were used to construct the Hulot icon in posters and other publicity materials are these: a soft hat, a pipe, trousers a few inches too short in the leg, and striped socks. There is something vaguely English, and definitely middle-class about Hulot's canonical dress; it certainly makes the figure internationally anodyne, in a way that François the postman was not. But again, the items that constitute the Hulot-sign could be read, point for point, as negative references to Chaplin: a Homburg instead of a bowler, a blazer in place of tails, trousers too short in the leg instead of ones too long and wide, and in place of the cane, a variety of similarly stick-like but functionally different accessories – umbrella, fishing rod, and butterfly-net. The striped socks, though, come from somewhere else: as Marc Dondey points out, they are borrowed from Keaton in *Parlor, Bedroom and Bath* – a film re-shot in French by Autant-Lara on his first Hollywood job, fifteen years before he made *Sylvie*.

There can hardly be a single detail of the Hulot-figure – from the position of his feet to the angle of his pipe, from the items he wears at the fancy-dress ball to the precise timing of his legs when he scampers off the beach – that was not thought out and decided in advance, in terms of a Hulot-concept that can perhaps never quite be written out.

In the shooting script, where the visual, corporeal characterisation of Hulot is barely sketched in, the main sense of the man seems to be that of a clumsy and solitary nuisance: he disturbs other guests by playing the gramophone too loud (shots 135–137, pp. 71–2), he muddles the two hands of bridge by swivelling the tables as he crawls after a lost table-tennis ball on the floor (shot 143), he lets the sea breeze into the lobby, playing havoc with the Businessman's correspondence (shot 152), he inadvertently inter-rupts health-and-beauty exercises on the beach (shot 156), and nearly causes a swimming accident by shaking the hand of a swimming tutor who had been keeping a pupil afloat (shot 211, cut from the available versions of the film). Indeed, the Swedish title of the film – *Semestersabotören*, "The Holiday Spoiler" – identifies this as the main subject of the film; the novelised version (by Jean-Claude Carrière) is similarly structured around the trouble that the clumsy yet loveable Hulot causes by mistake.

The script is also much clearer than the finished movie in respect of the romantic plot. Hulot is one amongst many suitors of Martine, the belle of the beach at Saint-Marc: Pierre, the narcissistic keep-fit addict, the Intellectual[224] and the unnamed youngsters who loiter in the street are all seeking Martine's attention and approval. Hulot seems to get nearer to his object than they do, since he does actually have a dance with the girl. But in the concluding sequence (no. 393), cut from the actual film, we see Martine and the others in a railway carriage on the way home, sharing their holiday snaps:

> On each snapshot Pierre's stationary and standard smile contrasts with Hulot, who is forever in movement, and thus has an arm or a leg out of frame.

The last [photo shows] Hulot all alone, with the white patch of a
bandage on his nose.

What mood the face of Martine might have shown in this shot – ridicule,
affection, hostility or regret – is not stated; but we can only surmise that the
sequence was intended to close off an "affair" that never actually began.

Although Tati always refused to make "Hulot sequels" and poured scorn
on ideas for titles like *Hulot Goes West* or *Hulot in Love*, there is in fact a
romantic thread that links the four Hulot films: a purely notional affair
engineered by Hulot's sister in *Mon Oncle*, a set of dreamy glances between
Hulot and Barbara in *Playtime*, and in *Trafic* – at last – a kind of embrace in
the closing shots, as Hulot comes back out of the subway to accompany
Maria Kimberley to her car, and holds up his umbrella with one hand whilst
putting the other around the girl's shoulder. Hulot, even or perhaps most
especially in his first incarnation in the script for *Les Vacances*, is not a sexless
figure, but a shy and self-effacing creature who fails to make any headway
towards the rather insubstantial object of his desire.

Hulot also seems designed to portray a kind of universal embarrassment.
On the first full day of the holiday week,[225] Hulot is on the beach when
the winch restraining a fishing boat slips on its ratchet. The boat, which is
still undergoing repainting, slides back into the water, to the great fury of
the painters, who cast angry glances around to find a culprit. The little
boy who might have loosened the handle for fun (Denis) is seen (shot 88)
helping a lady wind her skein of wool,[226] so he must be innocent; Henry
(*le Promeneur*), on whom the glance then comes to rest, is too far away; and
so suspicion is directed towards Hulot, seen drying himself with a towel
looped around a post. The script and the film never reveal who slipped
the ratchet on the winch (maybe nobody did it . . .) – but Hulot behaves
straight away as if he were the guilty party. As soon as he can, he scampers
off like a naughty child, despite the utterly indeterminate nature of his fault.

Other episodes have Hulot accepting guilt that is not, or not really, his
to bear. When he fails entirely to establish a civil relationship with a horse
for his riding excursion with Martine, the troublesome beast kicks down
a wooden door and then slams down the lid of the rumble-seat of a car,
apparently decapitating a passenger in a panama hat. Hulot runs away as if the
equine violence was all his fault, and he hides behind a beach-hut door to
watch the outcome, unseen.

Hulot's guiltiness is the flip side of the eagerness to please that his posture,
deportment and other actions suggest. It seems as though the character
imagined by Tati as the vehicle for a new kind of observational comedy has
something for which he needs to make up. Though most of his attempts to

do so go awry, Hulot embodies the abstract intention of making amends, irrespective of context. But he never does so by taking direct initiatives, or by entering into real interaction with the other character in the lobby, in the dining room, or on the beach. Hulot exists at one remove. An idea, an emotion, an insubstantial presence, Hulot is more like the ghost of *Sylvie* than the mumbling postman of *Jour de fête*.

TWENTY-FOUR

Gags, Jokes, and Switches

Few pleasures are more useful than a good comedy
QUEEN CHRISTINA OF SWEDEN[227]

Reduced to its simplest structure, *Les Vacances de M. Hulot* consists of a number of gags of the form: X (or somebody) takes Y (or something) for Z (or something else). What Noel Carroll calls the "switch image" and the "switch movement" in cinema sight gags[228] necessarily obey this underlying structure; but for the formula to be applied to the raising of a laugh, X's error in taking Y for Z has to be revealed, at some point, to someone, be it X (type A), another represented character (type B), or the spectator alone (type C). *Les Vacances* is the first of Tati's films to have regular recourse to the structure of dramatic irony as a comic device, but simple illustrations can be taken from nearly all his later films.

In *Mon Oncle*, Hulot, having realised that some of Mme Arpel's kitchen utensils are made of unbreakable plastic, bounces another pot on the tile floor just to check out his discovery. The pot breaks. X has taken Y for Z (has mistaken a glass pot for a plastic one), and discovers instantly the nature of his mistake. In such simple type-A gags, the "hero" is both the perpetrator and the victim of error. He deserves and obtains sympathetic laughter in proportion to the ease with which the spectator can imagine making the same mistake. Since no one finds it easy to tell plastic from glass at first glance, this simple gag can be taken as an elementary form of sympathetic irony, a form that can be endowed, in more complex articulations, with a great wealth of meaning.

Type-B gags, where a "wise guy" understands (and perhaps laughs at or profits from) the mistake made by X about Y, is very frequent in Hollywood burlesque (Laurel and Hardy shorts use almost no other type of gag), but are almost entirely absent from Tati's work. Type-B gags set one character above the other, even if only temporarily, and even if the roles can be reversed; they also require, or imply, some kind of interaction between characters. In Tati's world, though, characters do not interact, but pass each other by at a distance. Rivalry is never acted out, only implied; all that would make for dramatic interaction is left unsaid.

Most typical of Tati's comedy style are type-C gags, where only the spectator – provided he or she pays attention – is undeceived over the length of the joke. From the script of *Les Vacances*:

242. S.L.S.[229] In front of the villa. – Day
Martine says goodnight to Hulot and with her eyes still on him pushes the door open with her foot, bending her leg up from the knee, a gesture which could be taken as a come-on signal.
    Assuming this gesture was meant for him, Hulot is delighted, puts his hat at a roguish angle, and walks off.

243. – M.C.S – In front of the villa. – Day
Closer up, we can see the girl repeating her leg-movement, scraping away gravel that had been causing the door to jam.

Hulot has taken Martine's leg movement for a come-on; but the spectator is then given information that tells him that Hulot was wrong. This is exactly what Carroll means by a "switch movement". But in the film itself, there are many far more complex "switches" of image, movement and meaning. For example: with Martine and her aunt in the back seat, Hulot's broken-down Amilcar begins to roll down a sloping country road without its driver. The road bends left, but the Amilcar keeps straight on through gateposts into a driveway. The car's klaxon, attached to the spare wheel that has now also come unhinged and is dragged along by the car's gentle descent, bleats every couple of seconds. The sound of the quack-like horn runs over a cut in the image to the balcony of the chateau at the end of the drive, where a laird in a wheel-chair is trying to shoot fowl. He has his servant swivel him round to face the drive, for the laird (X) takes the car-horn (Y) for a duck (Z).

Sound is quite often the medium of misapprehension in Tati. At the Hôtel de la Plage, the gruff waiter has closed up the restaurant for the night. He puts on his overcoat, and the camera tracks him down the stairs towards the lounge, where most of the guests are now assembled. The grim-faced waiter's footsteps grow sharper as he descends, as if he were angrily stamping steel-tipped heels into the treads. But as he moves across the lounge and out of the frame, the staccato noises go on. Immediately, we correct our aural memory to dissociate the previously-heard sound from the idea of "bad-tempered footsteps". Only then do we see Hulot, backing into the lounge with dance-like steps from the table-tennis room to return a long ball. In this sound gag, X is the spectator: he has been made to take Y (the sound of ping-pong balls on bats) for Z (footsteps), and can only laugh at the error he has been deceived into making.

A visual version of this type of gag occurs in the script, but was either never shot, or has been removed from the versions currently in circulation.

The first tennis sequence (which has been cut) ends when Hulot is defeated and the ball goes off court into the vicarage garden. The English Lady, poking about in a bush, reveals in the depth of the field a priest snoozing on a deck-chair. Hulot sees his ball lying more or less at the feet of the priest; as he approaches, the priest awakes with a start, and immediately starts reciting a litany. Hulot takes off his hat as he bends down to get the ball, then stands up, puts his hat back on and moves off (shots 127–130, pp. 66–7). The joke intended must presumably be the resemblance of the scene to a man receiving benediction from a priest: a visual switch in which only the spectator is deceived and undeceived, and even then only in a symbolic or notional way.

An extremely elaborate gag of this kind, involving deceptions of sound, framing and camera angle, precedes Hulot's first arrival at the Hôtel de la Plage:

> The backfiring of Hulot's motor car bleeds under the first shot of the [hotel] lobby . . . As the sputtering dies away, the waiter moves from table to table establishing individual pockets of sound with every new reframing; then a squeal of someone trying to lock on to a radio signal comes up. We expect to see the source of the new sound, but instead of cutting to the radio operator, Tati cuts to a high-angle long shot establishing the space of the lobby, with the radio operator at the bottom of the frame.[230]

The point omitted from this otherwise accurate description is that when first heard the dreadful squawking of the radio is interpretable only as some kind of breakdown in the projection of Les Vacances de M. Hulot itself. Until the interpreting image arrives – not in the centre, but on the edge of the frame, where the spectator has to actively seek it out – the film plays with its audience in a daring and quite fundamental way, pointing to its own fragile status as a film, that is to say as a projection dependent on fallible equipment.

The typical Tati gag thus has the same ironical structure that underlies many more serious forms of theatre. Oedipus takes his father for a stranger, and tragedy ensues; Orgon takes Tartuffe for a saint, and on that misapprehension Molière builds a complex comedy of manners and beliefs. Tragedy and comedy both deal in errors of perception and their unveiling, a device known since the Greeks as anagnorisis. But in Tati, when a laird takes a honk for a quack, or when we take a clack for a footfall, or the search for a tennis ball as gesturally identical to a blessing – nothing happens. There are no neat resolutions to close off Tati's gags in Les Vacances, no punch-lines, no conclusions. Structurally perfect though they are, Tati's comedy gags do not drive plots or make stories. They just are: quirks of a world that is *just like that.*

A more elaborate XYZ structure is used in the sequence of Les Vacances where Hulot sees Mr Smutte's large, white-trousered backside close to Martine's changing hut on the beach, and from an angle that suggests to him that the fat banker is spying on a lady in a state of undress. Hulot approaches in righteous indignation, casts a huge long-legged kick at Smutte's posterior, and, in the instant of so doing, sees what the camera then allows us to see: Mr Smutte crouching over a tripod camera, taking a family snap. X has taken Y's position for that of a voyeur, whereas it is in reality the sign of something else. The "switch image" that prompts Hulot's knight-errantry is (we instantly grasp) the fault of framing and perspective; but we share his anagnorisis, since the camera had allowed us no other point of view from which to see Hulot's mistake before he could see it himself.

Fig. 53: *Hulot and the "peeping Tom".* (*This shot is seen for barely a second on screen*)

The persons and things that act as gag vehicles (Xs) and mediums (Ys) in Tati's film work are not infinitely varied. X is almost always either the formal hero (François in *Jour de fête*, Hulot in the subsequent films) or the spectator. Instances where false perception is attributed to another character on screen are really quite rare. For instance, in the opening sequence of the original *Jour de fête,* as the fairground horses leaning over the back of the trailer move to the left of the foreground, real horses in the pasture thus revealed canter away to screen right, tracked by the camera. If the village horses are taking X (their wooden simulations) for Y (a rival herd? new friends?) and are reacting accordingly, then Follainville is indeed a child's paradise, in which the real and the make-believe communicate with each other; and that is no doubt the message that Tati wished to give in the sequences establishing the mood and tone of the film. Another innocuous example of an alternative vehicle for a gag occurs in *Mon Oncle*, when Mme Arpel, about to welcome guests to her garden-party, seems to be trying to stop a carpet-seller from coming into the drive. What she first sees, and what we continue to see for just a little longer, is an arm bedecked in patterned tapestry, stretched out from behind the half-open front gate. The person who then enters despite Mme Arpel's initial protestation turns out to be the next-door neighbour (the bride she hopes her brother will wed), dressed in a loose-hanging caftan.[231] Here, Mme Arpel is (for a brief moment) the vehicle (X) of a gag, but for slightly less long than the spectator; and the medium (Y) of the gag – outlandish clothing – is far less grave than most of those for which Hulot himself is the vehicle.

One of the funniest and silliest gags in *Trafic* is when the leading lady, Maria Kimberley, is deceived by young, post-'68 Dutch frolickers who place a shaggy sheepskin body-warmer, with a dog-lead clipped on to it, beneath the wheel of her tiny runabout car. She falls into the trap and bemoans the death of her beloved pet terrier. Here, perhaps uniquely in Tati's work, a character is made fun of by other characters, and subjected to a "switch image" or visual deception of a type normally reserved for the spectator. For in nearly all other instances, the gags of Tati's films are instances of the humour of the world itself.

The gag which Tati used as his regular example of the difference between Chaplin's comedy style and his own is the "cemetery scene" in *Les Vacances*. Hulot and Fred have driven the Amilcar into a cemetery where a funeral is in progress. They have to sort out the car's canvas roof, but as a preliminary, Hulot looks for tools in the boot, and in the process, lays out a spare inner-tube on the leaf-strewn gravel. The leaves are wet and tacky; to set up the gag, Tati is careful to show Hulot himself annoyed by the way leaves are sticking to his shoe-soles.[232] So when the spare tube is turned over, we accept easily enough why leaves have attached themselves to it.[233] A funeral director passes by and takes the leaf-strewn inner tube for a wreath; he picks it up and hangs it on the memorial plaque. The gag becomes quite complex because the material misapprehension (tyre for wreath) prompts a human one – the two motorists are taken for regular mourners. Fred makes an embarrassed escape: but Hulot finds himself treated as a member of the family not just by the funeral director, but by the entire crowd of strangers lining up to offer condolences.

X becomes not any one character on screen, but a whole community, whose celebration of death goes way off-beam. At this point the tyre deflates on its hook; with a whoosh that is now heard by the assembly as Hulot's grieving sigh, it turns into a sadly sagging little thing.

Tati insisted that had this gag been Chaplin's, then the clever chap would have been responsible for the transformation of a rubber tube into a funeral wreath, and the spectator would have been invited to admire his ingenuity and to laugh with him at the gullibility of the world. Whereas he, Tati, made the comedy emerge not from the comedian, but from the situation; and that, he said, was a much more respectful and realistic understanding of life.

The follow-on from this gag is even more delicate. Standing in line shaking hands with po-faced and well-hatted "friends of the family", Hulot begins to smile, perhaps even to giggle. Michel Chion thinks that here, untypically, Hulot is sharing the comedy of mistaken condolences not with the characters on screen, but with us, the spectators of his film (and thus we would have a gag of type B, with the hero aware of the errors made by others, and sharing that awareness with us). In fact, Hulot's giggle is set off by another material gag: the tip of an ostrich-plume on a hat worn by a very short lady, wiggling about just under Hulot's chin.[234]

There are of course other kinds of comic episodes in *Les Vacances de M. Hulot*, unintellectual, physical jokes that have nothing to do with mistakes of interpretation. Like the acrobat-cyclist of *Jour de fête*, M. Hulot, in his first screen incarnation, is an agile and energetic fellow: he trips over a tow-rope and falls into a dock; he trips on the front stairs whilst carrying a pile of suitcases, and half-falls, half-runs all the way through the house and out the other side; he climbs a steep hill with a heavy rucksack on his back, and, when he reaches the scouts' hut, stands up straight to toast his achievement, forgetting that the weight on his back will topple him all the way back down the hill again. In another scene, on the beach, Hulot fails to mount a horse, gets his foot tangled in the reins, and is dragged backwards along the sand by the beast. These particular stunts are in the tradition of slapstick, but none of them are of the conflictual or "custard-pie" kind. Tati's physical comedy, in *Les Vacances* as before, is more related to the art of the music-hall mime and acrobat. It consists of solo acts, of turns and tumbles which make Hulot ridiculous, but do not damage or hurt anything much beyond pride – of which he seems to be peculiarly devoid.

Numerous other gags turn on material and mechanical objects, and most particularly on means of locomotion. Long before Hulot actually appears on screen,[235] his "living symbol", the antiquated Amilcar, announces his arrival in comic vein. Markedly smaller and slower than other cars on the road, the canvas-topped vehicle seems to waddle along like a lame duckling and to partake as much of the natural as of the mechanical world. Indeed,

Fig. 54: *Preparing to shoot the rumble seat joke. Note the hat, which will be crushed when the horse kicks the rear lid of the car*

other animals fail to react to it in the normal way: a dog emerges from a village porch to stretch itself out in the sun directly in front of the Amilcar, as if it were no more threatening than a toy mouse. (The sequence uses a standard trick of the trade: the brief medium-close shot of the dog settling down on to the otherwise empty stretch of tarmac is actually a more easily obtainable clip of a dog getting up – by reversing the shot, the illusion is given of the dog settling down instead.) But *Les Vacances* also includes more or less telling gags involving cyclists, trains, coaches, horses, road signs (a gag copied directly from *Gai dimanche*), a kayak, a hearse, and an inner tube, making the modes and paraphernalia of transport ubiquitous in the world depicted, and fundamental to its comic potential. Indeed, motor vehicles constitute an obsessive theme of Tati's work, in parallel to the pan-European fixation on automobiles throughout the post-war period.

But there is another type of gag, which hardly deserves the name, which involves neither the acrobat-mime nor the peculiarities of moving machines. In *Jour de fête*, there is just one such: when a local farmer, early in the morning of the "great day", collects his daughter's newly-laundered frilly blouse and, holding it aloft on its hanger so as not to soil it, tries to get back into the driving seat of his horse-drawn cart.[236] First he makes to mount in the normal manner, by stepping up on the cart-wheel, but as he is one-handed, he cannot get enough lift; so he goes to the rear, and tries to shin up, but can't keep the blouse high enough, away from the floor of the cart; finally, he finds a way of levering himself up by his knees. The scene is shot with a fixed camera, almost like a candid-camera scene. In *Les Vacances*, a similarly charming interlude occurs when a very young child slowly, delicately, and with great concentration, climbs the steps up from the beach holding a melting ice-cream cornet in each hand (shot 290, in the script). These charming vignettes seem designed to authenticate the more conventionally fabricated parts of both films, to make the whole composition seem more like a window giving on to the world as it really is.

It is in the hotel restaurant that the comedy of everyday life is orchestrated most fully. Henry and his wife arrive early for meals, because they have nothing else to do, and are manifestly bored out of their minds. Their blankly smiling, soup-plate faces give a comic surface to what is in truth a terrifying vision of life without aim. The surly waiter, on the other hand, demonstrates with extraordinary economy the workings of the social world: he adjusts the thickness of the slices he cuts from the roast to the girth of each diner as she or he enters the room. To him that hath . . .

Hulot has nothing. No wife, no words, no known employment or abode. On the beach, in the restaurant, in his car, he is clumsy, he is late, and he is often in a mess. Always eager to please, and never quite succeeding, he embodies the apologetic outsider, whose only real wish is to fit in. Unsurprisingly, he is most frowned upon in the restaurant, with its simple and harsh social ranking device. The only places where he can rise above his fate are the tennis court and the dance floor. For such reasons, it is really very hard to separate Hulot from the feelings and features of his creator. Hulot may not be an autobiographical figure, as Tati repeatedly declared, but he is linked to the man who imagined and performed him by an umbilical cord.

TWENTY-FIVE

On the Beach

The location for *Les Vacances de M. Hulot* was found after much searching amongst French and Belgian seaside resorts in the course of 1951. Lagrange accompanied Tati on these scouting trips, or else did them on his own, keeping a sketchbook of sites and especially of different styles of beach furniture. Saint-Marc-sur-mer, a few miles east of La Baule on the south coast of Brittany, which Tati already knew fairly well, was chosen for aesthetic and practical reasons, chief amongst which was that its bomb-damaged seafront had not yet been reconstructed, leaving empty sites near the beach on which to put up the set at little cost. But the styles of the beach-huts, wind-breaks, and even of the "Villa de Martine", amalgamate things seen by Lagrange all around the coast.

Saint-Marc also has a beach of firm sand set between two outcrops of rock that stretch into the sea. The sand was a problem. It got inside of everybody's shoes, it got into the machinery, and it scratched the film in many of the early takes.[237] But from the western arm of the rocks, the beach in front of the hotel takes on the shape of a gently-raked amphitheatre, almost too much like a purpose-built set to be true.

At Saint-Marc, Tati and Lagrange added a false entrance to the side of the hotel, since the main entrance remained in use during the filming; and they had a plywood platform set up on stilts to serve as Martine's balcony, and also as a perch for some of the high-angle shots of the hotel entrance and beach. Apart from that, however, what we see of the beach and environs in *Les Vacances* is the unmodified face of Saint-Marc in the summer of 1952.[238]

Tati was not an easy man to work with, and he did not mind letting his crew know. "I'll warn you in advance," he said to his recently-graduated script-girl, Sylvette Baudrot, "I don't need continuity. I have all the shots and connections in my head."[239] Nor did he need actors, and especially not stars. Jacqueline Schillio, whom he asked to play the role of Martine, was a friend of a friend (she adopted the stage-name of Nathalie Pascaud for the

Fig. 55: *Some of Lagrange's preparatory sketches for the villa*

Fig. 56: *Preparing to film on the beach at Saint-Marc*

role, but never acted again). She was the wife of a businessman with factories in Lille, and was unwilling to leave home for such a protracted period; so Tati got her husband to act in the film too: he plays Smutte, the man forever called to the phone, just as he was in reality called to the phone during the shoot. Tati also hired music-hall artistes, like Michèle Brabo, and little-known bit-part actors to fill in other roles; as for Fred, well, he was to be the next great comic star. Tati had met Louis Perrault at the "Gala du feu" in Lyon, where he had done his "Impressions sportives" in 1951. Perrault, a businessman of some standing, had been singing light opera as an amateur for years under the name of Bob Rochard, in local venues in Villeurbanne and Lyon.[240] Tati gave him a screen test, liked the results, and declared that a new star had been born. But despite the director's enthusiasm, Perrault did not really get enough space in Les Vacances to make his mark. Like every one of Tati's leading figures and many of his second-role casts, Louis Perrault never acted again, and returned to his business career.

The technical crew, on the other hand, included newcomers who would stay in the business, and also stay faithful to Tati, for many years: Suzanne Baron, the film editor, earned Tati's respect, and he never questioned her authority on technical details; Sylvette Baudrot, despite being "unnecessary", found she could cope quite well with the man, and was happy to return to work on nearly all of Tati's subsequent films; Cady-Films also took on a new administrative assistant, Bernard Maurice, who was to remain Tati's right hand man and "office sweeper" until the end of 1968.

Many of these youngsters were amongst the first graduates of IDHEC, the film school founded by Marcel L'Herbier in 1944, and originally housed only a few doors away from Tati's home in Rue de Penthièvre. Tati mistrusted people who had not learned their trade "on the job", but he was obliged by the rules of the CNC to employ properly qualified technical staff. The days of cinema as an art of amateurs were drawing to a close.

With a budget of about 105 million francs (Jour de fête had been made for a mere fraction of that sum, about eighteen million)[241] and a crew with an average age about half his own, Tati was in a quite different position making Les Vacances de M. Hulot than he had been on his first feature film. As director of Cady-Films, as a major individual backer, as director, co-author and principal actor, Tati considered himself not just as the man in charge, but as the owner of everything that moved.[242] Apart from the "historic chums" of Tati's own generation (Lagrange, Pierdel, Marquet), all location personnel addressed him as "Monsieur Tati";[243] crew and cast would not have dreamed of using the informal tu to such a daunting boss.

The whole team lodged at the Hôtel de la Plage, which continued normal service, with other regular paying guests, throughout the long shoot. The

Fig. 57: *Preparing to film Martine on her balcony*

restaurant and lounge that we see in the film, like the scout-camp hut and one or two other interiors, were recreated in the LTC studios at Boulogne-Billancourt later on (the scouts are extras roped in by Lagrange from the Ecole des Beaux-Arts, where he taught).[244] On some days at Saint-Marc, of course, real holidaymakers had to be asked to keep off the beach; but most of the time the film work proceeded without interrupting the normal summer life of the resort.

Like Sainte-Sévère, but to a much smaller degree, Saint-Marc and its hotel have become "places of memory": the main square has been renamed "Place Jacques-Tati", and in front of where the façade of Martine's house was put up there is now a concrete promenade graced with a life-size statue of M. Hulot looking out to sea (though his broken-off pipe makes it look as though he has a cigar-butt between his teeth). English tourists above all often try to book themselves in to "M. Hulot's bedroom", which does not exist (the skylight which appears to be Hulot's only access to the world outside was put in for the film: there never was a room behind).[245] No doubt the smaller scale of Tatimania by the seaside has to do with the fact that few locals were involved in making the film; in addition, Saint-Marc has been an altogether more prosperous and busy place than Sainte-Sévère over the last fifty years. In addition, of course, *Les Vacances* cannot easily be read as a celebration of Saint-Marc, even if the name of the location was widely known when the film first came out, and has remained well-known ever since. The film's broad subject is not that particular seaside resort, but the generalised idea of a holiday by the sea.

The abstract nature of Tati's second film is established by the credit sequence: waves lapping on the shore. The shooting script concludes: *irrésistible attrait du bain possible*, "the irresistible attraction of the dip to be had". Like the title sequence of *Playtime*, with which it has a family resemblance ("clouds, from right to left"), it paints a mood, not a place, and a story even less.

The people seen at the Hôtel de la Plage all move in peculiar ways reminiscent of the large gestures of grand opera, or of No drama, or the theatre of Brecht. Many of their movements are noticeably slowed-down and larger than life: the Commander points the off-road route to the picnic site from the open-top car with his arm outstretched horizontally for such a length of time that it is clearly a caricature of military manners; when Pierre plays against Hulot on the tennis court, his mime of the exhausted loser overstates the breathlessness that his actual playing could have caused; and the applause of the biased English lady umpire is like a demonstration of how to clap hands. These and many other artificial body movements (which the director tutored on the beach) bring to the cinema a kind of mime that displays itself as mime. At the same time, they are corporeal sculptures based on the way people actually move: Tati insisted that the physical caricatures he created allow us to see better what we really do see when we look around. In a sense, history has proved him right. Tati's direction of his "second roles" in *Les Vacances* has created a new category in the ways we see people in the street or on the beach: there are postures, deportments and gestures that we now call "Tatiesque". The adjective "Hulotian" has to my knowledge never been coined, in English or in French, and if it had been it would not mean anything like Tatiesque: for M. Hulot's antics have a fluidity and grace which is denied to everyone else on screen. Tati may have intended to depict his holidaymakers "without bitterness", as he said in a letter to one of his critics later on,[246] but all the same, *Les Vacances* is less kind to the rest of the world than many viewers have claimed.

Jour de fête is populated with characters who fill the social roles that make up small-town life: the barman, the barber, the postman and the priest, the widow, the butcher, and the farmer's wife; the mayor, the bandleader, the town-crier and a pair of gendarmes, mothers with children, and girls with sore feet. *Les Vacances* is a social comedy too, but the social reality of a seaside hotel is very different from that of a French country town. The world depicted is partly a personal vision of the human comedy, but also a realistic cross-section of international, middle-class life. Apart from the hotel proprietor, the lady who repairs Hulot's tennis racquet, and the duck-shooting laird and his son, the cast of *Les Vacances* is quite devoid of local colour. What Tati offers is a gallery of types that could be found in any hotel lobby of the Western World: the Businessman, the Retired Commander, the English Tourist, the Old Couple, the Serious Young Man of Ideas, the Pretty Girl, the Surly Waiter, the Latin Gambler. Alongside the mysterious M. Hulot, who is of course quite unique.

Maupassant put a smaller version of just such a middle-class world into the stage-coach of *Boule de suif*, where interaction between the characters reveals unpleasant truths about the nature of the bourgeoisie. But although there is a tiny bit of interaction amongst the guests at the Hôtel de la Plage, it soon peters out. The Intellectual does not get his way with the Pretty Girl, the Businessman does not do any deals, and the Commander is not unmasked as a fraud ... Like Flaubert's dream of a book about nothing, *Les Vacances* has all the machinery of narrative, but no story to tell; it seems to be held together by style alone.

TWENTY-SIX

Holiday Mood

The "atmosphere" of *Les Vacances de M. Hulot* is not a mere by-product of Tati's art, but an intricately constructed, entirely thought-out, social and aesthetic aim. Influential critics – André Bazin, Noel Burch, Kirstin Thompson – have puzzled over the film's handling of time – a timeless time, in which events or episodes ("cellular units", in Burch's term) have no natural order, could easily have happened in a different sequence. But that curious absence of directional, end-oriented time-flow is not curious at all in a film that aims to share with us the feeling of what a holiday is like. For we must not forget that a week by the sea was an aspiration, not a reality, for the vast majority of the film's first audiences in 1953, and there is in *Les Vacances*, as in *Jour de fête*, an element of documentary or even pedagogic intent, to show what the seaside (or a village fair) is actually like. Holidays are the very definition of suspended time; the daily hotel rhythm of breakfast, lunch, dinner and *soirée*, clearly marked out by the bell and the interior scenes, structures entirely random activities during the day.

Les Vacances is also, quite noticeably, a portrayal of boredom: for Kirstin Thompson that is in effect the "dominant" which allows us to interpret the film as a unitary whole. The main vehicle of the boredom effect is Henry, otherwise called *Le Promeneur*, the retired gentleman always dressed up to the nines, who arrives early for meals with his unspeakable wife, throws away the sea-shells that she gathers in an entirely trivial routine, and is often the "viewing eye" in shots that include actions by others, including Hulot. The master scenes in the hotel lobby are also visual constructions of collective boredom and civilised despair, as grand and depressing as any Russian country-house novel.

A good deal of the special atmosphere of *Les Vacances* comes from two different aspects of its form: the almost regular alternation between gag sequences and shots of nothing much happening at all; and the overlapping of visual details and especially sound between the two types of sequence. But it is a great pity indeed that none of the versions currently available in video have the original music composed and played on the piano by Alain Romains: Tati remade the sound track almost entirely when he re-launched the film in 1961, and he made further cuts and alterations to picture and sound in a second revision in 1978. The musical theme is wonderfully evocative even in the later orchestrations, but for those who saw and heard the original, it simply does not have the evocative magic of Romains's piano keys.

The tracks of the existing versions use sound bridges of vehicle noises, seagulls, and children's voices on the beach to link sequences of different types, held together by the common aural background noise of the seaside. But there are also several different exercises in switching music between non-diegetic and diegetic streams: the theme tune is played by Martine on her portable gramophone, for instance, and bridges from a shot of her room to a high-angle long shot of the beach as seen from that vantage point, where it reasserts the background theme; in a different way, the jazz music played by Hulot (and later on, by Denis) is first heard as an implausible background track before being revealed as diegetic sound.

It is in *Les Vacances*, too, that Tati abolishes language as a communicative device, and makes the least concession in all of his works to the conventional role of dialogue in film. Hulot says nothing audible throughout the film except when he presents himself, pipe in teeth, to the hotel reception desk. Because of his interdental impediment, he cannot articulate the middle consonant of his name, and utters something like "U-O", twice over. The proprietor removes the pipe for him (Hulot's hands are occupied by his suitcases and gear) and so we get to hear, just once, M. Hulot saying his name. And that is just about it. The light-footed, evanescent and apologetic enigma never says anything again.

The other characters have various language gestures of stunning banality dubbed over: calls to the telephone, calls to the children, remarks on the beauty of the view, but there are in the film no actual conversations, only tokens and simulations of that aspect of holiday life. With our ears as well as our eyes, we are made to be spectators of almost random fragments of a world seemingly devoid of action and significance.

However, it must already be clear that the elements from which *Les Vacances* is made mostly have clear roots in Tati's life and experience. Even the ping-pong match must have been thought up in memory of Bengt Grive; the tennis match is (more clearly) a reminiscence of Tati's own father's game; the picnic repeats part of the motif of *Gai dimanche*. Parcelled out in that way, the material of *Les Vacances* begins to seem almost autobiographical, or at least self-referential to a surprising degree. And this line of argument necessarily leads us to think that the guiltiness and embarrassment that Hulot incarnates must also come from a deep and personal source.

It is often forgotten that *Les Vacances* is the only place in his completed work where Tati simulates the experience of war, in a setting moreover that bore the scars of recent aerial bombardment. Hulot takes shelter in a hut used to store the fireworks that are to celebrate the end of the holiday week; it is dark, he lights a match, and the obvious consequence ensues. In this long sequence, the sound track actually mixes stock sounds of mortar shells and machine-gun fire: the fireworks parody of artillery bombardment (including a direct hit through the open window of Henry's room) is no mere academic fantasy, but a definite intention of Tati. (It was also one of the few physically dangerous sequences to shoot: Tati was quite seriously burned, and the single plaster on Hulot's nose in the morning-after sequence does not reflect the real injuries that the actor-director sustained.)

Fig. 58: *Tati's War? The commander leads the party*

Les Vacances is thus an extraordinarily paradoxical film. Its easily accessible humour made it a children's classic almost immediately; the film soon began a long and still-continuing career as a staple treat for French-language learners abroad (a considerable irony, considering the place that language holds in the film). Yet much of the film consists not of comedy gags, but of atmosphere, constructed by superbly crafted and subtle image- and sound-editing techniques. It has almost no story line, and despite its portrayal of boredom, it seems not to bore its audience at all. It appears to celebrate holidays by the sea, and yet it allows us to see just how trivial, pointless and depressing they are. And it presents a character that it is impossible to sum up or even to get to know or understand, yet whose name and silhouette instantly proved to have an almost universal appeal.

TWENTY–SEVEN

Accident

Les Vacances de M. Hulot was a huge success with critics and public alike when it came out in March 1953. Tati was now a star on the world stage, his every movement the subject of news items large or small in papers the world over. But the very success of the film set Tati at loggerheads with his producer Fred Orain, and thus laid the foundations for a long-drawn-out series of business disasters. From 1953 on, Tati became ever more entangled in legal thickets, and his work was seriously held back by a creaking business edifice that he never gave up trying to own outright. The aim was to remain independent, to be able to be always his own man. Even if that meant borrowing money from friends.

Tati and Orain had never been close friends, and from working together on *Jour de fête* and *Les Vacances* they had learned to trust each other no further than they could spit. The squabble that arose over whether Tati was receiving his proper share from the very substantial income that Cady-Films derived from *Les Vacances* grew so vicious that it ended up in court. Tati would certainly never make another film for Orain, whatever his "exclusive contract" with the company meant. Orain had no wish to work with Tati again, nor even to touch another fiction film.[247]

What, then, would Tati do next? "I have many ideas," he said at the time of the launch of *Les Vacances*, "and if the film does well enough, I will have a third go. But I won't change my ways ... If I have to fit in, then I would rather pack my bags with my music-hall gear and go back on the road with my act."[248]

From this point on, more or less, the story of Tati's career as a director is no longer really part of French cinema history as it is usually narrated and understood. He marched to the beat of his own drum. The success of *Les Vacances* enabled him thereafter to do his own thing, to owe very little to the general fortunes of the French cinema industry, and to avoid all engagement with its debates and its celebrated "movements", and even less to contemporary theories of film. Tati sought and enjoyed splendid isolation, which was also, at times, a fearful solitude. But if his talent and taste had been formed over forty years of practice and observation, he did not simply stand still after *Les Vacances*. As we shall see, the contrary is true: but from 1953 on, it is no longer really possible to approach Tati's work as part of French film culture as it changed and developed through the 1950s and 1960s. It became simply *le cinéma de Tati*.

However, the enervating burden of in-fighting with close associates must be counted a special misfortune in the 1950s when Tati was in every other sense in his prime. At the time, and even more in historical retrospect, *Les Vacances* proved Tati to be a master of his craft, and gave every reason for him to go on to make "Film N° 3" more or less straight away. But as he insisted on doing it on his own, and now without the help of a skilled producer, it was to take him five years.

The "many ideas" in Tati's mind in 1953 must have still included *L'Illusionniste*, the story about a conjuror described above (see above, p. 153);[249] an unwritten sketch on "The Occupation of Berlin", which would have shown how a group of French guest-workers in war-time Berlin got by with a thousand expedients, and cocked a snook at their German over-lords by eating better than they did and having a great deal more fun. Of course it was impossible to make such a film in the 1950s when the myth of *La France Résistante* was at its height. The third idea was a "family comedy", a project which had acquired the title of *Mon Oncle* by the spring of 1954 and must have already been well on the way towards being a shooting script. If it took four more years to get it from script to screen, it was partly because of Tati's clumsy tangle with Orain. With his young administrative assistant, Bernard Maurice, he instituted "Operation Clean-Up", to clean what he considered the Augean stables of the producer's accounts.[250] Tati also began to buy out the two per cent stake that Marquet held in *Les Vacances*, as well as the three per cent stake that had been ceded to his own lawyer, Kohlheim, and so he needed a regular supply of cash to keep up the staged payments.[251] But since the question of receipts from *Les Vacances* was pending in the courts, Tati's alleged share of it was held in escrow by the *tribunal de commerce*. So for the duration of the case, there was no ready money available to plough into a new film. There ought to have been a way out of a corner of Tati's own making, but he didn't find it for quite a while.

Fred Orain, whatever his accounting sins, remained president of the increasingly useful and active technical committee (CST) of the CNC, and was both a respected and an influential figure in the film community. By and large, producers and financiers had a greater long-term interest in the good will of Orain than they could possibly have in the genius of Jacques Tati. And so Tati's isolation – which had its roots in his refusal to mint repeats of Postman François and ramifications in the way he turned down ideas for *M. Hulot in Love*, *M. Hulot in London*, and so on – grew more extreme, even when his fame was at its height around the world.

He also had worries of a more personal kind. His father, Georges-Emmanuel, whose mind had been wandering for some years, at last agreed to retire, and to close down the old business of Cadres Van Hoof. The premises at 8, Rue de Castellane became "Home Service", a shop selling the very latest domestic appliances – vacuum cleaners, washing machines, and other kitchen gadgets that in the early 1950s were accessible only to the kind of wealthy shoppers accustomed to sauntering in the streets between the Madeleine and Place Vendôme. It fell to Jacques to dispose of his father's stock of over seven hundred antique and reproduction frames, and he contacted galleries in many parts of the world – London, New York, the Riviera – looking for the best price.[252] But he did keep back some of the best pieces, and a number of valuable paintings that would eventually decorate his own home.

Tati's growing concern with his parents clearly marks the script of *Mon Oncle*, and no doubt also explains in part why it was this comedy of family relations that Tati chose to make as his third feature film. But since the production company he had co-founded and to which he theoretically remained tied was now a hostile party, he had to set himself up in business all over again before he could even begin to find a way to return to the screen.

When *Les Vacances* appeared, Rue de Penthièvre was still the registered office of Cady-Films. By November 1953, the production company had moved out to Rue Pierre-Charron, giving the Tatischeffs more living space, but also marking a separation of the two entities. For his own use, Tati rented office space elsewhere – first in Rue de la Baume (off Avenue Friedland, near the Etoile), then in Rue Dumont d'Urville, in the same expensive area of central Paris. It was there, in February 1954, that he received out of the blue a letter from a young man in Roanne:

> Sir
> As an actor, director and set designer, I should urgently like to make your acquaintance.[253]

Tati must have received hundreds of more or less similar letters in the wake of M. Hulot's vast success; but to this particular one he had Bernard Maurice reply, after a month or so:

> As M. Tati has made no arrangements about the time and place of his next film shoot, he cannot consider any acting roles ... Nonetheless he grants you permission to telephone him.[254]

Pierre Etaix, who had many more talents than those listed above, was taken aback at the distant formality in which the reply was phrased: but he was overjoyed to get any answer at all. He had decided to write after hearing Tati speak in a radio interview of his admiration for people who could draw: and Etaix, trained originally as a maker of stained-glass windows, was a whimsical and skilful draftsman and cartoonist too. He made the kind of decision that perhaps only happens once in a lifetime: he piled all his belongings into a borrowed twenty-ton truck, and drove straight to Paris, where he made the "permitted" telephone call, and then hung around for months until the great man would finally see him.[255] "Do you want to be an actor?" Tati asked point blank at that historic job interview on 8 August 1954. "No, not at all," Etaix replied. "Good," said the director. "Because acting is the bottom of the pile," What he actually said in French was: *le dernier des métiers*, a stock phrase used by Tati's friend Boris Vian as the title of a recent little spoof he had written on the misery of the actors' trade.[256]

Tati took Etaix on to his staff – as office junior, dogsbody, errand-boy, cartoonist, assistant, sounding board, confidant, as a member of a "family", "whose sovereign and absolute patriarch was Jacques Tati".[257] Small, supple, sensitive and immensely talented, the modest Etaix did not grumble at the tiny allowance he was paid, and threw himself into every aspect of the work of preparing the next manifestation of M. Hulot. He also explored Paris, which he hardly knew, sketch-pad in hand, and came back to the office with drawings of some of the strange and quaint corners he had found. The effect of the steep slope of Montmartre on the lay-out of hillside houses preoccupied him for a while. Tati studied the drawings Etaix did of some bizarre staircases that led both up and down, depending on which side of the house you were on.

One of the purposes of Etaix's being on the payroll was to contribute to what Tati hoped would be a whole Hulot spin-off industry. Gallimard had already paid Tati 100,000 francs in advances for a novelised version of *Les Vacances*, but the money had to be returned when the chosen ghost-writer failed to produce any text. Another writer – Henri Colombet – was contracted, but he too made little headway in producing a story-book version of the film. Etaix's hoped-for role was to invent a Hulot strip-cartoon, perhaps even the designs for an animated cartoon featuring M. Hulot (an Amsterdam newspaper even reported that a series of that kind would soon be on the screen).[258] In the end, however, Etaix did charming illustrations for the novelised versions of *Les Vacances* and of *Mon Oncle* that were finally written by Jean-Claude Carrière, a very young man at the time, on his first commissioned job.[259]

Tati's attempts to stimulate Hulot derivatives as branches of his own

business activity contrast very strongly with his attitude towards other kinds
of commercial exploitation. He was asked by agents to appear in a series of
advertising shorts in Italy, and replied in pompous and haughty tone:

> May I merely point out that if I have a profession of which I am
> particularly fond I have never exercised it to sing the praises of a
> marque of motor car, nor will I use it to laud the quality of your
> spaghetti ... I would have you know that I turned down an offer of
> ten million [francs?] from American television to vaunt the comfort
> and joy of TWA.[260]

It was not until he had been bankrupted for real that Tati deigned to appear
in or to make advertising shorts (for Lloyds Bank, for the dairy-product
company Danone, and for Simca motor cars). But that did not mean to say
that he was not always interested in parallel business ventures, under his own
control, which would use his talents to exploit his own inventions to the hilt.

Tati was certainly believed to be immensely rich in the wake of *Les
Vacances*, and various people by the name of Hulot tried to extract compensation from Tati for his "unauthorised" use of their name:[261] one of the cases
('Tati called it his "custard-pie case") actually came to court, but was thrown
out by the judge.[262] A different Hulot in Enghien-les-bains took a kinder
approach, and invited Tati home for tea: the director used the occasion as a
photo-opportunity, making sure the press was there to see the two Hulots
smiling at each other.

As a public figure, Tati now had to spend a certain amount of time just
denying rumours: that he was going to film in England (though he might
have: see below, p.196), in Hollywood, in Rome ... One of the stories
that first broke in gossip columns certainly had some substance: the Italian
director Federico Fellini had asked Tati to play the role of Don Quixote,
and the Frenchman was quite inclined to accept.[263] Strange as it may seem,
given the very different character of their work, Tati was an unconditional
supporter of Fellini, and considered himself a faithful friend. As he wrote to
France Roche a couple of years later:

> As for the wars over Don Quixote, I had accepted Fellini's invitation
> because I like all he does, and because he has huge problems trying
> to keep his independence, and then because he asked me to help
> him. I hope for his sake that all the Cineramas, Cinepanoramas, and
> Cinetadeos in the world don't prevent him from showing us what
> he had to say with his Don Quixote. He can always count on me,
> even if he has to shoot in 16mm.[264]

To fund his new film in 1955–56, Tati turned first not to the film world, where he was already something of a black sheep, but to old friends. He wrote to Jean-Jacques Broïdo with full estimates for a colour and for a black-and-white version;[265] but Broïdo, who now had major industrial interests in Belgium and Holland, was not interested in muddling his friendship in financial deals. Borrah Minevich also declined the offer to get involved, since he thought Tati should simply franchise out his Hulot act and live off the income (in fact, Borrah was not nearly as rich as he liked to appear: his refusal may have been motivated more by the state of his bank balance than by the reasons he gave). Tati then turned to his foreign distributors, or at least to their Paris agents, since they were making very good returns indeed from his films. At Rue de la Baume, he shared a floor with Morey Getz, then the Paris representative of "GBD", an American distribution company.[266] He persuaded Getz to put up the first stake in his next film: 6.5 million (old) francs, that is to say maybe two or three per cent of what *Mon Oncle* might actually cost, in return for distribution rights in the Americas for *all* of Tati's films (it is not absolutely certain that these were still Tati's to sell; anyway, GBD promptly resold the Latin American rights for *Les Vacances* to Columbia Pictures). On the strength of this, he wrote contracts in his own name with a young writer, Jean L'Hôte, to co-write the scenario of *Mon Oncle*, and with Jacques Lagrange, to act as artistic consultant, in the summer of 1954. He also did tests of colour stock, renting his parents' house at Le Pecq for the purpose (and effectively routing 80,000 francs of Getz's money back into the family budget). But within a year Getz had changed his mind about working with Tati, and asked for all his investment back.[267] However, the film-maker did not have 6.5 million francs any more. As he reported in basic English to Jules Buck, another distributor-producer who, he hoped, would take on the mantle of Morey Getz:

> We have made an arrangement that [Getz] will receive sixty per cent of my own share from *Hulot's Holiday* and this until complete reimbursement. I was obliged to give him ride [sic] away one million francs . . . [268]

So by the end of that year, despite a temporary truce with Orain that had intervened in the preceding May, Tati was still no nearer to making *Mon Oncle* than he had been at the start, and he had even managed to cut his main income stream for quite some time to come.[269] Thus the project arose of making "Tati N° 3" in England, using British money (from Kenwood Films, most probably: letters to Kenwood and to Jan Sorley in Manchester in November and December 1955 make it seem as if the plan was already quite detailed). Tati was also still pursuing a Belgian track, and he submitted detailed costings for *Mon Oncle* to a Brussels production company called SIBI. The proposal shows Tati's very particular way of doing his sums. The estimated total production cost is set at 150 million francs for black and white, and 200 million francs for a colour version. Of this, Tati claimed to be able to provide the entire amount save for 25 million francs. This is how he proposed to find 125 million francs of his "own" money: the script, 10 million; services as director and actor, 30 million; pay-outs due from the *Aide au Cinéma* subsidy scheme (in proportion to seats sold for showings of *Les Vacances* in France), 20 million francs; personal advances from the UK distributor of *Mon Oncle*, 50 million francs; credit accounts at processing laboratories, 15 million francs. It certainly totals 125 million francs, but there is not a penny of Tati's "own money" in the sum! Not surprisingly, SIBI turned down a proposal that would have given Tati 83 per cent of *Mon Oncle* in return for a zero stake, beyond his ideas, his time, and his genius.

Something even worse came to pass in 1955 without Tati knowing at the time. The Eclair film processing laboratory, conducting one of its regular reviews of the stacks of cans of old films on its warehouse shelves, wrote to Cady-Films asking if it wished to continue to store the safety copies and unedited material of *Les Vacances*. Presumably because of the guerrilla war then prevailing between the production company and the director, nobody bothered to answer the letter. Eclair took silence for consent, and junked all the offcuts, double negatives and double positives with optical sound, and all the cans of magnetic sound tapes from which *Les Vacances* had been made, "in consequence of Cady-Films' non-response to our letter". It was a tremendous blow for Tati when he realised just what had happened. And that accidental disappearance of the basic constituents of much of his finest work is one of the main reasons why he came back to *Les Vacances* and to his other early films in the following years, to remake them again and again.[270]

A legal-financial truce with Orain arose in the summer of 1955[271] not so much because of this accident, but because of another, potentially even more serious disaster. Driving through a crossroads late one night in May, with Borrah Minevich quipping away in the seat beside him, Tati failed to see a coach that should not have been where it was, and the heavier vehicle slammed into the driver-side door of Tati's modest Peugeot Frégate. Cars were not equipped with airbags, side-protection bars or even seat-belts in those days, and the injuries Tati suffered were severe: double fracture of the left arm, a broken left knee, badly bruised chest and left eye. He was in plaster until November, and had several operations in the course of the autumn to adjust and then remove the pins in his bones. He left the hospital at Rueil-Malmaison in early July and convalesced at Berck-Plage, not too far away from his medical support, whilst Michou and the children (now nine and six years old) spent the whole summer on the Riviera. His recovery was painful and slow, involving long physiotherapy sessions and many hospital visits right up to the end of the year. He never recovered full rotation of his left wrist, and thus took to wearing his watch on the right. On his left, he now often hung a decorative bracelet or chain.

In later correspondence with his insurance company, Tati claimed that *Mon Oncle* had been ready to shoot when the traffic accident occurred.[272] In practice, Tati was far from being in a position to make a film in the summer of 1955: he had not yet even begun to put the financial backing in place, and there is no reason to believe that the shooting script had yet been written (*Mon Oncle* was registered for copyright and with the CNC in 1956). But if *Mon Oncle* really does belong intellectually and creatively to the earlier 1950s, it would be even more astoundingly prescient than it seems, with its official date of 1958, and its array of gadgets and decors that even now seem archetypes of the ultra-modern.

The great accident of May 1955 was not the first of Tati's smashes, nor was it the last: he seems to have had permanent bad luck on the roads, and was even to be treated to a noisy crash in Manhattan in a Yellow Cab he caught from his hotel. Though he never again suffered injuries quite so serious as those of May 1955, he and Micheline were forever in minor scrapes and traffic infractions, as the vast correspondence with auto insurance companies and not a few letters of apology to the prefect of police in the files of his film company show.[273] The 1955 accident was a turning point, though. It aged Tati considerably, and his hair now did turn completely white. It meant that M. Hulot would never again be able to trip over steps or fall headlong into water, race around a circular spray with a watering can in the dark, or deliver an elegant kick at a body-angle that almost defies the laws of physics. The very profound change in Tati's physical style in *Mon Oncle* is due to the consequences of the crash. And the irruption into Tati's film oeuvre of motor cars, from *Mon Oncle* through to *Trafic*, is a direct reflection of what was happening to the whole of France, and for which Tati's own accident serves as a banal, but personal, symbol.

The expansion of car ownership in 1950s France produced one of the most avoidable hecatombs of modern times, for it was not accompanied by a modernisation of attitudes about rights, roles and (mostly male) behaviour. Abstract doctrines of inalienable rights (unaltered in French law since the Napoleonic code put eighteenth-century philosophical reasoning into statutory form) gave rise to a disastrous organisation of French traffic movement. Driver behaviour was based not on what it was safe or sensible to do, but on manoeuvres one had the "right" to perform, producing a far higher level of mortality than in many similarly industrialised countries with equal or higher levels of car ownership. Attitudes inherited from an aristocratic world view, combined with a universal conspiracy to evade law-enforcement, legitimised behaviour which was often suicidal.[274] It cut a swathe through the French middle classes, killing and maiming many leading figures in cultural and intellectual life – Françoise Sagan (crippled, 1954), Roger Nimier (killed, 1955), Albert Camus (killed, 1960), Johnny Halliday (badly maimed) were amongst the most famous of the hundreds of thousands of road victims in 1950s France. Even the philosopher-novelist Simone de Beauvoir killed a pedestrian with her Simca Aronde.

The growth of motor-car use in post-war France is seen by some as the most visible aspect of the country's modernisation. But the actual behaviour of French drivers was more obviously a form of resistance to the new – they drove as if they were d'Artagnans with a bucking steed, not an inert lump of metal, under their shaky control. It is also not quite right to think of French automania in the 1950s as influenced by American models.[275] The cult symbols – the vehicles chosen by the rich and famous – were not American, but British and Italian, the only ones at the time to maintain that hand-made "quality" which had been the preserve, in pre-war years, of French-based automobile *couturiers*, like Panhard, Levassor, Salmon, and Hotchkiss.

In *Mon Oncle*, M. Arpel offers his wife an anniversary gift of a new, American saloon car, to replace their French-made Simca. American cars had a special status in 1950s France. They were either Belgian (which made them slightly ridiculous in "metropolitan" French eyes)[276] or second-hand purchases from the personal imports of the several hundred thousand US servicemen stationed in France; their size, their decorative features (fins, chrome) and their huge fuel consumption made them inherently absurd. That is the point of Robert Dhéry's charming, lightweight, and not entirely unTaticsque comedy, *La Belle Américaine* (*What a Chassis!*), the story of a white elephant rather than of an object of desire. M. Arpel's choice of a Chrysler underlines his pretentiousness and old-fashioned stupidity, not technocratic modernism, which would have been more pointedly figured by the flying-saucer-like Citroën DS (available from February 1956) or by any one of a number of streamlined European car designs that were then in production.

The modernisation of France through the motor car should much more be seen as a transference to the industrial plane of the secular rivalry with Germany. Those great symbols of the French industrial renaissance of the 1950s – the Renault 4CV and the Citroën 2CV – were Gallic Volkswagens, not French answers to the Town Car or the Mustang. And they were designed quite specifically to reconquer the French Empire in Africa and Asia, with the simplest and sturdiest mechanics imaginable, and very little weather protection. These "little monsters" hardly figure at all in Tati's comic realism of the roads. Moving vehicles in all of Tati's work are literally and metaphorically nostalgic ones: in *Gai dimanche*, he used an antique charabanc for the outing to the country; in 1947, he used a 1911 bicycle for Postman François; in 1953, a 1924 Amilcar for M. Hulot; in 1956–57, a moped (a *vélosolex*) and a regressive image of pretentiousness in the chrome-plated Chrysler; in *Playtime*, a vast array of very ordinary saloons and a Paris bus of a design first introduced in the 1930s; and in *Trafic* (1971), alongside a whole automobile exhibition, the main moving vehicle is an unreliable, antiquated truck, circa 1955.

But as he recovered from his own car crash, in the summer and autumn of 1955, with his script now in more or less final form, the sets more or less fully thought out by Lagrange, his team of young assistants on the payroll and the truce with Orain holding good, Tati still did not have a financial basis on which to shoot his next film.

TWENTY-EIGHT

My Uncle

The reception of *Les Vacances de M. Hulot* was enormously pleasing to Tati, who knew he had made a film of which he could be proud. But it also befuddled him to a degree, for he was now being taken seriously by intellectuals. Senior spokesmen of film art wrote detailed essays on Hulot: André Bazin, the mentor of François Truffaut, reflected at length on the treatment of time in *Les Vacances*;[277] a film historian exhumed Tati's pre-war shorts to explain how his genius had evolved;[278] Geneviève Agel, daughter of the Catholic critic Henri Agel, wrote a dithyrambic, book-length celebration of Tati's whole career, from music-hall to work in progress;[279] and Tati was interviewed in the already-august *Cahiers du cinéma* and in the liberal-Catholic monthly, *Esprit*.[280] Public response was also overwhelming, but simpler to understand: *Les Vacances* grossed no less than 384 million francs in its first three years, about three times what it had cost to make. Tati's audience now numbered many millions of ordinary people, young and old, the world over.

The impact of fame on Tati's obstinate but also hesitant personality is hard enough to imagine, even though he was in a sense prepared for it by the whole adventure of making films; but his sudden promotion to high rank in a cultural universe of which he had, for the most part, no more than a vague idea, must have taken him by surprise. Critics' comparisons of the countryside scenes in *Jour de Fête* to Raoul Dufy's lightly-coloured landscapes, of the views of the coast in *Les Vacances* to the promenade scenes of Eugène Boudin, and of the caricatural deportments of his characters to the human figures of Toulouse-Lautrec would have made sense to the picture-framer that Tati had been; he also probably knew the names of Sartre and Saint-Exupéry, both invoked by Agel to explain Tati's meaning in *Les Vacances*.[281] But he could hardly have measured the pertinence – or the pretentiousness – of her invocations of Rilke, Cervantes, Cocteau, La Bruyère, Desnos, Eluard, Gogol, Beckett, Kafka and St Francis to elucidate the style and meaning of his comedy films. It's not that these are inappropriate or misleading points of cultural reference in a serious attempt to explain the place and importance of M. Hulot; it's just that Tati had never read any of them, and never would. Yet, alongside Chaplin, Sennett, and Keaton, they were the figures in the landscape in which he was now placed by the cultural discourse of his day. An unsolicited testimonial from Harpo Marx ("I am very pleased you enjoyed *M. Hulot's Holiday* so much", Tati replied in English) came from more familiar terrain.[282]

In the spring of 1955, François Truffaut, a young critic who had not yet made his first film, published an incandescent pamphlet-length article denouncing almost the entire establishment of French film-makers. He divided eighty-eight representative names into five classes: the "intentionally commercial" (there were twenty-nine of these), the "commercial but decent" (another twenty-five were hit), a group of fifteen who "should try harder", and then a set of ten very famous names for whom Truffaut reserved his greatest ire, for they embodied the concept of *la qualité française* – makers of costume dramas, adaptations of literary classics, and of "filmed theatre", such as René Clair, Claude Autant-Lara and Tati's friend and early companion, René Clément. Not much of the great tradition of French film art was left after such an energetic clearing-out: just nine real "auteurs", whose names were Alexandre Astruc, Jacques Becker, Robert Bresson, Jean Cocteau, Abel Gance, Roger Leenhardt, Max Ophüls, Jean Renoir – and Jacques Tati.[283] Truffaut's simultaneously puerile, pedantic but not unintelligent ranking unleashed a period of intense polemic and vicious recrimination in the French film world, out of which the *nouvelle vague* emerged within a few years. Tati must have been both pleased and bewildered at the accolade he had received from Truffaut; but he never became part of the "new wave", nor did he participate in the arguments about film style that Truffaut provoked. It is hard to think of anyone less likely than Tati to indulge in the aggressive verbiage, self-ironising techniques, and "subversive" film practices of Godard, Rivette, and the early Truffaut. All the same, the respect in which he was now held by the rising generation of film-art gurus must have had an impact on Tati's conception of his place in the world, and of the value of his work.

In a decade of intensely intellectual preoccupations, in a country riven by its colonial inheritance, by its rivalry with the US and by a strongly left-leaning political culture, Tati did not fit any obvious public role or position, and he held himself aloof from most of the issues that were hotly debated in and around the cinema crowd. He signed a handful of the numerous petitions, protests and manifestos that occupied a great deal of public space in those years (in defence of Ophüls' banned film, *Lola Montès*;[284] in defence of striking Belgian film technicians; and in defence of Henri Langlois, in the later débâcle over the Cinémathèque,[285] and he liked to think of himself as being "on the side of the young". But there were many kinds of innovation of which he was intensely wary, for he knew that, alongside his receipts from Les Vacances, he had earned a symbolic and cultural "capital" that he needed to husband just as much; and to do that he had to avoid disappointing an audience more cultured, more intellectual, and far more political than he was. It must have seemed akin to walking a tightrope without a safety net (for in these domains Tati wasn't too sure how much distance separated him from firm ground) – but certainly much less fun than a real circus act.

Tati's first known trip to the US (a short visit in February 1952, for the launch of Jour de fête in New York) went unreported in France. But when he set off to the States to launch Les Vacances in June 1954, French newspapers treated the departure as an event of national significance: for Tati was now an ambassador for French film, the vanguard of a battle that had never really ceased between the fragmented industry of Victorine, Saint-Maurice, Boulogne-Billancourt and Joinville-le-pont, and the great behemoths of Hollywood. Even more widely publicised was his week-long stay in New York and Chicago in November 1954, when he appeared on a prime-time television variety show, "Fanfare" (NBC).

Television came to France in a particularly unfortunate way. During the Occupation, the German Propaganda department installed TV broadcast equipment in Rue Cognacq-Jay. The Provisional Government took over the still experimental station in 1945 and put it under the wing of the Ministry of Information, where it remained for twenty years. French television thus started life as a government service, and was long suspected of being a government propaganda tool. The Communist Party was as opposed to the spread and use of television as it was, initially, to the introduction of paperback books; but families of a much wider spectrum of political allegiance shared the left's mistrust of the new medium, and many of them forbade their children from ever watching it. Television thus spread more slowly in France than in Britain or the USA, and remained for many years a "suspect" medium, with a strikingly low level of cultural legitimacy.

In such circumstances, an appearance on American TV was a potential threat to Tati's new-found cultural status in France. On his return from New York, the director told stories that served to distinguish his approach to life and art from that of the Americans. He told how he had been invited to a luncheon with a clutch of film financiers, who all ordered steaks of a size not to be seen outside of a French abattoir. After chewing and drinking for a good hour, they said, now let's talk business. – Not until you finished what's on your plate! Tati retorted. And so the "negotiation" came to an end before it had begun. Tati made it sound as if he had scored a one-nil victory for French manners in an away-match against American money.

On the NBC show, Tati performed his "Sporting Impressions", just as he had earlier that year in London, on *Café Continental* (BBC-TV),[286] and in Rome, for a similar series, *Canzonissima*.[287] Tati was surprised to be asked to rehearse his act, which he never did. The producer said: "Too long, Mr Tati. You'll have to cut twenty-two seconds." Tati replied, with all the haughtiness of a prima donna: "It takes the time it takes, and I cannot cut a single second." Apparently, Tati got his way and did his act as he intended, amongst a medley of even more famous stars, including Judy Holliday and Frank Sinatra. True or false, the anecdote as narrated to French reporters let Tati's home fans know that the artist had stood up to the twin tyrants, television and the USA.[288]

Tati was slowly slipping into a kind of public persona, not as a real-life Hulot, but as a principled opponent of things modern and things American. No, he would not make a film in the US: he valued his independence too highly. No, he would not make television programmes, that was not compatible with the way he worked.

To make *Mon Oncle*, which had emerged by 1955 as the definite subject for "Film N° 3", Tati founded an entirely new production company, which he called Specta-Films. Financing for the film itself came from several complementary sources: a large advance from an Italian distribution company, cash from Alter-Films, or rather, from Alain Terouanne, whom Tati had met at a reception connected with the 24-hour motor race at Le Mans, a nominal involvement of Orain and Cady (to release the subsidies generated by *Les Vacances*, which of course still belonged to Cady), and investments from *L'Ecran français* and from Dollivet, of Gray-Films, who effectively did much of the work of a producer. But it was Specta-Films's film, that is to say Tati's; and he hoped, at least at the start, that Specta would be the film's exclusive distributor in France. The structure was no more complicated than many another film financing deal. But the work it was designed to serve was far more complex than anything Tati had attempted before.

The original sketch, dated August 1954, is focused on the relationship between the child, Daniel (the name Gérard was adopted later), and his two father-figures – the busy, efficient, businessman who is his real father, and his irredeemably disorganised and playful uncle, Hulot. The title would have us take "Daniel" as the "point of view" of the film, since only he can call Hulot *my* uncle; alternatively, we could take "Daniel" as a mere stand-in for Tati, who would then be representing his own (imaginary) childhood mentor in fun; but most viewers surely override such possibilities, and take the "my" for themselves, that is to say, they see

Hulot as a *universal* uncle-figure, a visiting angel that any child would love.

During the composition and making of *Mon Oncle*, Tati was in the middle of two quite difficult father-son relationships in real life. On the one hand, he was quite worried about the effect that his celebrity would have on his own children, and most concerned lest they grow up spoiled; so he shifted his son Pierre from school to school in search of a more protected and disciplined environment than a world-famous film star could provide in central Paris. On the other hand, he knew he did not have long to make peace with his own father; perhaps the time for such things was already past. The entire weight of the original sketch lies on the need for fathers and sons to find a way of being children together. Despite Tati's frequent claims that he "had nothing to say" in his films, he most certainly imparts a clear message about family feelings in the original sketch of *Mon Oncle*.

In French, there is a phrase for a rich relative who swims in from out of the blue, distributing largesse, or who acts as a kindly lender of last resort: *un oncle d'Amérique*, "an American uncle". The Hulot-role of *Mon Oncle* is quite clearly an inversion of it: a "French Uncle" who has no money, no job, no capacities for anything much apart from warmth, conviviality, tolerance and (fairly mild) fun.

The Hulot of the original sketch is not vastly different from the Hulot of the film, but there are a few details that link him more firmly to Tati's own past. The original Hulot spreads good humour by playing the piano (a compensation for Tati's own inability to respond to the lessons of Mlle Saulx), and it is through music, not through a street-urchin's gag, that emotional contact between father and son is made on the final page. Hulot has been packed off abroad (in the film, he is sent to the provinces) and Arpel returns home from the station (in the film, Hulot leaves by plane):

> His son, he can feel, needs him. So, putting his briefcase aside, for the first time he looks over his son's games, and takes part in them.
>
> He's not much good as a beginner but he is full of good will, and soon Daniel gains confidence and asks his dad for more.
>
> Now feeling quite at ease, the boy ventures to confide something in his father's ear. The latter accedes to the request, opens the piano in the lounge, and sight-reads the old tune that he had been asked to play: it's the one Hulot played for his nephew after their wonderful escapades and that he left behind him as a souvenir of something fantastical.
>
> Through this first exercise, M. Arpel, without realising it, appears to his son as a possible representative of his uncle Hulot.
>
> – The End – [289]

The original Arpel is also slightly different from his film incarnation – less a ridiculous figure than a fearsome one, in control of absolutely everything in his factory and in his home: "his enormous swatch of keys makes this obvious to the eye" (p. 7). As "the perfect image of the bourgois" (p. 2), Arpel clearly expresses some of Tati's resentment of his own father's strict control; just as the obsessively house-proud Mme Arpel must tell us something (though probably not a great deal) about Tati's attitude to his mother, of whom he remained extremely fond.

Fig. 59: *An early design by Jacques Lagrange for the Maison Arpel in* Mon Oncle

The scenario is also built around the distinction of the two different forms of urban life that we find in the film: the modern, suburban villa, and a traditional, cramped and twisted "old quarter" of Paris. The mere positing of the two quarters makes *Mon Oncle* a more complex – and a more expensive – film than either of Tati's two previous works. Tati might well have got the idea of making a drama and a comedy out of the post-war reconstruction boom from his conversations with Jacques Lagrange; but he could have got it just as easily from simply looking around.

Housing was perhaps the most acutely difficult problem in all European cities in the first decades after the war. In many places – notably Milan, parts of London, Frankfurt and Marseille – the solution imposed was the high-rise apartment building, using ferro-concrete and modular construction methods. In *Mon Oncle*, graceless blocks and towers of this kind are glimpsed in the background of shots of the "hole in the wall" through which Hulot, the stray dogs and the schoolboys pass as they cross between the two worlds. But the main image of the modern in the film is not at all characteristic of post-war housing in Paris and its suburbs. The Maison Arpel was designed by Lagrange as a pastiche of the International Style, which really dates from the years after the First, not the Second World War. It implements aesthetic ideas which were not up-to-date at all, and that is the often misunderstood point of Lagrange's work for the film. Le Corbusier's Maison Jeanneret of 1923, or others by Robert Mallet-Stevens backing on to the same cul-de-sac, are the classic instances of what Lagrange turned into the "Arpel Style".[290]

> I made a collage of illustrations from architecture reviews, with scissors and paste. I took bits from here and bits from there – port-hole windows, silly pergolas, winding garden paths to make the plot seem larger . . . It's an architectural pot-pourri.[291]

But the pastiche of what was indeed new thirty years earlier was also, in the view of Lagrange, an accurate history of one part of the post-war building boom. *Mon Oncle* gives a good account of the post-war years . . . "when young architects who wanted to be avant-garde . . . fell into the same mistakes as their grandfathers," Lagrange explained. Or in the more loaded account of an architectural historian: "With sharp irony, Tati revealed the transformation in the meaning of forms of classical modernism from avant-garde statement to petit bourgeois fashion item."[292] The irony was not evident to all the *petits-bourgeois* who saw the film: one of them liked the design so much that she ordered her architect to build her an identical home. Maison Arpel *bis* is still inhabited today, in a suburban street in Massy-Palaiseau.[293]

In the scenario, all that Tati calls for is a house that is pretentious, impeccably clean, and equipped with all the latest electrical labour-saving devices. He gives no other details of its appearance and internal design, calling it "a magnificent factory of cleanliness". Lagrange gave the Maison Arpel its actual form, going from his collage first to water-colours, then to real architectural drawings. It is perhaps a measure of the slow rate of change in twentieth-century architecture that the resulting construction still looks very modern. The Maison Arpel is now almost a classical design, yet it remains firmly associated with an idea of the avant-garde.

Tati's 1954 scenario gives far more detail about the garden, imagined rather differently from the courtyard actually constructed at the Victorine studios:

Fig. 60: *Le Corbusier – villas La Roche/Jeanneret (1923)* © *FLC*

Fig. 61: *A later stage of Lagrange's ideas for the Maison Arpel*

> A large pond with a fountain serves as a goldfish bowl, and to add
> a touch of reality, a small stream flows down from some recently-
> purchased rocks.
>
> A ceramic cat watches over the garden, which is actually not easy
> to use, since you are forever afraid of upsetting things, or dirtying
> or spoiling the decorations. (p. 1)

The fish-fountain that replaces the cat seems also to have been an idea by
Lagrange: he did numerous sketches that seem to offer alternative ways of
imagining a decoration whose pretentiousness overwhelms any aesthetic
dimension. The house itself is not at all ugly; the formal garden seems only
a slight exaggeration of French garden traditions; but the fish-fountain is
wonderfully absurd, a self-designating, vulgar and idiotic decoration. It alone
specifies the satirical intent of the entire composition. Without the fish,
indeed, we might have been fooled.

The water-spouting sea-bass that rises vertically from a pond far too small
for it was a nightmare to install, to operate, and to film. For a start, water is
transparent, and can barely be seen in a colour film. To make its gurgitations
visible, the fish-water had to be coloured dark blue; and to make it gurgle at
all, a whole complicated set of pipes and pumps had to be got to work, which
they rarely did properly when the cameras were running. On one occasion,
the reservoir tank burst; on others, the pipes sprang leaks all over the place.
From a practical, film-making point of view, the fish-gag was not remotely
efficient; but it could not be dispensed with, as the fish theme had been
firmly woven into the "text" of the old-quarter takes, shot near Paris ahead
of the main shooting at the Victorine studios at Nice.

The third location posited by the original script of *Mon Oncle* is Arpel's
factory: "His business consists of shredding a whole range of materials (rags
and bones, old shoes, old iron) and turning them into wonderful objects in a
new material ..." (p. 3). The fascination with plastics, polystyrenes and
recycling materials is a central part of the heroic myth of the post-war
industrial renaissance. Not for nothing does the slightly drunk uncle advise
the Graduate, in the American film of that name, to "get into plastics";
and in France, a poet no less distinguished than Raymond Queneau wrote
the commentary for a celebrated documentary on how plastics were made,
Le Chant du Styrène (a pun on the "The Siren's Song", *Le Chant du Sirène*).
It is far from certain that plastic products like the hosepipes of the "Plastac"
factory in *Mon Oncle* could be made from recycled waste; but the recycling
allows a channel of communication between the "old world" and the
"new", and is an important thematic and formal element in the film.

Tati the film-maker also recycles material of his own in *Mon Oncle*, which is the first of his films to introduce those kinds of allusion and self-reference that bind his half-dozen separate films into an oeuvre.

The cycling postman of *Jour de fête* is recalled in a tiny sequence which shows Pierre Etaix – in uniform, on a pedal-cycle – calling at the Hulot residence in the old town. The concierge is plucking a chicken in the front yard; Etaix makes a loud and convincing clucking noise, and for a split second, the concierge (and perhaps members of the audience) wonder if she is not pulling feathers out of a live chicken, in a tiny but transparent allusion to the farmyard sound deceptions of Tati's first feature film.

M. Hulot's permanently furled umbrella, in *Mon Oncle*, can also be seen as the re-deployment of a detail from *Les Vacances*. As a long, thin object implausibly protruding at an angle of thirty degrees off vertical from the rear panniers of Hulot's moped, it recalls the butterfly-net that sticks out in much the same way from the rear of the earlier Hulot's Amilcar, and both serve the same visual function of mimicking Hulot's gawky height and off-vertical posture (an iconic function reinforced by all the poster-designs for both films). But umbrellas had also been used in one of the shortest, tightest and most anthropomorphic gag sequences in *Les Vacances*. The spluttering Amilcar draws into a village square and stops in front of a *café-tabac*. Two men shoot out of the bar just as the car stops and swerve elegantly around its bonnet before crossing the road towards us (one of the men is in fact Tati, but you can only see that if you slow down the film or freeze the video frame). Each carries an attaché-case, and strapped to the top of each attaché-case is a furled umbrella with a traditional curved handle. In the next shot, they are at the bus-stop, in a milling crowd trying to find seats on the coach, which we presume will take them all to the seaside. There are two entrances, one at the front and one at the rear: each man makes for a different line, then, making no progress in the hectic rush, changes his mind and tries to join the other queue. As the two brush past each other in their reciprocating inversion of plan, the handles of their umbrellas lock together, and are thus pulled out of their retaining straps. We get a short, clear close-up of two embracing umbrellas on the ground, abandoned as the bus pulls away on its journey to a seaside resort where (for the duration of these timeless holidays) it never rains. It does not rain in *Mon Oncle* either, nor will it ever rain on the gleaming sets of *Playtime*, where the umbrella of *Mon Oncle* returns as an even more insistent icon of M. Hulot's old-fashioned demeanour. Only in Tati's farewell to narrative cinema, in the closing shots of *Trafic*, does his umbrella unfurl, together with a thousand others, bobbing spots of colour in a rain-swept car-park in Amsterdam. The embracing umbrellas of *Les Vacances* finally release a sense, constructed over twenty years and four movies: for in the rainy Dutch car-park, Hulot at last puts his arm around a young woman, and seems to find a happy, if not exactly erotic, end.

A third important "interwoven" element, first introduced in *Mon Oncle*, is the flickering glare of the television screen. After their hygienic dinner on the terrace, M. and Mme Arpel move their spidery metallic bucket seats to the salon and switch on the evening's TV programme (there was only one channel in 1956–58, so the question of choice does not arise). We see them from behind, but know they are watching television because of the unlovely, unstable blue glow of the cathode-ray tube that illuminates the entire frame. Similarly, in *Playtime*, the long sequence of Hulot's visit to Schneider in his "fishbowl" flat, seen exclusively in long shot through plate-glass windows, is illuminated by a flickering blue light from the television screens in his and his neighbour Giffard's apartment. In one short take, however, we do get to see what is being broadcast – a boxing match! The reprojected image is quite possibly (though the dimensions of the image make it hard to be sure) the sole surviving clip of Tati himself doing his boxing "impression" at the Bal Tabarin in 1938. Only in *Trafic* does Tati clearly show us a television screen front-on – in the back room of the border post, where no one is watching it, despite its showing one of the most fabulous images of our century: the clip of the first (and, still now, the only) men to set foot on the moon.

Fig. 62. *Lagrange's sketches for the dress of "The Neighbour" in* Mon Oncle

TWENTY-NINE

The Old World and the New

According to the papers, only eleven
per cent of Paris flats have bathrooms
RAYMOND QUENEAU,
ZAZIE DANS LE MÉTRO (1959)

Locations

Mon Oncle was shot between 10 September 1956 and 25 February 1957 at three separate locations – Saint-Maur, for the "old town" square scenes, Créteil, then barely more than an unlovely development site on the southern rim of Paris, for the "waste ground", school and Plastac factory sequences, and at the Victorine studios in Nice, where the Arpel house set was constructed.

More than half the sequences of the finished film are set in the Arpel house and barely more than a fifth in Saint-Maur, a proportion that seems surprising, so clear does the balance and opposition between old town and new house seem. The vast majority of the Maison Arpel scenes are exterior: as in *Jour de fête* and *Les Vacances de M. Hulot*, Tati only rarely takes his camera indoors. So although we do have two main sequences in the kitchen (Hulot's pot-dropping episode, and Gérard's antiseptic dinner), one in Gérard's bedroom, and two important visits to the main lounge, the Maison Arpel remains essentially an outdoor place, or rather, perhaps, an expressive object seen as a "thing in itself". The keyword for the interior design of the place, repeated three times by Mme Arpel, is: *tout communique*, "everything communicates". With its open staircase and its plate-glass sliding doors, the internal space of the Maison Arpel is indeed ill-defined. Since "everything communicates" in visual and spatial terms, the house requires constant tidying and cleaning throughout, since nothing can be hidden away. Lagrange thus produced a design which makes entirely plausible Mme Arpel's obsession with keeping order in the house, which was the basic constraint that Tati gave him in the original script.

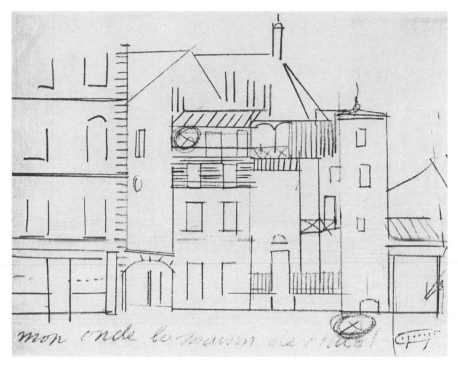

Fig. 63: *An early drawing of Hulot's house in* Mon Oncle *(Jacques Lagrange)*

Family relations

Tati's presentation of wives, mothers and matrons throughout his oeuvre is fairly consistent and not at all kind. In the pre-war shorts, he created an ambitious martinet in the wife of the gormless Roger (*On demande une brute*) and a rough-voiced farmwife as the mother of the other Roger, in *Soigne ton gauche*. In *Jour de fête*, fairman Roger's wife is a tense, suspicious, and domineering figure. In *Les Vacances*, with its larger cast and its subject of family holidays, there is a larger variety of wife-and-matron roles: Henry's wife (the Stroller), whose dialogue is perhaps the most comically banal of all Tati's characters; mothers knitting on the beach and squawking commands to a variety of children; and the prudish aunt of Martine, all give an image of wifely and motherly behaviour that seems to express not just a comical view of family life, but even a degree of resentment. But *Mon Oncle* is the first and only film of Tati's in which intimate family relations between wife, husband, brother, and child constitute the main theme.

The Hulot of *Mon Oncle* is some kind of poor relation of a successful middle-class family, but not a member of any other class. He remains a gentleman, and he remains *Monsieur* Hulot. Even whilst his sister calls her

Fig. 64: *The set of Hulot's house built into the main square of Saint-Maur*

husband "Charles", she manages never to address Hulot by a forename he does not have. He remains defined in the dialogue of the film exclusively by his relationships to others – "your brother" when Charles is talking to his wife, "your uncle" when she is talking to her son. This odd formality presumably derives from Tati's determination not to humanise his "lunar Pierrot" too much; but it leaves a distinct impression of oddness in the French-language version of the film, and even more so in the English.

The picture that Tati paints of a problematic family almost certainly has more to do with his home at Le Pecq than with his life as a parent at Rue de Penthièvre. All the same, Michel Chion is probably too clever by half when he sees the twin porthole windows of the Maison Arpel spelling out the two vowels – "o – o" – in the maiden name of Tati's mother, Van Hoof.[294] Mme Arpel, despite her sincere concern for the well-being of her son and her brother, is not the subject of any emotional or dramatic development: it is the father who is redeemed at the end when, released by the departure of Hulot from the jealousy that had come between him and his son, he can at last begin to express a degree of paternal warmth. *Mon Oncle* is not exactly a misogynistic work; but its affective focus concerns relations between men and boys, and it leaves women as no more than comic caricatures of them-selves – remarkably similar, in fact, to cartoons. Mme Arpel is the forerunner of the preposterous fat ladies of Tati's later television advertising films for Danone, and a representative of the mildly silly middle-aged blue-rinse set who fly in and out of the Paris of *Playtime*. Her husband, on the other hand, seems to have deeper personal roots, and to be in the film to express not a caricatural idea of fatherhood, but some of its problems and regrets.

The English version

A surprising and welcome piece of news reached Tati when he had settled in Nice, with Michou, Sophie and Pierre, who changed school once again. Even if GBD had been cheating him on what he was owed from the US distribution of *Les Vacances*, it had done a decent job of attracting critical attention, and Tati (with Henri Marquet) had received a nomination for the "Best Writing, Story and Screenplay" award of 1956 from the American Academy of Motion Pictures – the award more commonly known as the Oscars. Whether it was this news that prompted Tati to shoot *Mon Oncle* twice over – as an English-language and as a French-language film – is not known, but if the double shooting had already been planned, the news from Hollywood must have bolstered Tati's resolve. For it was the American market that held the key to his commercial standing, and, as many French writers and film-makers have realised, would also have a determining influence on his cultural position in France. For the superficial anti-Americanism of post-war French opinion-makers masks a deeper and more complex cultural dialogue, with historic roots in the eighteenth century: to be taken seriously in the only other country to have had a successful revolution lends enormous weight to your position inside France.

The American market has always been fairly unwelcoming to sub-titled films, and Tati – now a master in the art of dubbing, since he always used post-synchronised sound – could more easily and more cheaply produce an English-language version of the new film than a US dubbing studio, or so he thought. The English-language *My Uncle* is not just the same film with a different voice track: it is a curious attempt to create a visual and linguistic amalgam of America and France. All the shots where written language figures in the story – in the credit sequence, where the title *Mon Oncle* is scrawled on a wall, or outside the school, where we see ECOLE on the signboard, or in the factory parking lot, where SORTIE is painted on the ground – were reshot with English-language signs put in place; for many scenes with no translation requirement, different takes were used, and overall a great number of editing changes were made. As a result, the English *My Uncle* is about ten minutes shorter than the French, even though it includes some material never seen in France – for instance, the sinister, quasi-surgical disinfectant vaporiser device that Mme Arpel uses on Gérard's toast and boiled egg.[295]

My Uncle (re-titled *My Uncle Mr Hulot* for its later re-release in the US) is a more profoundly patronising film than *Mon Oncle*. It seeks to create the bizarre fiction of a French environment in which the middle classes speak a stilted, outrageously regal British English, whilst the populace – including Georgette, the Arpels' otherwise Spanish maid – babbles on in French. In that sense it reproduces a standard French nightmare with its roots at Omaha Beach, and behind that at Waterloo (if not at the Battle of Hastings, which produced the inverse result), of a country over-run by modernising, economically powerful, English-speaking overlords. But that nightmare vision also enhances what Tati imagined to be an English-speaker's perception of post-war France – a quaintly backward tourist paradise where you can perfectly well manage in English, except when you have to deal with the peasants. Thus Gérard speaks English, yet his companions in boyish crimes (the tricking of passers-by into walking into lamp-posts, the deception of motorists with a dustbin lid) speak to each other in French. Leather-jacketed chauffeurs who mistakenly believe they have been rammed from the rear expostulate with the other drivers in French; whereas a leather-gloved gentleman subjected to the same trick expresses his oily indignation to the lady driver behind him in upper-class British English.

British English has the sound of snobbery in American as well as French ears, and in a comedy we should perhaps not seek too much linguistic verisimilitude. Nonetheless, the language-fantasy-land of *My Uncle* is, it seems to me, an entirely French creation. It uses English in exactly the way French culture feared English would be used, as the vehicle of distinction, superiority, and wealth. It marks a particular moment in French cultural anxieties, one that would be superseded by the far more convincing mongrelisation of tongues in the truly Anglo-French dialogues of *Playtime*.

Tati took the opportunity of the re-dubbing to alter quite significantly one aspect of the "charming and authentic" market scene in Saint-Maur. Whereas in the French a lady buying grapefruit from an Italian costermonger gets cross because she thinks she has been overcharged, in *My Uncle* it is an English tourist from the Home Counties who gets cross with a French fruit-and-vegetable man. "Vous avez any grapefruit, s'il vous plaît?", she says, and then: "Vous avez cheated me, my good man!" Through this truly awful Franglais, Tati creates another one of his veiled windows on to the world – a distanced viewer of quaint goings-on in an archaic and (from this point of view) caricatural French town.

May 1958

It is partly because of the double dubbing to be done that it took Tati more than a year to bring out the two versions of *Mon Oncle* after the shooting was completed, but it is also partly because he liked to work slowly, and to keep on playing around with his celluloid material. When it did finally come out, in mid-May 1958, *Mon Oncle* could have been a disastrous flop – for its release coincided exactly with the collapse of the Fourth Republic, an only-just-averted outbreak of civil war, and the dramatic return to power of Charles de Gaulle. But the potential disaster turned to Tati's advantage. His much-trumpeted comedy had nothing to do with Algeria, with the army, with politics, or with de Gaulle, and for that very reason offered relief and release from the tense and volatile situation on the streets. These circumstances of the film's first reception also led reviewers and audiences to see *Mon Oncle* as *only* a comedy film, or else – equally erroneously – as a militantly satirical portrait of modern life, an onslaught on the French bourgeoisie, and an outright attack on modernism in architecture and design.

Idleness

The Hulot of *Mon Oncle* is more manifestly idle than his previous incarnation in *Les Vacances* because here he is not on holiday, but at the same time he is not exactly at work. And what is work, in Tati's world? It is presented more as a ritual than as productive activity. The secretaries at Arpel's factory spend their time chatting and doing their nails until "Dackie" passes by in the corridor ahead of his master and their boss; only then do they interrupt their convivial and natural activities and turn to their typewriters to create the clacking sound of secretarial work. The labour that Hulot performs in his brief employment at Plastac is to supervise a piece of machinery that does all the work by itself. Gérard is supposed to do his homework, but plays instead with a toy book that imitates and mocks the fish-fountain in his front garden. Mme Arpel certainly labours over her domestic space, but her exaggerated dusting and polishing movements are clearly presented as domestic rituals, not as productive work.

Hulot does not do nothing. He plays with Gérard, looks after him, and gives him a good time; he accedes to all his relatives' requests (to attend a garden-party, to try to get a job, and in the end, to leave Paris for some distant province); most of all, though, he entertains neighbourly relations with all the inhabitants of the old town, from the rag-and-bone men to the concierge. His idleness is not an absence of work, but a positive form of

Fig. 65: *Jacques
Lagrange in Paris,
around 1960*

social behaviour, and a clear pole of value in the world of the film. Idleness
has of course long been associated with culture, and with the cultivation
of values higher than those of production or enrichment. Tati was almost
certainly not aware of Goncharov's spectacularly inactive *Oblomov* or of
Samuel Beckett's *Molloy*. More likely as a source is the poet and novelist
Raymond Queneau, a long-standing friend, with as great an interest in idlers
and idling as Tati had. He too saw the right to do nothing very much as a
fundamental freedom of ordinary folk (see, for example, *Pierrot mon ami* and
The Sunday of Life). An even more explicit assertion of the right to idleness
can be found in René Fallet's extremely funny novel *Le Beaujolais nouveau est
arrivé*, where self-exclusion from the economy of labour is presented as the
very noblest form of resistance. In rehearsing the old town scenes of *Mon
Oncle* at Saint-Maur, Tati gave long and repeated lessons to the set photographer, André Dino, who plays the roadsweeper. The important thing, he
explained, was to make sweeping actions that are at each point interrupted
by something entirely plausible – a passer-by, a dog, a stray leaf blowing
the other way – so that without ever putting the broom down, the sweeper
never actually sweeps a single thing. Such a mime act is not meaningful
if it is done only once; like many of Tati's most signifying gags, the

non-sweeping sweeper only acquires significance when seen two, three, or four times over, at different points in the film. And the meaning is only recuperated by the spectator if attention is paid not just to the individual takes, but to their relationship and connectedness in the film. Tati clearly wants his viewers to read his film in the way that they might read a book. The proper observation of idleness is a kind of work – the work Tati claimed went into all his film ideas, and which his audience has to learn how to do.

Work

Making a film that values idleness was hard work for everyone involved, and Tati came close to exhausting the cast and the whole crew. Étaix was responsible for keeping the market stalls in the "old town" takes identical in appearance for every day of work at Saint-Maur. He would get up at the crack of dawn

Fig. 66: *Tati teaching André Dino how to not-sweep the streets*

to purchase fresh vegetables, fish and foliage, and then lay them out before the day's shooting could begin. Why were the stalls not decorated with plastic imitation fish and fruit, which a real-life Plastac could have turned out for a few pence? Ah, that would not have been "realistic", and Tati insisted every day on perfection in the achievement of realism in his kind of comedy film. In the studio set in Nice, many of the Arpels' domestic gadgets had to be simulated by painstaking, manual means. No functioning steak-flipping hot-plate device was available, so the slimmest of the crew (Etaix, once again) had to stay squeezed in the wall cavity at the rear of the kitchen set to pull a primitive lever at precisely the right moment for each of the takes of the kitchen scene. Nor was there a real photo-electric control mechanism for the garage door, which was pulled up and down by a hidden hand. Tati's demands on Etaix, Cottin and Marquet stretched the "gadget-men" to their limits. They invented the pedalo-lawnmower for their boss, but had unending trouble making it work. Tati was pitiless in his demands on his team, and seemed to enjoy making them run round in circles. In a not untypical outburst of frustration and anger, Marquet once said of his old chum and boss: "I would like to strip him, tie him to a stake, and cover him in shit!" [296]

Dogs play an important role in all of Tati's films, but nowhere more so than in *Mon Oncle*. The pack was not purchased, but adopted from the pound of abandoned beasts run by the SPA (the French version of the RSPCA). Tati, who always had a dog at home – and called each one of them Azor – needed a motley and scruffy pack because of the role that dogs play in the film. Alongside Hulot and the rag-and-bone men, they are the main channel of communication between the old town and the new, and it is they who, by playing with Dackie, provide a parallel to Gérard's escapades with his rougher, old-town playmates. Tati was good with animals, and saw no difficulty in getting dogs to obey his will. But it was the stunt-team that had to get the dogs to do the right thing at the right time, since Tati was either in front of the camera, or behind it, in most of the planned dog episodes. They just had to learn how to do it – from him.

Tati was particularly pleased with the way he disposed of the dogs at the end of the shoot. Instead of returning them to the SPA, he advertised in his usual newspaper, *Le Figaro*, asking for homes for dogs that were soon to be film stars. Of course he got a massive response, and was able to provide all his hounds with a comfortable life thereafter. All except for "Dackie", the Arpels' sausage-dog: he had belonged to poor Borrah Minevich, who had died suddenly shortly after the shoot began. Dackie went to Jean-Jacques Broïdo, who kept him in the family when they all moved to Geneva after de Gaulle came to power in 1958. A direct descendant of Dackie still lives in the Broïdo household.

Some of the gags in *Mon Oncle* seem almost designed to stretch stage-management skills beyond reasonable limits. For instance, Dackie had to be made to cross the magic-eye door-closing device with his narrow tail erect. This was necessary only because of the type of dog involved, and the height at which the magic eye had been set. It is an enormously time-consuming and frustrating exercise to make an untrained pet dog waddle *with his tail erect* precisely where you want it to go – and also, in this case, rather pointless, because exactly the same gag, and exactly the same effect, could have been achieved either by using a slightly larger breed of dog, or by setting up the electronic beam at a more appropriate height. Tati seems to have wanted to impose arbitrary and maddening difficulties on his team. As if to prove how good he was – with dogs, in this case, but also with much else besides.

The story of the "first factory gag" is exemplary in this respect. Arpel has found a job for the unemployable Hulot at a factory run by a friend. Tati thus

Fig. 67: *Tati and Pierre Etaix on the set of* Mon Oncle

needed a device by which Hulot, on his first day at the job, would get sacked in a minute or two of screen time. He asked Etaix to come up with something. The young man brought Tati an idea: no, that's not right, the director said. So Etaix devised another ploy for getting Hulot out of the job: no, too much like a custard-pie trick, said the director. And so it went on, until, in exasperation, Etaix declared the task logically impossible – Tati would have to invent a real *story* of how Hulot might lose a job before starting it, or else he would have to skip the sequence entirely. *I'll tell you something*, Tati said slowly, with his hand over his mouth, as it often was. *You think too much*. The gag finally used to manage this episode in the film struck Etaix as more complex and implausible than anything he had proposed. Hulot steps in loose dry plaster as he climbs the steps to the back door of the factory; his shoes thus leave white prints on the tiles; whilst waiting to sign on with the secretary, he tries to clean the soles of his shoes, and places them on the desk-top to do so, leaving what appear to be footprints there; when the secretary finally comes in, she deduces from the footprints on the desk that Hulot has been standing on it to look over the partition into the ladies' room; and so he is dismissed as a peeping Tom.

This is one of the small number of rather curious sexual notations in *Mon Oncle*, whose Hulot seems less bashful and less dumb than his seaside predecessor. At the garden-party organised by his sister – with a view to getting him to marry, moreover – Hulot appears to whisper a bawdy joke in the caftan-clad woman's ear. In his own lodging with the crazy stairways, Hulot encounters the concierge's daughter, making her way from the shower back to her room, wearing nothing but a towel. In other scenes, the same girl seems to have a crush on Hulot, who treats her kindly, but also seems to leave her without regret at the end of the tale. There is even a romantic interlude of a virtually traditional kind in *Mon Oncle*, when two lovers are seen at the canalside, exchanging sweet words by the light of the moon: the sequence quickly turns into another kind of traditional scene when the young man shows off his courage and skill by diving into the canal to save a drowning man – except that it is only a load of useless plastic tubing that has been shoved over the parapet. It would be an exaggeration to say that Hulot is at last given a sexual identity in *Mon Oncle* – for he remains essentially unspecified in that as in so many other domains – but it does seem that Tati wanted to incorporate at least a few morsels of the ingredients of more traditional narrative film. For *Mon Oncle* was going to be his bid for the Oscars, and for that he needed to persuade American viewers to watch, to understand, and to laugh.

From Cannes to Hollywood

Mon Oncle was shown at the Cannes Film Festival, just before its commercial release in Paris in May 1958, and it won the Special Prize (*Prix Spécial du jury*) for films not competing officially for the Golden Palm (won that year by the Soviet masterpiece, *Letaiut Zhuravli*, "The Cranes Are Flying"). Distribution deals for Belgium, Holland, Scandinavia and Italy were already in the bag, as was the Spanish-language version for Argentina and Mexico; *Mon Oncle* was clearly already set on a highly profitable international career, and on the strength of its very substantial advances, Tati felt able to set himself up in the manner to which he aspired. He also had family needs to attend to. His father Georges-Emmanuel had died on 23 December 1957, leaving his widowed mother Claire in the now half-empty "Ermitage" at Le Pecq. So Tati sold his quaint abode in Rue de Penthièvre whilst scouting around for a suitably commodious house in the western suburbs, and in the meantime moved with his whole family to live with his mother in his childhood home. These domestic moves describe a curiously parallel line to that of *Mon Oncle* itself, which celebrates – alas, just a few months too late – the reconciliation of an over-defensive father and a fun-loving son. By the time *Mon Oncle* began its victorious world career, the French Family Tatischeff had acquired a magnificent old house in Saint-Germain-en-Laye, which, if not quite as grand as the Tatischeff mansion that his great-grandfathers had ruled over in Moscow, was nonetheless a very tangible sign of significant wealth. Monsieur and Madame set about modernising the house in Rue Voltaire, and equipped it with all the latest gadgetry – but, unlike the Arpels, they had their kitchen cupboards, fridge and freezer panelled in old-fashioned, dark-stained oak.

The recognition that Cannes gave to Tati made him almost as newsworthy as Brigitte Bardot, whose latest role in *En Cas de malheur* (*Love is my Profession*), directed by Claude Autant-Lara,[297] persuaded even her co-star Jean Gabin that she was not just a sex-symbol but also a talented actress. American newsmen summoned Tati and "BB" for a television reportage. However, it was not at all clear in mid-May 1958 whether it would be safe to get a US camera crew into Paris and out again: there were well-founded rumours that parachute regiments – in Corsica, Toulouse, and Algeria – were about to seize Paris and impose military rule. Which is why Ed Sullivan conducted his television interview with the pair of them, on 19 May 1958, in the relative tranquillity of Brussels. A press photograph, now widely available as a postcard, commemorates the occasion, which helped to relaunch Tati as a symbol of French film art in America.

Tati was back in Brussels a few weeks later for an interview at the

Fig. 68: *9, Rue Voltaire, Saint-Germain-en-Laye*

Universal Exposition held to celebrate the recent signing of the Treaty of Rome and the inauguration of the "Euratom" sculpture. Then, after well-reported holidays in the high-class Alpine resort of Mégève, not far from Sauvy's regular haunt near Chamonix, Tati began an exhausting round of launches of his new film: Amsterdam, The Hague, and Rotterdam in August; New York in September (when he also did his mime act on the Steve Allen Show); Rome, then Milan, in October; and finally in November a two-week trip to America for the general US release of *My Uncle* in its English-language dress.

In Rome, Tati was granted an audience with Pope Pius XII, along with a number of other film personalities. But it seems that the group went to the audience chamber in the Vatican at the wrong time, or else that the Pontiff had been handed the wrong cue-cards by his staff, for the address that he gave was an elaborate celebration of the gas-fitting, plumbing and electrical trades. When he was asked by journalists what the Pope had spoken about during his audience, Tati said, simply and correctly, "about gas and electricity". Everyone thought he was pulling their leg. So he did, as he noticed a priest passing through the hotel lobby carrying an attaché-case: "Didn't you know that the Church takes a very great interest in energy supply? Can't you see (pointing to the Monsignor) that they've already started reading the meters?" This widely reported remark was construed as an anti-clerical joke. According to the local distributor of *Mon Oncle*, who must surely have been exaggerating, Tati lost about forty per cent of his Italian audience because of it.[298]

During Tati's US tour in November 1958, *Sports Illustrated* commissioned the French-American photographer Philippe Halsman to do a series of portraits of the man and the mime.[299] The imaginative and memorable studio photographs constitute perhaps the best record we will ever have of Tati as a comic mime. The city shots, showing Tati bemused by lifts in the hallways of modern skyscrapers and contemplating vast Manhattan building sites, build on the perception of *My Uncle* as a comical lament on modern architecture; but they also look forward to the themes of *Playtime*, the plan of which was perhaps already beginning to germinate in the director's mind.

The English version of *My Uncle* opened in New York and in Los Angeles in November 1958. It was well received in the press, attracted large audiences, and won the New York Film Critics' Circle Award for Best Foreign Film of 1958.[300] Rumours abounded that it would be nominated for the Academy Awards, which would take place in the spring.

Tati returned to France at the end of November at the peak of his career, with high hopes of soon taking the greatest prize of all. In the meantime, he had numerous other trips to make for *Mon Oncle*: another visit to beloved Stockholm (28 January to 4 February 1959), then Copenhagen (March 14), then a long flight to Argentina, for the first showing of *Mon Oncle* at Mar del Plata. Then came the delightful surprise: *Mon Oncle* was to be awarded the Oscar for "Best Foreign Film of 1958". The news was treated in France as a national triumph. Crowds came to Le Bourget airport to see Tati and Micheline set off on their journey to Hollywood; even vaster crowds attended his return. He held aloft the golden statuette as he walked down the aeroplane steps to the red carpet laid out on the ground.

The award of the Oscar for Best Foreign Film, in April 1959, does not make *Mon Oncle* a more remarkable film than it is: like Nobels and Goncourts, Oscars have distinguished many utterly forgettable works: but its significance for Tati, and through him for the French film industry as a whole, was very great. No less significant is how Tati handled himself as a celebrity during his fortnight in California. He was offered, as part of his prizewinner's due, any special treat that the Academy could provide. Tati asked simply if he could visit the nursing homes where the aged Stan Laurel, Mack Sennett and Buster Keaton now lived. The Academy was surprised, but laid the visit on nonetheless. Tati asked a few questions. Sennett stared at him and asked why he had bothered to learn English. "I understand you much better when you don't say anything."[301]

The visit was a homage to the masters of comedy film and, more specifically, to the masters of the *silent* screen. Keaton reportedly said that Tati's work with sound had carried on the true tradition of silent cinema. From that remark sprang Tati's ambition to add sound tracks to old silent comedy shorts and to relaunch them through his own company, Specta, which he intended to have a distribution as well as a production branch.

Fig. 69: *Tati with Buster Keaton and Harold Lloyd, Hollywood, 1959*

Tati returned from Hollywood with stories about America through which, in a sense, he sought to portray himself as a national figure. Warner Brothers, he said, had offered him unlimited financing to make his next film in the US, provided it starred Sophia Loren and was called *Mr Hulot Goes West*. "No, sir! Mr Tati Goes East!" was the director's widely reported reply. In the circumstances of the Cold War, that statement was easily misunderstood. Tati had meant to say that he would go on making films in France. But to American ears he seemed to have said that he preferred East to West, that he was more left than right, that he was, as people said of de Gaulle, "soft on the Reds". This is one of the sources of a persisting misconception of Tati's work as social criticism from a specifically left-wing point of view; and the apparently political edge to his rejection of Warner's bid meant that no further offers came to Tati from any Hollywood studio until the very end of his career. Tati's potential American career reached its zenith with *My Uncle*: then it suddenly died.

Between the death of his father in November 1957 and his trip to Los Angeles in April 1959, Tati's life was transformed. He had become rich, he had moved house, he was now the head of the family (his mother moved with them into Rue Voltaire) and head of his own company, Specta-Films. He had got rid of all association with Orain and Cady, just as he had got rid of all but a few of his father's old frames. But not everything was quite as rosy as it seemed. Pierre Etaix had come into the office one day to tell Tati that he was leaving. He had found what he really wanted to do in life – to be a clown. Anyway, he had to start earning a living, and he could not provide for himself, let alone a family, on the wages that Specta paid.

Tati seemed not to hear what the young man was saying. Pretending deafness like Balzac's Old Grandet, he laid out his new plans for the talented Etaix. "Did you realise?" he said. "You are going to work on my next film! You'll be my number one aide. That's your desk here – right next to mine. Do we have a deal?" Etaix had to repeat his resignation statement more than once. "I have to leave," he said. "I want to go my own way." Finally, Tati heard. And from that point on he never said another word to the younger man.

Tati treated Etaix's career move as if it were a betrayal; he made Etaix feel as if the parting had been worse than a divorce. It was something Tati could not control. The bad blood was never properly purged, and there was never a reconciliation between two men whose interests and talents were remarkably close.

De Gaulle's new regime was well established when Tati returned from his American triumph, and the only French winner of the Oscars was an obligatory guest at the Bastille Day Garden Party at the Elysée Palace. Tati did not like pomp and circumstance and was generally reluctant to accept official honours. The previous summer, just after the release of *Mon Oncle*, he had declined promotion to the *Ordre national des arts et des lettres*, with a well-turned, if thoroughly self-indulgent letter:

> I beg you to consider that the way I do my job and lead my life allows me to whistle as I walk down the street with my hands in my pockets, in less than formal attire, and I would feel obliged, if I had to wear this decoration with proper dignity, to change such habits which are the sole guarantors of my artistic and philosophical independence.[302]

But with his Oscar on the shelf at Saint-Germain, Tati felt obliged to accept the President's invitation, and so he went along to the traditionally vast garden-party on 14 July 1959.[303] With hundreds of celebrities and state officials to welcome, de Gaulle stood at the head of the *grand salon*, with the secretary-general of the palace at his side, whispering the name and the distinction of the next in line. Tati and Micheline finally arrived at the head of the queue. "Jacques Tati", the secretary whispered. De Gaulle looked down, as if to seek more information. "My Uncle", the secretary-general prompted. There are two versions of what the President then said. In version one, he is supposed to have declared that it was already his favourite film. In the other, perhaps more plausible, account, the President offered his sincere felicitations to Jacques Tati on the career of his charming and quite brilliant nephew.[304]

Fig. 70: *Jacques Tati and Charles de Gaulle*

THIRTY

Tati-Total

After *Mon Oncle*, Tati did not release another new film for nearly ten years. Moreover, he was not at all sure that *Mon Oncle* was really the film that he had wanted to make, and he confessed several times that he had in some sense lost his way: unlike *Les Vacances de M. Hulot*, *Mon Oncle* had a proper story, it had a firm narrative structure, and it had a message – fewer messages perhaps than those which became attached to it, but a message all the same, about fathers and sons, about inhibition and its release – in a word, about love. So for much of the time in the following few years, Tati turned back to his earlier and, for him, purer and more properly Tatiesque creations. But he must also have felt the first pangs of that awful fear that can come to people at the pinnacle of their careers – that they have nothing more to say. As Tati put it to a journalist in June 1959:

> I had come up with a really good subject, and wrote a well-shaped scenario with it. I thought to myself. "Now I'm really getting serious." But suddenly, looking at this too-well-made play, I felt old: to rejuvenate myself, I changed subject, took a different track, with something entirely lacking in construction. I like that, it makes me happy.[305]

Fears of ageing must have been drowned out most of the time by the comfortable size and complexity of the operation that Tati now commanded. By 1962, Specta-Films had acquired extensive premises at La Garenne-Colombes, near the LTC film processing laboratories, on the north-west industrial edge of Paris, much easier to get to from Saint-Germain than the smarter film-office district around the Etoile. There was a glass front door to the building with a disc-shaped brass knob, which he would use without amendment for the front door of the Royal Garden restaurant in *Playtime*; the offices were furnished with modern-style black synthetic-leather chairs that gave out a satisfying swoosh when you sat in them.[306] Tati had his administrative assistant, the meticulous and effective Bernard Maurice, to keep unwanted callers at bay, as well as his secretary, Juliette Wuidart, his assistants and his hangers-on. He liked to think of it as a family, of a convivial but traditional, basically patriarchal, kind. Or else you could think of it as a miniature MGM – a production company run by a director-writer-actor aiming to finance, to make, and to distribute not only his own, but also others' films.

Jacques Tati and Robert Bresson certainly came across each other at the LTC studios from time to time, and there were also quite a few people who belonged at one time or another to both their "teams" – Etaix, for example, who played the second thief in Bresson's *Pickpocket* (1959), and whose conjuring skills had been essential to train the other actors. Critics like Bazin had already pointed out the vague similarity between the two directors – their love of their craft, their independence, their rejection of easy effects, and their fondness for the long, slow shot. Perhaps because of these comparisons, perhaps because of a genuine mutual admiration, Tati toyed with the idea of financing Bresson's costume drama, *Lancelot du lac*, out of the profits from *Mon Oncle*.[307] Perhaps, though, Tati did visit the underfunded shoot of this mediaeval epic, with its amateur cast drawn from Bresson's circle of high-culture friends (the painter Luc Simon, for instance, and Laure Condominas, the daughter of the American poet and novelist Harry Mathews, play leading roles). Nearly twenty years later, Tati wrote an amiable spoof of the making of a costume drama, in which a Guinevere laments her long-lost beau. Clad in chainmail, helmet and visor, and all the metallic accessories of a comic-book knight, the missing prince returns on a white steed, swings his leg over the saddle to dismount, and, given the weight of his armour, sinks down to his knees in the sand ... [308]

Now that Cady had ceased to exist, Tati first sought to regain control of *Jour de fête* and *Les Vacances*, which he then withdrew from circulation entirely, in September 1959. For the first, he envisaged an almost entire remake; for the second, an entirely new sound track and a new cut, even though he had precious little of the original takes to work with after the disaster at the processing labs (see above, p. 197). He also dreamed of new subjects, as he confided to Paul Carrière in the early summer of 1960:

> I found the key to the "story" one Sunday morning, beside the motorway. I was watching thousands of cars go past ... [Drivers] have lost the ability to laugh, because inside their moving cages they no longer have any contact with nature or with their fellow-men.[309]

That idea would eventually turn into *Trafic*, which was not shot until the 1970s. But Tati's musings at the turn of the decade also foreshadow ideas that would be incorporated into *Playtime*, since he spoke of a plot which would involve "a great number of different Hulots" and a "ballet of characters sharing various features with Hulot". These dreamings were put aside when, not long after, Tati exhumed his old idea for a narrative film about a down-at-heel conjuror, and wrote it up into a full-scale shooting script, to be entitled either *La Grande Ville* or *L'Illusionniste*.[310] It contains a main role seemingly designed for someone just like Pierre Etaix: but the typescript was lodged with the CNC long after the two men had broken off all relations. Though Tati pursued negotiations with the Czechoslovak Film Office (and with the CNC for permission to shoot in Slovakia)[311] for quite some time after the "divorce", it is possible that he only deposited the script to protect it from being "stolen" by Etaix himself. Tati's long-standing anxiety about plagiarism, and more generally, about being cheated of his rights, had not diminished one bit.

In the years following the launch of *Mon Oncle*, Tati was not really in the business of making films, but of remaking those he cherished including a "job lot" of silent burlesque shorts purchased from Educational Pictures, to give them a non-speaking sound track that would enable Keaton, Sennett and the others to reach a new generation of spectators. And it was no doubt because he was not quite sure what he was really going to do next that Tati responded to a call he got from his old chum Bruno Coquatrix, now the owner-manager of the huge Olympia variety hall. Edith Piaf was ill: there was little chance of her recovering in time for her billed season, less than a month away: wouldn't you, Jacques, like to have one last go at live performance, and do a one-man-show to fill the gap?

Quite surprisingly, for a man in his fifties with no need whatsoever to earn a fast buck, Tati dropped everything, and said: yes, of course I will. It was perhaps a reminiscence of his great predecessor in French comedy film, Max Linder, who had also put on a live variety show at the selfsame theatre before the First World War.[312] More likely, though, the idea of trumping Charlie Chaplin must have appealed to Tati. *Limelight*, Chaplin's swansong film released in 1952, tells the sentimental story of an old trouper's last return to the music-hall stage. Tati's Olympia show would out-Chaplin Chaplin by making that fantasy come true.

France was once again in turmoil when *Jour de fête à l'Olympia* was conceived, rehearsed and put on. The Algerian conflict had come to haunt Paris. Independence fighters of the FLN planted suitcase bombs in left-luggage offices and cafés, whilst die-hard defenders of a French Algeria tried to assassinate Charles de Gaulle, and spread terror and random violence around the capital. The winter of 1960–61 was a sad and violent time. There were alerts on the metro, in cinemas and stations every week, if not quite every day. The economy was booming, a new airport had opened at Orly, and the beginnings of the motorway to the west had begun to snake out beyond Saint-Germain; but daily life in the capital was grim and fearful, as serried ranks of dark-blue police and riot-troop buses rushed down the boulevards, or parked menacingly in the main squares.

The show Tati imagined very quickly was the fullest expression of his desire to return to the very earliest sources of his art – but it was also an interesting attempt to innovate within the traditional forms of variety theatre. Its overall theme was the village fair, not yet quite a historical concept, but one which was even more nostalgic than it had been in its first incarnation in *Jour de fête*. The main material, of course, was Tati's first film – but with a difference. The director had recently discovered how touches of colour could be painted on to the original black-and-white stock, by a process called Scopachrome, and the Olympia show would provide a launch pad for the re-issue of his old film in this new polychrome dress. But the show-ing of the new-old film took up only the second half of the evening at the Olympia. The first half was a live variety show, a "village fair" brought to the Paris stage. He would have jugglers, trick-cyclists, a trumpet solo (Michèle Brabo), and the brass band from the Ecole des Beaux-Arts, as well as a conjuring act (by the banished Pierre Etaix, given a temporary reprieve), a few songs, and, above all, an act by Tati that had been done on film, but never before on stage: the "original" cycling lesson from *L'Ecole des facteurs*.[313]

The formal invention that was to frame this half-live, half-filmed spectacle was a kind of practical joke of preterition:

> It begins on screen with a sketch in which the celebrated M. Hulot is seen on his way to the Olympia. But suddenly the audience realises that Hulot is already there, in the auditorium. When the ballad-singer on stage comes to a halt because the double-bass is late, we see on a screen that has been discreetly lowered the selfsame double-bass, stuck in a typical Paris traffic jam – but the traffic policeman control-ling the flow turns out to be there, in the flesh, marching up and down on stage. And when sequences from *Jour de fête* are shown on screen, the characters come out of the film and on to the stage . . . even the village goat is live. The gags are strung along in a quite unpredictable order. "Live" and "filmed" are interchanged all the time, and the proscenium constantly breaks the bounds of the three walls of theatre and the four edges of a cinema screen.[314]

Thus did film, stage, star, and audience mingle, and overcome the separation – Tati would soon describe it as the "alienation" – of the silver screen. Of

course, it was not an entirely new idea – as Tati had been told by Maud
Linder after the success of *L'Ecole des facteurs*, Max Linder had experimented
with integrating film and live variety in much the same way,[315] and on one
of his rapid recent trips to Prague, Tati had seen the *Laterna Magica* troupe
using film inside cabaret in a perhaps even more startlingly inventive way.[316]
All the same, *Jour de fête à l'Olympia* expressed Tati's desire to include the
audience in the show and to include himself in the audience. He had
"false Hulots" planted around the auditorium, whose role was to walk out
seconds before it was Tati's turn to be on stage. Like some vague and popular
descendant of Wagnerian aesthetic ambitions, his aim was to create a *total
spectacle* that was indistinguishably a village fair, a film and a variety show.

The original *Jour de fête* shows one particular stage in the social history of
film – the film as the central and special attraction of a traditional village fair.
In the 1960s, Tati's recurrent desire was to bring the fair (or at least, the signs
and the atmosphere of out-door village entertainment) back to the cinema.
Thus many of the re-releases of his films, particularly in Holland and
Germany, were accompanied by brass-band parades in front of the cinema,
by external decorations of bunting and balloons, by mime acts on stage
before the start of the film, and by various forms of audience jollification.
(The re-release of *Les Vacances* at the Monte-Carlo cinema in Paris on St
Valentine's Day 1962 was enhanced by thousands of red button-hole
flowers flown up from Monte-Carlo, at the principality's expense . . .) For
Playtime's exclusive release in December 1967, Tati insisted on organising a
crèche in the cinema itself; and in the original plan for that masterwork,
the closing sequences would have projected the silhouettes of its characters
on to the walls of the cinema auditorium, mingling the imaginary with
the real, mixing viewers with the film itself. These disparate, not entirely
coherent ideas all express a nostalgia for the cinema as "total spectacle" – and
it can be no coincidence that a gala showing of *Jour de fête* in Amsterdam was
billed on Dutch hoardings as *Tati-Totaal*. But the underlying project, to
overcome the separation between performer and audience in the medium of
film, was utterly Quixotic, for the cinema is not and never can be a live act.
However, the 1961 show at the Olympia was much more than a convivial
decoration of a filmic event, and came perhaps nearer than anything else
ever has to a Wagnerian synthesis of all the popular arts which Tati practised
and enjoyed. "Outside" and "inside", performer and participant, screen and
stage, were, in principle, to be thoroughly muddled up, in the service not of
subversion, but of a peculiarly Tatiesque idea of convivial reality.

The first trace of the idea of a total spectacle in Tati's far from copious
paperwork is the original contract between him and his company, Specta, for
a film to be called *Récréation*, normally assumed to be the original working

title of *Playtime*, but which clearly covered something very different at the start. The contract, dated 17 November 1959, talks of preparatory work for a "spectacle cinématographique" with the following summary characteristics:

- long exclusive first-run showing, with bookable seats
- addition of a live stage-show that is part of the film
- simultaneous projection on several screens of additional filmed sequences without which the main film would be incomprehensible
- special sound equipment to be installed to allow the sound track to be controlled from a console during projection.[317]

If this is indeed the seed from which *Playtime* would eventually grow, then we must presumably count *Jour de fête à l'Olympia* as the branch on which most of these ideas flowered. Two years prior to the Olympia show, Tati was thinking of ways to make a cinematic spectacle more complex and varied, and looking towards new media, or at least, as yet uninvented technology, to involve and envelop the audience to a much higher degree than in an ordinary film projection. Coquatrix did not exactly prompt the invention of *Jour de fête à l'Olympia*, but provided a golden opportunity to try out ideas that had been in Tati's mind for some time.

The rehearsals for the show were crammed into a very short period, since this was an emergency event, made possible only by an unexpected programming gap. Tati slaved away in the Olympia for as much as twenty hours a day, often sleeping in the changing rooms instead of driving back home to Saint-Germain. But the overwork, combined with Tati's irrepressible habit of always showing others how to do their act, led to a physical mishap of some consequence. Unimpressed by the manner of one of the team of cycling postmen, Tati jumped on to the stage bicycle to demonstrate a properly comic pedalling style. But the machine was not locked on to the rollers at that point – and Tati's vigorous thrust on the pedals propelled him off the edge of the stage and into the orchestra pit.[318] He broke no bones on this occasion, but he bruised himself badly and twisted his back. He had to undergo intensive physiotherapy for a couple of weeks, delaying the opening night by as much; and even when the show finally opened, Tati was still in considerable pain.[319]

Everything seemed to conspire against Coquatrix at this point. He had lost Piaf to illness, he had nearly lost Tati to an accident, and then, on the opening night, just before the curtain was due to go up, riot and security police swooped in and cleared the whole house. They had been tipped off that the place was about to be blown up by terrorists.[320] It turned out to be a false alert, but the première had to be put off for another week.

Once it finally opened, on 24 April 1961, *Jour de fête à l'Olympia* filled the auditorium every night, and it could have run for many months. But Tati was already exhausted: he fainted in the wings after the curtain came down on the first night.[321] The daily routine did not make Tati any less tired; the matinées were a particular burden, since he rarely got to bed before dawn. The summer break was not far off, and he did not want his customary holiday by the sea with his family (although that year, sixteen-year-old Sophie would undergo the ritual *séjour linguistique* at Haslemere, to improve her command of English). So, to the great disappointment of many members of the troupe, who would perhaps never again have such a splendid framework for their variety acts, *Jour de fête à l'Olympia* closed.[322] Some of the troupe suspected that Coquatrix had been pressed into shortening the run by Tati not because the maestro was tired, but because he was ruffled by the success of acts which, on some nights at least, eclipsed his own. Tati's pride was undoubtedly hurt when the false Hulots in the audience were not immediately recognised; he also realised with sadness that the show he had devised was not quite the integrated spectacle he dreamed of; but it still seems most likely that the show closed primarily because the main star, with his old car-crash injury and his more recent back sprain giving him pain every night, just could not cope with accumulated exhaustion and needed a long rest. All the same, he was delighted to have a live audience once again, and in the summer of 1961 told one old friend that the Olympia show would reopen in the autumn (it did not),[323] and wrote to old friends that he was going to get a music-hall team back together again to take Europe and show-business by storm (he never did).[324]

After *Jour de fête à l'Olympia* folded, Tati carried on remaking *Jour de fête*, and shot the extra scenes with the Dutch painter later on in the summer of 1961 (see above, p.148). He also continued to hanker after a framework in which a film show would also be a celebration, a fair, a convivial and sociable night out: and to this end he eventually took out a lease on a vacant cinema in Rue de Rennes, the 500-seat Lux. Max Linder, long before, had also owned his own cinema in Paris, which he called, for simplicity's sake, Le Max-Linder, since it was destined only to show the "King of the Kinema" on screen. Tati, more modestly, called his enterprise L'Arlequin, and had its interior redesigned and redecorated by a well-known architect, G. Peynet.[325] At L'Arlequin, *Jour de fête* would be shown in its new colourised version, of course, but in a special way: first a comic short, then the advertisements, then an interval – with the Bagnolet brass band in the foyer, balloons released in the auditorium, and a whole set of gags to recreate all the fun of the fair. As Tati explained in an interview in a local community

newspaper, he wanted to create a different experience of film and to overcome the "alienation" of the darkened room:

> A different kind of cinema, a cinema in which the spectator can
> remain himself once he has come in ... I would like the viewer
> to feel that he is in some sense part of the spectacle, that there has to
> be a dialogue between him and the director; in a word, what I want
> is a human exchange.[326]

In principle, L'Arlequin would show not only Tati's films, but also comic
shorts by others, and films that Tati admired, and, in some cases, had
acquired. It was at L'Arlequin that the Dutch documentarist, Bert Haanstra,
first found a French audience: indeed, Tati liked *Zoo* (1962) so much that he
required or requested, whenever he could, that it be shown together with
Jour de fête throughout the world. (The colourised *Jour de fête* was indeed
shown in London in that way, with *Zoo* as the "warm-up" film.)[327]

Zoo is a film about people: filmed by a hidden camera located inside
the chimpanzees' enclosure at Amsterdam Zoo, it is a montage of people's
faces through the bars of the cage – faces grimacing, smiling, scowling,
and bored, a gallery of untutored and unconscious comedy acts. Its family
resemblance to Tatiesque comedy derives from its strict reliance on observation and its refusal to intervene directly in what the spectator has to see;
but it is not made with Tati's concern for the recomposition of the world
through mime. Haanstra, who had been bowled over by *Les Vacances de
M. Hulot* when he first saw it at the Cannes Festival in 1953, was overwhelmed and delighted by Tati's view of him and his work. With his pliant
and unpretentious personality, Haanstra considered himself to be at Tati's
command.[328]

Running a *cinéma de quartier* was an odd turn for Tati to take – but as he told
reporters, no doubt to cock a snook at other directors who invested their
earnings in country estates, "It's just as much fun as buying cows".[329] It
was also rather less long-term than running a farm: the lease only lasted
six months, and when it ran out Tati did not feel inclined to renew it. To
thank his backer in this venture – a textile magnate from Troyes – Tati
invented his "inflatable towel device", a beach or bath robe with an incorporated inflatable cushion that could serve as a head-rest or pillow, for reading
on the beach. A few hundred of these eventually found their way to one
of the Club Med's resorts, and may perhaps even now be in use, with labels
saying "Brevet Jacques Tati".

Tati also kept a weather eye open for talents that were compatible with
his, a habit that sometimes came close to ensnaring and controlling potential
rivals. In early 1964, he went to Holland to see Bert Haanstra's latest film,

Alleman (*The Human Dutch*, 1963), was enthralled by it, and sought to buy the rights for France, so as to be able to adapt it in his own way. To begin with, it all had to be done in a hurry to allow Specta to get a French *Alleman* into the 1964 Cannes Film Festival; but as Simon Carmiggelt, the Dutch scriptwriter, has reported elsewhere, working quickly with Jacques Tati turned out to be a contradiction in terms.[330] In the meantime, *Alleman* had had a rapturous reception in London; Haanstra felt that the "international" version shown there was quite good enough for the rest of the world; the German version, being dubbed in May, was identical; but still Tati dithered and dallied about making his own changes for France. And did nothing. Over the whole summer, as Haanstra's film attracted large audiences all over the world, evasive and yet pernickety letters from Bernard Maurice and René Silvéra continued, until, in the autumn, Specta-Films informed the Dutch director that it was no longer interested in distributing *Alleman* in France, as it could "only reach a small part of the audience".[331]

Tati's behaviour in these years with respect to his old companion and disciple Pierre Etaix is more mysterious. In collaboration with Jean-Claude Carrière, who had written the novelisations of *Les Vacances* and *Mon Oncle*, Etaix pursued a career in film that seemed to mimic, or to honour, Tati's own path: first, comic shorts (*Rupture*, 1961; *Heureux anniversaire*, 1962, which won an Oscar in 1963), then a hugely successful comedy feature film, *Le Soupirant* (*The Suitor*, 1963), which, like *Les Vacances* ten years earlier, won the Prix Louis Delluc. Tati organised private screenings of all these, and, in front of his assistants and staff at Specta-Films, gloated and raged over details, ideas, gags and whole scenes which, he said, Etaix had stolen directly from him, or from those Buster Keaton and Mack Sennett films that Specta was supposed to be re-releasing with Tati-designed sound tracks.[332] *Yoyo*, which appeared in 1965, drove Tati really wild: with its circus setting and its sentimental plot, it certainly has something in common with *L'Illusionniste*; it is also a very funny, touching and beautiful film, and Tati – at this point struggling to keep the *Playtime* shoot going – must perhaps have feared for his laurels. But *Yoyo* got panned, in almost libellous terms, in much of the Paris press. Etaix suspected Tati of having written the harshest of the articles, or, at the least, of having prodded subservient journalists into writing them. He now readily admits that at the worst point he became a victim of persecution mania, suspecting Tati of pulling strings not just in the Paris press, but in the chance events of daily life, which for a time seemed not haphazard at all.[333] Etaix's obsession with Tati's malevolent power may well have been beyond reason, but it was not entirely without grounds. Tati had not been well disposed towards Etaix from the moment the young man had left the employment of Specta-Films, and thereafter he certainly did nothing to promote or to encourage his ex-protégé. Some critics and commentators came to Etaix's side in the end, in a dispute that had all the rancour and irrationality of a long-drawn-out divorce. When *Playtime* finally appeared, some said that the paucity of real comic turns in the film was easy to explain: having lost his gagman, Etaix, Tati just could not come up to the mark.

From 1958 to 1963, Tati diversified himself, not always in directly profitable ways. Plans to make *L'Illusionniste* were finally abandoned. His return to variety was cut short. His career as a cinema-proprietor did not last long. He bought options on film scripts by others, but never shot or produced any of them.[334] Specta-Films never really established itself as a distributor, and sound tracks of the Keaton, Sennett and Harold Lloyd shorts were never done. Tati threw vast amounts of his and others' money into remaking the sound track of *Les Vacances*, but many viewers who remembered the original thought that he had simply spoiled the film. He poured an even vaster fortune into reshooting, colourising and remaking the sound track of *Jour de fête*, again without convincing most critics that he had really improved it a great deal.[335] All this kept him busy, to be sure, as did his frequent trips abroad to attend the launches of the various versions of his three films. It also kept his "home team" – Bernard Maurice, Juliette Wuidart, Jean Reznikov, and a few others – in decent and productive jobs. In his mid-fifties, with a comfortable fortune and a high reputation, Tati could have left it at that, and gone on enjoying his double life as an artist with a set of fairly Bohemian chums, and as a *grand bourgeois* of Saint-Germain, mixing with art-collectors, financial directors, surgeons and industrialists. But though he took a long time to find what it was, and even longer to give it form, there was something else that Jacques Tati still had to say.

Part Three

Playtime

1960–1970

*The history of film as an art is mainly
a history of films that lose money*

CHARLES EIDSVIK
Cineliteracy. Film Among the Arts
(New York: Random House, 1978), p. 177

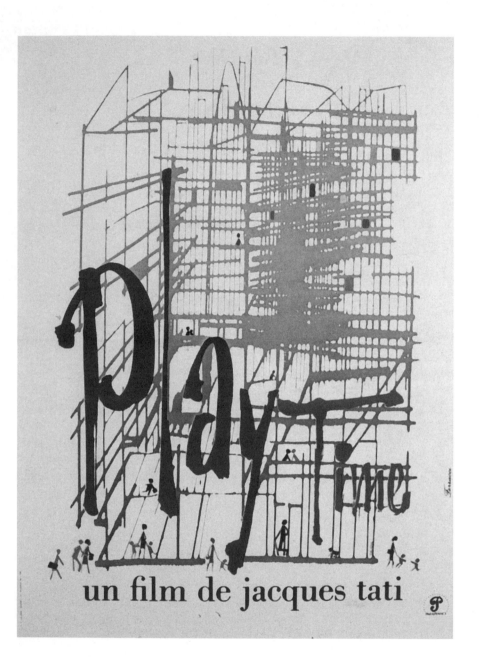

un film de jacques tati

THIRTY-ONE

Edifice Complex

Writing to his distant Russian mistress in 1846, as he began to launch himself into his last great novels, *Cousin Bette* and *Cousin Pons*, Balzac declared that "circumstances demand that I write two or three capital works ... which prove that I am younger, fresher and greater than ever!" Tati did not express himself in such heroic terms, but what he said as he started making his fourth and greatest feature film boils down to much the same thing:

> *Playtime* is the big leap, the big screen. I'm putting myself on the line. Either it comes off, or it doesn't. There's no safety net.[336]

Playtime is Tati's most ambitious and magnificent film by far. It was also a monumental disaster; and almost every stage in its development, its making, and its release was clouded over by the foreboding of an unhappy end. Tati seemed to have designed for himself an exit from the world's scene that echoes M. Hulot's departure from the screen, at the end of both *Les Vacances de M. Hulot* and of *Mon Oncle*, as a solitary, unresolved enigma.

Everything had to be big. From the beginning, "Film Tati N° 4", as it was still called on the cast-rosters drawn up for the start of shooting in late 1964, was to be a wide-screen super-production, exploiting the beauty of sun and clouds over real, modern exteriors, and dissolving M. Hulot amongst crowds seen from afar in vast airport halls, along interminable glass-walled corridors, and lost amongst simultaneously labyrinthine and unenclosed office booths. Where could such a real set be found? On a promotional trip to Germany for the relaunch of *Jour de fête* in 1964, Tati inspected the Ford factories in Cologne, then made a special trip to Munich, and on to Belgrade, to look at possible large sites under construction. He flew to Arlanda, the brand-new airport near Stockholm, to see if that could be used,[337] and contacted businesses in and around Paris to cast an eye over possible megablocks recently completed or still under construction. But there was a fundamental problem, one which he had been able to solve with firmness and tact for his previous shoots, but which seemed insurmountable for Film N° 4. The village square in Sainte-Sévère, the Hôtel de la Plage at Saint-Marc, and the centre of Saint-Maur had all been places in regular daily use, which film-making would most certainly disrupt. For *Jour de fête*, Tati had persuaded the villagers to become part of the film project; for *Les Vacances*, he had been able to persuade the hotel guests to keep out of the way when it mattered; and at Saint-Maur, it had not been too difficult to persuade local people to take pride in the use of their town square in a film. But Tati could not so easily persuade a car factory, a bank or a conglomerate headquarters to down tools and telephones for a month – or a year – or perhaps more – whilst its building was over-run by actors, lighting men, hordes of extras, hairdressers, electricians, carpenters and caterers. All imaginable large steel-and-glass structures representing the world of tomorrow were necessarily in daily use; the cost of occupying the real Orly airport, for example, even if it had been permitted to a now-acknowledged master of the French screen, would have been prohibitively high even for a project aiming to take cinema architecture to the very limit. Tati's principal director of photography, the celebrated French-Hungarian cameraman, Jean Badal, was also adamant: if you want to shoot scenes of reflected clouds moving across the glass panes of a skyscraper, you will have to have the skyscraper all to yourself.[338]

Lagrange had what still looks like the best idea for making the vast ambition of Tati's script a financially viable project. He proposed setting up a regular development company, building a real steel-and-glass structure, making the film in it, and then, after minor alterations to the building, selling it off as flats and offices.[339] "Tati could have built the same set for real instead of fake. It would have cost the same."[340] It was, after all, a period of building mania all around Paris, and fortunes were being made by even run-of-the-mill architects and property developers. If the set-building was thought out in the right way, there should be no problem about disposing of it profitably at the end of filming.

Tati took this advice, but went one disastrous step further: he would build his set not for resale as flats, but for future use as a *cinecittà*: he would thus endow the French film industry with a purpose-built, fully-equipped studio complex. It was in principle a magnificent, even magnanimous, and certainly megalomaniac plan. It might even have worked. The Paris city council agreed to lease Specta-Films a large patch of waste land in the south-eastern corner of the capital, just next to the recently-completed Boulevard Périphérique. That was where Tati's studio-set would rise, a short drive from the old heart of the Pathé empire at Joinville-le-pont. But there was a fatal catch. The land had long been scheduled for a clover-leaf intersection between the ring road and one of the several radial motorways soon to be built, linking Paris with the east of France.

There never was the slightest chance of the French state abandoning its road-building plans, not even if a gold mine or a Roman palace had been found under the ground that Tati held on a short lease. In 1961, Paul Delouvrier, one of the great technocrats of the rebuilding of France, had accompanied President de Gaulle on a helicopter trip to inspect the lay-out and the "circulation problems" of Greater Paris. On seeing the tangled, strangled web of the suburbs, the President declared: "This clap-house has to be sorted out!" Delouvrier was given full authority to rationalise traffic flows along the lines of the recently-completed PADOG (*Plan d'aménagement et d'organisation générale*).[341] Prime Minister Georges Pompidou, a notorious motor-car fanatic, told Parisians without the slightest circumlocution or embarrassment that their city now had to be adapted to the automobile.[342] He ploughed the right-bank expressway through the historic heart of the city, along the picturesque quayside of the Seine, and straight under the Louvre; not even the frantic protests of the Ministry of Finance (housed in the Louvre) or the wealthy and well-connected inhabitants of riverside apartments could stop the onward march of the bulldozers in those road-happy days. How could Tati have thought that the zoning of Tativille would be altered just because he had built a wonderful studio-set on the land? He may have accepted all along that his project was doomed; but if he had not realised it from the start, then he must have been oddly out of touch with the realities that he nonetheless portrayed in his films, and which he had shown implicitly in the credit sequences and explicitly in the nearly last sequence of *Mon Oncle*: buildings in the "old town" being demolished to make way for new roads.

The budget for "Film N° 4" was rumoured to be monstrously large from the early days of its conception. Five million,[343] six million,[344] ten million,[345] twelve million[346] – journalists bandied all sorts of figures about. There is no sure way of knowing precisely how much Tati spent, especially as many of the key bills went unpaid in the end. But he did assert, probably correctly, that the total cost of building the set was no more than what it would have cost to hire Sophia Loren or Elizabeth Taylor for the leading role. But there are two sides to every equation. Even if Tati had not been obliged to have most of the set built twice over, Sophia Loren, unlike Tativille, would have ensured a US release for the film.

The first real disaster to strike, in the autumn of 1964, was a large gust of wind. Tativille had been under construction since September, and was nearing completion. The wind knocked large parts of it down. Tati discovered that his insurance cover for "acts of God" had been cancelled the previous week because his initial backers had "forgotten" to pay the premiums. The repairs cost 1.4 million francs, according to Tati,[347] inaugurating

Fig. 71: *Tativille. Start of construction*

the long train of delays and cost over-runs that would plague *Playtime* for the rest of its (far too many) days.

Three years elapsed between the gust of wind and the first showing of *Playtime* at the Empire on the Avenue Wagram. The set was not properly finished until March 1965. Shooting proceeded in good order in April, May and June. In July, unseasonal rain held up filming for several weeks, and by September Tati's money had run out. That was when he got new advances from the Crédit Lyonnais, and he began shooting again in November ... and carried on, sporadically, until October 1966. Three hundred and sixty-five days' shooting in all, which must be close to a world record for a commercial film.[348] Then came no less than nine full months of editing before the film was finally ready for showing in December 1967. Even then, the film was not entirely finished, or rather, public response prompted Tati to carry on cutting his film night by night in the cinema's projection room, so that the versions seen by its first audiences were never quite the same twice over. In those thirty-six months, there were days, whole weeks, even a period of a couple of months, when nothing happened on the waste land at Saint-Maurice. The light was not right. Or the clouds were going in the wrong direction. Or, more frequently, the money supply had run out, and Tati had to devote himself to raising more backing before he could summon the cast and restart the shoot. And with each interruption,

Fig. 72: *Tativille. The
city rises*

the world moved on, and new sequences, new props, new observations
had to be invented and integrated to keep the film to its remit of portraying
the absolutely contemporary state of the world.

As his own producer, and because he insisted for as long as he could on
retaining distribution rights as well, Tati, through Specta-Films, contracted
large debts with the state-sponsored film finance company UFIC and with
several other banks too; these loans were secured initially against the
company's assets, but then, increasingly, against Tati's personal wealth.
Regular financiers had become wary of putting money into a company run
by Tati, who was in any case now being sued by Orain for cost over-runs
on the remakes of *Les Vacances* and *Jour de fête*. When his collateral ran out,
Tati turned to relatives and friends to back him up, and fairly soon he was
in debt to almost everyone he knew. Mme Tatischeff *mère*, who lived with

the family at 9, Rue Voltaire, had a comfortable sum in savings, the fruits of Georges-Emmanuel's long business career. On her death, Jacques could expect to share it with his elder sister Nathalie, who was now approaching retirement age. But Jacques, who loved his mother dearly, had a persuasive case, and so the entire Van Hoof-Tatischeff family inheritance was invested in Specta-Films. For those in the know, Tati's situation was alarming: he looked like a drowning man. Jean Badal put Tati in touch with Darryl F. Zanuck, who seemed quite willing to take on the entire production, and who certainly had the means to do so; but nothing came of it.[349] The Communist millionaire, Doumeng, made a charitable contribution when he heard what a mess Tati's finances were in.[350] Norbert Terry, a product placement consultant for the film, also tried to help, at the other end of the political spectrum. He spoke to his neighbour on the Ile Saint-Louis, Georges Pompidou, and the Prime Minister agreed to come to Tativille to view the rushes. Not only did he and his wife Claude have an artistic interest in the work of Tati, but the politician also judged the survival of France's most celebrated Oscar to be in the national interest.[351] As a result, Pompidou gave a nod to his *chef de cabinet*, Michel Jobert, who instructed the state bank, Crédit Lyonnais, to extend its credit line to Specta-Films.[352] It was probably for that large advance that Tati was obliged to mortgage his great house in Saint-Germain. Even at that stage few people realised that Tati really had mortgaged everything else that he owned – even the rights to *Les Vacances* and *Mon Oncle* – to finance a single film set. Yet that was precisely what he had done.

> *You really did invest your own wealth?*
> I had to. They said: You want to finish the film? Yes. Well, then you'll have to sign here. So I signed. *Jour de fête*, *Les Vacances*, my house, everything went.[353]

He had also done it in a rather complicated way, by not drawing what his company owed him as his percentage of the income from all his previous films. But the tax authorities were not concerned with whether Tati had in fact drawn his income or not: income was income, and he owed large amounts of tax on it. His personal overdrafts began to mount, and long before *Playtime* was finished, Tati was in substantial debt to the least forgiving of all creditors, the Collector of Taxes.

The set, though, was truly magnificent. It had its own power-plant and its own approach road. It consisted of two main buildings in steel and concrete, one for the exhibition hall, airport lounge, office building, and restaurant scenes; and one for the supermarket and drugstore scenes. The main one was properly weatherproof, with industrial-standard lighting, heating and power;

the escalator that we see in the hotel and office sequences is a perfectly real, operational one, bought for the sole purpose of shooting those scenes. Given the scale of the set, many of the "trick" effects had to be similarly outsize: the aeroplane fin seen moving across the background picture window of the airport-lounge sequence is admittedly not a real-life Caravelle, but a model on a scale of 1:3 – a very large piece of plywood on wheels.

Fig. 73: *Tativille. The city functions*

The rest of the set was ingenious in the extreme. Large wood and plastic flats mounted on railway tracks allowed streets of skyscrapers to be created, in different arrays, to give the visual semblance of a whole city of glass and steel. Each "storey" painted on the flats is slightly smaller than the one beneath it, so that a straight-on image creates the illusion of looking up towards the top of a great tower. But the roads between the simulated blocks were perfectly real – proper macadam on a properly constructed base, equipped with standard-issue traffic lights, in full working order.

Tati claimed that he would have liked his wonderful toy to be used for all sorts of other things – but at the same time he was extremely cagey about letting strangers on to his set. He allowed Nicolas Ribowski, whom he took on for a time as an assistant, to make his first short there (*Cours du soir*, starring Jacques Tati, in one of his least exciting performances ever); he hired out the building for a very 1960s fashion show by the accessory designer

Esterel;[354] Jean Badal started to make his own film about the construction
and the magic of Tativille. René Clément considered using it for some
sequences of *Paris brûle-t-il?*; and Ken Harper, the British producer,
investigated making a musical there.[355] But most of these ideas for putting
Tativille to use came to nought; and none of them improved Specta's
cash-flow position, and none of them could hold back the bulldozers
waiting to raze Tativille to the ground, which they began to do even whilst
the last takes of *Playtime* were being filmed, in November 1966. Tati did
not like being disturbed during a shoot. His reputation as a moody and
difficult person did not help; nobody was much inclined to get in the great
director's way.

The financial folly of Tativille, which cannot be omitted from the story
of the making of *Playtime*, should not mask the magnificence of the
concept, nor its aesthetic and social purpose. The rebuilding of Paris and its
suburbs was under way: even in Saint-Germain, older houses in Rue Voltaire
were being knocked down by developers intent on erecting seven-storey
blocks "in Milanese style", as Tati put it in his protest to the departmental
authorities.[356] But a new Paris of steel and glass had not yet really emerged
from building sites. The great towers of Maine-Montparnasse and the
Défense business zone did not yet exist. Tativille was a construction of
the *future* of the city – a future that has now arrived, but not one that Tati
could readily find in physical form at the time he planned and made his film.

Of course, pressure for the rebuilding of the city along "American" lines
had been present for most of the century, most notably in the well-publicised
and thankfully imaginary projects of Le Corbusier, who would have built a
vast avenue of free-standing Chrysler Buildings all the way from Paris to
Saint-Germain, and whose "Plan Voisin" of 1925 projected the total dismant-
ling of the centre of Paris and its replacement by eighteen geometrically
spaced towers. But Depression, defeat, German Occupation, and the colonial
wars had put all such plans on hold for more than thirty years: the fabric of
central Paris had changed remarkably little since Tati's youth. Even those
special symbols of the post-war era, the UNESCO headquarters and the
Maison de la Radio, exempted from planning restrictions, were not properly
finished until 1962. Since much of the urban fabric had deteriorated in the
meantime, the accumulated pressures for modernisation and expansion were
all the greater as France grew more prosperous by the day.

It was only in 1961 that building regulations were changed to allow high-
rise construction in the city itself, and it was several more years before large
structures resembling the set of *Playtime* actually appeared on the horizon: the
Science Faculty at Jussieu, on the site of the old Halle aux Vins (for which
Jacques Lagrange designed the floor mosaics) was begun in 1965 (Tativille

was complete by then) and finished in 1967, more or less coinciding with
the release of Tati's film. The plans for the business area around La Défense
were approved in 1964, but not much of it was visible above ground until
around 1970, and the scale and ugliness of the site did not become a matter
of public concern until 1972. But in the virulent debate that then arose,
one architect at least seems to have been inspired by Tativille, long since
demolished: Emile Alliaud proposed to complete and to humanise La
Défense by putting up two curving blocks covered with mirror glass, in
which Parisians might see the reflected images of the city's more familiar
monuments. This is precisely what Tati allows us and his American tourists
to see of the city in *Playtime*: the Sacré-Coeur, the Eiffel Tower, and the
Arc de Triomphe reflected in the plate-glass doors of the travel agency.

Tativille was also a construction of a particular kind of beauty. Unlike
the Arpel House in *Mon Oncle*, which is a heightened image of a rather

Fig. 74: *Playtime,
1967: The Eiffel Tower
captured in reflection*

old-fashioned idea of modernism, the Strand Building is a standard tower block, which Tati's genius, Lagrange's advice, and Badal's technical skills turned into an almost abstract canvas. The winking lights of the tower that Hulot looks upon when he gets off his old Paris bus hark back just a little to the lights-on/lights-off routine of Martine's villa in *Les Vacances* and to the cross-eyed porthole windows of *Mon Oncle*; but they also celebrate the fearsome, uplifting beauty of a skyscraper city that Tati had glimpsed in Manhattan, but which was still no more than an artist's dream on the waste land of Saint-Maurice. *Playtime* is not fundamentally or essentially a satire of high-rise architecture: it is more a celebration of the beauty of large edifices, and an expression of wonderment at humankind's ability to create.

THIRTY-TWO

Le Gadget

Much of the straightforwardly satirical thrust of Tati's film work is focused on the accessories of modern life, on those gimmicks, novelties, toys, and trinkets for which the French borrowed an English word: *le gadget*.[357] Whereas the Arpels' house in *Mon Oncle* is, as we have seen, a barely heightened exemplification of modernist design, their mode of living is dominated by excessive and frequently pointless use of gadgets. But *le design* and *le gadget* are not mutually exclusive categories, and Tati makes several telling points by taking the one for the other, and vice versa.

The strange curved sofa in Mme Arpel's salon has no obvious use when it is first seen. M. Hulot, baby-sitting for Gérard on the Arpels' anniversary night out at the restaurant, turns it on its side and uses it as a bed. But as we discover Hulot sleeping in the next day, what we see is not just a subversion of a curious domestic gadget, but a satire of *le design*: for the inverted sofa is exactly isomorphic to the famous chaise-longue created by Charlotte Perriand, the notoriously modernist interior decorator whose career ran parallel for many years to that of Le Corbusier.

By no means all of Tati's gadgets are art-historical jokes of this kind. Some, like Hulot's antique Amilcar in *Les Vacances de M. Hulot*, rely on visual analogies for their humorous effect (the little car looks and moves more like a duck than a wheeled vehicle); some are only really funny because of the circumstances of their use, like the pedal-powered lawnmower driven at an extremely low gear (and thus with comically rapid leg-movements) by the Arpels' snobbish and overdressed neighbour in *Mon Oncle*; some are rendered absurd only by consequences of their use, such as the (now very ordinary) photo-electric door-opening device, or by a malfunction superimposed by post-synchronised sound (such as the opaque babble of the PA system at the station in *Les Vacances*, and of the office intercom in the Strand Building foyer in *Playtime*); and yet others, such as the devices displayed and demonstrated at the "Ideal Home" exhibition in the same film, are barely perceptible as comic in themselves.

Fig. 75: *Le Corbusier – Pierre Jeanneret – Charlotte Perriand, chaise longue (1928)* © FLC

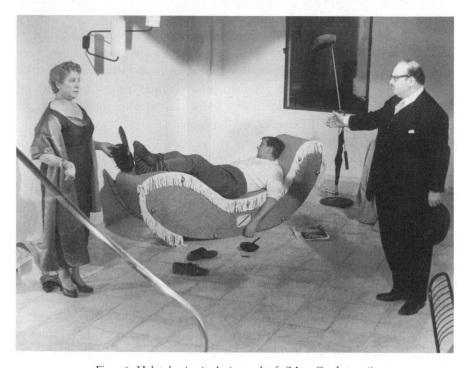

Fig. 76: *Hulot sleeping in the inverted sofa* (Mon Oncle, *1958*)

At least one of these gadgets was not invented for the film, but borrowed from the show that Esterel held on the set in 1966: articulated eye-glasses that allow short-sighted women to put make-up on each eye in turn.[358] But this perfectly practical little device is progressively derealised by a whole series of inanimate mimicries which begin when the German businessman, angered by the false Hulot, apologises to the real one and vigorously shakes his hand, forgetting that he has his black-rimmed spectacles in his fist. The sound track makes the crack of the frame quite audible, so that when Rainer Kohldehoff, a real German businessman roped in for the task, puts his spectacles back on, we are amused to see them twisted in a way that precisely imitates the ladies' click-lift frames. It is not too much of a stretch of the imagination to accept that the businessman – who perhaps has one eye less myopic than the other – does not know that he has only one lens to see through.

It is likely also that the illuminating broom, with built-in battery-powered headlights for sweeping out dark corners, was at one time a marketable device; and there can be little doubt that the "Greek-Style" flip-top disposal bin, made to look like a section of a fluted column, has been at some time (and perhaps still is) available from some real design store. Only the straight-backed, doll-like posture of the demonstrators, their slow, repeated, mechanical gestures of display, and their rigid smiles make it clear that these are comic displays of gadgets held up to ridicule. Similarly, the probably fictional silent door sold under the slogan "Slam Your Doors in Golden Silence" is the vehicle of a complicated gag, but not in itself a subverted, exaggerated or satirised object. The human joke built around the noiselessly closing door (which even its inventor cannot make bang when he slams it in anger) is a circuitous kind of cinematic self-reference: as the entire film has post-synchronised sound, all doors slam in golden silence unless and until Tati decides to dub over a specific noise.

To treat the new as ridiculous is a risky game, for it is never clear in advance which piece of innovation will "take" and become an object of continuing desire and affection, and which will sink into oblivion. But it is of course a standard tactic of the conservative resistance to modernisation: trains, bicycles, cars, planes, and more or less every minor accoutrement of industrialised living were subjected on their first appearance to satirical presentation in cartoons, stories, fiction and film, some of which (such as Villiers de l'Isle Adams's *Contes cruels*, or Chaplin's imagination of the conveyor-belt factory in *Modern Times*) belong to the mainstream of the artistic tradition. Tati's use of gadgetry and innovation is remarkable for its ambiguity: especially in *Playtime*, but also to some degree in his earlier films, he exploits the new almost equally for its comic potential and for its aesthetic pleasure.

Fig. 77: *The Lonely Labyrinth.* Playtime's *perspective on the world of work*

There is perhaps no more joyously amusing and simultaneously beautiful sequence in all of Tati's films than the installation in *Playtime* of a large pane of glass in a building under construction. Five men, knees bent, arms outstretched, hold the huge pane upright on a high storey and, under the gaze of the crowd that has gathered in the street below, gingerly move it, with hesitant but co-ordinated dance-like steps, towards its final home. A jazzy sound track bleeding over from the previous sequence introduces the glaziers' complicated dance; when it falls silent, two likely lads in cloth caps in the crowd below – instances of Tati's unceasing use of viewers inside the frame – strike up a triumphant fairground marching tune ("In a Persian Market") on plastic combs or kazoos. The back-lighting of the imaginary pane makes the object of the glaziers' attention a shimmeringly magical transparent thing – for it is in fact a pure creation of mime, not an actual pane at all. Body-language thus transforms a banal industrial-constructional act into ballet, and gives us a highly crafted glimpse of the accidental beauty of modern life. Far from making glass-based design an object of ridicule, the glaziers' syncopated two-step transforms and heightens the joy of the new.

Playtime also transforms a mere traffic jam into an epiphany of reconciliation. The penultimate sequence of the film brings the coach-load of departing tourists to a roundabout, crammed with a cross-section of the human and mechanical population of a modern city: delivery vans, motorcycles and motorised bicycles, parents with children, regular buses, construction traffic, ladies with luggage, saloon cars, taxis, and an open-top Sunbeam Talbot Alpine. (Because Tati had virtually run out of money when shooting this sequence, the traffic is partly a cross-section of his own social world – he roped in all his remaining friends and relatives to drive round and round in their own cars, and the Alpine is in fact his wife's – Micheline can just be made out, for the second and last time in Tati's oeuvre, behind the wheel). But this magnificently choreographed scene is far more than a merely convivial traffic jam. A girl on the pillion of a motorcycle bounces gracefully up and down behind her beau. The front wing of an "ugly duckling" Citroën 2CV, with its extraordinarily springy suspension, bounces up and down to exactly the same beat. The whole fleet of vehicles caught in the circle stops and starts to the eye-rhythm established, and a loud fairground hurdy-gurdy on the sound track synchronises all the movements into an unexpected, ravishingly beautiful and joyous merry-go-round. The central prop of *Jour de fête* returns, transformed but immediately recognisable, to demonstrate the continued presence in modern life of the simple pleasures of riding round and round.

In a shot taken as from the inside of the American tourists' bus, we see a pair of hydraulic car lifts in a service station rising and falling on the beat of the music. The most magical sequence of all, though, begins with a shot from inside a building giving on to the roundabout: a window-cleaner climbs his step-ladder and begins to wipe the already transparently clean pane of a wide, tall window that opens by swinging vertically on pivots. He pulls the pane in towards himself, and we cut to a shot of the same pane, seen from inside the tourist bus. Through the bus window we see the reflection of the bus itself and of the sky, whilst also seeing through the pane to the cleaner on the other side – just as on a train you can often see both the landscape outside and the reflection of yourself and fellow-passengers in the compartment. But as the cleaner pushes the pane up, the bus-passengers have the impression of being swung up into the sky itself, and as it rotates down again, we come back to land with a swoop, as on a fairground ride. The *oohs*! and *aahs*! of the voice track are the ladies' reactions to the general scene, we suppose, but they are synchronised with our spectator's experience of a simulated Big Dipper. This is not what is generally called a "special effect" in the cinema: it is perhaps best seen as an instance of poetic realism, where a really occurring phenomenon – the prismatic possibilities of optical glass – is observed and exploited to express and create a sense of joy and pleasure.

Tati's first appearance in a professional film – as the ghost in *Sylvie et le fantôme* – had been filmed in the same way, through a mirror set at an angle to the set, making him seem to float across the world depicted without coming into contact with it.[359] The viewer may or may not know that Tati is borrowing a technique learned from Claude Autant-Lara in 1946. But the "re-inscription" in *Playtime* of elements from Tati's entire career surely underpins the sense of plenitude that we cannot but feel in the closing sequences of the film. The ghost of Tati's ghost is utterly benign.

A more perceptible reference to Tati's earlier work comes in a shot of the roundabout from the pavement. The music track subsides and stops; a man approaches a parking meter and puts in a coin, and immediately the hurdy-gurdy music track starts again, transforming the street furniture into a juke-box, or the traffic into a recognisable "switch image" of a fairground ride. This is almost a remake of a sequence in *Jour de fête* where Postman François enters Bondu's café: the background music bridging over from the previous shot comes to a stop in mid-bar, then the postman gives a hefty kick to the pianola, and the dance-tune starts again, no longer background sound but "switched" into the diegetic musical track.

The gadgets of *Playtime*, from articulated spectacles to parking meters, from self-lighting brooms to hydraulic car-ramps, are thus not remotely sinister, nor are they generally presented in a satirical light. M. Hulot may well dissolve in this expansive, expensive celebration of the future of the city, but he spreads through it an attitude of kindly subversion, as if to recuperate even its most brutal and messy aspects as sites of convivial, simple, and child-like fun.

THIRTY-THREE

The Wide Screen

A pin drop

All Tati's films except *Playtime* are made on celluloid film 35mm wide, the almost universal standard for professional film work since the 1920s. The width of celluloid available for the photographic image on such film is rather less than 35mm, since some space on the two sides of the strip is taken up by perforations, and also, after the advent of optical and then magnetic sound, by another 3mm strip for the sound track. From around 1930 on, therefore, the standard photographic image on 35mm film was 15.6mm high by 20.8mm wide, a proportion of roughly four by three. The same proportion of height to width (the *aspect ratio*) is obtained on the screen when such a frame is projected, and this shape of image (ratio 1:1.33), came to be called the "Academy ratio". But substantial variations are possible even on conventional 35mm film. Masks or caches can cut the height of each frame, and thus increase the aspect ratio of the projected image; alternatively, special lenses can be used which "squeeze" a wider image on to the film (through a procedure called anamorphosis, often used by Renaissance painters) and "unsqueeze" it again when the film is projected. A French optical scientist called Chrétien invented the anamorphic lens and its application to the cinema in the 1920s; Autant-Lara experimented with it in a film version of Jack London's *To Make A Fire*; but the Hypergonar, as Chrétien called his invention, failed to catch on, and development work on it was stopped.[360]

Cinemascope was a US development of the Hypergonar idea. It was introduced in 1953, and was the first widely-used anamorphic procedure, allowing 35mm film to project images with aspect ratios of 1:1.66, 1:1.85 and even 1:2.35. It was tremendously popular. But why should spectators want to see panoramic, wide-screen images anyway? The human eye has an angle of vision of about 64° to either side of the perpendicular; when we look at something, we also see without looking, in the field of peripheral vision, what there is to either side of it, in an arc of about 128° from edge to edge. So in the cinema, the wider the screen image or aspect ratio, the greater the illusion that you are looking at something real, since more peripheral vision is engaged. In the very widest formats, you actually have to turn your head to see all that there is to see, as in the real world. In the early days of cinema, Abel Gance famously tried to simulate such "vision in the round" with a triptych screen (requiring three films and three projectors) for his *Napoleon*, which has an aspect ratio overall of 1:4.

Cinemascope quickly drew large audiences, and thus led to a proliferation of imitations and sub-licensed adaptations – "Dyaliscope", "Franscope", "Totalvision", and so on, with various different wide-screen aspect ratios. The film industry tried to impose standards at its Stockholm Congress of 1955, and again a couple of years later at Harrogate, and laid down a new, standard aspect ratio of 1:1.65, close to the Golden Mean. But in some eyes, the technical squeeze and stretch involved in making 35mm film project a wide-screen image led to a loss of image quality (more significant when the magnification ratio was high, as it was in those days when films were regularly shown on very large screens in auditoriums holding two and even three thousand spectators). A clever idea for using 35mm sideways-on without anamorphosis (Technirama) failed to catch on. So, with audiences now accustomed to wider images, the field lay open for the Rolls-Royce of all celluloid technologies, 70mm panoramic colour film.

On such a wide strip of film, the individual frames are 22mm high and 48.5mm wide, and have an aspect ratio of 1:2.2 without anamorphosis. In the US, 70mm film was used with anamorphosis of coefficient 1.25, giving a huge screen ratio of 1:2.7. Even from the middle of the auditorium, spectators watching such a screen have to turn their heads to follow cavalry charging, aeroplanes plunging, or Moses and his people crossing the Red Sea.

Because it fills a little more of the reality of human vision, the wide screen allows the camera to be a little less directive of the spectator's glance than was traditional in the older, squarer formats. Instead of using shot and counter-shot to show two cowboys walking towards each other down the dusty main street of a lonesome desert town, for example, you can show both of them together in a single long shot on a very wide screen. By the same token, takes can also last longer, since there is more information available, and more going on for the spectator to recognise and absorb. Such a style of pre-dominantly long shots, with long takes and more than one thing happening on the screen, is of course entirely characteristic of Tati's work from the start. Wide-screen technology seems to have been invented for him. Seventy-millimetre film was a dream come true.

Given its significantly higher cost, 70mm film was generally used only for grand spectaculars featuring box-office celebrities in visually sumptuous locations or decors. Tati wanted to use it for a quite different purpose:

> What I like in wide-screen film are not cavalcades, gunfights, crowd scenes and so on, what I find extraordinary is that the device allows the viewer to have a fuller appreciation of a mere pin dropping in a large empty room . . . [361]

There is no scene in *Playtime* that is quite so provocative, but many where perfectly ordinary things – traffic on its way to and from the airport, people standing in a bus queue, and so forth – are filmed in washed-out colour on the wide stock. But most of the shots are chock full of different and parallel things – people moving in the foreground and the background, sounds "located" in actions on the margin of the frame, tiny jokes or gags happening in a corner, or half obscured by something else. For Jean Reznikov, indeed, the "challenge" that Tati set himself with the panoramic screen was based on a "shockingly basic mistake" about human vision: for whatever the size of the screen and its ratio, the eye can only take in so much at a time, and always at the same natural angle of sight. Tati tried to fill all of his wide screen, and did so to an extent that makes it impossible to follow all the action at one viewing. Fine for film buffs who go back to watch it three times in a row, but too confusing for members of the general public who see the film only once.[362]

Lost illusions

Tati was acutely aware of the problems that variable aspect ratios created for the aesthetics of the frame. When shooting *Mon Oncle* in 1956, for example, on standard 35mm colour film, he left margins at the top and bottom of each frame (that is to say, visual space containing no significant action or detail) so that if the film were projected through an anamorphic lens on to a cinemascope-type screen, the audience would lose nothing essential.

> I am keeping to standard format, but trying at the same time to keep a safety margin at the top and the bottom of the frame, for the barbarians who keep on showing standard-format films on a panoramic screen, and thus slice off the top and the bottom of the picture.[363]

Tati also imagined the wide screen as a new way of drawing the audience back into the cinema, and away from TV screens. Simple scenes perfectly filmed on 70mm and projected with multi-track stereo sound provide an extremely rich visual and aural experience, significantly more enveloping than 35mm, and vastly more entrancing than the front end of a cathode-ray tube. Tati's hope was that the sheer lavishness of his new film would bring spectators back into cinemas, and would throw up one more hurdle in front of television's steady advance. But that forward march has come to corner Tati's most magnificent film, for when *Playtime* is shown on a TV screen, with its nearly-square ratio of 1:1.33, the loss of image content (the left and right edges disappear) makes it a mere shadow of what it was intended to be, and hardly worth taking out from a video store. Improvements in "scope" technology have allowed 35mm film to create wide-screen effects that are now just as good, and far less cumbersome to shoot and to project. As a result, 70mm projectors have now almost disappeared the world over, and it is rarely possible to watch the film that Tati actually made. The original *Playtime*, into which Tati poured all he had in order to raise a lasting monument in film, has all but disappeared.

Even the copies of *Playtime* in 35mm anamorphic format that are now sometimes shown are not copies of the original film that Tati made. Criticised as it was for being too long on its first release, Tati – now completely insolvent, and working entirely on his own – edited his film down from 140 to just under 120 minutes, cutting pieces out of the copies shown at the Empire cinema, and then out of other copies, one by one. The general-release version of *Playtime* was thus a rather shorter film than what Tati had intended. A certain Mr Lofthouse wrote from London, after the film's UK première, to protest that he had not been able to see all that Tati had made. "I can assure you," Tati replied, "that the negative of *Playtime* being in my possession, I will have the opportunity to lengthen it by two minutes each year, which will not be noticeable at all, and will enable you, in five or six years, to view the film as I have imagined it".[364] Despite this assertion, the version re-released in 1977 did not restore the cuts made ten years earlier; nor did the new 35mm anamorphic print released in the early 1990s. About twenty minutes of the original film seem to have vanished.[365]

The screen and the canvas

Tati's use of the wide frame and the wide screen is a challenge to the spectator, because it subverts and attacks comfortable habits of "film language". The camera does not lead the eye to where the "action" is. On the contrary. There is far too much to see on the screen; the "action" is not in a single narrative event, but in a multiplicity of details and movements whose significance is not always obvious straight away. Tati believed that it was the wide-film format that gave him this liberty; Badal didn't bother to explain that it was only the ratio, and above all the mise-en-scène, that created this radically new form of film art. For it is at last truly appropriate to talk of Tati's screen images as one would talk of a painting: he quite consciously used the screen as if it were a canvas, over which the eye could roam, instead of as a simulated glance, constructing a single line of vision in each take.

The early scene in the airport lounge is a magnificent case in point. The shot is filmed from a crane and shows the whole length and breadth of a large hall. In the foreground, a man and a woman on a plastic bench, looking crouched and hunched, because of the angle of the shot. To the right, a set of anonymous partitions, from which various characters emerge. In the middle ground, a sweeper, clearing up rubbish from the floor. Further back, other characters, seated and standing; and in the far depth, uniformed men and women – only on second or third viewing can you see that they are actually life-size cardboard cut-outs, not moving figures – and behind them, through a plate-glass window, the tailfin of a large passenger plane. Nothing is immediately obvious in this huge panorama. It might be a hospital waiting room: the hushed conversation of the foreground couple might signify that they are expecting the results of some test, or that the man is soon to go in for an operation. A straight-backed, uniformed woman who marches on to screen from lower right and exits behind one of the partitions could be a nurse: she is holding a white bundle or package (we cannot really tell) that might be a new-born child. (There is a child screaming somewhere – but the stereo sound track makes us unsure whether it is on or off screen.) The sweeper's equipment trolley also has a medical look; and we have been deceived, if we are French, by the film's opening pan of a pair of nuns in habit, into thinking of either an ultra-modern convent, or, more plausibly, a hospital scene. Only if we focus on the background detail – and there is no visual or aural prompt to make us do so – can we see that it is an airport lounge, and this ambiguity is maintained for far longer than most viewers easily tolerate. After sequences showing the arrival of a VIP and then of a group of American tourists, we cut back to the large hall, now slightly more crowded, and see Hulot enter from the right, in middle field, where, given the perspective, he fills not one hundredth part of the screen. He drops his umbrella, picks it up, and exits again. The panoramic ratio is combined with depth of field, and it is in the background or on the edges of the frame that many of the actions take place.

But why does M. Hulot turn up for his third filmic entrance in an airport hall? *Mon Oncle* had ended with Hulot's banishment to the provinces, and although the script called for a closing sequence at a railway station, the film actually ends with an airport scene. This, then, is Hulot's return to Paris: and just as on his departure he had become entangled with a coach-load of departing tourists, so on his return he coincides with a gaggle of American ladies passing through the hall. The "continuity" is minimal, but it is real, and for those with long memories, it is underscored by the family resemblance of the jazzy music track used for the departure scene in *Mon Oncle* and the "African Theme" used for the title sequence of *Playtime*.

More and more, as he made *Playtime*, and then spoke about it after its release, Tati used metaphors and anecdotes of painting to explain his aims, his approach and his art. "I like my films just as a painter likes his paintings," he would say to ward off invitations to express regrets about his own work. Interviewed by the *Cahiers du cinéma* in 1968, Tati likened his earlier work (*Jour de fête* in particular) to what Godard and others had done ten years later and named the "New Wave"; and with *Playtime*, he said, he had brought something quite new to the cinema again; he felt he belonged more with the younger generation of film-makers than with colleagues of his own age.[366] Ten years later, in his last long interview with critics from the *Cahiers*, Tati likened himself more explicitly to a painter – "I am in the position of a painter painting his canvas" (*je me place sur le plan d'un peintre qui fait sa toile*), and compared *Playtime* to modern abstract art.[367] Abstract art abandons figuration, and replaces it with the aesthetic organisation of colour and line; *Playtime* organises colour, shape, and light without the figurative backbone of a narrative, and, in that sense, Tati's film could be called "abstract". But in other ways it is equally important as a work of realist art – as a painting of modern life on the screen.

THIRTY-FOUR

Economic Airlines

If *Playtime* has no real story, it does at least have a narrative frame which resembles that of *Jour de fête* (which takes place over not much more than twenty-four hours) as well as the arrival-to-departure plot of *Les Vacances de M. Hulot*: a group of American holidaymakers come to Paris for a twenty-four-hour city-break in their grand European tour. They pass, in turn, through the airport, the hotel and an Ideal Home exhibition, and then have a night out at a brand-new, up-market restaurant. They see the sights, but only through a glass door, brightly; and they appear not to get a wink of sleep.

"Film N° 4" was first titled *Récréation*, meaning a play-time break in the school routine. In this form, as under its definitive international-English name of *Playtime*, the title does not at first sight seem as natural, as necessary or as directive as those of *Jour de fête*, *Les Vacances*, or *Mon Oncle*. "Playtime" does not really tell us what the film is about. What it states is more an attitude than a subject – modern life seen not as labour or activity, not in terms of relations or events, but as recreation. Tatischeff's only real talent at school had been in the breaks, and his life as rugby-man had lain essentially in the after-match entertainments; and though he had acquired a capacity for intense and meticulous effort as a mime and as a film-maker, his greatest work celebrates what he most valued in life, which was play.

Tati's reluctance to use professional actors had not abated one bit, and he wanted real American ladies to act themselves on his set. Until de Gaulle pulled French forces out of NATO in 1967, Saint-Germain-en-Laye housed the Supreme Headquarters of Allied Powers in Europe (SHAPE), and a great number of high-ranking US military personnel were housed with their families in and around the town. Tati was thus fully aware that all the "talent" he needed for his group of tourists was on his doorstep. But he wasn't quite sure how to get hold of it.

A young woman, speaking French with an American accent, turned up one day in the cafeteria of the studio complex at La Garenne-Colombes where Specta had its splendid HQ, and pertly introduced herself to the great man. She was eager to get into film, she said. Tati took her back to his office, sat her down on his vast U-shaped sofa, and offered avuncular advice. "Don't try to get into the business," he said. "Make your first short by yourself, as I did." Then: "By the way – do you know any Americans in Paris I could use for a group of tourists?"

Marie-France Siegler eagerly took on the task of unearthing a suitable group for Tati's next film, a job far exceeding what she had hoped to come by on her first trip to a film studio. She went straight to the PX in Rue Marbeuf, and read the small-ads on the social announcements board. The Officers' Wives Club was holding a cake-baking contest in two days' time. She went along, and found herself amongst a whole crowd of American housewives. She rang Tati at once, and told him to drive over as soon as he could. And that was how the squad of genuine-false American tourists was recruited for *Playtime*. "*For-mi-dable*," said Tati in his characteristic way, stressing each syllable separately; and he appointed Marie-France Siegler to her first proper job on the spot, with the title of "assistant wardrobe mistress". She soon became something more akin to a personal assistant; the two remained associates and warm friends for the rest of Tati's life.[368]

Tati took rather longer to find his leading lady, or rather, to finalise a decision that had been made in his head or his heart several years earlier. In 1961, he had got to know the German au-pair working for his neighbours in Rue Voltaire – a long-legged brunette with a pleasant face and a natural modesty that he found attractive. When he saw her at the bus-stop on her way to her afternoon French lessons at the Alliance française, Tati often picked her up in his car and gave her a lift into town. On one of these trips he asked her if she would like to act in his next film. Barbara Denneke had never thought of acting as a career. Her Bavarian parents would certainly be alarmed by their daughter abandoning her aim of becoming an air hostess, or, failing that, a bilingual secretary. But then the spirit of adventure caught her. "Why not?" she said, not knowing whether the offer was entirely serious.[369]

Barbara returned to Germany in the summer, failed to find work with Lufthansa, and got a job as a secretary in Frankfurt. She continued to keep in touch with Tati – New Year greetings, the occasional change-of-address card – but the film project remained quite uncertain. In the meantime, Specta-Films was scouting around Europe for a non-actress to play the leading lady in "Tati N° 4". The specification must have been hard to meet:

> A girl about 20–25 years old, coy, a little awkward, but with intelli-
> gent eyes, a pretty smile & a pleasant face. She must be rather tall
> (at least 1m68), have a great freshness and simplicity, and be very
> feminine. She must not look athletic.

An important point: she must not be an actress.

It matters little whether she is fair or dark. The most important is the reserved appearance, due to a good education ... [370]

Tati certainly auditioned a few aspiring non-actresses, but his mind kept coming back to the au-pair: "I have not yet definitely chosen the foreign girl who will hold the part to which, as you know, I attach a great importance. The candidates I have contacted, if they have not your defects, are most of the time lacking your qualities," he wrote to her in May. But in June 1964, with the *Playtime* project now set to begin fairly soon, Tati renewed his acquaintance with Barbara Denneke when he needed an interpreter on his visit to Düsseldorf and Cologne. He asked her again if she would like to audition for a role in a film he was now sure to be making very soon. Since the job she was doing (at Findus, the frozen food suppliers) was not very fascinating, she said yes, and was hired forthwith, on a ten-month contract to run from August 1964. Tati did not offer her an Eldorado: the salary of 3,000 francs a month was not a great deal more than what she was earning already, but it came with a free flat at Saint-Maurice, not far from Tativille, and the use of a brand-new Volkswagen car.

Tati's affair with Barbara may or may not have been his first infidelity, but it was the one which he failed to keep entirely private. The filming lasted not the ten months originally planned, but nearly twenty-four – much longer than the affair, whose break-up added palpably to the tension and gloom hanging over that interminable and ill-starred shoot. To begin with, Tati spent his week-day nights at Saint-Maurice, and returned to family life at Saint-Germain at weekends. On the surface, he seemed to cope very well with a life divided in two.[371] For there was never the slightest question of his leaving Micheline; he remained devoted to his shy and infinitely supportive wife.

Alongside his leading lady and his tourist group, Tati began to collect together his technical team in the early months of 1964. Once the decision was made to use purpose-built and not already-existing buildings for the set, he contracted the architect Eugène Roman to design and build Tativille, using design ideas long cooked up by Lagrange. He took on Claude Clément (the younger brother of the more famous René) as his first assistant. He hired Jean Bourgoin as his director of photography, and had him do a series of tests, both in colour and in black and white. But he soon came to disagree with Bourgoin, and replaced him with a celebrated proponent of "dramatic colour", the Hungarian cameraman Jean Badal.

Another important figure in the adventure of *Playtime* also came into contact with Tati in the summer of 1964. Norbert Terry, a former UN interpreter in New York, had settled in Paris in the early 1960s to bring the fairly common American practice of product placement to France, where it was still unknown. Product placement is a form both of advertising and of commercial subsidy: it seeks to bring together the makers of props, equipment and services needed in a film (from motor cars to liability insurance, from service-station chains to office-furniture suppliers) and to arrange the free or below-cost provision of the objects in return for making the product-name visible in the film itself. Both film-maker and product supplier have a joint interest in product placement, for it reduces the outlay on the film whilst providing effective exposure for the product or for its name.

Tati had set himself against the use of his talents for advertising so many times already that he was initially very hesitant to allow *Playtime* to be funded by placed products. But he got along very well with Norbert Terry, and had to concede that the young man's argument was irrefutable: given that *Playtime* was going to show cars, petrol stations, an exhibition of consumer products, a hotel, a restaurant, an airport and much of the rest of modern life, it could not very well show unnamed or unrecognisable cars, objects, gadgets and so forth; and given that names had to appear, they might as well be the names of companies decent enough to provide their products for free.

There was also a more general and perhaps deeper point in Tati's acceptance of Terry's services. Advertising was absolutely integral to the modern world that *Playtime* was aiming to depict and to undermine, as much a symbol of the new as the steel-and-glass buildings or the traffic jams and street-lighting that were about to be constructed at such huge expense. Not only would it be far more realistic for advertisements to appear on the sides of buses, on hotel walls, at the travel agent's desk, and so on, but the film itself needed to be imbued with the "spectacular" ethos of product naming and commercial image-making.[372]

From this point of view, Terry was only half-way successful. About twenty companies signed up for Tati N° 4: BP built and equipped the garage seen in the penultimate sequence at the roundabout; Simca provided nearly all the saloon cars seen in the earlier parts of the film;[373] Béhin provided some of the furniture. But rather few advertisements are seen *as advertisements* in the film: Avis (the car-rental company) gets its name on screen for a few seconds, as do Phillips, Remington, San Pellegrino, SNC, Thomas Cook, Vitos, 3M, Groupe Drouot (an insurance company) and Trigano (the camping-gear firm);[374] we hear *The New York Herald Tribune* being touted in the street, and "Quick Cleaner" being advertised on the radio in Barbara's hotel bedroom. In the supermarket scene a few other product names occur – "Ideal Cheese", "Cheese Delight", "Miss Marvell", "Pullover Parade", "Silver Match" and Pirelli, but these do not really add up to anything like the quantity of product names that a real visit to a store would reveal in a few seconds. Surprisingly, and strikingly, most of the walls of Tativille are bare: there are no advertisements on the sides of the buses that pass by, nor are there any hoardings on the streets. The density of commercial insignia, company logos, and product posters in *Playtime* is nowhere near the reality of the contemporary world, or of what it was like thirty years ago. It is probable that this had less to do with Tati's aesthetics than with Norbert Terry's failure to convince large numbers of advertisers that *Playtime* was going to be seen by large audiences. For the rumour of the disaster of Film N° 4 preceded its completion and release by several years.

The props and services supplied by the score of willing advertisers covered perhaps ten per cent of the film's total outlay, Terry believes, and thus constituted a quite significant alleviation of Tati's financial problem. But Terry simply could not find an airline willing to pay a suitable price to have its name on the luggage labels of a German au-pair and a group of US Army wives. The tourists of *Playtime* arrive not by Air France, but by the fictional and, in retrospect, ironically named "Economic Airlines". For the producer and his many creditors, it would have been far more economical if they had flown TWA.

THIRTY-FIVE

Situations

Playtime's first night at the Empire Cinema on the Avenue Wagram in December 1967 coincided with the publication of Guy Debord's *La Société du spectacle*, a book that Tati certainly never read, but which is linked with his film work in curious ways.

Debord was the *Gauleiter* of a violently fractious left-wing splinter group called the Situationist International. Its disparate ingredients, grafted on to a common attachment to the early Marx, included surrealist renegades, abstract artists of the COBRA movement (notably, Asger Jorn), and would-be town-planners and architects, such as Raoul Vaneigem. Though it soon had minute and disproportionately noisy branches in London, Copenhagen, Munich, Milan, and New York, the centre of the SI was Paris, whence it distributed its journal *Potlatch* and, from around 1957, *L'Internationale situationniste*. The SI was never very specific about what it would do when the Revolution came. Its main concern was to analyse, to describe and to denounce – in often brutally aggressive terms – the inauthenticity, alienation, and hollowness of "spectacular society".

In its disagreeable and provocative way, Debord's quarrelsome faction was an essential element in the turn towards everyday life that constituted one of the most important intellectual adventures of post-war France. Henri Lefèbvre's *Critique de la vie quotidienne* was the philosophical source-book for much non-Communist Marxist thinking of the 1950s and 1960s; but it was through Situationist tracts, very probably, that ideas for constructing, or at least imagining, alternative, "unalienated" forms of living found their way into the minds of large numbers of people who were themselves in no sense biding their time until the next revolution.

For Debord, what characterised modern society was its panoply of devices for transforming authentic life into alienated spectacle, and for making passive spectators out of citizens who by rights should be participants in their own lives. Situationist recipes for resisting this disaster focused both on the physical environment and on mental disciplines. An early tract by one of

the German members of the network, for example, called for functional
buildings to be replaced by "accidental architecture", in which emotion,
not rationality, would be the determining criterion. It gave a mad and
inspirational blueprint for the "Impractical Dwelling" which would reconcile
man with his environment and make his life immeasurably more convivial
and authentic:

> We must therefore spread the impractical dwelling. A few sharp
> corners to bump into, an extended route from bed to cupboard, so
> as to inhabit your flat more fully, a creaking door, a lock that does
> not work, a wobbly table, an uncomfortable armchair . . .
>
> Accidental architecture allows change and even aims for histori-
> city. The age of a house should not be readable only in terms of its
> style. It should also be noticeable in the advance of rust, in the
> decomposition of the concrete, in the flaking of the plaster. Classical
> modernist houses become sordid as they age. Accidental construc-
> tions acquire patina, like mediaeval buildings.[375]

But the revolution could also be made in the head as well as in brick and
plaster. To reconfigure the urban landscape, Situationists practised the "drift"
or *dérive*: a purposeless perambulation which allowed the city itself to shape
the route and to create what they called "psycho-geographical situations".
Stripped of its revolutionary rhetoric, "drifting" is much the same thing
as idling with an entirely open mind, and with heightened sensitivity to the
reality, and not just to the signs, of the city.

To undermine the false surface of modern life, the Situationists also
proposed and practised the ambiguous and enthralling technique of *détournement*. The French word has a range of meanings – misappropriation,
embezzlement, kidnapping, and the corruption of minors are the main
ones – but in Situationist usage, which became quite widespread and is now
effectively the word's primary sense, it means twisting things into shapes and
forms they were not meant to have, and it covers such schoolboyish fun
as intentional misquotation as well as barely less grown-up stunts like
redesignating double yellow lines on the kerbside as authorisations for
double parking. When Georges Perec asked in one of his slighter texts
why you cannot buy cigarettes at the pharmacy, or why subway tunnels are
not reserved for cyclists,[376] he was indulging in a minor but recognisably
Situationist exercise. And when Tati falls asleep at his desk in the Plastac
factory, in *Mon Oncle*, in response to the regular sighing-breathing noise of
the machinery, he too, though he probably did not know it, is turning
détournement into a comedy gag that can be seen by those with a revolutionary mind-set as an implicitly subversive act.

Situationist writing is not intentionally funny at all, and only those who are amused by verbal violence in the service of a lost cause can smile when they read Guy Debord. Nonetheless, the supposedly revolutionary techniques promoted by IS are easily recognisable as the very tools of Tati's subtle comedies of observation. It is no surprise to learn that Guy Debord was a great admirer of his films;[377] but it is much more difficult to explain how a sixty-year-old denizen of Saint-Germain-en-Laye with a literary and political culture no richer than that of an average accountant's clerk could invent a film which echoes and implements many of the ideas of an uncompromising underground guru of the permanent revolution.

Mon Oncle expresses quite a few of the theses of Situationist architectural thought – Hulot's house in the old town, with its illogically lengthy stairs and passageways, is a virtual demonstration of Feuerstein's "accidental architecture", and as Hulot keeps his door key in a roof-gutter clearly visible in long shot from the middle of the village square, his "insecurity system" echoes some of the more political ideas of the IS too. But *Playtime* is imbued with Debord's critique of modern society in a more fundamental and pervasive way. The whole of the first part, from Hulot's arrival at the airport in the morning through to nightfall, when he visits Schneider's apartment, has the exact form of a "drift" or *dérive*; and the whole of the second part, in which a pretentious restaurant falls to pieces and generates a night of authentic enjoyment, is an elaborate exercise in *détournement*. This is not a question of direct influence or of inspiration; a meeting between Debord and Tati in the early 1960s is about as likely to have happened as the chat in a Zürich bar between Lenin, Tristan Tzara and James Joyce that Tom Stoppard cooked up in *Travesties*. But the striking confluence of the Situationists' understanding and of Tati's observation of social realities suggest that they were both in touch with the deeper currents of French national anxieties. *La Société du Spectacle* is commonly held to be a harbinger of the outbreak of youthful anger and joy that captured the world's attention six months later, in May 1968. Like most people of his generation, Tati probably saw those "events" as the near-collapse of French society; and he seemed to some to be merely trying to clamber on to a bandwagon when he declared that in *Playtime* he too had been on the barricades. But he was not wrong to say that at all. His masterpiece is indeed a critique of the inauthenticity and alienation of modern life, but it is a far more effective and humane one than can be found in the sybilline utterances of Guy Debord.

The "Royal Garden" restaurant is the chosen site of Tati's own joyous revolution, which in his mind, it seems, was specifically French:

The general theme of *Playtime* can be summed up thus:

In the planned and organised world that is being got ready for us, where everything is directed towards improving working conditions and infrastructure, there remains a place for individuals, as long as they keep enough of their individualism and personality, and that is what is peculiar to the French, who can adapt anything available to their own needs and natures . . . [378]

The curiously "national" ambition of the whole project had been stressed by Tati even in interviews that preceded the start of shooting:

[Our role] is to make people laugh, and also to show that, whatever the architecture, and however much one town may look like another, *l'esprit français* will always survive![379]

The dinner dance at the Royal Garden, from the arrival of its first distinguished customer in a silver Rolls-Royce to the departure of the Tubby American from breakfast at the drugstore, lasts all night, and also for almost half the length of the whole film. The choice of a restaurant is no doubt in part a reminiscence of Tati's first professional engagements as a mime, when he did a "clumsy waiter" routine at Louis Leplée's no doubt equally pretentious establishment in the early 1930s; and it also provides a chance to remake in a magnificently lavish setting the frightful meal that forms the centrepiece of *Gai dimanche*. But it also provides a cunning way of presenting Tati's own commentary on the *société de consommation*, an expression far more suggestive of eating and drinking than its English counterpart, "consumer society".

The first overdressed diners order the speciality of the house, *Turbot à la Royale*. The fish is brought to them, but has to be warmed up, basted in its sauce and seasoned on the mobile grill that is placed by the diners' table. In a sequence of gags of extreme complexity, the fish is prepared for its *consommation* not once, not twice, but three times over, owing to confusions among the waiters and to diners changing their tables. The turbot looks quite delicious. *Vous allez vous ré-ga-ler*, the maître d'hôtel declares three times over in deep-throated, salivating tones. And yet no one does make a meal of it. The triple repetition of the preparation, presentation, and description of a succulent dish that never gets near a hungry mouth is a long-drawn-out, almost agonisingly funny commentary on the insubstantiality of the objects of desire in a consumer society: what is sought after and offered is but an appearance of a dish – a shop-window fish – a hollow *spectacle* of life.

Hulot gets into the Royal Garden not because he is part of the tourist group, nor because he has booked a table, but simply because he is recognised and roped in by his old army pal, now working as the doorman. Tony Andall, who plays the role, was indeed an old pal of Tati's, though not from army days: he lived on a river-barge moored at the Ile de la Jatte in the Seine, and the inner circle of senior chums on the Tativille set often spent their evenings having at least as good a time *chez Andall* as they had had during the day shooting the Royal Garden episodes.[380]

The restaurant is barely finished for its opening night, and the harassed assistant architect is held responsible for all that seems to go wrong. A floor-tile in the centre of the dance floor sticks to a waiter's foot; the serving hatch from the galley is not wide enough for the fish-platter; the heating control is over-sensitive and difficult to adjust; eventually, the trellis decor collapses with a little help from Hulot. However, the biggest flaws in the design of the restaurant are due neither to shoddy workmanship nor to functional miscalculations. The flashing neon sign beneath the street canopy, a spiral ending in a directional arrow, like a convoluted question mark in lights, is designed to attract customers into the place. What it actually does is to cause drunks ejected from the restaurant to follow the direction of the gyrating lights and to be drawn, willy-nilly, straight back into the place.

The other huge mistake is the restaurant's central design feature, a four-pronged "royal" crown that is integrated into the wrought-iron backs of the diners' chairs. Gentlemen's jackets become impressed with the insignia, as do the bare backs of ladies wearing evening dress. As the restaurant collapses, the Tubby American who takes charge of the night allows only those bearing

Fig. 78: *The neon sign*

the brand-mark of the Royal Garden to enter his improvised *guinguette*. The accidental by-product of thoughtless and pretentious design becomes a ticket to a more convivial world.

Nobody, least of all Hulot, actually seeks to disrupt the evening at the Royal Garden, for the place falls to pieces all on its own. That collapse of

Fig. 79: *Lagrange's sketches for the Royal Garden seats*

the physical environment, however, is what permits stilted, pretentious and aggressive behaviour to give way to calmer, warmer and more popular forms of fun: an old tune – *Nini peau de chien* – on the piano, jokes and laughter at a table with a red-checked cloth ... *Sous les pavés, la plage!* students wrote on Paris walls a few months later; beneath the posh restaurant, there is a *vrai petit bistrot* waiting to be found, seems to be the message of the Royal Garden episode of Tati's *Playtime*.

Fig. 80: *The Royal Garden, just before the collapse of the decor*

Not the least paradox of Tati's film is that it suggests both a revolutionary sensibility, and a rather nostalgic, not to say reactionary view of the world. Just as paradoxical is the thoroughly globalised dialogue (characters speak English and German as well as French, and many sentences are indeterminate mixtures of two if not three tongues), and the almost explicit assertion of a specifically French ability to survive the pressures of modern life by sub-verting them. Like *Jour de fête*, but on a far grander scale, *Playtime* provokes political and historical interpretations, but avoids giving simple confirmation to any one of them.

Perhaps the most mysterious gag of all in the immensely rich canvas of *Playtime* is the story of the "clothes-peg man", the waiter whose trouser-leg is the first piece of clothing to be damaged by the sharp angles of the Royal Garden's furniture and decor. The manager has him stand outside on the balcony, so his embarrassingly torn trousers should not be seen by the guests. But other accidents occur to waiters at roughly five-minute intervals. One tears his white jacket on a chair, and comes outside to switch it with the banished waiter's on the balcony. Then another waiter splits open his shoe on the badly-lit step of the restaurant's mezzanine level, and comes out to exchange it for the scapegoat's still good shoe. The excluded waiter acquires a bow tie that has fallen into the sauce, a soiled napkin, and so on, in a

Fig. 81: *The* guinguette *at the Royal Garden (at the piano, Barbara Denneke; in a cap, the set carpenter; seated, middle, Michèle Brabo)*

long-drawn-out, typically Tatiesque gag structure, which becomes funny through repetition and incremental exaggeration. But who or what is this bizarre dirty-clothes-hanger of convenience? Tati may only have been able to conceive of him as a joke about a restaurant. What we can see in the victim's slowly-constructed plight, however, is the very process of scape-goating, or the comic creation of an entirely unfunny truth: from him that hath not, shall be taken away. The waiter-on-the balcony routine is in the end a subtle and surprising variation on the themes of marginalisation and social exclusion which provide *Mon Oncle* with its narrative line and its tragi-comic ending. The Hulot role is indeed shared out in *Playtime*, just as Tati intended.

Playtime is the only one of Tati's films that is populated almost entirely by

Fig. 82: Playtime: *The Excluded Waiter*

humans (or by cardboard cut-outs of human figures): the absence of the dogs, cats, horses, chickens, geese, and goats that are important and often central figures in all of Tati's other work is a mark of what is deeply wrong with the world portrayed. The loss of the natural, animal world is underlined by the wonderfully implausible crowing of a cock that greets the Seriously Drunk Young Man as he exits from the Royal Garden in the grey light of a summer's dawn. Does he just imagine it in his stupor? Is there really a chicken-coop in the backyard of some hovel hidden by the great towers of Tativille? Or is it one more little reminder of Tati's earlier work, the animal-farm sound track of *Jour de fête*? But the comic irony of the cock-crow is also a notation of sadness, a reminder of precisely what it is that has been lost in the world of *Playtime*.

There is a small, but perhaps significant exception to the general absence of animal life in *Playtime*. Whilst Hulot is being entertained by Schneider's display of domestic trinkets and an account of his winter holiday, Giffard, the office factotum from the Strand Building, returns home – with a plaster on his nose, identical in shape and position to the plaster on Hulot's nose at the end of *Les Vacances* – to the flat next door. He is tended by his wife and presumably his mother-in-law, gets into leisure wear, and then takes the dog for a walk. The dog, which has no other role in the film, thus allows Giffard to come across Hulot in the street, and to establish contact with him in a way that the Strand Building had itself prevented. It is a plausible sequence of events, but also a self-indulgently sentimental episode. As in a Tintin comic or many a children's cartoon, a four-legged friend provides the opportunity and the excuse for an outbreak of human interaction and warmth.

THIRTY-SIX

Fish in Water

Tati abandoned Postman François once he had created him, and he would have liked to do the same with Hulot. Unlike Chaplin's bowler-hatted persona, Hulot was not just a comedy act that could be repeated in a different environment, nor was he quite a character with a potential for development through time. Hulot was more like a principle or an idea: Tati would have liked him to be a presence in works other than his own, but only Truffaut ever took up the suggestion, using Tati's regular double, Jacques Cottin, to play a cameo Hulot role in *Domicile conjugal* (*Bed and Board*, 1970). Commercial logic dictated that Hulot had to be in *Playtime*, and all the more because Tati had not invented any other human vehicle to carry his vision of the modern city. But to compensate for an obligation that he said he would rather be without, he tried to find ways of making Hulot dissolve in the film. The means chosen for this paradoxical project was to *multiply* Hulot into a set of episodic characters, each seen for a few seconds in different scenes.

An original-cast roster for what was planned as a 178-day shoot lists three "alternative" Hulots alongside the real one – an English Hulot, a Swedish Hulot and a "false Hulot", each required to be on set for four or five days of shooting, whereas Tati-Hulot would be needed on 100 days in all. In the draft script, the narrative begins when the "pretty foreigner" thinks she recognises M. Hulot in the airport hall – but finds it is only his English look-alike. Nearly all of this disappears in the finished film,[381] which took far more than 178 days of shooting, and ended up using many characters and several set locations not mentioned in the script or rosters. What remains of the multiple Hulots is a scarf-wearing youngster who causes confusion at the exhibition because his hat, coat and pipe make him vaguely resemble Tati's screen image when seen from behind; a "false Hulot" seen leaving the Strand Building by Giffard (who runs into the glass door in pursuit), and another false Hulot seen later on outside the Strand by the same Giffard, and who turns out to be black.

Hulot is moved off-centre in *Playtime* not just by being multiplied, but by not being given any of the major comedy turns. The dance of the glaziers, the travel agent's heel-and-toe routine, the journalist's reverse-walk and the news photographer's ballet posture, Giffard's ski-mime and Claude Schurr's outrageous dance steps, Billy Bourbon's drunk act, and the dancer whose high heel snaps as she walks through the Royal Garden – all these physical comedy gags that enhance the dream-like quality of the film are done by others, not by Tati. Hulot is almost nothing more than a presence and a posture in *Playtime*, and he is almost never in the centre of the wide screen. One of the most daring reversals of "normal" comedy practice is the sequence that follows Hulot's arrival at the Strand Building. The concierge, centre screen in front of his vast communications panel of winking lights and buzzers, tries to establish contact with Hulot's business partner. Hulot himself is seated behind the concierge, virtually blocked off from our view, except that he stretches his long neck out to the side, trying to see what the concierge is doing, but also allowing us to see him. It is a composition that is on the verge of clumsiness and incompetence, yet it works extremely well, making both the baffled concierge and the hesitant, obedient, but curious Hulot alternative centres of visual and comic effect.

Tati often declared that his aim was to make the comedy gag more "democratic": funniness, he said, should not be the sole apanage of the comedy star, but distributed amongst all the participants in a film, as it is in life.[382] Tati certainly did not mean by this that he wanted to make fun of everybody else in *Playtime*, nor that he simply wanted to invite his spectators to observe the comedy of life. None of the gags in *Playtime* is a mere observation, even less is it the accidental fruit of candid-camera techniques. What Tati parcels out in *Playtime* is not comedy itself, but the comedy *gag*, which is an altogether more constructed affair.

Few of the gags in *Playtime* are of the aural, visual, or mental double-take kind that virtually defines the humour of *Les Vacances* and *Mon Oncle*; indeed, some of them are so unmarked as to be barely comic turns at all. At the roundabout sequence towards the end of the film a milk van stops near the curb, a delivery boy hops out, places bottles on the pavement, and springs like a gazelle back into his van. This was supposed to be shot with a real delivery man: but Tati worried all night long before the take. Would he be able to do it properly? he asked Badal. Would a delivery boy be able to imitate himself to perfection? And so he cancelled the shoot, and started looking for a ballet dancer, which took several days to find. The gag, if it is such, is to have the springy step of a delivery boy imitated with such grace and timing that it rises to the level of ballet, a comic vision of ordinary life enhanced by its re-enactment in mime.

Tati himself performs some of the comic mimes in the film. Captured on the pavement by his parvenu army pal (whose physical appearance and manner make him almost a repeat of M. Arpel in *Mon Oncle*) and taken into the lobby of the "fishbowl" apartment building, Hulot wipes his feet, as Schneider does, on the mat. The wiping continues as what we imagine to be a lively conversation goes on – and it goes on, and on, and on. Tati's long legs, coupled with his peculiar posture, make the scene an *imitation* of a man wiping his shoes, and, also, quite unexpectedly, a picture of a man miming the motions of a dog's hind legs.

The Hulot of *Playtime* also finds himself off balance on a couple of occasions, which seem to echo and answer each other in the film. First, when introduced by the concierge to the glass-sided waiting room of the Strand Building, he tests his weight on the floor, in the manner of a man with time to waste – and, finding the thermoplastic tiles more highly polished than expected, slips forward and falls over, arms and umbrella asplay. Then, when being silently entertained to Schneider's winter-holiday anecdotes, he makes as if to copy the amateur skier's demonstration of what fun it is to schuss down the slopes, and instantly collapses on to the floor. Combined with Hulot's bewildered pursuit of Giffard through the open-plan office spaces, his capture by the unsuspected lift, and many other tiny sequences where he is so to speak taken unawares by his environment, the Hulot of *Playtime* is even less at home in the physical world than his previous incarnations in *Mon Oncle* and *Les Vacances*.

Some of the more straightforwardly comic turns are played by non-professionals used entirely as themselves. The concierge was given little instruction about how to operate the blinking-buzzing panel in the Strand Building foyer: most of the takes are the "genuine" reactions of a retired Paris porter to the equipment put in front of him.[383] Similarly, the carpenter hauled in to account for the inadequate width of the serving hatch in the Royal Garden galley is the regular set carpenter, who did not at first know he was being used as a comedy turn. And the plumbers in the Drugstore sequence using their syphons and piping to appropriate supplies of wine are actual workmen, not actors pretending to be on to a good thing.

Most of the imitation gags were carefully and intensely rehearsed. The cleaner, the officers, the journalists and the tour guide in the opening airport scenes, the pivoting secretary in the labyrinthine open-plan office, the girls demonstrating the various gadgets in the ideal home exhibition, the travel agent dancing on his seat, and the American businessman with his nasal spray, mouth spray, document-case and perfect crease, all took mime lessons from the director, who spent long hours showing them how to perform themselves. (In the restaurant sequences, a few professional mimes are used, notably the clown, Billy Bourbon, who repeats his already-famous drunk act.) The physical style of Tati the mime artist is distributed through the huge cast of *Playtime*, and the effect is indeed to dissolve M. Hulot into a whole world through which his spirit moves, like a fish through water.

The one character in the film who does no obvious miming and who has no comic dimension at all is the leading lady, Barbara, who in this respect repeats the role of Martine, in *Les Vacances de M. Hulot*. All she really does is to allow Hulot to occupy the margins of the screen, since she is centred so much of the time. Attractive and charming as she is, Barbara cannot really be said to add much to the film as a whole; her simplicity and sincerity is utterly overshadowed by the constructed reality of the almost uncountably many mimes.

But it is not just the characters who imitate themselves in Tati's most grandiose film: the inanimate world also seems inclined to represent itself as another. The clearest examples are the roundabout that turns into a merry-go-round, and the parking meter that mimics a coin-in-the-slot music box; but there are of course also major features, such as the airport hall that seems to be masquerading as a hospital waiting room, and minor props, like the lamp-standard taken for a vertical hand-rail in the old Paris bus. In *Playtime*, almost everything is – in some sense – *playing* at being something else. And it is this subtle humour of mimicry that makes *Playtime*, despite its lack of a real plot and its absence of any straightforwardly comic exploits, a comedy film. It does not hit you in the eye. To spectators geared up to see the sequel of *Les Vacances* and *Mon Oncle*, it seemed an overlong, often boring, failure. Audiences at the Empire smiled, but few of them laughed outright.

THIRTY-SEVEN

Towers of Babel

Tati would have liked to rule over his set and crew as a benevolent despot: "I like team work, as long as I'm in sole charge of the team . . . And then, I prefer directing to acting . . ."[384] However, it became apparent after a time that Tati could not quite meet the basic requirement of authority – regular pay. So the technical staff responded in kind, and were not always regular with their work, putting the film back a little more every day. They insisted on downing tools for every regulation break, and finishing dead on the hour of six, whatever the stage of the shoot. Even so, when Tati was short of money and equipment, film stock, or props were not available, the crew would turn up nonetheless, and sit around, or else use the set and its facilities to get on with work of their own. Barbara Denneke, for instance, filled in her many spare hours by learning to sew on the wardrobe department's sewing machine.[385] Sylvette Baudrot did her knitting. One of the craftsmen developed an interesting sideline in abstract wrought-iron decorations. Over the two long years of shooting, from early 1965 through to the end of 1966, Tativille was a very undisciplined place of work.

More senior technical staff could not afford to hang around waiting for Tati's next loan or advance. Sylvette Baudrot, the continuity editor, had taken on other engagements for 1966, as had Jean Badal: both needed jobs that would pay them a decent wage. Andreas Winding stood in for Badal for much of the Royal Garden shooting; and Marie-France Siegler replaced Sylvette for a time. These discontinuities are barely visible in the final cut; more perceptible are the additions made to keep the film up to date, such as the long-haired louts with the ghetto-blaster who interrupt the attempts by an American soldier to get a good snap of Barbara with the "typically French" street flower-seller. But history would not stand still, even for Tati: when *Playtime* was finally released in December 1967, de Gaulle had pulled France out of NATO, and uniformed US soldiers were never more to be seen on Paris streets.[386]

Tati also ran through a whole set of assistant directors, none of whom could really afford to spend years earning a pittance on a single film. Claude Clément, René Clément's younger brother, left the set in high dudgeon at Tati's dictatorial manner; Nicolas Ribowski lasted only a few months; and Marie-France Siegler, who had no real experience of the trade but could now earn her nickname of *CinéSiegler*, emerged as assistant director as well as continuity girl to plug the gap that had been left.

Henri Marquet and Jacques Lagrange remained faithful to their old friend to the end, even if they could not do much to help him out of the hole he had dug. The worse it got, the more Tati slowed down, and the more he pursued not the best shot available, but the perfect one. He could not really believe that he would be abandoned by everyone; for a while, he trusted an off-hand comment made by André Malraux, the Minister of Culture, that something would be done to save Tativille; but he must have known, if only dimly, that nothing would come of it. The first expulsion order had come in early 1965. No Paris studio would allow him in to complete the shoot.[387] Only a great deal of obstinacy and luck would allow him to finish the film; only vast public enthusiasm all over the world could save it from disaster.

The original project for the film was for a special kind of filmed entertainment – a show that would run in a single house, with pre-booked seats and audience involvement, more like live theatre than regular cinema (see above, p. 234 for the terms of the original contract). Specta-Films retained first-run Paris distribution rights, even after general-release rights had been sold; and what remained of Tati's original plan resulted in *Playtime* being launched at a very expensive cinema, serving not a popular, but an elite clientèle. But it was not the Paris audience that would make or break Specta-Films: it was the US.

Hulot says nothing in the whole of the film, and almost none of the narrative is conveyed through its dialogue, but that does not mean to say there is no speech. On the contrary, "talk" is all around, all the time, in *Playtime*. "The dialogue is background sound as you hear it when you're in the street, in Paris or New York," Tati said to Jonathan Rosenbaum.[388] It consists of fragments of formal and informal greetings (*Hulot! L'armée! L'armée!*), of functional and directional commands (This way, ladies!), of telephone calls, loudspeaker announcements, expostulations, enquiries, orders at the travel agents, radio advertisements, newspaper hawkers, and so on, a wonderful mosaic of all the phatic functions that human speech can perform without ever constituting a finished sentence. But language-snippets of precisely that kind are more than ordinarily dialectal, and have to be adjusted quite precisely to the social and regional situation of the speaker. Tati could get his *titis parisiens* quite right, because he knew exactly what a concierge or a plumber might say. But what about all the rest? He needed help. And he turned – at a late stage, and in quite a rush – to perhaps the most famous American in Paris, the columnist Art Buchwald, who had long been writing about French topics for the *New York Herald Tribune*. But Buchwald had by then gone back to the States. So Tati caught the next plane to Washington, taking unedited cans of *Playtime* with him, and spent a week of intense work adjusting the English language-gestures of his as-yet undubbed film.

Buchwald claims to be surprised by the large credit he got in the title sequence – *Dialogues anglais: Art Buchwald*, in huge letters on the screen – since he regarded his role as not much more than that of copy-editor. It is likely though that Tati thought that Buchwald was really famous in the US, and that his name on the screen might function as a kind of guarantee when it came to getting US distribution for the film. If that was so, then all that can be said is that it didn't come off.

What does come off spectacularly well, however, in both the "French" and "international" versions of *Playtime*, is the portrayal of a world where languages mingle and, to some extent, merge. Tati had used the comedy of semi-polyglottery in *Les Vacances*, where the Commander begins sentences in English and finishes them in French, but in the 1960s, in Gaullist France, the issue of "language purity" was no longer generally seen as a comical subject. René Etiemble, despite his own great wit and erudition, had made *Franglais* – the progressive incorporation into French of English terms and even turns of phrase – a political as well as a linguistic issue.[389] Language purists, of which the French have always had many eminent examples, and never more than in the late 1960s, could see *Playtime* as a filmed polemic against what they thought of as the bastardisation, the mongrelisation, or even the creolisation of French. Yet the language-games of Tati's film and of Buchwald's dialogue do not really justify such a view. Most of the characters speak one language in native form, and a second language – either English or French – imperfectly; when speaking their second language, they often break down and lapse into their native tongue – for example, Rainer Kohldehoff, the "inventor" of the silently slamming door, who falls back on German when he gets really angry, or the Tubby American in the Royal Garden party scene, who reverts to English when he gets over-excited; but nobody much – not Schneider, not Giffard, not Barbara – comes out with actual sentences in Franglais. Tati's portrait of an international and multilingual world is more realistic than polemical, and comical only in pointing up the strange clashes and mix-ups that occur when several tongues are spoken at once. The language-world of *Playtime* is indeed that of any European airport or hotel lobby; but it also recreates on a small scale the language-world in which Tati lived in the later 1930s as an international touring performer.

THIRTY-EIGHT

The End of the Road

Critics were not blind to the beauty of *Playtime*, but most treated it in their reviews as the confirmation of a disaster foretold. There had been too many press trailers already for Tati's "film-tortue, film-monstre, film-mystère", as *Paris-Jour* called it.[390] The director had moaned to journalists already that he was on the verge of bankruptcy, that he was going to give up and go away, that he would rather face raging tigers on safari than the critics of his greatest film, because it was bound to be misunderstood.[391] In the summer of 1967, he declared:

> I'm fed up playing Don Quixote. I've ruined my health in this adventure and I've really got everyone against me. After *Playtime*, I would really like to stop.[392]

Tati also made himself very unpopular with film journalists by keeping them as far away as he could from the set and the editing studios, and by allowing only a very few interviews in the final stages prior to the launch. He must have got on the wrong side of a good number of them, for in their annual "awards" for 1968, they granted Tati (*ex aequo* with Marlon Brando) the "Lemon", their booby-prize for the least amenable, not to say the rudest, of the subjects they had had to treat.[393] Haughty, defensive, and often silent, Tati was not a good interviewee. He expected to be treated as the genius that he undoubtedly was. But given the plight he was in, his poor relations with not necessarily very competent or admirable publicists did not help this *enfant terrible* to reach the wide audience that he, and Specta-Films, desperately needed.

A month before the first night, *Minute* headlined: *Tati au bout du Hulot*, a clever pun on "Tati at the end of his tether". Tati's appeal against the court judgment in favour of Orain also took place at the wrong time, on 30 October 1967, and was widely reported in the press in early November.[394] It really did not help *Playtime* to have Tati's financial dirty washing in the news just before the launch. Moreover, *Playtime* did not go on to general release straight away: for several weeks it could only be seen at the Empire, which, though it was equipped at Tati's insistence (and funding from a children's clothes designer) with a crèche for young children,[395] charged higher prices than other cinemas in Paris. Creditors who had not already grown wary and weary of Tati could now see very clearly what was coming.

Rights for the UK and Scandinavia were sold, and the film met a more enthusiastic response in those countries. In England, houses were eighty per cent full for *Playtime*, at least in its first weeks of showing. A British producer, Dmitri de Grunwald, who had met the Tatis on holiday at La Baule, seemed keen to come up with the finance for another Hulot film. The press coverage in Mexico, Uruguay, Argentina, and Ecuador was more than satisfactory. But French audiences, and above all US distributors, were unconvinced.

> There's one good reason: out of every ten spectators asked, one claimed to have enjoyed the film, three admitted to having been made to smile, but the remaining six, as they emerged from the two-and-a-half hour show looking as glum as the grave, had the same refrain: *Tati c'est fini!* (It's all over for Tati!)[396]

For Germany, Tati decided to dub a special version, and worked with a German translator in Paris through the weeks of April, May and June 1968, when Paris was in a state of siege. For this version, Barbara, Reiner Kohldehoff and the manager of the Royal Garden were dubbed by German speakers (in the first two cases, the same actors were used, since they were German). But for all the other roles, Tati made the *original* actors read the German translation, that is to say, to speak a language they did not understand. It was a daring experiment in the mongrelisation of tongues, in the service, presumably, of Tati's notion of comic realism.[397]

It is not uncommon for six months or more to elapse before a new foreign film finds an American distributor (and even more common for foreign films to find no way into US cinemas at all). But six months after *Playtime*'s Paris première, student demonstrations in the Latin Quarter turned into riots and all of a sudden France seemed once again to be on the brink of revolution. The "Events" of May 1968 made headlines world-wide, and displaced all other kinds of news from France. *Playtime*, like Georges Perec's novel, *Things*, and many other cultural exports from France, lost even a marginal hold on American attention, since they came from "before". The connection between Tati's vision of the new and what was actually happening on the streets was far from obvious: in the context of what for a while seemed like a massive turning point in European history, *Playtime* had no obvious relevance, and US distributors simply ignored it. Writing to his bankers at the start of the following year, Tati explained that the events of May 1968 were the main reason for late payments from overseas distributors of *Playtime* and thus for Specta-Film's increasing indebtedness.[398] But the main reason was not late payment, but the fact that no payments at all were due from the US, since no distributor had been or ever would be interested in the film. Only American money could have saved Specta-Films from default, and it never came. It was not until late 1970 that a copy even found its way to the US, and was given a "sneak preview" at an out-of-centre New York cinema (the Continental Theater, in Queens). Tati was disappointed not to be invited to come and talk to the audience about "the qualities and faults of this difficult child, who lacks violence as well as sex appeal, but who expresses a certain gentleness", as he wrote in his curious English to his contact at the Walter Reade Organisation.[399] But it would have been to no avail. *Playtime* never has had a full commercial release in the US, even now (1999).[400]

Bankruptcy is not a happy event, and the collapse of Tati's empire left many sore feelings. Not only the French rights, but also the prints and negatives of all Tati's films were seized and held in escrow by the courts: from late 1967, *Jour de fête*, *Les Vacances de M. Hulot*, *Mon Oncle*, and even *Soigne ton gauche* were taken out of circulation, and would not be seen legally in France for nearly ten years. None perhaps felt more abused by the disaster than Bernard Maurice, who had run the administrative side of Tati's operations for more than fifteen years. He had become a stakeholder in Specta, and as its Managing Director, found himself liable for its outstanding debts to the relevant parts of the social security system (URSSAF).[401] He and Tati parted company at the end of 1968 on the very worst of terms; and many other people to whom Specta owed money began to think of Tati as a crook and a cheat.

Tati swallowed his pride and asked anybody who would listen to him for help and, more especially, for money, since he now had nothing to live on at all. His old rugby captain, Alfred Sauvy, was glad to respond. He had long before set up a fund for impecunious scholars, the Association Etudes et Recherches, and he may well have used that to tide over his old friend. But he did more. He sent a round-robin to all the surviving members of the Sauvy Fifteen and got them to make (quite significant) contributions to an endowment for Micheline.[402] Jacques was kept out of this (quite wisely, since any money given to him would have gone straight to the Crédit Lyonnais, the UFIC, and other creditors). As a result, there was at least enough income to keep the Tati family in groceries. Many other anonymous well-wishers sent Tati money: postal orders came from schoolchildren all over France, and from further afield. But donations from fans and admirers were drops in an ocean of debt. They could not possibly save the Tatischeffs' beautiful home at Saint-Germain.

Number 9, Rue Voltaire was repossessed by creditors and auctioned off in 1969, just after the death of Tati's mother, Claire Van Hoof. His sister Nathalie, now aged sixty-five, who had moved to Rue Voltaire after retiring from her lingerie business a few years before, lost her home just as much as Jacques and Micheline did. Her companion, Fernande Plé, could afford to rent a flat in Saint-Germain, which gave her at least a place to live. However, what would otherwise have been her share of the family legacy had been invested in Specta-Films, which was now insolvent. Nathalie thus had nothing to look forward to in her retirement and old age.

Tati and Micheline moved back to Rue de Penthièvre, where they rented a small flat a few yards from their old home. Sophie and Pierre, now in their early twenties, could fend for themselves. It was a terrible defeat. Tati wanted to give up entirely. Leave Paris, go on safari, get away from it all. It is hardly surprising that he sank into a long and deep depression.

The end of the road came in 1974. After long-drawn-out legal procedures Specta-Films was dissolved, and its few remaining assets sold at auction. Potential buyers were alerted by the following advertisement in the "Miscellaneous" section of the film industry's professional weekly.

Adj. **AU TRIBUNAL DE COMMERCE PARIS**, le 25 AVRIL 1974 à 14 h 15 - **FONDS**
En -un
seul lot   **L'ENSEMBLE DES DROITS**   pouvant appartenir à :
                                                       sarl • SPECTA FILMS •
sur les films de long & court métrage, parlant, Noir & Blanc, Couleur
ci-après : **PLAYTIME - MON ONCLE - LES VACANCES DE M. HULOT - JOUR DE FETE**
et **SOIGNE TON GAUCHE - L'ECOLE DES FACTEURS - COURS DU SOIR.**
Mise à prix : 120 000 F (NE pouvant être baissée). Consign. 50 000 F.
S'ad. Me DEMORTREUX. Not. 67, bd St-Germain - M· PINON. Synd. 16, r. Abbé-Epée.

Fig. 83: *Official announcement of the sale of Tati's work*
(From Le Film français *n° 1528, April 1974)*

The starting price of 120,000 francs was barely more than it would have cost to buy the same amount of blank celluloid. At that price, there was at least a starting bid. But the traditional auctioneer's candle burned down before a second bid came, and Tati's entire oeuvre – the physical cans of films as well as all rights to exploit the work – fell to Nino Molossena del Monaco, an Italian property speculator with no experience, and up to that point, no particular interest in film. The cans went straight into a bank vault. There was no special reason to hope that they would ever be screened again. Hard to see how even Jacques Tati could have made a joke or a gag out of such a cruel turn. It was a very bitter end.

Part Four

Confusion

1970–1982

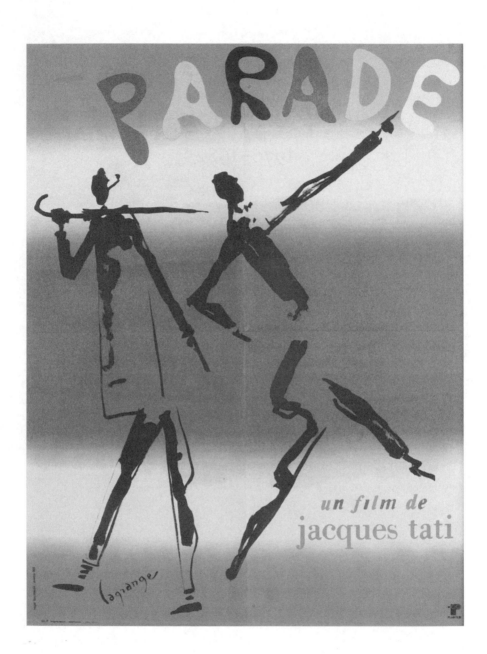

THIRTY-NINE

Tati-TV

In the wake of the *Playtime* fiasco, Tati did not blame his film for the plight he was in. He had made the film he had wanted to make in the way that he wanted to make it. That was a privilege not given to many, a privilege for which it was almost reasonable to pay all that he had.

He was hurt by the public's unwillingness to love the film as much as he did, and by the blindness of most critics to the "romantic" shape he had given to the film. When the American tourists arrive in Paris, one of them notices how the lamp-standards on the motorway resemble the shape of lily-of-the-valley; and at the end of the film, Barbara finds a little plastic lily-of-the-valley in the gift that Hulot has managed to get to her. Cut to an exterior shot, as through the window of the bus returning to the airport for departure, and we see those same street-lamps lighting up as dusk falls, like so many flowers opening in the night. For Tati, this visual theme was proof positive that he was not a reactionary critic of modern life, but a sentimental celebrant of its potential for beauty and joy.

What hurt him far more, however, was to be treated like a leper simply because he was bankrupt. Old acquaintances from business, even neighbours from Saint-Germain, crossed to the other side of the street so as not to have to ask him how he was. Staff left Specta-Films, of course; but many others abandoned him too. "I found myself alone and deserted in the midst of the problems caused by that *enfant terrible*, *Playtime*," he wrote to one of his acquaintances, who was probably also a creditor. "I won't hide the fact that I was on the brink of giving up the struggle . . ."[403]

But the family stood by him. Micheline was his solace and support. "Without Mme Tati, I could never have got anywhere," Tati declared to a journalist. She would go without new dresses, without grand holidays, and even without her smart cabriolet:[404] indeed, her stylish Sunbeam Talbot (seen in the roundabout sequence towards the end of *Playtime*) was traded in for a modest Citroën runabout.[405] Sophie, who had learned the trade and the skill of sound and vision editing at her father's side, started out on her own career, and Pierre looked to find his own niche in the production side of the business.

Lonely and moody as his plight made him, Tati did not carry out his threat to "give it all up", nor did he do anything so silly as to go on safari. Alfred Sauvy, still Tati's "captain" in this time of need, urged his old team-mate to go back to the music-hall: "You have so many resources, so many riches!" Sauvy wrote.[406] But Tati's health had taken too many knocks. He must have had warnings in earlier years. During the filming of *Playtime*, for example, he had stopped smoking for a time, and had mentioned it in a way strongly suggestive of a response to medical advice. In the spring of 1969, he had to go into hospital for observation; his complaint, he told a journalist at that time, was nephritic colic.[407] But by 1970, if not rather earlier, he knew that he had some kind of cancer. A return to live performance, whatever Sauvy thought, would involve a routine that Tati simply could not take any more. The future was not bright. But there was hope.

Tati actually made more films in the 1970s than in the 1960s, though none of them had the vast scope of *Playtime*, nor the perfection of his earlier work. He shot a comic advertising short for Lloyds Bank in London, which the bank refused to release: according to one of the actors involved, Jonathan Cecil, it displayed a comic invention remarkably like the ATMs or hole-in-the-wall cash dispensers that would be introduced a few years later, but had not yet been thought up by the banks.[408] In France, he made a series of cinema "spots" for the milk-product firm Danone, which stressed the slimming virtues of the firm's low-fat yoghurt. (These are recognisably Tatiesque productions, but are cast in a crueller comic style than any of Tati's feature films. They poke fun at fat ladies in a way that is unacceptable nowadays, and exploit sexist assumptions that have become quite obsolete.) However, even before *Playtime* was released, Tati had hatched plans for an entirely new adventure, and for working – at last – outside of France.[409]

Despite the unsatisfactory out-turn in 1964 of Specta-Films's involvement with *Alleman* (*The Human Dutch*; see above, p. 237), Bert Haanstra stayed in touch with Tati and, in his own modest view, remained an admiring friend. He had done some scouting for *Playtime* locations on Tati's behalf in Amsterdam, and was greatly moved to be invited to attend a gala showing of the film in Paris, in December 1967.

It must have been then – perhaps even at the after-show dinner, *chez Moustache* – that Tati first came up with a strange idea: to make a series of twenty television shows, about twenty minutes each, featuring M. Hulot in a variety of comic situations. Haanstra was surprised. Indeed, Tati had so often declared television to be his "enemy number one", had so publicly set himself on the side of film art against the visual and creative poverty of the small screen, that the proposal for a "Tati-TV" series even now seems almost shocking. What was more, *Playtime* was supposed to show the dissolution of M. Hulot, the end of the role of the comic character as such, the arrival of a new, "democratic" form of film comedy, which a resurrected Hulot as the central feature of his own TV series would flatly contradict.

In response to a letter from Tati that laid out the plan in more detail, Bert Haanstra picked up the telephone and told the great director what he thought.

> "Jacques, you want to make these episodes fast," he said, "but you won't. You are constitutionally incapable of doing anything at high speed."
>
> "No, no," Tati replied, "I'm not going to make them, you are."
>
> "All right," Bert replied. "Maybe. But let me give you some advice. You should make another Hulot movie, but not a series for TV. Find a story in which the Hulot character would logically arise. Not a big-budget thing like *Playtime*. Your other films are just as great."[410]

Haanstra was in a disappointing professional position himself in early 1968. He had invested a great deal of money and time in a documentary feature on professional football, a film which was to have followed the Dutch Ajax team through the 1967 European Cup tournament to the final, which the team was expected to win. But, like politics, football is a funny game. Ajax got knocked out in round one by Real Madrid, and by the same token knocked out Haanstra's film.[411] At the same time, a major film sponsored by UNICEF on "The Children of the World" (*Kinderen in de wereld*) had to be abandoned for lack of financial backing, and so Haanstra found himself, if not at a loose end, at least open to new projects. So discussions with Paris continued – mostly on the telephone, as far as can be told – over a possible venture in tandem with Tati. The idea was to create a joint structure that would be entitled to subsidy from the Dutch national production fund, using Haanstra as director (and also his own regular crew and editing studios), and Tati as author and principal actor. And from that structural idea came the theme itself – lines of communication between France and Holland, and more specifically the recently-opened A1 motorway that ran north towards the Belgian border. A film about traffic had been in Tati's mind for some time, in any case (see above, p. 230).

Unbeknownst to Haanstra, Tati was simultaneously in discussion with Svensk Filmindustri in Stockholm, hoping to obtain subsidies there too for his next project. But Haanstra and Tati got together in Saint-Germain in June 1968, and drew up a formal contract to prepare a full-length comedy film in colour, entitled not "Tati N° 5" as might be expected, but "Hulot Production N° 5". The contract stipulates that most of the film would be shot in Holland, using a Dutch crew. A few weeks later, the Tatischeffs joined the Haanstras for a ten-day cruise on the latter's boat, plying slowly up and down the canals and inland seas of the Netherlands. A much more modest vacation than those that the Tatis had taken in the past, at La Baule or on the Riviera, and, by all accounts, a great deal less fun. But Jacques and Bert got on with planning the future film, for which Tati was still prepared, at this stage, to forgo his role as director. After all, without Bert, there could be no Dutch subsidy. And as Tati said in a thank-you letter from Paris, "the fact to have lived at four people in the same room for ten days appears to me as the proof our collaboration can be carried on in the most friendly way".[412]

But still there was no script, for N° 5 was conceived in purely visual terms. Haanstra asked a cartoonist (one of whose drawings had caught his eye, and which Tati had liked a lot too) to come up with a set of drawings of cars and traffic on the general theme of modern travel. The whole set – forty-three car sketches and twenty-eight comic cartoons of travel incidents – were supplied by the end of August 1968, and were to constitute the "raw material" for the whole film. But it was also already agreed that the film's journey from Paris to Amsterdam would end at the great Amsterdam automobile show held in the exhibition space called RAI. Haanstra got permission to use the hall before the show was set up, after installation, before public opening, and during the public days too: the management of the hall seemed only too eager to have a Haanstra-Tati movie made on the premises.

Despite these positive steps, the project had not quite taken shape by the end of 1968, when Tati declared his Swedish hand and proposed to restructure the project as a three-way co-production with Svensk Filmindustri underwriting the first $200,000, the Dutch film fund underwriting the next $150,000, and "France", that is to say, Tati's theoretical backers, coming up with $100,000, but retaining fifty per cent of the rights in view of Tati's personal contribution as actor and author. But Svensk Filmindustri would not move without having a script; nor could Bert submit his subsidy bid without a clear plan and a text. So Tati finally sat down to write a scenario. He came up with an outline only six pages long, an untitled, unattributed and, frankly, rather scrappy piece of work.

Nonetheless, it was on the strength of this vague snippet that Haanstra eventually shot the empty-hall sequences of *Trafic* (in a hangar at Schipol airport), the opening shots of the automobile show, and other sequences (notably, the candid-camera views of nose-picking motorists caught in a traffic jam) in April–May 1969. He did so on the understanding that Tati was an honourable man and that the financial and legal niceties would be sorted out properly in the end – and for that reason, though perhaps with a heavy heart, he did the filming on his own responsibility, and using his own resources.

Tati did not seem overjoyed. Indeed, he did not seem anything at all: he was most often unobtainable on the telephone, and letters from Haanstra often went unanswered. The only news from Paris in mid-1969 was that Tati had at last found a backer, Robert Dorfman, who seemed willing to put his money in, and to leave Tati to get on with the rest. But none of the money had yet found its way to Holland, where the filming was going on. Eventually, Tati did send Haanstra a formal contract for the film – but Haanstra's lawyers would not let him sign it, since it would have left him personally liable for most of the risks. All the same, Haanstra did more filming at the DAF car plant, and scouted for more locations in Antwerp and elsewhere. He had a good idea what the film was supposed to be about: but save for the six-page "synopsis", there still was no shooting script, even if there now was a new title: *Yes, Mr Hulot!*

Haanstra's patience ran out in mid-July, when there were indeed barely two months left during which it was sensible to schedule outdoor shoots. He was horrified to learn that Tati, who was supposed to be working night and day on the script, had actually taken off for the Moscow Film Festival without even telling him he would be away for two weeks. So he bypassed Tati and wrote directly to the backer, Dorfman, with a clear ultimatum that unless there was some real progress very soon, he, Haanstra, would have to back out of the project. And he did, towards the end of August 1969. From then on, "Hulot Production N° 5" was Jacques Tati's film.

Of course, it is possible to account for Tati's dilatory and clumsy behaviour by the emotional turmoil that his financial problems were causing him. He was very prone to bouts of gloom in post-*Playtime* years, and as we have seen he had a bad health scare in the first half of 1969. He must have wondered, too, if he really had anything more to say. He didn't have a Broïdo or an Etaix to prompt and spark his wit, and Bernard Maurice was no longer there to keep a grip on office business. Marie-France Siegler, Tati's assistant and companion, and Juliette Wuidart, the office secretary, were just about all that was left of the old "family" team. Tati was a very lonely old man.

On location, though, the old Tati came back to life – rather more than Haanstra liked. In March 1969, during the filming of the automobile show in Amsterdam, Tati had insisted as usual on using non-professionals for the walk-on roles, and, as always, he had insisted on showing them how to be themselves. His mime acts of how the extras should walk had the entire crew and cast falling about with laughter. Then it was the extras' turn to do it: and

Fig. 84: *Tati and crew shooting* Trafic. *Amsterdam, March or April 1969*

nobody laughed at all. Haanstra felt embarrassed on behalf of these people, who were first made ridiculous by Tati's flamboyant exaggeration of their deportment and gestures, and then made doubly foolish by their failure to recreate themselves as comedy acts. This, then, was the unseen cruelty of films which, in their finished form, seemed to be all kindness and grace. *Les Vacances* and *Mon Oncle* must also have been made in that way, Haanstra thought. Tati must have manipulated and humbled a host of ordinary folk whom he had hired ostensibly just to be themselves. This realisation helped Haanstra to take his distance from a man he had admired too much. He grasped that Tati's directing style was not compatible with his own way of working with people. He had already spent his own money on the project, but he had signed no contract, and had every right to back out.

When Haanstra told Tati of his decision, the maestro at first pretended not to have heard, just as he had feigned deafness when Etaix had tendered his resignation in 1958. He then behaved as if he had not had even an inkling of what Bert had been trying to tell him, at first directly and then in more formal letters to the producer, Dorfman, over the previous weeks. He had been well aware of his reputation as a "difficult person" for decades, and was even quite proud of it at times (see above, p. 181). But the ups and downs of his long career do not seem to have given him any mature understanding of the reasons why most people sooner or later turned away. As a result, Tati never ceased to treat professional partings as divorces, or betrayals, or worse.

Svensk Filmindustri had withdrawn from the Tati–Haanstra project in June 1969. In December, Tati's long-insolvent company, Specta-Films, went into formal receivership. The half-shot *Yes, Mr Hulot!*, now code-named *Trafic*, was abandoned at the year-end. As one of the most creative and revolutionary decades of the century came to a close, Tati's career was on the rocks.

FORTY

Rescue from the North

In Stockholm, in the early dark months of 1970, Karl Haskel, who had worked for Swedish TV virtually since its inception, had a curious problem. He needed a programme concept that would somehow justify the use of a light aircraft, because one of his friends, a sound engineer, needed flying hours to qualify for his pilot's licence. Necessity is the mother of invention, and Haskel and the talented young Lasse Hallström, then still a cameraman,[413] came up with "Springtime in Europe", a show-business magazine that would consist of interviews with artists and celebrities throughout Europe, focusing on what spring meant for them. (For Swedes, of course, it means more or less everything.) The proposal was accepted by the head of administration of Swedish TV's Channel 2, the financial wizard Gustaf Douglas, and so a team of three set off to Malmö, Copenhagen, Amsterdam, and finally Paris, where they interviewed two international stars, Mireille Mathieu and Jacques Tati. Why Tati? "Because Sweden was Tati's most beloved country," says Karl Haskel. His films – including *Playtime* – were enormously popular there, and he was generally known to like Sweden.

Lasse Hallström fell ill with a stomach bug on arrival in Paris, and stayed in bed in his hotel, so the interview was conducted by Haskel, with the sound technician manning the camera. Why, Tati asked, have you young men bothered to come so far just to ask me about springtime? Haskel explained the hidden agenda – getting the soundman more flying hours – and Tati laughed out loud. But he sent Marie-France Siegler, now his permanent assistant and companion, to Hallström's hotel, not with chicken soup or aspirin, but with flowers, grapes and wine.

The filming of *Trafic* was due to restart fairly soon, and Haskel asked if Tati would allow him to make a TV documentary on location, a "making-of" Tati's fifth feature film. Tati's loathing of television was no secret, nor was his dislike of having strangers on his set. But he warmed to the young Swedes and to their as-yet invisible cameraman. Haskel had no idea that Tati had been secretly thinking about television for a couple of years already, nor that he had been engaged in discussions with Svensk Filmindustri only a few months before. So he was more surprised than he would otherwise have been when Tati agreed entirely to the proposal. It was quite a coup for the young producer. It would be the first and probably the only documentary to be made on an active shoot of a Tati film.

Gustaf Douglas, who had grown up with Tati's films and counted himself a "Tatifan" through and through, was enthralled by Haskel's project, and gave it all the backing it needed. And so, in January 1971, Haskel, Hallström and a comedy writer and Tati-admirer by the name of Lars "Brasse" Brännström, came to La Garenne-Colombes with a 16mm cine-camera, to begin interviewing Tati and the *Trafic* team in the offices rented by CEPEC, the new company set up to handle Tati's affairs in TV and film. Once again, Lasse Hallström fell ill on arrival and took to his bed. This time, Tati sent "CinéSiegler" to find a doctor for the ailing Swede.

Haskel recorded long conversations with almost everybody he came across at the office: Michel Chauvin, the financial administrator of CEPEC; Sophie Tatischeff, now a proper film editor, working for her father; Marie-France Siegler, actors working on *Trafic*, and of course Tati himself. In these conversations, conducted partly in English, partly in French, and often made obscure by the medley of tongues, Tati mentioned that he would like to make something for TV himself; or rather, to find a way of *using* TV to pursue his argument with the modern world. It was just an idea, he said, with a code-name of "Tati TV" or *TTV*. Something to think about for the future, after *Trafic* . . .[414]

These Paris interviews were of course only the groundwork and preparation for the real project, a location documentary. *Trafic* had been in the making since spring 1969: and still it was not finished. With Dorfman's tolerant backing, with the involvement of two other production companies, Tati had struggled on in the summer of 1970, shooting the road sequences on the motorway itself, and the long episodes at the garage in Belgium. It was beginning to add up to a real film, but as it had been made throughout with no proper script – almost improvised "on the road", according to Marie-France Siegler, the assistant director – it was not easy to tell when it would be complete. But the few days' shooting planned for March in Amsterdam would have to be the last. The budget had been over-run already.

Haskel and Hallström returned to Stockholm, and met Tati and the crew as planned at the location site in Holland in March 1971. When they arrived, Tati took them aside to explain the situation. He had run out of money for the film. In actual fact, the cameraman had just been recalled to Paris by the producers. So it was not possible to shoot, and by the same token just as impossible for the Swedes to film Tati shooting. Unless . . . Well, yes, of course, Lasse knew how to operate a 35mm cine-camera, and this time he was not confined to bed with a stomach bug. Wonderful! said the director. Then we can start tomorrow ... but there is one other problem to attend to. Ahem. Er ... Well, you see, the cameraman took his equipment back to Paris when he left. You wouldn't happen to have, well, to have brought along a ...

The situation was quite extraordinary. Here was a world-famous film-maker, an Oscar prizewinner, a national institution, reduced to behaving like a scrounger at the age of sixty-five. For youngsters like Hallström and Haskel, the opportunity – no, the obligation – to help a stranded giant was overwhelming. It had to be done. In retrospect, though, there is also something sordid about the scene, and the situation. How could a man with Tati's experience, with his skills, with his influence and stature, have allowed himself to sink to such a state? Maybe he was exaggerating the drama of his plight; maybe he had invented a stratagem to prevent the documentary being made; but it is most likely that what he told the Swedes was indeed the literal truth.

Haskel had come equipped with a 16mm camera and monochrome film stock to make a film intended for television broadcast: there were no portable video cameras yet, and all location work for TV was done in 16mm and directly broadcast. As *Trafic* was being made in 35mm colour, he could only help if Swedish TV was willing and able to provide the right equipment – but it had to be immediate, since Tati had no money to prolong the shoot. Haskel telephoned Douglas, and put the problem to him. Within hours, a 35mm camera and the appropriate cans of film were on board an aircraft and were delivered by courier to the Amsterdam set the next day. It was an extraordinary act of generosity, but not a stupid one: Gustaf Douglas could think of no more appealing deal than to become part of Jacques Tati's production team, and maybe even to involve Swedish TV more fully in Tati's future work. Of course, it was also of some concern that the documentary that had already been started should not be abandoned; and the only way to pursue it was to get *Trafic* moving once again. But these interests, though real, in no way diminish the spectacular generosity and effectiveness of the Swedes' response.

In return for this unhoped-for assistance, Tati allowed Karl Haskel to film anything he wanted, whilst Lasse Hallström manned the cameras for the last three days' shooting of *Trafic*. With his streaky long hair, old cat-fur coat, and post-'68 attitudes, Hallström did not correspond one bit to Tati's ideas of style and decorum in professional life. At a dinner for the whole crew after two days' shooting, Hallström had the cheek, or the revolutionary zeal, to disagree with something that the Great Director had said. The table fell silent. For the mostly young and mostly French crew present that evening, disagreeing with Tati was one thing, but saying so to his face quite another. A major storm was expected, and it came. Tati flew into a rage, stood up, and marched out of the restaurant, leaving the Swedes to pay the bill. Lasse Hallström was furious, and declared he would not do another minute's work for such a pig-headed monster.

But there was another day's filming still to do. That night, in the hotel, Karl Haskel was given an instant tutorial in the manipulation of 35mm cameras, and he turned up on set the following morning, bleary-eyed but ready for work. Tati was at first taken aback, and then very professional. Good, he said. Let's get on with it. The rift with Hallström was never healed, and all of the takes which he filmed were junked. Two or three of Haskel's takes, on the other hand, remain in the finished version of *Trafic*.

During the shooting in Amsterdam, the idea of a co-production with Swedish television was broached again, and in the following weeks Haskel was in touch with Tati by letter and phone in order to make the project more precise. Tati had an English translation made of his draft "TV scenario", under the title *TTV*, and sent it to Stockholm, where it was read with great interest.

This English-language scenario does not seem at all related to the original television series idea that Tati had first put to Bert Haanstra in 1967–68. On the other hand, it has a great deal in common with the project later entitled *Confusion*, of which it seems to be the earliest surviving draft. But the "series" idea was a recurrent fantasy of Tati's in these years, and it re-emerged in the summer of 1971 in Tati's discussions with his interlocutors in Stockholm. At one point, Tati seemed to be on the verge of agreeing to do a series of twelve or perhaps fifteen short television films suitable for editing into a 90-minute feature film. At other times, it seemed more like the reverse: to devise a 90-minute feature film constructed in such a way as to make it divisible into a dozen or so television shorts. But *Trafic* was still not quite finished. With Maurice Laumain and Sophie, Tati was still busy in the editing studios.

Nobody had yet tried to make anything that was simultaneously a television series and a cinema film, for an obvious reason: TV screens had and still have an aspect ratio of 1:1.33, and the cinema screen uses 1:1.65 when it does not use the wider formats allowed by anamorphosis and/or 70mm film (see above, pp. 257–9). Tati's first discussions of his project with Swedish TV concerned the aesthetic and technical challenge of working simultaneously for the two different media. The bustling, energetic Gustaf Douglas came to Paris in 1971 for one of these initial discussions, and also had the pleasure of dining with Jacques Tati. After dessert, Tati stood up and did an impression of a young man on his way up in the world: though he had known Gustaf Douglas for barely a couple of hours, he mimed the man to perfection, and with such grace that even the boy-genius of Swedish TV was flattered, entertained, and amused.

Television cameras of the early 1970s were large, heavy machines requiring three operators, and thus entirely unsuitable for anything but studio work. Tati wanted to know if he could film in 16mm (the norm for TV broadcast), and then blow it up to 35mm, so that he could edit a cinema film in his habitual manner. He asked Swedish TV to test the process, and pursued discussions of its practicability and aesthetic consequences with technicians and administrators in Stockholm, when he visited for the long-delayed première of *Trafic*.

It was obviously going to be an expensive way of doing things. Douglas was a sincere admirer of Tati the creator, and not even half his age: all the same, he was in charge of public money, and was not going to let an old man waste it. As a result, one of these technical "TV-ciné" discussions turned into a shouting match. Tati and Douglas calmed down and made a pact: they would allow each other to utter insults and curses in the language they commanded the best, the one in which they had the greatest resources of invective. Douglas swore at Tati in English, and the director responded in like vein in French. He knew that at bottom he had a real friend in the north. And that he would somehow find a way of making his next film in the royal city that had helped him out once before, in 1948, when his first feature film, *Jour de fête*, had seemed destined to sink without trace.

FORTY-ONE

Mirrors of Motors

Throughout the protracted and fragmented filming of *Trafic*, Tati's reputation as a film-maker ten years ahead of his time continued to grow amongst intellectuals and serious film critics. *Les Cahiers du cinéma* devoted most of issue 199 (March 1968) to *Playtime*, with contributions from widely respected film critics and theorists, such as Noel Burch. Such consecration was not a consolation prize for Tati's financial fiasco; it was seen, more and more, as his due.

For the launch of *Trafic* at the brand-new Gaumont cinema on the Champs-Elysées, in April 1971, Tati – perhaps prompted by Lagrange – had a brilliant idea: the film's title was set up not in the usual neon lights over the theatre awning, but drawn out in elongated lettering, like a map of traffic flows, on a large mirror. Thus through the word "Trafic" the stroller on the great entertainment avenue could see the reflection of . . . actual traffic.[415] It was a device of such simplicity, and such ironic impact, that it rose above the mere commercial function of self-advertisement. The cinema sign, in a quite profound sense, *was* the meaning of the film.

The opening night was a grand affair, attended by many public figures, including Raymond Marcellin, the Minister of Transport of the day. It is not likely that he found much inspiration for the road-building programme in the film that he saw.

For *Trafic*, Tati had turned Hulot from an unemployable fringe figure of Christ-like simplicity into a draftsman for a car-customising firm, Altra. The firm's sole design is a diminutive camping-car, a distant descendant of the Amilcar of *Les Vacances de M. Hulot*, a comically gadget-laden get-away-from-it-all fantasy vehicle that mocks the very idea of personal independence and of economical holidays. Built around a standard Renault 4L chassis and body-work, the Altra was actually displayed in the Renault showrooms opposite the theatre for the first few weeks of *Trafic*'s release, adding even more to the intended confusion of the real and the imaginary in the Champs-Elysées.

But in the film we see relatively little of the diminutive marvel on wheels, and we certainly never see it on the road: it remains throughout no more than an idea of a car, a universal dream of a self-contained world that is nonetheless unmistakably French – the electric grill hidden behind the front bumper is custom-made for *steak-frites* ("with a garnish of loose chippings", quipped one reviewer) and the striped-canvas awning is just like the beach furniture of *Les Vacances,* which itself re-uses designs from the animated films of Emile Reynaud and the seaside paintings of Eugène Boudin.

The film tells the story of the journey from the Altra factory somewhere near Paris to the motor show in Amsterdam. Hulot accompanies the lorry carrying his design, and the structural comedy of the film is the age-old, creakingly obvious comedy of a journey that goes wrong. The lorry is late loading. The lorry runs out of fuel. The lorry is searched from top to bottom by Belgian border guards. And of course, the lorry breaks down in the middle of nowhere, and has to wait for lengthy repairs in a bucolic garage-junkyard, beside a Flemish canal. At the exhibition hall, the commercial representatives of Altra grow more frustrated as the days go by, and, in the end, are forced to abandon their empty stand. By the time the vehicle reaches the hall, the exhibition has closed. Hulot, though, does not pay a real price for failing to be on time: the pert and infuriatingly fashionable PR girl who has darted back and forth along the motorway in her minuscule bright yellow open-top runabout finally allows Hulot to express a little ordinary warmth, and in the film's closing shots, we see Tati's long arm around her shoulder as he escorts her through the rain back to her car.

For a film almost improvised as it was being shot, *Trafic* has a fairly clear and firm plot, and one which, in an obvious sense, also tells the story of the film's own making, and of the film-maker's own fundamental flaw: his inability to do things on time. Shot by several different cameramen – Haanstra, Paul Rodier, Hallström and (for one sequence) Haskel – the final edited film is not too obviously a patchwork of styles, even if the candid-camera sequences are quite new to what was taken to be Tati's art. But what is worth a thousand blemishes, what justifies and redeems the sad dissensions and muddle that presided over its making, are the extraordinary sequences in *Trafic* where Tati makes men, cars and umbrellas move with the meaningful grace of a perfectly-rehearsed ballet.

In the great hangar where the exhibition is to be held (a sequence shot at Schipol, not in the RAI itself), dark-suited men with attaché-cases measure out the sites of individual stands. We see them in a very long crane shot, in a field several hundred feet deep. The floor-space is marked out with some kind of string or wire, over which the officials have to step whichever way they go. And so we see these distant mannikins marching in almost military, business-like step for a few paces left, then raising the knee high to step over the wire, then continuing their habitual stride. They go this way and that – for they are examining the whole lay-out of the great show – and at points that are logical, but unpredictable to us, they raise their knees, and step over wires we cannot actually see. It is a gag entirely opposite to John Cleese's contemporary invention of the Ministry of Silly Walks. What Tati's officials do is entirely reasonable and realistic; it is surreal only because we have never previously looked at something like that with the careful, distant attention of Tati.

Fig. 85: Trafic: *The Accident*

The visual centrepiece of the doomed journey along crowded motorways to the Amsterdam exhibition is the Great Crash. It is at a four-way crossroads controlled by a policeman. The initial accident between the Altra lorry and a car is caused by a combination of bad driving by Maria in the runabout, and the contradictory signs made by a flustered traffic policeman. But this first collision sets off a chain reaction on the crowded road, and at least a dozen vehicles "drift" into each other, or the ditch. A flying-saucer-shaped Citroën DS brakes so hard that it rises on to its two front wheels, and glides forward at an angle of forty-five degrees to the road, as if on tip-toe. There is something implausible, impossible even, about the exact sequence of vehicle movements that we see in that shot. Like the car-and-dog sequence in *Les Vacances*, the key element in this stunt was performed backwards – it is apparently easier to keep a Citroën's tail off the ground when it is in reverse.[416] Here, however, the artifice of reversed film is far more visible than in *Les Vacances*, since we see not just the dancing Citroën, but another car zooming *backwards* at high speed on the left hand side of the screen. Then a different car loses a wheel, which rolls on and on; a Volkswagen "Beetle" runs behind it, out of control, with its loose and damaged bonnet flapping up and down. It suddenly seems to be a predatory beast – a crocodile perhaps – lazily pursuing a giant bagel rolling on its edge. When the cars have all come to rest, the passengers and drivers emerge on to the roadway, stretching themselves, testing for broken bones, bruises and torn muscles – and perform, quite realistically but also quite magically, a set of callisthenic exercises on the junk-strewn macadam. Of course Tati is marking the memory of his own accident, abreacting the emotions still attached to that painful disruption to his life. This is not just a comic enhancement of an all-too-common scene on the roads. Something about it – its complex choreography, its slowed-down grace – makes it also a personal memorial. It was Tati's way of finally dealing with his own Great Crash.

The final sequence of *Trafic* seems to have been conceived as a visual farewell to the entire oeuvre of Jacques Tati. The Altra team has been

Fig. 86: Trafic: *After the Accident*

dismissed from the exhibition because of late arrival; Hulot has, for the last time, been given the sack by his boss. He walks off, with his springy, ostrich-like gait to the subway entrance, and says farewell to Maria, the PR girl, before going down the steps. She turns, but does not move on, for the rain has begun – the first and only rain in any film made by Tati. More people come to shelter in the subway, and so Hulot, as he comes back out, having changed his mind, has to struggle up the steps through a growing crowd. He finds Maria, who was waiting for him; and at last, he unfurls the furled umbrella that has been the Hulot prop and symbol for twenty years. As he holds it over Maria's head, with his free hand around her shoulder, we get a crane shot of the whole, huge car-park in the rain, which turns into a field of flowers as here, there, and now everywhere, red, blue, black and pink umbrellas unfold between the vast ranks of motor cars. Hulot dissolves into the crowd, but in contrast to his exit from *Les Vacances*, *Mon Oncle* and *Playtime*, he is not left alone. There could hardly be a clearer way of saying that this is indeed the last of Hulot.

Fig. 87: Trafic: *Umbrellas in the rain*

FORTY-TWO

On Tour, On Show

The last takes of *Trafic* were shot in March 1971, thanks to the generosity of Swedish television, and the film was launched in Paris barely a month later – an unusually rushed job for a man like Tati. But over the previous two years he had certainly taken his time with his return to Hulot, and not just driven Haanstra off the project, but pushed even the resilient Gustaf Douglas near to distraction. In the long-drawn-out sequence at the Belgian customs post, Tati invented semi-domestic scenes of custom-house life, including a shot of a buxom woman with enormous breasts and a highly visible cleavage. An old-style, X takes Y for Z kind of joke: for the woman changes her angle to the camera, and we see that she is in fact nursing a naked infant. For this shot, Tati needed a pair of infant buttocks that would match up to the build and skin-texture of the actress's bosom. And of course the two had to match *exactly*. Tati had the shooting stopped whilst he and his inner team scoured nurseries and crèches up and down the land: it took them a whole week to find the right babe. "Dutch buttocks!" is what Gustaf Douglas replies when you ask him why Tati took so long to make his films.

The music track of *Trafic* has a curious, but characteristic, history. Tati's son Pierre was friendly with a certain Maxi Walberg, whose father happened to be a good friend of the composer Charles Dumont, best known as the author of Edith Piaf's most famous song, *Je ne regrette rien*. A social event was thus engineered to make Tati and Dumont get together, sometime in 1970, whilst *Trafic* was in the midst of its long making. After being introduced to the song-writer, Tati said, almost as an off-hand remark: "If you like, you can write the music for my film." Dumont was amazed, but jumped at the opportunity, and promised Tati he would come up with something as soon as he had seen the pictures.

> But not at all, my dear friend. You think of some themes and then come and play them for me. When you come up with something I like, I'll take it for my film . . . [417]

Tati assured Dumont that the subject of his film was of no importance for the composer, though he did let out that it was about motor cars. Dumont brought along this tune and that, and each time Tati said, well, it's OK, but maybe a little too jolly ... or, it's fine, but I don't think it's really jolly enough ... Until one day, having drafted a tune without a real thought for the film at all, Dumont found Tati exclaiming, "That's it! That's what I wanted! How did you guess?"

Tati had always behaved in a similar manner with his juniors, giving them little direct instruction and waiting until they came up with something he felt he could use. It created an atmosphere of great freedom, and at the same time of almost Kafkaesque authoritarianism in the offices and studios of Cady, Specta and CEPEC. What Tati's collaborators could never quite grasp was the degree to which the director was manipulating them gently in the right direction, but also to what extent the maestro really did not have a clue.

Dumont's music plays an important role in *Trafic*, but it is also drowned out for long sequences of the film by the disagreeable, painfully loud noise of traffic. Indeed, perhaps the most lasting impression of the whole film is of the exhausting experience of having spent a couple of hours by the side of a motorway. And what is even odder about this sound track is that the sound effects are slightly, but consistently, out of synch. The minuscule disjunctions of sound and image had already been noticed by sharp-eared viewers of *Playtime*, but in *Trafic* the effect is more noticeable, partly because the noises themselves are less agreeable, and much louder. The reason is not any lack of editing skill on Tati's part or those of his assistants, Maurice Laumain and Sophie Tatischeff. Those closest to Tati believe that the non-synch sound was not intended as a distancing device, but derived from the fact that in his sixties, Tati actually heard things that way – with a slight delay. It is indeed quite possible that with advancing age, and with his generally sluggish personality, Tati's ear had grown slower, even if his approach to sound and noise was no less subtle and creative.

Tati also used *Trafic*, as he used all his films, to "recycle" stunts and gags that had got left out of the final cuts of his previous work. One quite noticeable re-use joins the Maison Arpel of *Mon Oncle* to an otherwise irrelevant little house in the Belgian countryside in *Trafic*. In the earlier film, Hulot, creeping out of the house at night, carefully lifts the metallic gate to the street so that it should not scrape or creak: but he gives a little too much lift, and the gate comes off its hinges, leaving Hulot stuck with a gate in his arms. In the finished movie, the sequence ends there.

In the script, however, Hulot attempts to repair the damage by climbing a tree and trying to drop the gate back into place. In so doing, he misses his hold, slips, and falls, remaining attached to a fork in the tree by his ankles,

Fig. 88: *Hulot stuck with a gate in* Mon Oncle

completely upside down. In *Trafic*, Hulot fails to rouse the inhabitants of the house from their slumbers, so he climbs up the front to knock at their bedroom window, using a conveniently thick mass of ivy for hand- and footholds. The creeper fails to take his weight entirely, and comes away from the wall, leaving Tati suspended, once again upside down, in mid-air. The sequence is a straightforward replication of the episode cut out of *Mon Oncle*, and one has to presume – especially given Tati's age and ill-health – that he really wanted to give the world an image of himself in this strange and painful position: Hulot, the lunar Pierrot, hanging in the air, like a comic angel descending but not quite making it to earth.

Trafic was not made in French, but through the muddled medium of film-crew English. The leading lady, an American model living in Paris, Maria Kimberley, spoke her lines in English, the Dutch and Belgian extras spoke in Flemish and Dutch. Like so many more recent French films, the French-language version cannot really be considered the "original", and *Trafic* is as much a linguistic "Euromovie" as *Playtime* was intended to be. But where *Playtime* has some splendid inter-language jokes in all its versions ("Comment dit-on *drugstore* en anglais?" versus "How do you say *Drugstore* in French?"), *Trafic* does not have much memorable dialogue: indeed, it has little dialogue at all. Its first origin in a set of commissioned cartoons remains very visible in the finished product. Tati gives us in this last feature film a series of almost caricatural images of the real conditions of road traffic – and its ubiquitous, unbearable noise.

Trafic got a rather mixed reception in Paris. "There was laughter, but also puzzlement in the audience",[418] "an impression of conscientious and laboured work",[419] "it's not hard for Tati's new film to be better than that interminable *Playtime*".[420] The vaguely left-wing *Nouvel Observateur* thought the film ideologically suspect: its critique of motor-car culture was not harsh enough, it said, and its gentle comedy was more likely to reconcile people to cars than to make them give up on driving. All Tati's work, we must add, is essentially angled towards reconciliation, not revolt. Tati was not out to change the world, but to help us look at it with less horror.

Nonetheless, the circumstances of *Trafic*'s release were very different from Tati's previous launches. The producers had given distribution rights to Gaumont, which made sure the film got a rapid national and international release, and for much of the next twelve months, Tati was on television, on tour, and on show the world over. After Paris, there was the première in Bordeaux, then Tel-Aviv, then Rome. In July, Tati was the guest of honour at the Berlin Film Festival, and his visit – as well as his new film, called *Stoßverkehr* in German – received wide coverage. He was snapped alongside Shirley MacLaine and Anna Karina, and had a whole feature to himself in the tabloid *BZ*, whose photographer used him to make fun of paternoster lifts. He must have had some sort of summer break, but was back on the road in October, for a fanfare appearance in Stockholm, where, *pace* the theme of *Trafic* if not of *Jour de fête*, he led a cyclists' night time demonstration against new road construction in the city. And so to London, for the première of *Trafic*, rebaptised *Traffic*, at the National Film Theatre, where Tati gave a brief talk and performed for the first and only time in public his celebrated impersonation of Charles de Gaulle. The former president had died less than a year before.

Trafic is not a revolutionary film like *Playtime*, nor is it as loveable as *Mon Oncle* or as dreamily beautiful as *Les Vacances*. This no doubt explains the rather luke-warm reaction of French critics, and the now conventional view of the film as a "step backwards" in Tati's art. He himself admitted that in terms of techniques and material, *Trafic* could have been made before *Playtime*, which would always remain his "last" film, the culmination of all he wanted to do in the cinema. But if it is put in that position – let us say, as a film located in the history of Hulot straight after *Mon Oncle*, but nonetheless shot when the first French motorways had been completed – it is by no means an insignificant satire of modern life. It deals not at all with the "fast cars and clean bodies" which Kirstin Ross sees as the central topics of the culture of everyday life in the 1950s and 1960s, but with the imperfect state of modern communications (Mme Arpel's theme sentence in *Mon Oncle*, after all, is *tout communique*) – and with the greater pleasures of taking a break.

Fig. 89: *Jacques Tati in London for the launch of* Traffic, *1974*

FORTY-THREE

A French Fortnight

Charles de Gaulle resigned after losing a referendum on regionalisation in 1969, and under the presidency of Georges Pompidou, Franco-American relations grew warmer in the early 1970s. One of the lesser fruits of that change of climate was the organisation of a great "French Fortnight" throughout the US in the autumn of 1972, a fanfare of events that incidentally brought Jacques Tati to the US as a roving ambassador for French film culture. Indeed, Tati thought that he ought to be considered equal in status to a real ambassador, and be given a state pension commensurate with his services to the nation. He should have been so lucky! But the French fortnight did at least get him a little of the US audience that had been so badly missing.

On arrival in New York in November, he took a taxi down Fifth Avenue. A car ran through a red light and struck the taxi side-on. Micheline's arm was cut, Tati was bleeding from his forehead. The police called an ambulance, and pretty soon the Tatischeffs were being rushed to hospital by a stout middle-aged driver who turned round and said: "Hey, you're Mister Hulot, aren't you?" Tati was delighted.[421] In France, he could no longer command that kind of instant public recognition. (He once got very cross with a policeman who refused to allow him to park on yellow lines simply because he was M. Hulot.) Tati declared himself at last to be really fond of America. And yes, he would love to make a film in the States . . .

The trip turned out to be not much of a holiday. After spending an afternoon in hospital, Jacques and Micheline lost all their travel cash when their hotel room in New York was burgled. The French consul tided them over, but as Tati had not taken out an insurance, he lost over $1000.[422] *Trafic* was released in New York, in its "original" version, with Maria Kimberley's voice in English, and the Dutch voices in Dutch. It got a far more enthusiastic response than in France. "The world Tati sees is slightly mad," Vincent Canby wrote in the *New York Times*, "full of mimetic rhythms which say less about the dehumanisation of society than about the resilience of its members."[423] Which is precisely the point Tati had been trying to make, in *Playtime* as in *Trafic*.

The New York première had been previewed and prepared by an entire festival devoted to the work of Tati in that most French of American cities, New Orleans. All five of Tati's feature films were shown in repertory for a week, including the 70mm (but shortened) version of *Playtime*. From New Orleans, Tati flew to Dallas, where the huge Nieman-Marcus department store was hosting its own great "French Fortnight", and was able to show *Playtime* once again. Tati had to attend dinners and events, since his role was to "embody Frenchness" for the greater benefit of parfumiers, champagne producers and other high-value export industries, and he was not always the most convivial of guests. Marie-Claude de Brunhoff, a French publisher's representative, recalls sitting next to him at one of those occasions, and not hearing him utter a single word.

But by the time he got to New York, Tati had been contacted by one studio at least, and perhaps more, and his mind was working on a real project for the US. And he was happy to flatter his hosts as much as he could:

> The city where I feel closest to what is happening in the world is New York. I've already got ideas, there (he points to his forehead), it's an American scenario which could happen anywhere else. Like in *Trafic*, it's a topical subject, without a nationality.[424]

But what project was it? It could only have been the very same satire of television *mores* that had originally been submitted to Svensk Filmindustri in 1969, and had now been contracted to Swedish television for a year already, and would eventually come to be known as *Confusion*. Tati claimed to be watching lots of American television in his hotel room, and to be disgusted by most of what he saw. He also claimed to have turned down a lucrative American offer to make a TV comedy series out of *Les Vacances de M. Hulot*. "I must hang on to my freedom," he repeated. "I've got to the age of grey hair without making any compromises ..."[425]

As soon as Tati got back to Paris, in late November 1972, he had a visit from an American film journalist, who interviewed him for a couple of hours. "It was easy enough to be liked by Tati," Jonathan Rosenbaum recalled. "All one had to do was to say that *Playtime* was one's favourite film."[426] Such was the goodwill created by appreciation of the maestro's *enfant terrible* that Tati said that if Rosenbaum ever needed a place to stay in Paris, he could always kip on the great sofa in the office at La Garenne-Colombes. But it would be for quite another reason that the long-haired American was soon to spend many hours in that seat.

FORTY-FOUR

Circus Time

The Stockholm première of *Trafic* in October 1971 – a gala performance in which Tati appeared on stage doing some of his "Sporting Impressions" once again – had also provided the opportunity for serious negotiations with Swedish TV, towards which Tati owed a serious debt of gratitude, if not of actual cash.

The deal that was made as a result of those talks hardly hints at what the finished product would turn out to be. Tati actually contracted to make thirteen short television comedy programmes, under the title *TTV*.[427] Shooting was supposed to start almost straight away. The producer was to be Karl Haskel, who had had the first idea to interview Tati for "Spring-time in Europe" and who had conducted most of the interviews for the abandoned location documentary on the creator of *Trafic*. Tati quietly insisted that he wanted the great Gunnar Fischer, Ingmar Bergman's director of photography until 1960, to do all the takes. That was arranged without any fuss. In addition, Tati proposed to begin by making what would be the closing sequences of all thirteen episodes, a jolly circus act, a short display of acrobatic delights. He knew precisely which performers he wanted – *Veteranerna* ("The Veterans"). Perhaps it was their name that appealed – what better catchword could there be for Tati's own position in the world of entertainment? But he had never entirely lost contact with the world of circus performers, and his choice may have been based on inside information, if not on direct knowledge of the troupe.

Tati kept to schedule, to begin with at least, and slotted in a week's shooting in Stockholm in November 1971, in between his US trip and his visit to London. He filmed twelve versions of The Veterans' act in 16mm (the usual format for television re-broadcast), but in colour, and did a thir-teenth take of the same material in 35mm: presumably, the last was for the cinema-film version that Tati still hoped to make, even if there was no mention of such a thing in the contract with Swedish TV.

Shortly after, the same Europa Film Studios in Stockholm were used by another world-famous circus master and film comedian, though of a rather different kind. Jerry Lewis came to Sweden to make a controversial, and still unreleased, movie, *The Day the Clown Cried*. Its hero is a German clown who has taken to drink to hide his hatred of the Nazis; he is interned in an extermination camp, where his job is to keep the children amused whilst they are being led to the gas chambers.[428]

For Gunnar Fischer, the doyen of Swedish cameramen, and his son Jens, who was at the time his apprentice, the Tati project was a mystery and a mess. There was no story-board. Neither Karl Haskel nor Tati could tell them whether they were framing their shots for a television programme or for a feature film: but Tati wanted images that would go into 1:1.33 and 1:1.66 *at the same time*. That just can't be done, the cameramen told him. Tati thought about it. He sat beside the camera for hours, trying to think through the numbers, the shapes, the requirements, muttering to himself as if no one were nearby. The Fischers held Tati in great respect, and admired the intellectual effort that he put into the conception and design of each shot. (Few film directors they had worked with had anything approaching Tati's command of framing.) But they could see he was confused by technical aspects that they themselves understood with great ease. It was a rather sad mess.[429]

Fig. 90: *Tati musing over aspect ratios in the Europa Film Studios, Stockholm, 1971*

Still, The Veterans' act was a tremendous turn, and Tati kept them all at it, sometimes for twenty hours a day, getting just the right takes on their physical jerks and musical jokes. At one point he decided that he needed a drummer. All right, said Karl Haskel, I'll get hold of Janne Carlson. He rang him: it turned out that it was around midnight, and even the famously wild Carlson was in bed. But for Jacques Tati? OK! He called a taxi and came out to the studios, not exactly pleased to be up in the middle of the night. He entered the studio in his long sleeveless sheepskin coat and his black hair in a bandanna, walked up to the tall gangling man who must be M. Hulot, and grabbed him quite hard between the legs. It was Carlson's "signature", an aggressive act for which he was well known. The 64-year-old Tati was taken aback, but controlled himself, and, after a few moments' complete silence, flung his arms around the jazz drummer. From then on, the Fischers recall, it was like a love affair between the distinguished director and the wild man of Swedish jazz.

"So where are the drums?" Tati asked.

"What drums? I got a call to come out here to meet you. Nobody said anything about drums . . ."

So Carlson had to go back and come out again with his gear. And by that time it was nearly 3 am, and even Tati needed to get to his bed.

Next day, and every day thereafter, Tati kept Carlson there drumming just as background music, far beyond what was actually needed for the takes. It seemed that Carlson's mere presence helped Tati to work: though his mood, for much of the time during that long week, was melancholic and withdrawn.

Tati returned to Paris "to write the rest of the script", since the original *TTV* scenario, involving a Tatiesque satire of life in a TV studio, had now definitely been put aside, and there was no other script for the series project still called "TTV" but necessarily of a quite different order. It was probably at this stage, if not earlier, that Tati gave a ring to his old friend Jacques Lagrange, and got down to designing circus gags with him. Lagrange's papers contain a number of undated sketches of clowns and decors that seem retrospectively like echoes of *Parade* (and were no doubt planning documents for it). The Swedish producers visited Lagrange in his studio in Paris; the painting of the two acrobats on top of each other in the finished film is, if not by Lagrange, certainly after an idea by him. The credit given to him as co-author of *Parade* was inserted at Tati's insistence.

Beyond a scenario, the project now also needed co-producers, since the original estimated budget of between two and three million crowns had grown to between three and four million, well beyond the means of Swedish TV, which had never before been involved in financing and producing a project of such a size. There were consultations with Swedish Film Industry, and with German studios, but nobody took the bait of becoming involved with Tati's next film, and so nothing much happened throughout 1972.[430] By early 1973, Swedish TV was getting impatient, for it had already invested a substantial sum in the Europa Studios filming of The Veterans. Messages were sent to Michel Chauvin, and then a consultant producer, Bo Jonsson, visited Paris and put a new proposal direct to Tati: scrap "TTV" and honour your obligations by making a 52-minute "special" for Swedish television, intended for international resale, and focused quite specifically, if not exclusively, on Tati's own performances as a mime. Tati would thereby take back the rights to the longer film (which would become Confusion, in fact): the "Tati special" would be designated as a quite different project. To this Tati agreed, and in September 1973 a new contract was signed. He was certainly sad to abandon the original project; he would have liked to make that longer satirical film about TV itself; and perhaps he already knew that this Swedish "special" would be his last real work for the screen.

From this point on, things moved fast. François Bronett, a Swedish circus master, was hired as artistic consultant, and he helped to select and to hire circus artists; the old Circus Theatre in Stockholm was hired for a week in late October, and a set of acts, an audience and a few very special actors were rapidly engaged. The most special of those actors were two children, Anna-Karin Dandenell, aged three, and Juri Jägerstedt, aged six, who were picked from a nursery class at Halen, not just for their looks, but because when the casters came round Anna-Karin and Juri were the least obedient to requests to carry out various actions.

This rapidly composed circus opened on 29 October 1973, to an audience half composed of extras (mostly found from inside Swedish TV) and half composed of real spectators bringing their children to the circus. Apparent numbers were swelled by life-size board-mounted photographs of seated spectators wearing real scarves, hats and glasses.

The circus sequences were filmed by three video cameras: no celluloid, be it 16 or 35mm, was shot during this second phase, though there was the possibility that the finished product, once it had been broadcast, would be transferred to 35mm for release as a cinema film. But Tati wanted it edited in the time-honoured way, that it is to say with scissors and sellotape, on celluloid film. Karl Haskel lugged the heavy cans of videotape to London week after week, where a small lab barely a mile from Heathrow Airport had the technology to transfer video to 35mm negative film.

And then ... in the midst of the circus work, Tati declared that what he was shooting was in the first place a feature film, and secondarily a television special. The primary material therefore consisted not of the videotapes, but of the 35mm celluloid to which they had been transposed, or rather of the 16mm work prints which had been made of the negatives, which Tati was now editing, and with which he was exhausting his editors. He ran through four in all before the project was finished.

Tati returned to Paris in November 1973, where he managed to hire a super-16mm camera to shoot some additional sequences with a troupe of music comedians he could not get to come to Stockholm. On that shoot his cameraman was once again Jean Badal, and he used his daughter Sophie in the cutting room. There were therefore now four separate "sets" of material for *Parade* (the title had been found before the circus filming in Stockholm) – 35mm film of The Veterans from the Europa Studio filming in 1971, 16mm film from the same shooting, 35mm film created by transposition of video shots of the Stockholm circus performance, and super-16mm film of the additional Paris shooting.

These last sequences were of course in 1:1.66 format and they could not be edited into the film as they stood, since the musical trio turned into a duo in the screening room back in Stockholm. The Norwegians claimed to have a sophisticated device that allowed wide-screen to be reshot on to the narrower format, and so Karl Haskel set off once again with cans of film to turn them into something else . . . The Oslo equipment turned out to be pretty rudimentary (you had to *kick* the device to make it pan left or pan right!), but it worked.

However, as often happens, the editing threw up the need for some more transition shots, and the Stockholm circus was hired again in early 1974 for "completion shooting". The audience was reassembled, as were the child actors – though if you look carefully at the finished movie, you can see that Anna-Karin and Juri vary in age quite substantially from sequence to sequence. The Fischers returned to man the cameras for this last set of takes in the circus, and were still just as unclear about what they were supposed to be doing as they had been in the Europa Studios two years before.

Parade was Tati's last film, but not the crowning glory of his career. From a technical point of view, it is the least good work he ever did, and can be seen as a tragic mistake for a man who for three decades had exhausted all around him in the search for perfection in image and sound. It is also a public exercise in personal nostalgia. Tati's early career in music-hall mime was widely known by the 1970s. Like a film star hired to act a role that refers to the star's own publicised life (like Philippe Léotard playing an alcoholic in Claude Lelouch's "free adaptation" of Hugo's *Les Misérables*, or indeed Chaplin playing an old music-hall performer in *Limelight*), Tati's role in

Parade is to be himself, and thus to invite his audience to see his film at least in part as a sentimental self-depiction. This too is utterly unlike what Tati had done in film art up to that point: you could even call it a heart-rending capitulation to a system Tati had sought to avoid, at great personal cost, throughout his career. These objections to *Parade* cannot be simply dismissed. But there are two sides to every coin.

In *Parade* Tati found a way of implementing one of his long-standing aesthetic and social ambitions, to cross the boundary between *film* and *spectacle*. He had attempted such a thing many times, at film launches introduced by a live mime act, or when he put film sequences inside a variety show (*Jour de fête à l'Olympia*, see above, pp. 231–3), and he had dreamed of even more radical ways of doing it in the first sketch for the work that became *Playtime* (see above, p. 234). In *Parade*, he abolishes the distinction between "film" and "show" by shooting a live performance, but for all sorts of reasons the experiment is much more interesting than "filmed theatre" of the traditional French kind.

Tati's circus special also gives substance to his much-touted aim to "democratise the gag". The means he uses for this are not entirely original: he can hardly be the first circus master to put members of the troupe in the audience, and every popular entertainer has always tried to get audience members on to the stage or into the ring. However, Tati uses these fairground devices on film, and to my knowledge he was the first director to think of doing so. Considerable artifice is required to achieve the appearance of spontaneity. When members of the circus audience are challenged to ride one of Karl Kossmayer's bucking mules, a bald and bespectacled husband in a crumpled office suit breaks away from his anxious wife and meets what must be the first great dare of his life. The illusion is quite perfect – for the hen-pecked husband is actually an acrobat in disguise. But we cannot be quite so sure about the other volunteers who come into the ring to get thrown about by the mule. How "composed" is this sequence? How natural? In the end, we do not know if we are watching a show or a film, and that blurring is precisely what Tati wanted. The uncertain boundaries between spectator and performer, between spontaneity and composition, between "show" and "film" add up to Tati's last real word on the paradox of art that had worried him for more than twenty years.

Tati the mime is the star of the circus show, and by the same token the centre of the film. The director had no choice in the matter: it was a requirement of the contract with Swedish TV, and the only way Tati had of getting off the hook of an earlier contract he had failed to fulfil. *Parade* thus provides the only extensive visual record that we have of the mime acts that got Tati's career launched around 1935. Though his slightly stiffened movements are visibly those of an ageing man, his sense of rhythm and of mime are wonderful to see, and they fully explain why Colette had thought him so striking forty years before. The performances filmed for *Parade* were Tati's last public mimes. And the last of them all is the repeat of his famous imitation of the horse-and-rider, in which Colette had seen the recreation of the legendary centaur. As he comes to the end of his ride and moves towards the wings, the house-lights dim and the spot focuses on the elegant, angular rear of an old man in tails and top hat. It is a beautiful mise-en-scène of the end of a long career, perhaps the most perfect exit that the old trouper could have conceived for himself.

Fig. 91: *The centaur's last stride, Stockholm, 1973*

Seconds after the photograph shown above was taken, Tati, exhausted by his act, passed out cold. Maybe the memory of Molière, who died as the curtain went down on his most famous role, as the *Malade imaginaire*, will have flashed through his mind. Or he may have seen the sad beauty of ending his public life with the act that had launched it in the first place. But the doctor brought him round, and packed him off to hospital for a check-up and a rest.[431]

In *Parade*, Tati also integrates techniques that he had first learned to admire in the films of Bert Haanstra. After the circus show, the "spectators" leave, but the two children, Juri and Anna-Karin, stay behind, and are set to play amongst the props and equipment in the wings. The "child's-play" sequence was filmed only once, without rehearsal or completion shots (and it was filmed only on video, not on celluloid film), in the manner of a documentary or candid-camera film. Most of it consists of tracking shots of some length, and most of it is filmed not in Tati's habitual long-shot style, but in close-up. The children do nothing very elaborate, do not perform any gags, follow no script: they just play around amongst the pots of paint, musical instruments, and accessories left on the empty set. There is no post-edited sound, and no music, just the direct sound of the noises that the children make with their new-found toys. The closing sequence of this 85-minute film (Tati paid no attention at all to the contractual limit of 52 minutes, conventional for TV programming schedules) could be seen as an ironic self-reference, for in this strange and haunting episode the metaphorical title of Tati's masterwork is given a literal turn. The old performer has left the ring, the centaur, like François, like Hulot, is gone for good. A new generation is now learning what *playtime* means. It is not necessarily tragic, or even sad, to note that they are playing for TV.

During the making of *Parade* in Stockholm, Tati seemed to some to be a rather glum and confused old man. He was certainly not very well; he suffered not just a fainting fit in the wings, but also a minor stroke when taken up for a ride in a private plane. But he was well enough to enjoy one quite splendid treat, a grand *soirée* at Gustaf Douglas's castle on a private island in the Stockholm archipelago. He was in such good form that night that he put on a repeat performance of the "Tennis at the Turn of the Century" sketch which can be seen in *Parade*.

During his stay in Stockholm, Tati seemed very dependent on particular kinds of people. "He needed people who could stand up to him," says Elisabeth Wennberg, "because people like that could also stand up *for* him." The drummer Carlson, the administrator Gustaf Douglas, and Wennberg herself clearly came into that category; but Tati also got on well with the costume director, Inger Persson, who knew (so people say) exactly how to make Tati imagine that her ideas were ones he had thought up himself. Outside of the filming, Tati had virtually no contacts in the city – he was there without Micheline, on a work assignment, and he went back to his hotel only to sleep, of which he did rather too little for his own good.

Tati met Gustaf Douglas again some time later in London, at a dinner for potential buyers and distributors of *Parade*. Having adopted the turtle-neck in the late 1950s, when it was still a clear fashion statement of informality of a mildly Bohemian kind, Tati found shirt-and-tie functions quite irksome. But for London producers, he had had to put on a tie, and was thus ready to be disruptive and irreverent at dinner with his Swedish sparring partner. He had told Douglas long before about some of his japes – for example, how, when he had been asked to taste the wine at some pretentious dinner, he had carefully sniffed his glass of water, then taken a sip, then swished it around his mouth before nodding measured approval – and the wine-waiter hadn't even noticed! In London, though, and perhaps because of the unwonted constriction about his neck, Tati went a bit further. A po-faced *sommelier* in tails poured the regulation finger of wine into Tati's glass for tasting. The maestro began to go purple in the face, shifted uneasily in his seat, clutched at his throat, made as if to stand up, pretended to go rigid, knocked over his chair, and fell full-length backwards on to the floor. A disaster! Was the wine as bad as that? Or was it another stroke? The restaurant manager was rushing to dial 999 when Tati got up, with a broad grin on his face. Tati must have known that he was playing with fire. He really could have dropped dead any minute.

FORTY-FIVE

Confusion

Between 1967 and 1975, all Tati's projects seem to have been diversions from a single, original, long-running idea to make something for, or about, or involving television. As we have seen, *Trafic*, shot from 1969 and released in 1971, was the fall-back from an original plan to produce a TV series with Bert Haanstra. *Parade*, begun in 1971 and not finished until 1974, was the unexpected end-result of an original plan to shoot a television series for Swedish TV, which quickly got muddled with a more elaborate idea for a film about television to be called *TTV*. Throughout this period, though beset by debts and ill-health and distracted by unceasing travels to launch films, receive prizes, and represent the art of French film abroad, Tati continued to brood, most often with his old chum Lagrange (but never before noon, it must be said: Tati did not become an early riser in his advancing years), about the underlying and rather confused project which would be the ultimate vindication of his art, a sequel or equal to *Playtime*, a project which eventually acquired its proper name of *Confusion*.

Tati had his assistant, of course, the faithful "CinéSiegler", but to develop a script that would, he hoped, make a truly international film, he sought other hands, and most particularly American ones. Jonathan Rosenbaum was involved in one of the earlier patches of work on *Confusion*. He was "flattered, even awed but also rather bewildered" to be summoned to La Garenne-Colombes in January 1973 to draft the gags that Tati was going to invent for his next film. Not a great deal got written during that long month of work. On some days, when what Tati called his "Slavic side" predominated, a cloud of melancholia would descend over the director, and it would become hard for Rosenbaum to get anything out of him at all. Sometimes Tati would take down his large scrapbooks devoted to the production of *Playtime*, and linger over photographs of the sets . . . But on good days, Tati acted out his ideas in front of his amanuensis, and used him as the spectator that he always needed to create a new gag. But though Tati was paying the young American a good fee, he seemed happy

Fig. 92: *The first direct appearance of a television set in Tati's work: the "fishbowl" flats in* Playtime *(1967)*

enough to spend a fair amount of time with him just chatting about this and that.

> He wasn't much of an intellectual or someone who read much . . .
> During one of our first sessions, while I was still trying to figure out
> why he had hired me, I ventured that, because the principal subject
> of *Confusion* was television, it might perhaps be worth thinking
> some about, say, Marshall McLuhan. The suggestion brought blank
> stares from Tati and from Marie-France [Siegler]. After a brief
> explanation . . . it quickly became clear that they weren't interested
> in the slightest.[432]

All the same, the 123-page scenario in French that emerged at some point – perhaps quite a few years later – from this long-simmering ambition is far from unintelligent, and is at least as amusing and interesting to read as the scripts of Tati's other films: and it is, at last, a truly Tatiesque script in which M. Hulot does not appear at all. Tati had been trying to do without Hulot for at least a decade, but had never yet quite found the way. In the very last working session that he had with Rosenbaum, Tati speculated about starting off *Confusion* with something "truly outrageous: Have the screen go dark, for instance, so that the kids in the audience would start whistling" (Debord's

Hurlements en faveur de Sade ("Screaming for Sade", 1952) had gone much further: in this legendary "anti-film", the screen remains dark throughout!); or else begin the film by killing off Hulot once and for all.

> Suddenly Tati got up from his desk – he always thought best on his feet – and started pacing about his little cubicle, blocking out a scene. Yes, they would be transmitting something like a live soap opera or a melodrama from a TV studio, and real bullets would accidentally be inserted in a prop gun instead of blanks. Hulot would be a studio technician, or, even better an innocent bystander . . . and when one hammy actor pulls out his gun to blast another hammy actor, he misses and instead shoots an out-of-frame Hulot . . . Consternation . . . the show must go on . . . the melodrama continues while the crew frantically conspires to remove Hulot's corpse without the TV cameras picking it up . . . the actors have to keep stepping discreetly over the dead body every time they have to cross the set . . . Tati was playing all the roles, including the Hulot corpse, and he had me in stitches . . . [433]

Tati's work has its fair share of dead-man jokes: in *Jour de fête*, François delivers a letter to a townsman dressed up in Sunday best, and congratulates him on his fine get-up for the fair – and as he exits the room, he and the spectator see a corpse laid out on the bed previously obscured by the inward-opening door, and reinterpret the clean suit and shirt as mourning wear. In *Les Vacances*, of course, an entire sequence is set in a cemetery, where a funeral is turned into a surreal comedy of errors; and even in *Playtime*, a life-size wire-framed dummy of a chef-de-cuisine intended to advertise the restaurant's opening night has to be carried inside when the tables are all taken, and in horizontal portage looks remarkably like a poisoned cook being removed from the scene of the crime. (No corpse jokes occur in *Trafic*, maybe because road traffic is all too literally lethal.)

But Hulot does not need to die in the final version of *Confusion*, for though his spirit lives on in a character defined as having "un certain hulotisme",[434] there is no role in the film for Tati-Hulot at all. The setting is a vast futuristic audio-visual factory, COMM (Compagnie d'Ordinateurs et Matériel Multivideo), and the action concerns pretty much all the "media industries" Tati could think of: fashion photography, television sports reporting, shooting a costume drama, a communications device remarkably like the as-yet uninvented internet (text-messages appear on office consoles), miniaturised wrist-watch television sets, in-car telephones, remote controlled video screens on the backs of tourist bus seats, and, above all, in central and final position, the comic failure of a new "magic" lens to deal competently with the real colours of the world.

Early colour television to the original American standard, the only colour TV Tati had seen much of, is of course pathetically unreliable (Europeans accustomed to PAL and SECAM take its acronym, NTSC, to stand for "Never The Same Colour"), and *Confusion* could be taken narrowly to be no more than a joke about that. But for a film-maker thwarted by the Thomsoncolor scandal at the start of his career, a satire of science-fiction colour technology has a more personal and sharper motivation. *Confusion* might have been almost an autobiographical film.

The film would have been far cheaper to shoot than *Playtime*, since the COMM HQ is not a skyscraper block, but an underground bunker, and nearly all the scenes of the script (apart from the comic costume drama location sequences, and a few introductory shots of travel by limousine and bus) are designed to be made in studio. But what is striking, and probably unrealisable, in the script, are all the jokes about bodily functions. *Confusion* has a degree of scatological vulgarity that is quite unlike anything Tati had envisaged or made before.

For instance, on the tourist bus which keeps plunging into the new Paris tunnels just as its passengers try to take snapshots of the Eiffel Tower or the Concorde obelisk, a very large Dutchman tries to use the on-board lavatory. The roomette is so tiny he has to go in bent double, but he can't relieve his bladder in such a posture; so he comes out, bends over backwards, and tries to enter the WC in reverse (p. 33). In the COMM offices, the toilets as well as the cloakrooms are coin-operated, and even a visiting VIP has to find the right change to relieve himself (characteristically, it is the Portuguese cleaner who comes up with the requisite penny); similarly, at the airport where the "see-through" X-ray machine is in use, there are several lavatory-queue gags, involving women as well as luggage-laden men. One wonders what this is all about. It is probably true that bladder problems afflicted Tati rather more as he grew old; but the motivation of the jokes is probably a little more general, even if now of only historical interest. Paris had for many decades been plentifully supplied with open-access and free *urinoirs* (of the type known as *vespasiennes*). In the name of hygiene, these were fairly rapidly removed from Paris streets in the 1970s, and replaced by a far smaller number of hideous, aluminium, coin-operated and unisex "comfort stations". The script of *Confusion* bears the clear mark of an old man made cross by the disappearance of what, for him, were real conveniences.

The most surprising excretum gag in the script occurs in the office of the director of COMM. A spotlight makes a pool of colour on his large desk, a round shape that is easily confused with a plate. When his breakfast is served, he puts a dollop of marmalade on the non-plate, but as he is soon called out, he forgets all about it. In a later sequence, he returns to his office: the breakfast tray has gone, and the lighting has changed, so the dollop of marmalade on his desk looks like "less palatable matter" (p. 116).

One of COMM's new products is a kind of X-ray machine designed to increase airport security (precisely the kind of thing that is used on luggage nowadays). Passengers passing through it can be seen without any clothes on at all, and Tati proposes to use this device several times over to create numerous comic gags – a chap with padded shoulders revealed to have a puny thorax (p. 101), a stiff-necked managing director in a dark suit and tie looking just as stiff-necked and rigid in his birthday suit (p. 101), a woman arranging her dress as she passes through the machine made to look as though she is scratching her naked body all over (pp. 101–2).

Perhaps the mild obscenity of these sequences is a measure of Tati's outrage at what was being done to the natural world outside of the media firm's headquarters. *Confusion* contains an exterior sequence by the local river bank, between which flow great clumps of plastic waste, polystyrene boxes, half-digested fast-food lunches, and old boots ... The scene seems pretty much identical to the suburban canal in which Debedeux and his friends fish, in René Fallet's *Le Beaujolais nouveau est arrivé* (1975). That novel also articulates many of Tati's dearest themes – the conviviality maintained by French *copains* in the face of New Brutalist architecture, and a generalised resistance to modernisation through cultivated idleness. But whereas Fallet also makes fun of the militant French branch of the Friends of the Earth (the first election they contested was for the council of the highly politicised fifth arrondissement of Paris, in 1974), Tati seems, in *Confusion*, to be more in sympathy with the ecologists. It is quite extraordinary how the old man seemed to be able to keep up with his times.

There are many other elements in the text of *Confusion* that look backwards, and recall scenes from Tati's earlier films. The visiting VIP makes a speech which would have resembled the party-political radio broadcast we hear in *Les Vacances*:

> Amongst the burps and gurgles transmitted, we can grasp only a few words, such as: information, future, invention, communication, technology, peace, which the speaker stresses from time to time (p. 72)

As in *Playtime*, there are long sequences where characters get lost in search of each other in labyrinthine corridors, and other long sequences of comic chaos in an airport departure lounge. As in the Royal Garden restaurant sequence, too, one of the main comic devices in the underground factory is the unreliable heating system. As a result, some office workers are in shorts and tee-shirts, and others in scarves and fur hats. And the imagined film ends in a way remarkably similar to *Jour de fête*, as the long-haired *cinéastes* making their costume drama about Guinevere and her knight, after an open-air beanfeast celebrating the end of the shoot, set off in a jolly caravan, led by a horse-drawn dray, and backed up by two motorcyclists whose winking tail lights fade into the darkness at the close of the film.

A script, of course, is only a script, and it is quite impossible to know how many of the ideas in what is still only a sketch would have eventually been realised. But it is clear that the material proposed would have allowed Tati to include references to pretty much everything he had ever done. In different sequences, and in different media, there are opportunities for mimes of football, wrestling, boxing, weight-lifting and show-jumping; there are views of different kinds of blocks of flats, and of a mix of cars, buses, motorbikes and mopeds; there are roles for floor-sweepers, for café waiters, for pert office girls, and for a character – surprisingly, called Luther – who has no real luck with his great invention, the colour-modifying lens. Hulot had certainly been killed off, but the idea of an outsider wandering through a world that does not quite know what to do with him lives on.

The "key" to *Confusion*, stated at the start of the scenario, is to use two distinct qualities of image. Scenes designated in the margin by the letter C (presumably, for "camera") are intended to represent reality, and would have normal image definition. Scenes to be shown as images in the monitors inside the COMM offices and elsewhere, signalled in the script by the letter V (presumably, for "video"), would have fuzzier definition and less stable colours. Obviously, here, Tati is putting the recent muddle of *Parade* to expressive purpose. It would have been a very neat device. Grain and texture would declare the "reality level" of the sequence, without the need for flashes forward or back, and without the stock-in-trade of Hollywood cinema, parallel editing. Like all of Tati's films, *Confusion* would have a single temporal thread, but unlike all the others, it would have two distinct, intertwined and self-representing image tracks.

Parade was first shown as a cinema film at the Cannes Film Festival, in early May 1974. Jérôme Savary, the star and director of a "new age" circus troupe, *Le Grand Magic Circus*, decided to make a great fuss of Tati, and held a parade for *Parade* along the Croisette, with clowns, balloons, a brass band, and tumbling acrobats – with a seventy-year-old ex-mime in stone-washed denims and a Hawaiian shirt at the head. For some, it was a wonderful homage of the circus to one of its masters; for others, a sad, demeaning spectacle imposed on Tati solely because he needed the launch and the buzz.

Released in Paris in December 1974, *Parade* certainly got Tati back into the news, and for a short time it looked as though his career was about to take off once again. David Frost, the English television personality and media mogul, announced that his company, Paradine Productions, would put up most of the $1.6m budget to allow Tati to make his new film in Los Angeles, through a local firm called North-Levinson Productions. "Jacques Tati to Make First Hollywood Film!" screamed the banner headline in *The Hollywood Reporter* in the summer of 1975.[435] The aim was to have *Confusion* "in the can" for Cannes 1976. "Tati may be sixty-eight," the journalist said, "but he has the mind and the activity and the life in him of Steven Spielberg, who's twenty-eight . . . A number of big names in cameo roles is envisioned in *Confusion*, but Tati has renounced all slavishness to celebrity power. 'I can work with anybody', Tati remarks in the presentation for the film. 'I can make a chicken on a farm funnier than any star.'"

As often happens in the cinema world, the trumpeted project fizzled out, and nothing was ever heard of it again. Tati continued to traipse through airport lounges on his way to festivals and launches – to London and Moscow in 1975, London and Bologna in 1976, Neuchâtel and again London in 1977, Rio de Janeiro in 1979, and Barcelona in 1982 – but he never did manage to find the right backers to make his last film.

Nino Molossena del Monaco, who had bought the rights, and the very cans, of Tati's films numbers 1, 2, 3 and 4, did not leave his property to mature in the bank safe where it was stored. He actually worked very hard to disentangle the financial, administrative and legal constraints which prevented public showings of the films, and eventually succeeded in freeing Tati's oeuvre from its chains.[436] By 1977, *Jour de fête*, *Les Vacances*, *Mon Oncle* and *Playtime* were once again available for distribution.[437] Tati no longer had any direct financial stake in them, of course, but he had not lost any of his moral and aesthetic interest in his early works. Naturally, he wanted to make them just a little bit better before they were seen again. It would have taken a brave man indeed to finance Tati's umpteenth remake of anything at all. But against all the odds, a British friend did just that.

After a ten-year interval, the 1961 version of *Jour de fête* was re-released in France in February 1977, and the 1963 remake of *Les Vacances* and the still-unaltered *Mon Oncle* came out in April of that year. *Playtime* was first re-released in London in June 1978, in its "international" version on anamorphic 35mm film, and shortly after in its "original" French in Paris. What with *Parade* and *Trafic* still in circulation, and a whole host of television documentaries and interviews appearing all over Europe, Tati, as he passed his seventieth birthday, was more visible than he had been for many years. Not as part of the French film scene, nor really as part of French film culture, to which his career relates only very indirectly. By the end of the 1970s, Tati was an international celebrity, which must have been agreeable to him, and also a historic monument, which was perhaps not quite so easy to bear.

Tati first returned to Saint-Marc-sur-mer in 1976 at the behest of the
BBC, whose reporter, Gavin Millar, conducted long interviews with the
director as he strode over the sands and sat in the dining room of the largely
unchanged Hôtel de la Plage. The hotel and the little town had done very
well out of Tati, and most especially out of his British admirers: almost all
the rooms were always booked (and still are) many months ahead by
holidaymakers from the Home Counties wanting to stay in "M. Hulot's
Hotel". But it was perhaps that return to the site of *Les Vacances* that gave
Tati the itch to add just one more scene. Two years later, he returned with
a small crew, to shoot a new sequence that would make *Les Vacances* seem
like a new film once again. It was awfully complicated. The idea was to insert
a satirical reference to a "beach movie" that had supplanted *Les Vacances* and
had famously turned the very idea of seaside vacations into a nightmare. For
this, Tati had to have the kayak which folds in two when Hulot paddles it
out to sea completely remade. He also had to assemble a large crowd of
beach extras, wearing exactly the same costumes as those of the original
film, and thus twenty five years out of date. In the reshot sequence with the
remade kayak, the inner lining of the craft tears into jagged shreds as a
capsizing Hulot tries to free himself from the "jaws" closing over him, and
the shreds are so shaped as to resemble – rather vaguely – the teeth of a Great
White Shark. Cut to a long shot of the beach: someone stands up, pointing
out to sea; the crowd takes fright, and flees from the shore back up to the
hotel. End of sequence. If you've seen Spielberg's *Jaws*, you might laugh. If
not, the sequence seems odd, if not meaningless.

Fig. 93: *The original sketches (circa 1951) by Jacques Lagrange for the collapsing
canoe gag in* Les Vacances de M. Hulot

Like the 1961 remake of *Jour de fête*, the version of *Les Vacances* now in
circulation thus contains contradictory, incompatible "datings". It is a
confusion that annoys, amuses, and can also delight. The time-warp of 1960s
jeans alongside 1940s steam trains, of 1950s beach-wear alongside a swipe
at Steven Spielberg, puts Tati's stories into a generalised, almost abstract
chronological space. He had always meant M. Hulot's holidays to take place

in "anytime", and the "day of the fair" to happen in all possible worlds. The remakes and re-insertions dehistoricise Tati's works to a degree; but precisely because they create contradictions and disjunctions in the time reference of the film, they also remind us of passing time, and put the films' own histories on screen.

Epilogue

Old age does not become an acrobat or a sports mime. By the time he made the last sequence of *Les Vacances* in the summer of 1978, Jacques Tati knew that his cancer, even if it might allow him a few years' more life, would never be cured. He continued to discuss *Confusion* with Jacques Lagrange, and often called him on the telephone (*Jacques? C'est Jacques* . . .) but they both knew the film would never be made. He spent many an afternoon with his friend the cartoonist Sempé, in his studio giving on to Place Saint-Sulpice; he spent time with the Bergerons, with the Broïdos in Geneva, with his other old rugby-chum Gorodiche: friends such as these, and many others, including the restaurateur Moustache, helped Tati ward off bouts of gloom, which sometimes came close to clinical depression. He seemed to have become resentful of others' fame, and to take it amiss if he was not recognised in restaurants and around town. For Tati, who got little pleasure from reading or from watching others' films, old age was not a happy time.

Through these years, Tati continued to appear as a celebrity judge, or just as a celebrity, at film festivals of all sorts, in France and abroad. He was keen to support young film-makers, and also to promote the making of shorts, which he thought the best training and initiation possible for a budding director. When he was awarded a "César" – the French equivalent of an Oscar – for lifetime achievement, he surprised everyone by speaking vigorously, almost angrily, in favour of new subsidies for short films by young directors. That was how he had made his start in cinema, he said, but nowadays a young film-maker has not got even that much of a chance . . . He stumbled in what he had prepared, and his diction, which had never been very good, and was now further impeded by his clumsily-fitted set of false teeth, clouded his words even more . . . The chairman interrupted, and the audience gave a standing ovation to Jacques Tati, the maker of M. Hulot, once famous as the only French film-maker to turn a profit, later famous for going bust . . .

When he had learned that he was to receive a César, Tati had told

Lagrange that in truth he owed one half of it to his painter-friend. He would say so in his acceptance speech. "This César also belongs to Jacques Lagrange ..." But whether it was because he just forgot, or because the chairman's interruption came too soon, the statement was never made. It is also hard to know how true it would have been. Tati owed some part of what he had been able to do to a great many people, from Henri Marquet to Pierre Etaix, from Alfred Sauvy to Jean Badal, from Bernard Maurice to Bert Haanstra, from Sylvette Baudrot to Karl Haskel ... The task of a director is in large part one of choosing, co-ordinating, and managing the skills of others. But Lagrange certainly belonged to that small set of partners whose talents had sparked off Tati's own, and without whom he might never have realised his full potential. Sauvy, Broïdo, Marquet, and Etaix had played that role for a time, but no one had played it so consistently, nor for so long a time, as Jacques Lagrange.

Tati died in November 1982. He had asked to be cremated. He had also insisted that the burial of the ashes be a very modest affair. He did not want a priest of any kind to officiate. Indeed, in the memory of some, if things had been left entirely to Tati's discretion, he would have had his body stuffed into a bin-bag and put out with the rubbish. Tati had always been very proud of his work, and rightly so. But he had never thought much of himself.

Fig. 94: *Jacques Tati, Stockholm, 1973*

Notes

One. French Family Tatischeff

1. In many newspaper articles and even in some reference works, the date is wrongly given as 1909 (more rarely, as 1908).
2. Interview with Sophie Tatischeff, Paris, 29 June 1998.
3. Conversation with Germaine Meunier, Saint Germain-en-Laye, November 1998.
4. "Cette tristesse dont vous me parlez", Tati said to the *Cahiers du cinéma* in 1968, "c'est un peu mon côté slave" (*CC* 199, p.20), but he must have been pulling the leg of the journalist who reported (in "Aux Quatre Coins de Paris", *L'Aurore*, 23 March 1969) that the creator of M. Hulot would definitely make his next film in Russia, on a "Slav story" told to him by "my other grandfather, General Tatischeff, who was the Tsar's Ambassador in Paris . . ."
5. See for example his answer to Max Favalleli, in *Ici-Paris*, 16 March 1953.
6. Anon., "Artisan numéro 1 de l'écran français . . .", *Tribune de Genève*, 6 June 1958. This source also describes Tati's grandfather as "Toulouse-Lautrec's regular framer"; there is at least one early photostat of a Toulouse-Lautrec pen-and-ink portrait (perhaps of Tati's grandmother?) in AJT, which lends some support to this claim.
7. Conversation with Germaine Meunier, Saint-Germain-en-Laye, November 1998.
8. Marc Dondey, *Jacques Tati* (Paris: Ramsay, 1987), p. 15. Dondey was able to interview Tati's sister Nathalie; some details of Tati's childhood come from this source alone.
9. Dondey, p. 15.
10. *New Yorker*, 29 August 1971, p. 45.
11. AJT video cassette 111, clip 4, my transcription; the interview (conducted in English) is undated, but probably took place in Stockholm around 1975.

12. The clip is excerpted in Sophie Tatischeff's excellent documentary on her father, *Tati sur les pas de M. Hulot*. See also H. G. Woodside, "Tati Speaks", *Take One* 22.6 (1970), pp. 6–8.

13. "Vingt questions sur les vacances posées à Jacques Tati", *Les Cahiers d'Elle* 10 (May 1953).

14. Notably, in an interview with Eric Lejeune ("Avec *Playtime*, Jacques Tati entre dans l'ère des loisirs", unidentified press cutting circa 1967, in AJT). Here, Tati allows his interviewer to assert that *Les Vacances de M. Hulot* was directly inspired by childhood holidays at Mers-les-bains, and that M. Hulot's odd dress derives from his father's visits during the war, clad in his fancy uniform.

15. Letter from Nathalie Tatischeff to James Harding, 13 May 1983; BFI, Harding Collection.

16. Interview with Ira Bergeron, Paris, November 1996.

17. Like his birthdate (see Note 1 above), Tati's reported height and weight vary in newspaper articles and reference sources, but within a plausibly narrow range: from 1m88 to 1m92 (6'1" to 6'4"), and from 92 to 100kg (14st. 7lb to 15st. 10lb).

18. Conversation with Pierre Etaix, Paris, November 1996.

19. Alfred Sauvy, *Légendes du siècle*. Paris: Editions Economica, 1990, pp. 125–6.

20. Will Tusher, "Jacques Tati to make first Hollywood film", *The Hollywood Reporter*, 237.21 (24 July 1975).

21. Fred Orain, for instance, interviewed in December 1996, described Tati as *bête comme un clou* ("as thick as a plank").

22. Jean-Claude Carrière, "Comédie à la française", *American Film* 11.3 (December 1985), p. 18.

23. Letter to Suzanne Legoueix, 6 February 1957 (AJT, Specta-Films Correspondence file).

24. Letter signed Max Duravy, dated 22 March 1939; original and several contemporary photostats in AJT.

Two. The Framing Business

25. Interview with Jean Reznikov, Paris, August 1997. The same anecdote crops up in Tati's interview with Jacqueline Vandel in *Le Figaro littéraire*, 19 November 1964.

26. Paul Guth, interview with Tati, *Le Figaro littéraire*, 29 September 1956.

27. Jacqueline Vandel, "Jacques Tati", *Le Figaro littéraire*, 19 November 1964.

28. Claude Schurr, private correspondence, 1997.

29. Quoted in French by Morando Morandini, "Il mimo Tati legge gli nomini", *Cinema* XII.135 (10 June 1954).

30. Anon., "Tati distributeur de Mack Sennett", *Le Figaro*, 16 October 1964.

Three. The Cavalier

31. This observation, and some of the preceding material, is taken from a manuscript transcription of Tati's memoirs as dictated to Jean L'Hôte, circa 1980, pp. 63–4 (kindly supplied by Gilles L'Hôte). Tati also spoke at length about Lalouette and the Sixteenth Dragoons in an interview broadcast by the ORTF (in the series called *Cinépanorama*) on 3 March 1956.

32. Ibid., p. 41.

33. See for example Philippe Trétiack, "La Fille de Mon Oncle se souvient", *Elle*, 12 December 1994.

34. See Fig. 15 on p. 39.

Four. Tati's University

35. See Olivier Merlin, *Tristan Bernard ou le temps de vivre*. Paris: Calmann-Lévy, 1989.

36. L'Hôte, op. cit., p. 6. See Note 31 above.

37. L'Hôte, op. cit., p. 9.

38. Charles Ford, *Histoire du cinéma français contemporain*. Paris: Editions France-Empire, 1977, pp. 242–4.

39. L'Hôte, op. cit., p. 4.

40. Alfred Sauvy, *La Vie en plus. Souvenirs*. Paris: Calmann-Lévy, 1981, p. 237.

41. Correctly spelled Katharine (née Hyde). See *Who's Who in France, 1955–1956*.

42. Christian Guy, "La vie difficile . . . du créateur de M. Hulot", *France-Dimanche*, 18 September 1958, p. 34.

Five. Les Copains

43. Alfred Sauvy, letter to Jacques Tati, unidentified publication (copy kindly provided by Anne Sauvy-Wilkinson).

44. L'Hôte, op. cit. p. 14.

45. Geneviève Agel, *Hulot parmi nous*. Paris: Editions du Cerf, 1955, p. 13.

46. Sauvy, p. 237; see Note 40 above.

47. See Note 43 above.

48. Sauvy, p. 238; see Note 40 above.

49. Ibid.

50. In a letter dated 7 April 1939, Sauvy stated that the revue was first performed on 28 April 1930, but the programme of that show has not been found.

51. Geneviève Agel describes a rather different mime sequence under the title "Le Voyage en Tramway" in *Hulot parmi nous* (Paris: Editions du Cerf, 1955, p.16). This may have been developed for Tati's occasional returns to the music-hall stage for one-night celebrity shows in the late 1940s; no other sources mention it.

52. Max Favalleli, interview with Jacques Tati, *Ici-Paris*, 16 March 1953.

Six. Down and Out

53. Pierre Bost, *Le Cirque et le Music-Hall.* (Les Manifestations de l'Esprit contemporain.) Paris: Au Sans-Pareil, 1931. See in particular pp. 40–2.

54. Pierre Billard, *L'Age Classique du cinéma français*. Paris: Flammarion, 1995.

55. Raymond Chirat & Jean-Claude Romer, *Catalogue. Courts-métrages français de fiction, 1929–1950*. Paris: Editions Mémoires du cinéma, 1996. Item 176.

56. See Paulette Coquatrix, *Les Coulisses de la mémoire*. Paris: Grasset, 1984, pp. 23–5.

57. Martine Danan, "French Patriotic Responses to early American sound films", *Contemporary French Civilization* XX.2 (1996), 294–303, provides fascinating detail on the strategies employed to "naturalise" foreign films in France between 1929 and 1933.

58. Freddy Buache, *Claude Autant-Lara*. Lausanne: L'Age d'homme, 1982. *Parlor, Bedroom and Bath* became *Buster se marie*, and *The Passionate Plumber* was transformed into *Le Plombier amoureux*.

Seven. Oscar, Roger and Rhum

59. Chirat & Romer, op. cit., item 38.

60. "Le Cinéma des cinéastes", broadcast 17 April 1977; INA, Archives sonores, cassette no. K1707.

61. Chirat & Romer, entry 1026. In 1977, Tati recalled that he did indeed start shooting *Oscar champion de tennis*, but that it was so "childish" in conception and execution that it was stopped before being finished.

62. These speculations are not confirmed by Tati's later reminiscence that the Blue Riband Gala was his very first paid engagement, "mon

premier cachet", in C. Guy, "La vie difficile ... du créateur de M. Hulot", *France-Dimanche*, 18 September 1958, p. 35.

63. Sauvy, letter to Jacques Tati, unidentified publication (copy provided by Anne Sauvy-Wilkinson).

64. Sauvy, pp. 237–8; see Note 40 above. Sournia, in the far south-west of France, was the home of Sauvy's maternal grandfather. See Michel-Louis Lévy, *Alfred Sauvy. Compagnon d'un siècle*. Lyon: La Manufacture, 1990.

65. Interview with Max Favallelli, *Ici-Paris*, 16 March 1953. What Tati does not mention here is that the *gérant* in question was called Hulot.

66. René de Laborderie, "Tête à tête avec Tati", *Lui* (October 1967), pp. 5–15.

67. Interview with Tati in *Arts*, 13 May 1953, p. 4.

68. The rest of the cast and crew were similarly professionals: Jean Clairval acted in Barrois's *Trois de la Marine* and also wrote his own scenarios; and Raymond Turgy (also known as Rémond or Raymond Vilmont) can be found in several features of the period, notably *Le Juif polonais* (Jean Kemm, 1931).

69. Carbon copy of letter from Bernard Maurice to Henri Langlois, 6 March 1961 (AJT, Correspondence file).

70. Ginette Vincendeau, "From the *bal populaire* to the casino: class and leisure in French films of the 1930s", *Nottingham French Studies* 31.2 (1992), pp. 52–69 (p. 52).

71. *Action cinématographique* n° 37, 10 October 1937.

72. For example, in an interview broadcast on Canada 1 in 1971 (AJT, video cassette n° 20).

Eight. Sporting Impressions

73. These details mostly from Jacques Feschotte, *Histoire du Music-Hall*. Paris: PUF, 1965.

74. Information from Lucile Terouanne (formerly Mrs B. Minevich), Paris, January 1998.

75. Pascal Sevran, *Le Music-Hall français de Mayol à Julien Clerc*. Paris: Olivier Orban, 1978.

76. Nathalie Tatischeff, letter to James Harding, 13 May 1983. BFI, Harding Collection.

77. Letter to Tati, signed Max Duravy, 22 March 1939. AJT.

78. See Colette, "Spectacles de Paris", *Le Journal*, 28 June 1936.

79. C. Constantin Brive, "Le Sport considéré comme un des beaux-arts", *L'Auto*, 17 October 1935.

80. Pierre Audiat, "Lavalisons . . .", *Paris-Soir,* 21 September 1935.
81. C. Constantin Brive, see Note 79.

Nine. A Day in the Country

82. Carbon copy of letter dated 7 March 1963 (AJT, Correspondence file).
83. Carbon copy of letter dated 27 March 1959 (AJT, Correspondence file).
84. See Jacques Richard, "Quand les gens du cirque inventaient le cinéma burlesque", *Le Cirque dans l'univers* nº 179 (1995), pp. 5–8. Tati met Loriot when both were performing at the *Européen* night-club in 1936.

Ten. The Centaur

85. Confirmed by Germaine Meunier, Saint-Germain-en-Laye, November 1998.
86. Letter from Jacques Tati to his lawyer, 1 February 1956 (AJT, Correspondence file).
87. Jean Queval, "*Jour de fête*", *Sight and Sound* 19.4 (1950), pp. 165–6.
88. Colette, "Spectacles de Paris", *Le Journal*, 28 June 1936.
89. 4 March 1937; then the same double act in Brussels, the following day. See *Conferencia* 24 (1 December 1937): pp. 671–676, which includes a description and review of Tati's act.
90. These details from Tati's own press-cuttings and collection of posters and programmes (AJT) and (for the dates) from André Sallée & Philippe Chauveau, *Le Music-Hall et café concert.* Paris: Bordas, 1985, pp. 116, 151.
91. See Robert Delaroche and François Bellair, *Marie Dubas.* Paris: Candeau, 1980, which includes a one-page preface by Jacques Tati.
92. The *Berliner Zeitung* of 17 January 1964 reproduces a 1938 publicity photograph from the KadeKo, showing Tati in a white suit surrounded by Tatjana Sais, Rudolf Platte, Loni Heuser, Werner Fink, Günther Schwerkolt, and Edith von Ebeling.
93. The clip is included in Gilles Delavaud's short film on *Mon Oncle*, *L'Ecole du regard* (Ministère de la Culture/Totem Productions, 1994).
94. "Cinq colonnes à la une", dir. Guy Labrousse, broadcast by ORTF in 1966.
95. Recalled by Tati in an interview published (in Italian) in *La Nuova Stampa*, 22 May 1954; see also letter dated 25 March 1983 from Eileen de Brandt to James Harding (BFI, Harding Collection).
96. *New Yorker*, 17 July 1954.

97. Bruno Dumons, Gilles Pollet, Muriel Berjat, *Naissance du sport moderne*. Lyon: La Manufacture, 1987, pp. 15–16.

98. Ibid., pp. 23–37.

99. See Florence Pizzorni Itié, *Les Yeux du stade. Colombes, temple du sport*. Thonon-les-bains: Société Présence du livre, 1993.

100. See Bruno Dumons, etc., pp.57–63; Note 97.

101. Pierre Chazaud, "Le Sport et son expression culturelle et artistique dans les années 1920–1930", in Pizzorni Itié, op. cit. pp. 100–14.

102. Michel-Louis Lévy, see Note 64.

103. Conversation with Jean Reznikov, Paris, August 1997.

104. Conversation with Ira Bergeron, Paris, November 1996.

105. See Robert Storey, *Pierrots on the stage of desire. Nineteenth-century literary artists and the comic pantomime*. Princeton, NJ: Princeton University Press, 1985. Alongside a psycho analytical interpretation of Pierrot plays, Storey provides an extensive, detailed, and authoritative account of mime and dumb show in France from the romantic era to the very end of the nineteenth century.

106. Jacques-Charles, *Cent Ans de Music-Hall*. Paris: Jeheber, 1956, p. 56.

107. See Thomas Leabhart, *Modern and Post-Modern Mime*. London: Macmillan, 1989, p. 26; and also Decroux's own course-book, *Paroles sur le mime* (Paris: Librairie théâtrale, 1963), which has many telling illustrations.

108. Jean Laurent, in *Les Nouveaux Temps* (24 June 1943) explicitly accused Maurice Bacquet of having copied Tati's act.

109. Letter dated 11 October 1948 to the President of the Association des Auteurs de Film (AJT). The dating of this letter is probably correct, as the original is filed with other business correspondence about *Jour de fête*, shot in 1947. However, other items of correspondence concerning the historical priority of Tati's mime act, apparently connected with an attempt to obtain compensation for infringement of "copyright", bear dates from the late 1930s. The dispute with Barrault probably originated before the war; there were certainly other imitators of Tati's imitations at that time.

110. Marc Bernard, "Visite à Jacques Tati", *Le Figaro littéraire*, 29 April 1961.

Eleven. Make-Believe

111. Confirmed by Didier-Jacques Broïdo (Jacques Broïdo's son) in conversation in Geneva, July 1998.

112. Extracts can be seen in Gilles Delavaud's pedagogic video on *Mon Oncle*, *L'Ecole du regard* (Ministère de la Culture/Totem Productions, 1994).

113. Information from Jean Guihou, November 1998. M. Guihou's old school friends acted in the film. With thanks to Sophie Tatischeff. The farm belonged to the Gobin-Daudé family, wealthy industrialists who were friends of the Tatischeffs in Le Pecq and Saint-Germain.

114. *Soigne ton gauche* was the only one of Tati's pre-war films which was re-released by his own company, Cady-Films, in the post-war period. The credit sequences and (very probably) the sound track of the current copies were added in the 1940s and have nothing to do with the film's original production.

Twelve. Tati's War

115. "Vingt questions sur les vacances posées à Jacques Tati", *Les Cahiers d'Elle* 10 (May 1953).

116. Michel-Louis Lévy, p. 40; see Note 64.

117. A recently-rediscovered box of Tatischeff family photographs includes a set of snaps showing military trains in snow-covered sidings, with legends on the reverse (no dates or place-names are given, of course) in Tati's hand. These are almost certainly postcard messages to Nathalie from the winter of 1939–40 and are entirely consistent with Tati's supposed posting to the north-eastern border.

118. Christian Guy, "La vie cocasse et difficile du créateur de l'inoubliable M. Hulot", *France-Dimanche*, 18 September 1958. There are many variants to the story: Tati may have spent more than one night in the cells.

119. For example, to the cartoonist Jean-Jacques Sempé, as late as 1980. Interview with Sempé, Paris, January 1998.

120. From "TTV", a scenario by Jacques Tati. Typescript, 76pp, Swedish Television Archives, Stockholm. This passage from p. 10.

121. Ministère des armées, service historique, *Guerre 1939–1945: Les Grandes Unités françaises. Historiques succinctes*. Paris, Imprimerie nationale, 1967, vol 1, p. 370. Tati's *livret militaire* has been lost.

122. See, for example, Julien Gracq's novel, *Un Balcon en forêt* (translated as *A Balcony in the Forest*) for a powerful evocation of the atmosphere of futility and confusion at the front.

123. Guy Teisseire, "Monsieur Tati", *Elle*, 5 March 1979. This statement is perfectly consistent with the official records of the French Army for the 3rd DLC; Note 121 above.

124. One member of the audience was a soldier called Ernst Günther Klein, who became a journalist and interviewed Jacques Tati for an unidentified newspaper in 1963 ("Eine herrliche Privatvorstellung", clipping dated 22 August 1963).

125. Press cuttings from *Paris-Midi, L'Oeuvre, Le Matin, Je suis partout, Les Nouveaux Temps,* etc. for these dates are pasted into pp. 25–7 of Tati's cuttings book (AJT).

126. Jean Laurent, in *Les Nouveaux Temps,* 24 June 1943.

127. Archives nationales (Paris), F42, box 142.

128. See Jacques Evrard, *La Déportation des travailleurs français dans le IIIe Reich.* Paris: Fayard, 1972, for fuller details.

129. Interview with Didier-Jacques Broïdo, Geneva, July 1998; some information drawn from a manuscript memoir in Mme Broïdo's hand.

130. Hans-Dieter Schäfer, *Berlin im zweiten Weltkrieg. Der Untergang der Reichshauptstadt in Augenzeugenberichten* (München: Piper, 1985) contains several first-hand accounts of the influx of foreigners in war-time Berlin; Howard Kingsbury Smith, *Last Train from Berlin* (New York, 1942) paints a gloomy picture of Berlin's entertainment world just before the US entered the war.

131. *Ici-Paris Hebdo,* 19 April 1961.

132. Interview for the series "Le Cinéma des cinéastes", broadcast on 17 and 24 April 1977. Audio cassette no. K1707, "Tati par Tati", Archives Sonores INA.

133. Interview conducted by François Ede in 1994, in Ede, *Jour de fête de Jacques Tati ou la couleur retrouvée* (Paris: Cahiers du cinéma, 1995), p. 83.

134. For example, in *France-Dimanche,* 18 September 1958, Tati allows it to be said that he had harvested wheat and beet for three years in Sainte-Sévère "pour ne pas aller faire son numéro en Allemagne".

135. Sophie Tatischeff, interview in *Cinémascope* 2 (January 1995); information based on interviews with Mme Vialatte and others at Sainte-Sévère during 1987–88.

136. Interview with Ira Bergeron, Paris, November 1996.

Thirteen. The Way Back

137. Marcel Carné, *La Vie à belles dents.* Paris: J.-P. Olivier, 1975, p. 224. The same anecdote is told by Edward Baron Turk, in *Child of Paradise. Marcel Carné and the Golden Age of French Cinema.* Cambridge, MA: Harvard University Press, 1989.

138. Fred Orain, interview with François Ede, January 1988, in François Ede, op. cit. pp. 42–3.

139. Ede reports that the role of the ghost in *Sylvie et le fantôme* had also been offered to Barrault, who had conflicting engagements elsewhere.

140. Claude Autant-Lara, "Entretien", in *Cinématographe* n° 37 (1978), pp. 22–3.

141. BiFi, CN 811 (Archives du Crédit national) contains a document dated 29 November 1948, signed by Fred Orain, referring to *L'Ecole des facteurs* as "Film d'essai du film *Jour de fête*".

142. See *L'Ecran français* n° 50, 12 June 1946.

143. Paul Guth, interview with Tati, *Le Figaro littéraire*, 29 September 1956. Tati stresses the connection in this interview because he had just hired Max Martel to act a small role in *Mon Oncle*.

144. On Demange's career, see R. Chirat & O. Barrot, *Les Excentriques du cinéma français* (Lausanne: Veyrier, 1983), p. 216.

145. He may also have been ill at the time the shoot was planned. See Paul Davay, "L'Extravagant Monsieur Hulot", *Elite*, February 1968. The clipping in AJT is annotated in what I take to be Tati's hand as "bonne biography de JT" [sic].

Fourteen. Mr Byrnes and M. Blum

146. See Jean-Pierre Bertin-Maghit, *Le Cinéma français sous l'occupation* (Paris: Olivier Orban, 1989); also Charles Ford, *Histoire du cinéma français contemporain, 1945–1977* (Paris: Editions France-Empire, 1977).

147. As a result, most of the archives of this unusual bank are now housed in the BiFi.

148. See Patricia Hubert-Lacombe, *Le cinéma français dans la guerre froide, 1946–1956* (Paris: L'Harmattan, 1996), pp. 7–43, for a detailed account of the agreement and its reception in France.

149. *L'Ecran français* n° 54, 10 July 1946.

Fifteen. Local Colour

150. Three undated typescript draft scenarios (respectively of 2, 14, and 18pp.) are in the AJT; a fourth variant was published in A.-J. Cauliez, *Jacques Tati* (Paris: Seghers, 1962) and is reproduced in François Ede, *Jour de fête ou la couleur retrouvée*, Paris: Editions Cahiers du cinéma/INA, 1995, pp. 94–6.

151. Rodolphe-Maurice Arland, letter to Karim Ghiyati, 18 May 1996, reproduced in Karim Ghiyati, *Panoramique sur la carrière de Fred Orain*. Unpubl. thesis, Université de Paris-Sorbonne, 1996.

152. Letter from Fred Orain to Paul Wagner (Maison Dubail), 27 March 1947, in Karim Ghiyati, op. cit., p. 73.

153. Reported by François Ede, op. cit. p. 43 (see Note 133). This remarkable book gives a gripping account of how the long-abandoned honeycomb negatives were finally coaxed into releasing their colours;

it provides more detail on the technical nature of the Thomsoncolor process than can be included here.

154. Benoît Noël, *L'Histoire du cinéma couleur*. Croissy-sur-Seine: Editions Press-Communication, 1955.

155. Chirat, item 389. The catalogue does not record which colour process was used: presumably one of the Agfa- or Gevaert-derived methods, such as Rouxcolor or Gevacolor.

156. See Ede, op. cit., (Note 133) for technical details.

157. Included in Jérôme Deschamps, Les Couleurs de *Jour de fête*, © INA/ Son pour Son, 1995.

158. Interview with Didier-Jacques Broïdo, Geneva, July 1998. See also Patrice-Hervé Pont, *Caméras légendaires* (Neuilly: Fotosaga, n.d.) for details of Broïdo's proudest achievement, the design and launch of the Webo and Carena "pocket" movie cameras in the years after the Liberation. The Webo remained in production until the early 1980s.

159. Or 1940, if André Delpierre's account is to be preferred; see p. 86 above.

160. Despite this, Mercanton's name does not appear on the credits of the film, nor in Dondey's technical entry for it. See *Jacques Tati* (Paris: Ramsay, 1987), p. 263.

161. In Ede, op. cit., p. 38.

162. Jacques Tati, interviewed by Fernand Seguin in "Le Sel de la Semaine", Canada 2 TV, 1968 (AJT cassette 21).

163. Claude-Marie Trémois, "Mon Oncle? C'est M. Hulot", *Radio-Cinéma* 351 (7 October 1956).

164. Jacques Tati, speaking to Noëlle Chaval in a television programme on "les films coloriés", 1977; clip included in Jérôme Deschamps, Les Couleurs de *Jour de fête*, © INA/Son pour Son, 1995. Very similar remarks were made in an interview with A. Y. Serge, *Radio-Cinéma*, 15 August 1954, quoted in Ede, op. cit., p. 79 (see Note 133).

Sixteen. Sounds and Words

165. Michel Chion, *La Toile trouée. Le son au cinéma*. Paris: Editions des Cahiers du cinéma, 1988. See, for instance, pp. 22–3.

166. Jean-Claude Carrière, "Comédie à la française", *American Film* 11.3 (December 1985), p. 18.

167. Kurt London, *Film Music: A Summary*. London: Faber and Faber, 1936, p. 27.

168. In *Komposition für den Film* (Frankfurt: Suhrkamp, 1947), Theodor Adorno and Hans Eisler relate film music to ritual practice and the creation of a quasi-magical "aura". They also speculate that the

function of music in early silent movies was to make the magical moving pictures less frightening to the audience. See Tom Levin, "The Acoustic Dimension", *Screen* 25.3 (May–June 1984), pp. 60–3.

169. See, for example, the analysis of Delerue's score for Truffaut's *Jules et Jim* in the third edition of David Bordwell, Kristin Thompson, *Film Art. An Introduction* (New York: McGraw-Hill, 1990), p. 250.

170. In the 1949 b/w version, shots of François at the sink are intercalated. These were cut from the 1961/64 remake, and not restored in the 1995 colour version.

171. I am not convinced that the existing sound tracks are entirely original. *Gai dimanche*, in particular, seems to me to have been at least partially re-recorded after the war (there are electronic "bleeps" filling in for the commentaries Rhum is supposed to be making on the sights that the tourists, but not the audience, can see).

Seventeen. Back-Up

172. It was also one of the earliest uses in France of magnetic instead of optical sound. Karim Ghiyati, op. cit., p. 35 (see Note 151).

173. The technicians, at least, continued to receive royalties for many years.

174. See Bertin-Maghit, *Le Cinéma français sous l'occupation* (Paris: Olivier Orban, 1989), p. 53.

175. R. Chirat & O. Barrot, *Les Excentriques du cinéma français* (Lausanne: Veyrier, 1983), p. 227.

176. Letter from Orain to Paul Wagner, 5 July 1947 (AJT, Correspondence file).

177. "Jour de fête" , *L'Aurore*, 9 May 1949, p. 2.

178. *L'Aurore*, art. cit.

179. Maine Vallée, interview in *Le Figaro*, 7 January 1995.

180. Dondey, op. cit., p. 263 (see Note 8).

181. In her documentary film, *L'Homme au chapeau de soie*, Maud Linder points out that her father's burlesque shorts provide "an on-the-spot record of the sports of the day" – skiing, skating, horse-riding, bathing and boating, for the most part.

182. Jean Rougel, in *L'Ecran français*, 2 September 1947; reproduced in Ede, op.cit., p. 44 (see Note 133).

Eighteen. US Go Home!

183. The telephone system was a branch of the Post Office at that time (and until the 1970s).

184. Lucy Fischer, "*Jour de Fête*: Americans in Paris", *Film Criticism* VII/2

(1983):pp. 31–44, makes much the same point; see also D. Bellos, "Tati and America", *French Cultural Studies*, June 1999.

Nineteen. Deepest France

185. *The New York Times Film Reviews, 1913–1968* (New York: Arno Press, 1970), p. 2591; review originally published on 20 February 1952.

186. Aurélien Ferenczi, "Aujourd'hui c'est Jour de fête", *L'Information*, 11 January 1995. Deschamps (distantly related to Micheline Tatischeff) is the creator of the comedy series, *La Famille Deschiens*.

187. Some of the "agricultural" ambience shots in the 1949 release – a ploughman tilling a field, a shire horse at rest – were cut from the 1964 remake to make time available for the additional sequences. The original is distinctly more peasant-oriented than the remake.

188. Jacqueline Michel, "Sainte-Sévère-sur-Indre est devenu Follainville", *Le Parisien libéré*, 20 June 1949.

Twenty. Windows and Frames

189. Claude Ventura, quoted by François Ede, op. cit., p. 12 (see Note 133).

Twenty-one. A Slow Release

190. *L'Aventure est au coin du bois* (1948), *Deux Petits Anges* (1948) (Chirat, items 149 and 483). Both are shorts about children.

191. *Les Vagabonds* (1948). According to Chirat (item 1412), the director of photography for this contemporary comic short was Jacques Mercanton.

192. See also E. Eckert Lundin, in *Expressen* (Stockholm), 28 January 1959: "Tati was not the star of the show (in 1948)."

193. China Teater, Stockholm. July 1948 programme booklet. Drottningsholm Theatre Museum Library, Filmhuset, Stockholm.

194. According to an anonymous article in *Svenska Dagbladet*, 28 January 1959, Tati had good friends in the coffee business with cash to spare, and they were the initial backers of *Jour de fête*. No mention of the "coffee connection" has been found outside of these Swedish sources.

195. Bengt Grive, *Glitter och Stänk* (Stockholm, 1989), pp. 57–60: "Tati och blåa svenska ögon". The same anecdote can be found in *Aftonbladet*, 27 January 1959.

196. *Upsala Nya Tidning,* 18 June 1964.

197. On 19 May 1951. Tati could by this time command a very high fee:

150,000 francs for a single appearance (AJT, Correspondence file, letter dated 11 May 1951).

198. BiFi, shelfmark SCEN 1115 B333.

199. Tati referred to this story as his "next film" as soon as *Les Vacances* had been released. At that time, if only briefly, he also had in mind a film on sport in 1900. See his long interview in *Franc-Tireur*, 21 March 1953.

200. Claude Deparsac, "Monsieur Tati", *Bonjour Bonheur*, December 1962. The "smuggled" showing lasted one week.

201. Anne Manson, interview with Jacques Tati, *L'Aurore*, 18 December 1967. Not everything in this article can be taken seriously.

202. Art Buchwald, in *New York Herald Tribune*, 23 May 1949.

203. Louis Chauvet, "Vers un renouveau du cinéma burlesque", *Le Figaro*, 13 May 1949, p. 5.

204. Jeander (Georges Sadoul), "Un Film burlesque français", *Libération*, 16 May 1959, p. 2.

205. André Lang, "Les Films de la semaine", *France-Soir*, 14 May 1949, p. 4.

206. Claude Lazurick, in *L'Aurore – France Libre*, 22 May 1949.

207. *Le Monde*, 20 May 1949, p. 9.

208. *Le Canard enchaîné*, 18 May 1949, p. 4.

Twenty-two. Declarations of Independence

209. According to an article by Orain written in 1957 (reprod. in Ghiyati, op. cit., p. 96, see Note 151) Tati received 22 million francs as his share of the takings of *Jour de fête*.

210. See H.M., in *Le Monde*, 1 June 1950, for a fairly devastating and possibly exaggerated critique of the history and significance of the prize. The jury of 21 included Tristan Bernard's son Raymond, the director Corniglion-Molinier, the comedy actor Noël-Noël, and a host of society ladies. See also *l'Époque*, 31 May 1950.

211. Transcript of an interview with Lagrange, circa 1975, kindly supplied by Hyacinthe Moreau-Lalande.

212. Conversation with Lucile Terouanne, Paris, January 1998.

213. See also *New York Times*, 20 February 1952, reprinted in *The New York Times Film Reviews, 1913–1968* (New York: Arno Press, 1970), p. 2591.

214 "Maxi", *Jour de fête*, *Variety – Film Reviews*, 1949, p. 53.

Twenty-three. Waiting for Hulot

215. See for example issue 1199 [BN M-482], for 23 August 1879.

216. *Exposition Emile Reynaud, Inventeur du dessin animé*. Cinémathèque française/Conservatoire national des Arts et métiers, January–March

1946. Walt Disney himself came to Paris to attend the exhibition. See Dominique Auzel, *Emile Reynaud et l'image s'anima*. Paris: Editions du May, 1992, p. 110.

217. *Emile Reynaud, peintre de films*. Exhibition catalogue, Cinémathèque française, coll. Les Maîtres du cinéma, 1945, pp. 68–9. According to this catalogue, the original film strip is in a museum in Prague.

218. Article signed F. B-R., in *Le Monde*, 24 July 1947.

219. Kindly supplied by Hyacinthe Moreau-Lalande.

220. Interview with Jean-Jacques Sempé, Paris, January 1998.

221. Michel Chion, *Jacques Tati* (Paris: Cahiers du cinéma, 1987), p. 32.

222. Letter to M. Hulot, "concierge au lycée Gassendi, Digne", 30 June 1958: "To be precise about the origin of my character, I must tell you that the name was chosen with the full approval of the manager of the block where I live, and whose name is also Hulot" (AJT, Correspondence file).

223. An iris is a fade which uses a diminishing circular spot.

224. American critics (e.g. Thompson, see Note 225) call this character "The Communist". But as Sartre had already firmly answered the question "Peut-on être un intellectual de droite?" in the negative, they are – in a sense – quite right.

225. Kirstin Thompson, "Boredom on the Beach: Triviality and Humor in *Les Vacances de Monsieur Hulot*", in: *Breaking the Glass Armor* (Princeton, NJ: Princeton University Press, 1988), pp. 89–109, provides (p. 103) a schematic chronology for the film.

226. This shot was cut from the English-language version seen in the US.

Twenty-four. Gags, Jokes, and Switches

227. In Johann Arckenholz, *Mémoires concernant Christine reine de Suède*. Amsterdam & Leipzig, 1751–1760, vol 2, p. 53. Quoted by Monica Setterwall, "Queen Christina and Role Playing in Maxim Form", *Scandinavian Studies* 57 (1985) pp. 162–73.

228. Noel Carroll, "Notes on the sight gag", in: A. Horton (ed.), *Comedy/ Cinema/ Theory*. Berkeley, CA: University of California Press, 1991, pp. 25–42.

229. In this script, S.L.S. is used for "short long shot" (showing a number of characters in full height against a larger background); M.S. for "medium shot" (characters seen with only a little space above and below); and M.C.S for "medium close shot", characters seen from the knees up.

230. Donald Kirihara, "Sound in *Les Vacances de Monsieur Hulot*", in Peter

Lehman (ed.), *Close Viewing. An Anthology of New Film Criticism.* Tallahassee, FL: Florida State University Press, 1990, pp. 150–70.

231. For all its apparent innocence, this gag also represents and perhaps mocks a fundamental issue in French society of the day: the assumptions of the middle classes about North African immigrants, "marchands de tapis ambulant en France", as Romain Gary put it in *La Vie devant soi.*

232. These key elements of the gag are not present in the film-script, which has a briefer and less convoluted cemetery scene.

233. Noel Carroll (art. cit. in Note 228; p. 41) makes the pertinent remark that the gag works only because the film is in black and white: in a colour film, dead leaves attached to a black rubber tyre could not easily be made to resemble a wreath. Consequently we have to accept that the characters on screen *also* see things in black and white. This provides a rather curious negative confirmation of Tati's various pronouncements on the irrelevance of colour.

234. In the original version of the film, Hulot meets the four undertakers the following day on the beach – one of them still wearing his working (mourning) clothes. This was one of the many sequences lost when the negatives were destroyed (see p. 197). From Tati's interview with Jean-André Fieschi and Jean Narboni, *CC* 199 (1968), p. 19.

235. Tati himself appears as an anonymous traveller in a tiny snippet that can hardly be seen, rushing in front of the parked Amilcar to catch a bus – the prelude to the "locked umbrella" gag.

236. The cart-driver was a local farmer, Gaston Chaignon. See *Le Parisien*, 11 January 1995.

Twenty-five. On the Beach

237. Letter from A. Joubert (Saint-Marc) to James Harding, 10 March 1983; BFI, Harding Collection.

238. With the exception of the dock into which Hulot trips and falls: that sequence was shot at La Baule.

239. Conversation with Sylvette Baudrot, Paris, November 1996.

240. Details from *Combat*, 4 June 1952.

241. See Ghiyati, op. cit., p. 71. The average cost of making a feature film in France around 1950 was between 45 and 50 million francs.

242. Finance for the film came in small part from *L'Ecran français*, in part from the distributors, Discina (a company controlled by André Paulvé); another significant input consisted of subsidies available from the French state in proportion to the seats filled to date by *Jour de fête*.

Again, Tati took no fee as author, director or star, but allocated a proportion of the receipts to himself in respect of his contribution to the film. It seems true to say that more or less everything he had earned from *Jour de fête* went into *Les Vacances*; and that the way he sorted the finance made his second film a personal "double or quits" operation. As a result, Orain's financial interest in the success of the film was less than Tati's.

243. Tati's formality extended to his family life. Like Simone de Beauvoir, who only ever addressed Jean-Paul Sartre in the polite plural *vous* form, Michou always referred to her husband as "Monsieur Tati". Information from Sophie Tatischeff.

244. *France-Soir*, 17 June 1952. The bunks in the scout-hut are borrowed from the set of Albert Schweitzer's leper-colony at Lambarene, the subject of a better-funded film being shot at the same time.

245. Some sequences in the shooting script are located in "Hulot's bedroom", but these were never shot; no bedroom set was constructed.

246. Tati to Gilles Jacob, 16 December 1962 (carbon copy in AJT).

Twenty-seven. Accident

247. Cady-Films and Armor-Film, its successor under the ownership of Orain, went on to produce literally hundreds of documentary shorts, but never ventured into full-length or fiction film again.

248. *Arts*, 13 March 1953.

249. Although the full scenario that has survived was probably not typed up for many years and was not deposited at the CNC until 1961, the main ideas of the plot certainly go back to the period 1950–55; the idea of shooting it in Eastern Europe (probably Czechoslovakia) was in the air before *Mon Oncle* was on the screens.

250. The term first used in a letter from Bernard Maurice to Tati, 18 July 1955 (carbon copy in AJT).

251. These details from a letter from Bernard Maurice to Morey Getz, 28 February 1955 (carbon copy in AJT).

252. Letters to D. Matt (4 January) and E. Schweitzer Galleries (22 April) in New York; prices asked range from 25,000 to 45,000 francs per frame.

253. Ms. letter dated 3 February 1954 (AJT, Correspondence file).

254. Carbon copy letter dated 16 March 1954 (AJT, Correspondence file).

255. René Marx, *Le Métier de Pierre Etaix* (Paris: Edition Henri Berger, 1994), p. 24, for some of these details. Others from conversations with Pierre Etaix, Paris, November–December 1996.

256. Boris Vian, *Le Dernier des métiers*, not published until after Vian's death (Paris: Pauvert, 1965).

257. Etaix's words.

258. *De Telegraaf*, 12 October 1955.

259. Jean-Claude Carrière, "Comédie à la française", *American Film* 11.3 (December 1985), pp. 18,19, 22, 80. Carrière went on to become a scriptwriter for Pierre Etaix and many others, and remained a close friend of Tati's.

260. Letter to François Burnier, Milan, April 1957 (AJT, Correspondence file).

261. The more restrictive concept of privacy in French law makes it possible for people to believe in good faith that they "own" their own names, like the Ancient Egyptians in Ismail Kadare's *The Pyramid*.

262. Tati reacted the same way when a French-Algerian family chose to operate their cut-price clothing store under the name of TATI. He tried to take the "name-stealers" to court, but was advised to desist, since Tati is not uncommon as a family name in French-speaking Africa. It is also the name of a group of languages.

263. Carbon copy of letter from Jacques Tati to "Molto caro Fellini", 24 March 1955 (AJT); see also Tati's explanation and denials in *Paris-Match*, 24 and 30 May 1955.

264. Letter to France Roche (*France-Soir*), 16 March 1957 (AJT, Correspondence file).

265. Estimates sent on 1 February 1954 (AJT, Correspondence file).

266. A letter from Bernard Maurice to Morey Getz, dated 4 May 1955, lays out the details of Getz's investment, paid in stages from August 1954 (AJT, Correspondence file).

267. After Getz's death in 1958, his executors tried to obtain rights in *Mon Oncle*. Tati seems to have been successful in his counter-claim that Getz had lent him money on a personal basis and had not invested in *Mon Oncle*. This would suggest that Getz's 6.5 million francs was never fully paid back. Letter from Tati to Lester Guterman, 9 July 1958 (AJT, Correspondence file).

268. Letter dated 3 October 1955 (AJT, Correspondence file). A few days later, Tati sent "technical samples" to Gevaert for laboratory testing. Broïdo's cameras were at that time being manufactured in Antwerp by Gevaert.

269. Relations with GBD also turned sour quite soon: by the following spring, Tati was threatening to seize all prints of *Les Vacances* in circulation in the USA unless GBD paid what it owed him already ... (Letter from Tati to Jules Buck, 19 March 1956, AJT, Correspondence file).

270. See Tati's comments on this in "Le champ large. Entretien avec Jean-André Fieschi et Jean Narboni, *CC* 199 (1968), p.19.

271. Tati retained a vestigial share in Cady-Films until July 1959, when he sold his stake to Fred Orain's father-in-law for a mere 99,000 francs. Cady-Films was wound up in November of that year, and all its continuing business was thenceforth handled by Orain's other company, Armor-Films.

272. Letter dated July 1958 (AJT, Correspondence file).

273. Here is a small selection: 11 May 1959, accident at Passage Denfert, Paris (Tati injured again); 29 May 1959, fine for speeding in Saint-Cloud; 12 August 1959, crash at Magny-en-Vexin; 10 November 1960, a crash involving Micheline; 15 February 1962, collision damage, Rue Pierre-Charron, Paris; 2 June 1964, most of Tati's staff fined for parking offences, Saint-Germain; 4 September 1967, another collision involving Micheline.

274. French road deaths, measured by all and any of the available criteria, were about five times higher than in Britain in the 1950s; even today they are more than double.

275. Kirstin Ross's *Fast Cars, Clean Bodies. Decolonization and the Reordering of French Culture* (Boston: MIT Press, 1995), despite its high reputation in French cultural studies, is not well informed about French car culture of the period.

276. Belgium, having no automobile industry of its own, imposed lower taxes on US car imports than any other European nation, and it became the international clearing house for second-hand Chevrolets, Oldsmobiles and Cadillacs.

Twenty-eight. My Uncle

277. A. Bazin, "M. Hulot et le temps", *Liens*, May 1953, repr. in *Esprit* (same date), repr. in *Qu'est-ce que le cinéma?* Paris: Editions du Cerf, 1975, pp. 41–8.

278. Claude Beylie, "Jacques Tati inconnu", *Cinéma 57*, n° 23 (December 1957).

279. Geneviève Agel, *Hulot parmi nous*. Paris: Editions du Cerf, 1955.

280. See issues for April and August 1953 (*Cahiers*) and August 1953 (*Esprit*).

281. Even so, her claim that Sartre's famous dictum, *l'enfer c'est les autres* (from *Huis Clos*) could be taken as a motto for *Les Vacances* must have seemed then, as now, to be a wild exaggeration.

282. Reply sent 17 May 1955 (AJT, Correspondence file).

283. François Truffaut, "Crise d'ambition du cinéma français", *Arts*, 30 March 1955.

284. *Arts*, 6 January 1956.

285. See Antoine de Baecque, Serge Toubiana, *François Truffaut*. Paris: Gallimard, 1996, p. 347.

286. Broadcast 20 March 1954.

287. Broadcast 5 July 1954.

288. Art Buchwald, "Jacques 'Hulot' Tati's American Spectacular", *New York Herald Tribune*, 23 January 1955.

289. *Mon Oncle*. Résumé du scénario de Jacques Tati. Paris, août, 1954. Typescript, p. 14. My translation.

290. The Maison Jeanneret is in Square du Docteur Blanche (16th arrondissement), a cul-de-sac off Rue Mallet-Stevens. See Norma Evenson, *Paris: A Century of Change, 1878–1978* (New Haven, CT: Yale University Press, 1979), p. 165.

291. Transcript of an interview with Jacques Lagrange, circa 1975, kindly supplied by Hyacinthe Moreau-Lalande.

292. Dietrich Neumann (ed.), *Film Architecture. Set Designs from "Metropolis" to "Blade Runner"* (Munich/New York: Prestel, 1996), p. 136.

293. Marie-Hélène Contal, "Lagrange Peintre et Architecte", unattributed press cutting, circa 1985.

Twenty-nine. The Old World and the New

294. Michel Chion, *Jacques Tati*, p. 110.

295. Gilles Delavaud, *L'Ecole du regard. "Mon Oncle" de Jacques Tati* (Ministère de la Culture/Totem Productions, 1994) shows some of the key sequences that differ in the two versions.

296. Conversation with Pierre Etaix, 12 December 1996.

297. Shown at Cannes in May 1958 but not released in France until September, because of the political situation.

298. Guy Teisseire, "Monsieur Tati", *Elle*, 5 March 1979.

299. *Sports Illustrated*, 20 December 1958.

300. A sub-titled French version also played simultaneously in New York in the winter season of 1958–59.

301. Jacques Tati, "Une Visite à Mack Sennett", *L'Express*, 10 November 1960.

302. Letter to the Minister for Education, 23 August 1958 (AJT, Correspondence file).

303. Tati attended several other receptions at the Elysée Palace in the 1960s.

304. Günther Seuren, "Wenn ich nicht pfeife, stimmt was nicht mit mir" (includes an interview with Jacques Tati), *Christ und Welt* (Stuttgart), 4 October 1964.

Thirty. Tati-Total

305. *Le Parisien*, 12 June 1959; much the same material in *L'Aurore* for the same date. The two films referred to may be *L'Illusionniste* (the "well-constructed piece") and *Playtime*, but Tati may also be referring to other sketches now lost.

306. Jonathan Rosenbaum, "The Death of Hulot", *Sight and Sound* 52 (1983), pp. 95–7 (p. 95).

307. Reported by F. M Bonnet, "M. Hulot als Onkel", *Film-Telegramm* 24/59, 9 June 1959. A reprint of the same article in *Kölnischer Rundschau* on 13 June 1959 omitted the reference to *Lancelot du lac*.

308. The spoof is a sequence in *Confusion*, written with Jacques Lagrange in the 1970s. See Chapter Forty-five.

309. Paul Carrière, "Jacques Tati. diverti plus que jamais", *Le Figaro*, 26 May 1960.

310. The two script fragments were registered with the CNC separately, on 8 June 1961 (*L'Illusionniste*) and 7 September 1962 (*La Grande Ville*). However, in the script that is now archived at the BiFi (SCEN 1115 B333) under the name "Tati N° 4", *L'Illusionniste* and *La Grande Ville* figure simply as the names of two parts of the same project. Despite its name, *La Grande Ville* does not seem to be in any way a pre-figuration of *Playtime*.

311. Letters of 30 and 31 May 1961, respectively, to Ladislav Kachtik (Ceskoslovensky Filmexport) and the CNC (AJT, Correspondence file).

312 See Maud Linder's television film, *L'Homme au chapeau de soie*.

313. A film record of the act performed on the stage of the Olympia can be seen in Nicolas Ribowski's *Cours du soir* (1966).

314. *France-Soir*, 5 May 1961.

315. Conversation with Pierre Etaix, Paris, November 1996.

316 Woody Allen's *Purple Rose of Cairo* plays games with the same idea – inside the film, not within an actual show.

317. Carbon copy contract, included in the AJT Correspondence file for November 1959.

318. Marc Bernard, "Visite à Jacques Tati", *Le Figaro littéraire*, 29 April 1961.

319. Tati underwent surgery in November 1961, quite possibly in connection with the injuries he had sustained in rehearsal the previous spring.

320. Reported at length in (for example) *The Times*, 1 May 1961.

321. *Le Figaro* (24 April) and *France-Observateur* (27 April 1961).

322. The last night was 19 June 1961.

323. Letter to Mlle Charron, 19 July 1961 (AJT, Correspondence file).

324. Letter to Naudy, 3 May 1961 (AJT, Correspondence file).

325. See *Le Monde*, 25 November and 4 December 1964, and *L'Ecran français*, 27 November 1964, for details of the theatre's new design.

326. Juliette Hacquard, "Un Grand Homme tout simple", *Montparnasse mon village* n° 46 (April 1965).

327. Peter Cowie, *Dutch Cinema. An Illustrated History*. London: Tantivy Press, 1979, pp. 35–46.

328. Freddy Sartor, "Haanstra en Tati", *Film, Televisie en Video* 466 (November 1966), pp. 30–1 (in Dutch).

329. Honoré Bostel, "Mais qu'est-ce que fait donc Jacques Tati?", *Paris-Match*, 12 December 1964.

330. Simon Carmiggelt & Peter van Straaten, *Mooi kado*. Utrecht, 1979, pp. 21–3.

331. Bernard Maurice to Bert Haanstra, quoted in English in Jo Daems, "De Tati-Episode" (extracted from Daems's biography of Bert Haanstra), *MediaFilm. Tijdschrift voor filmcultur en filmkunst* 214 (1996), pp. 12–23 (p. 15).

332. Interview with Jean Reznikov, Paris, August 1997.

333. Conversation with Pierre Etaix, Paris, November 1996.

334. For example, J. Lefèbvre, *Calcul de probabilités*, option purchased 26 September 1962.

335. The German-language version was a particular disappointment: its voice-overs, Tati said, were pretentious, stupid, and badly spoken, and as a result he tried to cancel Atlas Filmverleih's distribution contract. Letter to Eckelkamp, 9 August 1963 (AJT, Correspondence file).

Thirty-one. Edifice Complex

336. *Le Figaro littéraire*, 19 November 1964.

337. Reported in *Upsala Nya Tidning*, 18 June 1964.

338. Conversation with Jean Badal, Paris, August 1997.

339. Information from Hyacinthe Moreau-Lalande, Paris, October 1996.

340. Transcript of an interview with Jacques Lagrange, circa 1975, kindly supplied by Hyacinthe Moreau-Lalande.

341. See Eve Jouennais, "La Pré-histoire des villes nouvelles", *Urbanisme* 301 (1998), pp. 51–3.

342. Quoted by Norma Evenson, *Paris. A Century of Change*. New Haven, CT: Yale University Press, 1979, p. 58.

343. *Paris-Jour*, 15 July 1965.

344. Guy Teisseire, *L'Aurore*, 24 February 1965.

345. Hélène Mara, in *Arts*, 14 October 1964.

346. Thomas Lenoir, "Tati et le temps des loisirs, *L'Express* 815 (30 January 1967).

347. Claude-Marie Trémois, "Tati-Playtime", *Télérama*, 22 October 1967.

348. This schedule given by Trémois, see previous Note.

349. Conversation with Jean Badal, Paris, August, 1997.

350. Danièle Heyman, Michel Delain, interview with Jacques Tati, *L'Express*, 1 June 1979, pp. 47–8.

351. See Note 350.

352. Confirmed in private correspondence with Michel Jobert, 18 April 1997.

353. See Note 350.

354. Marcelle Poirier, "Gimmicks Galore from Esterel", *Yorkshire Post*, 24 January 1966; see also *Le Figaro*, 24 January and *Le Monde*, 25 January 1966.

355. *France-Soir*, 27 August and *Minute*, 10 September 1965.

356. Letter to the Préfet de Seine-et-Oise, 8 June 1962 (AJT, Correspondence file).

Thirty-two. Le Gadget

357. First attested in conversational French circa 1946, and still categorised in standard French dictionaries as an Americanism. But the English word was probably borrowed centuries before from the French *gâchette*, meaning a trigger, and then, by extension, any small mechanical device.

358. Almost identical gadgets are currently available in many mail-order catalogues.

359. See Chapter Thirteen on *Sylvie et le fantôme*.

Thirty-three. The Wide Screen

360. See André Barsacq, *Les Décors de film* (Paris: Seghers, 1970), pp. 133–40 for the technical considerations; David Bordwell, Kirstin Thompson, *Film Art. An Introduction* (New York: McGraw Hill, 1990), pp. 168–73, for the aesthetic issues involved, with useful illustrations.

361. Honoré Bostel, "Mais qu'est-ce que fait donc Jacques Tati?", *Paris-Match*, 12 December 1964.

362. Conversation with Jean Reznikov, Paris, August 1997.

363. Claude-Marie Trémois, "Mon Oncle? C'est M. Hulot", *Radio-Cinéma* 351 (7 October 1956).

364. Letter to Mr Lofthouse, 18 September 1968.

365. Interviewed on French radio on 17 April 1977, Tati said he would "like to have" the complete version back in circulation, but he remained evasive about the practical prospects for such a thing. The 70mm version currently under restoration will also be 119 minutes long. It is rumoured that a complete, 140-minute 70mm copy resides in a film archive in Moscow; we have not been able to substantiate this, nor by the same token to see the original film.

366. *CC* 199 (1968), p. 11.

367. "Propos rompus" (Interview with Jean-Jacques Henry, Serge Daney, Serge Le Péron). *CC* 303 (1979), p. 15 & passim.

Thirty-four. Economic Airlines

368. Based on a conversation with Marie-France Siegler, Château de Pécany, December 1996.

369. Conversation with Barbara Denneke-Ramponi, La Queue-en-Brie, July 1997.

370. Letter dated 5 February 1963 to Lena Rydhagen (Norrköping) (AJT, Correspondence file). Similar letters throughout 1963 to friends in England and to Bert Haanstra in Holland.

371. See Note 369.

372. Conversation with Norbert Terry, Cannes, December 1996.

373. Despite this, Tati at first refused to make a TV commercial for Chrysler, the owners of the Simca marque (AJT, Correspondence file, 25 March 1963).

374. Edgar Schneider, "Pour Tati, *Playtime* is Money", *France-Soir*, 20 December 1967, mentions in addition Waterman (pens), Prisunic (super-markets) and Moët et Chandon (champagne) as product advertisers in the film. According to this article, the whole electrical plant of Tativille was sold off to the Victorine studios in Nice.

Thirty-five. Situations

375. Günther Feuerstein, "Thèses sur l'architecture accidentelle", 1960; repr. in *Archives situationnistes* (Paris: Contre-Moule, 1997), vol 1, pp. 60, 66–7.

376. See D. Bellos, *Georges Perec, A Life in Words* (London: Harvill, 1993), p. 280.

377. Information from Vincent Kaufmann and Andrew Hussey, both currently engaged on biographies of Guy Debord.

378. Letter to Michèle Lecluse, 13 April 1965 (AJT, Correspondence file).

379. Interview with Jacqueline Vandel, *Le Figaro littéraire*, 19 November 1964.
380. Andall opened a restaurant, Le Petit Véfour, after he had finished acting for Tati.

Thirty-six. Fish in Water

381. An analysis of the film published in March 1968 shows that Barbara's recognition of the "English Hulot" was retained in the now-lost long version of the film. See Pierre Leroy, "Play Time", *Téléciné* 140, vol 28, fiche n° 482.
382. See Tati's interview with Jonathan Rosenbaum, entitled "Tati's Democracy", *Film Comment* 9.3 (May 1973), pp. 36–41.
383. Conversation with Barbara Denneke-Ramponi, La Queue-en-Brie, July 1997.

Thirty-seven. Towers of Babel

384. Quoted in *Marie-France* n° 134 (April 1967).
385. See Note 383.
386. In addition, Tati could not keep the same team of "ladies" over such a long shoot: many were posted back to the States, or to other NATO locations, in the course of the filming, and had to be replaced. Some were bussed back to Paris from Brussels for the last takes. See *Panorama* n° 91 (March 1966) and *L'Aurore*, 18 December 1967
387. *Paris-Jour*, 29 September 1965.
388. See Note 382.
389. R. Etiemble, *Parlez-vous Franglais?* appeared in 1964, just as Tativille rose from the ground.

Thirty-eight. The End of the Road

390. Jacques Chancel, "L'Homme qui se cachait derrière Jacques Tati", *Paris-Jour*, 17 September 1967.
391. Thomas Lenoir, "Tati et le temps des loisirs", *L'Express* 815 (30 January 1967).
392. *L'Aurore*, 31 August 1967.
393. *Le Parisien*, 4 April 1968, p. 15.
394. See for instance Jacqueline Vandel, in *France-Soir*, 4 November 1967.
395. *France-Soir*, 19 December 1967, *Le Figaro*, 5 January 1968. In the event, it was only ever used by twelve children.

396. "Tati ne fait pas la conquête de l'Ouest", *Minute*, 17 January 1968.

397. Werner Schwier, "Pariser Tagebuch", *Münchener Abendzeitung*, 14 August 1968.

398. AJT, Correspondence file 7 January 1969.

399. Letter to Sheldon Gunsberg, 28 November 1970 (AJT, Correspondence file).

400. The Walter Reade Organisation bought US rights in December 1970, but never secured general distribution.

401. Private correspondence with Mme B. Maurice, July 1997. Bernard Maurice eventually paid the several hundred thousand francs owed by Specta in respect of social security out of his own earnings, to avoid personal bankruptcy.

402. The story, which by its nature cannot be properly documented, has been confirmed by Jacques-Didier Broïdo, amongst others.

Thirty-nine. Tati TV

403. Letter to M. Morgaine, 31 December 1970 (AJT, Correspondence file).

404. Jean-Marie Fitère, "Le Sacrifice de Madame Hulot", *Ici-Paris*, 9 January 1968.

405. (AJT, Correspondence file, 20 August and 9 September 1968).

406. Ms. letter, Sauvy to Tati, 17 December 1968. Copy kindly supplied by Anne Sauvy-Wilkinson.

407. Anne Manson, "Aux Quatre Coins de Paris", *L'Aurore*, 23 March 1969.

408. Jonathan Cecil, "A Memory of August 1971", unpublished ms., James Harding Collection, BFI.

409. The chronology of the following episode proves beyond reasonable doubt that Tati knew in advance that he would lose everything with *Playtime*.

410. Adapted from Haanstra's own account, as reported verbatim by Freddie Sartor, "Haanstra en Tati", *Film, Televisie en Video* 466 (November 1966), pp. 30–31 (in Dutch).

411. A short was salvaged from the material already shot: *Retour Madrid* (*Return Ticket to Madrid*, 1967).

412. Letter dated 12 August 1968, quoted (in English) by Jo Daems, in "De Tati-Episode", *Mediafilm. Tijdschrift voor filmcultur en filmkunst* 214 (1996), p. 17.

Forty. Rescue from the North

413. He went on to make *ABBA The Movie* (1977), *The Children of Bullerby Village* (1987) and many other films in Sweden before beginning his current and continuing career as a director in the USA.
414. Thanks to Karl Haskel, the unedited, only partly translated, and annotated transcripts of these conversations have survived, but the film itself has been junked. The documentary was never made, despite all this preparatory work.

Forty-one. Mirrors of Motors

415. Octave Burnett, "*Trafic*", *Télèciné* 173 (October 1971), pp. 17–23.
416. The special suspension of this particular model made it particularly suitable for "acrobatic" stunts. Many attempts were made to meet the challenge of driving a Citroën on two wheels only from New York to Los Angeles.

Forty-two. On Tour, On Show

417 Charles Dumont, *Non je ne regrette rien* (Paris: Guy Anthier, 1977), pp. 192 3.
418. G. Langlois, in *Les Lettres françaises*, 21 April 1971.
419. Jean Fayard, in *Point de vue/Images du Monde*, 16 April 1971.
420. *Minute*, 28 April 1971

Forty-three. A French Fortnight

421. *New York Post*, 6 January 1973.
422. *France-Soir*, 18 November 1972.
423. Vincent Canby, "Tati's Terrific *Traffic*", *New York Times* (Sunday), 17 December 1972.
424. Reported in *France-Soir*, 18 November 1972.
425. Ibid.
426. Jonathan Rosenbaum, "The Death of Hulot", *Sight and Sound* 52 (1983), p. 95. Tati hired other English-language writers from time to time, for *Playtime* as well as for *Confusion*: Michael Hargraves, Gene Moskowitz, and maybe others.

Forty-four. Circus Time

427. Conversation with Karl Haskel, Stockholm, November 1996.
428. *Le Nouvel Observateur*, 15 October 1998.

429. Conversations with Gunnar and Jens Fischer, Stockholm, November 1996.

430. Conversation with Gustaf Douglas, Stockholm, November 1996.

431. Conversation with Marie-France Siegler, Pécany, December 1996.

Forty-five. Confusion

432. Jonathan Rosenbaum, see Note 426.

433. Ibid.

434. *"Confusion" de Jacques Tati.* Roneo booklet, undated, 122pp. kindly made available by Hyacinthe Moreau-Lalande, p. 2.

435. Report by Will Tusher, in volume 237, issue 21 (24 July 1975).

436. According to Carol Lawson, in the *New York Times*, 6 November 1977, he also paid off $1,600,000 owed by Specta-Films and other parties in respect of Tati's films.

437. Andreas Freud, "Jacques Tati and his movies return after Enforced Vacation", *New York Times*, 9 February 1977.

Sources

The Films of Jacques Tati

The most reliable filmography of Jacques Tati's work for the screen can be found in Marc Dondey, *Jacques Tati* (Paris: Ramsay, 1987), pp. 263–5.

No copies of *Oscar champion de tennis* (1932?) and *Retour à la terre* (1938?) have ever been found. Video copies of *On demande une brute* (1934), *Gai dimanche* (1935) and *Soigne ton gauche* (1936) can be seen at the Vidéothèque de Paris. The sound track of this version of *Gai dimanche* was almost certainly amended after 1945. The credit sequence of *Soigne ton gauche* was inserted after the foundation of Cady-Films in 1946. A single copy of the original 1936 film may still exist in private hands in Geneva.

Copies of the original version of *Jour de fête* (1947/1949) are very hard to come by. Most videotapes purporting to be the "original" version of Tati's first feature film give the colourised version of 1961/63. More widely available are video cassettes of the colour version, as restored by François Ede and Sophie Tatischeff in 1995. This latter version also has an entirely re-recorded sound track.

The original version of *Les Vacances de M. Hulot* with piano-solo sound track has been lost. The 16mm and 35mm copies in distribution give the 1963 remake or else the 1978 version, which is the same save for the inserted "shark-tooth" sequence in the collapsing-kayak episode. Video copies available in Britain and the USA are all of the 1978 version.

Mon Oncle is widely available in 16mm and 35mm colour and in VHS video. The English-language version, *My Uncle*, has become rare, and is not available in video. Tati never "remade" *Mon Oncle*.

Playtime is available in 16mm colour, in wide-screen 35mm colour, and in VHS video in France, Britain and the USA. A 70mm copy also exists and is shown from time to time in the USA and elsewhere. All versions available last 119 minutes. It is rumoured that a single 70mm print of the original, 150-minute film is located in a Moscow film archive. A restored 70mm print is expected to be released for cinema showings in 2000.

Trafic and *Parade* are both commercially available in France as SECAM VHS video cassettes. In the case of *Parade*, this is a transfer of the film, not a direct recording of the programme broadcast on Swedish television.

Texts by Jacques Tati

Mon Village. Unpub., typescript, 2 pp., circa 1945

La Fête au village (with Henri Marquet). Unpub. typescript, 14 pp., circa 1946

Jour de fête (with Henri Marquet and René Wheeler). Unpub. typescript, 18 pp., 1947

Jour de fête (unattrib.), in François Ede, *Jour de fête ou la couleur retrouvée* (Cahiers du cinéma, 1995), pp. 94–6

Les Vacances de M. Hulot (with Henri Marquet), unpub. typescript, 70 pp., 447 sequences. 1951

Film Tati N° 2: Les Vacances de M. Hulot (with Henri Marquet and Jacques Lagrange), roneo booklet, 202 pp., 396 sequences. Cady-Films, 1951

"Allez! . . . Pas d'histoires" *Arts*, 13 March 1953

Mon Oncle. Résumé. Unpub. typescript, 14 pp. 1954

Mon Oncle. Scénario. With Jean L'Hôte and Jacques Lagrange. Roneo booklet, 157 pp., 410 sequences. Specta-Films/Gray-Films/Alter Films, 1956

Contribution to "La mode vue par six cinéastes", *Le Nouveau Femina-l'Illustration* 24 (1956), p. 53

"Un bon conseil à M. Hulot", *Marie-Claire* n° 16 (1956), pp. 102–3

L'Illusionniste. Découpage technique en 311 séquences. Typescript, 136 pp., signed but undated (1958?)

Film Tati N° 4 (*L'Illusionniste – La Grande Ville*), unpub. typescript, circa 1961.

Letter to the editor, *New York Herald Tribune*, 16 November 1958

"Prix Jacques Tati du film humoristique amateur", *Loisirs-films* N° 18 (October 1960)

"Une Visite à Mack Sennett", *L'Express*, 10 November 1960

Film Tati N° 4. With Jacques Lagrange. Unpub. typescript, 148 pp. Specta-Films, 1960(?) (first draft of *Playtime*)

Letter to the editor, *Le Figaro*, 1 February 1962

Untitled ("A Amsterdam, dans un building . . ."). Typescript, 12 pp. (several blank), 1971

TTV. Scénario de Jacques Tati. (Text in English) Typescript, 76 pp., circa 1972

Confusion. With Jacques Lagrange. Typescript, 123 pp., circa 1975. Extracts published in *L'Avant-scène cinéma* 400 (1991), pp. 9–17

Preface, in Robert Delaroche and François Bellair, *Marie Dubas*. Paris: Candeau, 1980. p. 11

Novelisations and By-products

Jour de fête. Illustrations by E. Lamotte. Hachette, 1950. (Children's picture-book version of the film)

Les Vacances de M. Hulot. Text by Jean-Claude Carrière. Cartoons by Pierre Etaix. Paris: Laffont, 1958. Repr. 1985

Mon Oncle. Text by Jean-Claude Carrière. Cartoons by Pierre Etaix. Paris: Laffont, 1958

Playtime. Un film de Jacques Tati. Paris: Dargaud, 1967. 2 vols, unnumbered pages

Bibliography

Fischer, Lucy, *Jacques Tati. A Guide to References and Resources*. New York: G. K. Hall, 1983

Books about Jacques Tati

Agel, Geneviève, *Hulot parmi nous*. Paris: Editions du Cerf, 1955

Louis, Théodore, *Jacques Tati*. Bruxelles: Club du livre de cinéma, 1959

Cauliez, A.-J. *Jacques Tati*. Paris: Seghers, 1962

Gilliatt, Penelope, *Jacques Tati*. London: Woburn Press, 1976

Maddock, Brent, *The Films of Jacques Tati*. Metuchen, NJ: Scarecrow Press, 1977

Nepoti, Roberto, *Jacques Tati*. Florence, 1979 (in Italian)

Harding, James, *Jacques Tati Frame By Frame*. London: Secker & Warburg, 1984

Chion, Michel, *Jacques Tati*. Paris: Cahiers du Cinéma (Collection Auteurs), 1987. English translation: *The Films of Jacques Tati*, transl. M. Viñas, P. Williamson and A. d'Alfonso. Toronto: Guernica, 1997

Dondey, Marc, *Jacques Tati*. Paris: Ramsay, 1987. Repr. 1993

Kermabon, Jacques, *"Les Vacances de M. Hulot", de Jacques Tati*. Crisnée: Yellow Now, 1988

Ramirez, François and Rolot, Christian, *"Mon Oncle" de Jacques Tati*. Paris: Nathan, Collection Synopsis, 1993

Ede, François, *Jour de fête ou la couleur retrouvée*. Paris: Cahiers du cinéma, 1995

Fieschi, Jean-André, *La Voix de Jacques Tati*. Strasbourg: Limelight/Editions Ciné-fils, 1996. 26 pp.

Abela, Emmanuel, *Présence(s) de Jacques Tati*. Schiltigheim: Editions Ciné-films, 1997. 25 pp.

Principal documentaries about Jacques Tati

"Jacques Tati". Omnibus, 13 May 1976. Written and directed by Gavin
    Millar. BBC archive, VC 165352

"Tati sur les pas de M. Hulot". Directed by Sophie Tatischeff. CEPEC/La
    Sept/Antenne 2/INA, 1989

"L'école du regard. *Mon Oncle*, de Jacques Tati". Written and directed by
    Gilles Delavaud. Paris, Magimage, 1994 (with a 72 pp. pamphlet)

"Les Couleurs de *Jour de fête*". Written and directed by Jérôme Deschamps.
    INA/Son pour Son, 1995

Tati's long radio interview with Claude-Jean Philippe, originally broadcast
by France-Culture on 17 and 24 April 1977, is also available as an audio
cassette published by Radio-France under the title "Tati par Tati" (K1707)

Tati in Les Cahiers du cinéma

n° 32/34 (1954):
    Barthélémy Amengual, "L'étrange comique de M. Tati"
n° 82 (1958):
    Jacques Doniol-Valcroze, "Tati sur les pattes de l'oiseau"
n° 83 (1958):
    Interview with André Bazin and François Truffaut
n° 199 (1968):
    Articles by Jean-André Fieschi, Noel Burch, Jean Badal, Paul-Louis
    Martin
n° 239 (1979):
    Serge Daney, "Eloge de Tati", and other articles by Jean-Louis Schefer,
    Bernard Boland, Jean-Jacques Henry

Other important articles on Jacques Tati

Aroso, Mario, "Il Play-Dialogo di Monsieur Hulot", *Rivista del cinematografo*
    8 (August 1968), pp. 450–7

Bazin, A., "M. Hulot et le temps", *Liens*, May 1953, repr. in *Esprit* (same
    date), repr. in *Qu'est-ce que le cinéma?* Paris: Editions du Cerf, 1975,
    pp. 41–8

Beylie, Claude, "Jacques Tati inconnu", *Cinéma 57*, n° 23 (December 1957)

Carrière, Jean-Claude, "Comédie à la française", *American Film* 11.3
    (December 1985), p. 18

Carroll, Noel, "Notes on the sight gag", in: A. Horton (ed.), *Comedy/
    Cinema/ Theory*. Berkeley, CA: University of California Press, 1991, pp.
    25–42

Daems, Jo, "De Tati-Episode", *MediaFilm. Tijdschrift voor filmcultur en filmkunst*
    214 (1996), pp. 12–23

Fischer, Lucy, "*Jour de Fête*: Americans in Paris", *Film Criticism* VII/2 (1983)

Heyman, Danièle & Michel Delain, interview with Jacques Tati, *L'Express*, 1
    June 1979, pp. 47–8

Kirihara, Donald, "Sound in *Les Vacances de M. Hulot*", in Peter Lehman (ed.),
    Close Viewing. An Anthology of New Film Criticism. Tallahassee, FL: Florida
    State University Press, 1990, pp. 150–70.

Morandini, Morando, "Il mimo Tati legge gli nomini", *Cinema* XII.135 (10
    June 1954)

Rosenbaum, Jonathan, "The Death of Hulot", *Sight and Sound* 52 (1983),
    pp. 95–7

Sartor, Freddy, "Haanstra en Tati", *Film, Televisie en Video* 466 (November
    1966), pp. 30–1

Subiela, Michel, "En laissant couler la guimauve," *Positif* n° 6 (1954)

Thompson, Kirstin, "Boredom on the Beach: Triviality and Humor in *Les
    Vacances de M. Hulot*", in: *Breaking the Glass Armor* (Princeton, NJ:
    Princeton University Press, 1988), pp. 89–109

Truffaut, François,"Connaissez-vous *Mon Oncle*?", *Arts*, 6 April 1958, pp. 2–3

Reference sources

Auzel, Dominique, *Emile Reynaud et l'image s'anima*. Paris: Editions du May,
    1992

Barsacq, André, *Les Décors de film*. Paris: Seghers, 1970

Bertin-Maghit, Jean-Pierre, *Le Cinéma français sous l'occupation*. Paris: Olivier
    Orban, 1989

Billard, Pierre, *L'Age Classique du cinéma français*. Paris: Flammarion, 1995

Bordwell, David, & Kristin Thompson, *Film Art. An Introduction*. New York:
    McGraw-Hill, 1990

Bost, Pierre, *Le Cirque et le Music-Hall*. (Les Manifestations de l'Esprit
    contemporain.) Paris: Au Sans-Pareil, 1931

Buache, Freddy, *Claude Autant-Lara*. Lausanne: L'Age d'homme, 1982

Carmiggelt, Simon, & Peter van Straaten, *Mooi kado*. Utrecht, 1979

Carné, Marcel, *La Vie à belles dents*. Paris: J.-P. Olivier, 1975

Chazaud, Pierre, "Le Sport et son expression culturelle et artistique dans les
    années 1920–1930", in Pizzorni Itié, pp. 100-14

Chion, Michel, *La Toile trouée. Le son au cinéma*. Paris: Cahiers du cinéma,
    1988

Chirat, Raymond & Jean-Claude Romer, *Catalogue. Courts-métrages français de
    fiction, 1929–1950*. Paris: Editions Mémoires du cinéma, 1996

Chirat, Raymond & O. Barrot, *Les Excentriques du cinéma français*. Lausanne: Veyrier, 1983

Coquatrix, Paulette, *Les Coulisses de la mémoire*. Paris: Grasset, 1984

Cowie, Peter, *Dutch Cinema. An Illustrated History*. London: Tantivy Press, 1979

Danan, Martine, "French Patriotic Responses to early American sound films", *Contemporary French Civilization* XX.2 (1996), 294–303

de Baecque, Antoine & Serge Toubiana, *François Truffaut*. Paris: Gallimard, 1996

Decroux, Etienne, *Paroles sur le mime*. Paris: Librairie théâtrale, 1963

Dumons, Bruno, Gilles Pollet, Muriel Berjat, *Naissance du sport moderne*. Lyon: La Manufacture, 1987

Dumont, Charles, *Non je ne regrette rien*. Paris: Guy Anthier, 1977

Emile Reynaud, peintre de films. Exhibition catalogue, Cinémathèque française, coll. Les Maîtres du cinéma, 1945

Evenson, Norma, *Paris: A Century of Change, 1878–1978*. New Haven, CT: Yale University Press, 1979

Evrard, Jacques, *La Déportation des travailleurs français dans le IIIe Reich*. Paris: Fayard, 1972

Exposition Emile Reynaud, Inventeur du dessin animé. Cinémathèque française/Conservatoire national des Arts et métiers, January-March 1946

Fallet, René, *Le Beaujolais nouveau est arrivé*. Paris: Gallimard, 1975

Feschotte, Jacques, *Histoire du Music-Hall*. Paris: PUF, 1965. (Que sais-je? N° 1169)

Feuerstein, Günther, "Thèses sur l'architecture accidentelle", 1960; repr. in *Archives situationnistes*. Paris: Contre-Moule, 1997, vol 1

Ford, Charles, *Histoire du cinéma français contemporain, 1945–1977*. Paris: France-Empire, 1977

Ghiyati, Karim, *Panoramique sur la carrière de Fred Orain*. Unpub. thesis, Panthéon-Sorbonne, 1996.

Grive, Bengt, "Tati och blåa svenska ögon" in: *Glitter och Stänk*. Stockholm, 1989, pp. 57–60

Hubert-Lacombe, Patricia, *Le cinéma français dans la guerre froide, 1946–1956*. Paris: L'Harmattan, 1996

Jacques-Charles, *Cent Ans de Music-Hall*. Paris: Jeheber, 1956

Jouennais, Eve, "La Pré-histoire des villes nouvelles", *Urbanisme* 301 (1998), pp. 51–3.

Leabhart, Thomas, *Modern and Post-Modern Mime*. London: Macmillan, 1989

Levin, Tom, "The Acoustic Dimension", *Screen* 25.3 (May–June 1984), pp. 60–3.

Lévy, Michel-Louis, *Alfred Sauvy. Compagnon d'un siècle*. Lyon: La Manufacture, 1990

London, Kurt, *Film Music: A Summary*. London: Faber and Faber, 1936

Marx, René, *Le Métier de Pierre Etaix*. Paris: Henri Berger, 1994

Merlin, Olivier, *Tristan Bernard ou le temps de vivre*. Paris: Calmann-Lévy, 1989

Ministère des armées, service historique, *Guerre 1939–1945: Les Grandes Unités françaises. Historiques succinctes*. Paris, Imprimerie nationale, 1967, vol 1

Neumann, Dietrich (ed.), *Film Architecture. Set Designs from "Metropolis" to "Blade Runner"*. Munich/New York: Prestel, 1996

Noël, Benoît, *L'Histoire du cinéma couleur*. Croissy-sur-Seine: Editions Press-Communication, 1955

Pizzorni Itié, Florence, *Les Yeux du stade. Colombes, temple du sport*. Thonon les-bains: Société Présence du livre, 1993

Pont, Patrice-Hervé, *Caméras légendaires*. Neuilly-sur-Seine: Fotosaga, n.d.

Richard, Jacques, "Quand les gens du cirque inventaient le cinéma burlesque", *Le Cirque dans l'univers* n° 179 (1995), pp. 5–8

Romains, Jules, *Les Copains*. Paris: Grasset, 1922

Ross, Kirstin, *Fast Cars, Clean Bodies. Decolonization and the Reordering of French Culture*. Boston, MA: MIT Press, 1995

Sallée, André & Philippe Chauveau, *Le Music-Hall et café concert*. Paris: Bordas, 1985

Sauvy, Alfred, *La Vie en plus. Souvenirs*. Paris: Calmann-Lévy, 1981

Sauvy, Alfred, *Légendes du siècle*. Paris: Editions Economica, 1990

Schäfer, Hans-Dieter, *Berlin im zweiten Weltkrieg. Der Untergang der Reichshauptstadt in Augenzeugenberichten*. München: Piper, 1985

Sevran, Pascal, *Le Music-Hall français de Mayol à Julien Clerc*. Paris: Olivier Orban, 1978

Smith, Howard Kingsbury, *Last Train from Berlin*. New York, 1942

Storey, Robert, *Pierrots on the stage of desire. Nineteenth-century literary artists and the comic pantomime*. Princeton, NJ: Princeton University Press, 1985

Truffaut, François, "Crise d'ambition du cinéma français", *Arts*, 30 March 1955

Turk, Edward Baron, *Child of Paradise. Marcel Carné and the Golden Age of French Cinema*. Cambridge, MA: Harvard University Press, 1989

Vincendeau, Ginette, "From the *bal populaire* to the casino: class and leisure in French films of the 1930s", *Nottingham French Studies* 31.2 (1992), pp. 52–62

Other sources used – the vast majority of which are shorter film reviews and newspaper cuttings – are referenced in Notes. Copies of almost all such smaller items are kept at the AJT.

Index

The Index is in overall alphabetical order but with sub-headings in chronological order.
Jacques Tati's film titles are in bold capitals, other film titles are in plain capitals.
Titles of books, plays, and journals are italicised.
Page references to illustrations are italicised.